Opel Ascona
Service and Repair Manual

I M Coomber and Mark Coombs

Models covered

Opel Ascona front-wheel-drive models with petrol engines, including special/limited editions;
Saloon, Hatchback and Estate

1297 cc, 1598 cc, 1796 cc & 1998 cc

Covers major mechanical features of Convertible
Does not cover Diesel engine

(3215-240-11X7)

© J H Haynes & Co. Ltd. 2014

A book in the **Haynes Service and Repair Manual Series**

ISBN 978 0 85733 929 4

British Library Cataloguing in Publication Data
A catalogue record for this book is available from the British Library.

**J H Haynes & Co. Ltd.
Haynes North America, Inc**

www.haynes.com

Contents

LIVING WITH YOUR VAUXHALL CAVALIER

Introduction to the Vauxhall Cavalier	Page	**0•4**
Acknowledgements	Page	**0•4**
Safety First!	Page	**0•5**

Roadside Repairs

Jacking and vehicle support	Page	**0•6**
Towing and wheel changing	Page	**0•7**
Identifying leaks	Page	**0•8**
Booster battery (jump) starting	Page	**0•9**

MAINTENANCE

Weekly checks

Introduction	Page	**0•10**
Underbonnet check points	Page	**0•10**
Engine oil level check	Page	**0•12**
Coolant level check	Page	**0•12**
Screen washer fluid level check	Page	**0•13**
Brake fluid level check	Page	**0•13**
Power steering fluid level check	Page	**0•14**
Electrical system check	Page	**0•14**
Battery check	Page	**0•15**
Wiper blade check	Page	**0•15**
Tyre condition and pressure check	Page	**0•16**
Lubricants and fluids	Page	**0•17**
Capacities	Page	**0•17**
Tyre pressures	Page	**0•17**

Routine Maintenance and Servicing

Maintenance schedule	Page	**1•1**
Introduction	Page	**1•7**
Maintenance procedures	Page	**1•8**
Servicing Specifications	Page	**1•17**

Contents

REPAIRS & OVERHAUL

Engine and Associated Systems

Engine	Page	2•1
Cooling and heating systems	Page	3•1
Fuel and exhaust system - carburettor models	Page	4A•1
Fuel and exhaust systems - fuel injected models	Page	4B•1
Starting and charging systems	Page	5A•1
Contact breaker ignition system	Page	5B•1
Electronic (breakerless) ignition system	Page	5C•1

Transmission

Clutch	Page	6•1
Manual transmission	Page	7A•1
Automatic transmission	Page	7B•1
Driveshafts	Page	8•1

Brakes and Suspension

Braking system	Page	9•1
Suspension and steering	Page	10•1

Body Equipment

Bodywork and fittings	Page	11•1
Body electrical system	Page	12•1

Wiring Diagrams

	Page	WD•1

REFERENCE

Dimensions and weights	Page	REF•1
Conversion Factors	Page	REF•2
Buying spare parts	Page	REF•3
Vehicle identification numbers	Page	REF•3
General Repair Procedures	Page	REF•4
Tools and Working Facilities	Page	REF•5
MOT Test Checks	Page	REF•7
Checks carried out from the driver's seat	Page	REF•7
Checks carried out with the vehicle on the ground	Page	REF•8
Checks carried out with the vehicle raised	Page	REF•9
Checks carried out on your vehicle's exhaust emission system	Page	REF•10
Fault Diagnosis	Page	REF•11
Glossary of Technical Terms	Page	REF•18

Index

	Page	REF•23

Introduction to the Vauxhall Cavalier

The front-wheel-drive (fwd) Cavalier was introduced in August 1981 and replaced the earlier range of rear-wheel-drive Cavalier models. The bodywork was also revised to distinguish it from the earlier models and was initially available in a two or four-door Saloon version, or a five-door Hatchback. The five-door Estate variant was introduced in 1983.

The engine and transmission on all models is transversely mounted. Initially available with a 1.3, 1.6 or 1.8 litre engine, the 2.0 version was added to the range for the 1987 model year. A 4 or 5-speed manual transmission, or a 3-speed automatic transmission will be fitted.

The 2-door Convertible variant was introduced in October 1985.

Various levels of trim and equipment are available depending upon the model selected from the range.

These vehicles should present few problems for the home mechanic. They are of straightforward construction with good access to all service points.

Vauxhall Cavalier SRi 130

Vauxhall Cavalier L Estate

Acknowledgements

Thanks are due to Champion Spark Plug, who supplied the illustrations showing spark plug conditions, to Holt Lloyd Limited who supplied the illustrations showing bodywork repair, and to Duckhams Oils, who provided lubrication data. Thanks are also due to Sykes-Pickavant Limited, who provided some of the workshop tools, and to all those people at Sparkford who helped in the production of this manual.

We take great pride in the accuracy of information given in this manual, but vehicle manufacturers make alterations and design changes during the production run of a particular vehicle of which they do not inform us. No liability can be accepted by the authors or publishers for loss, damage or injury caused by errors in, or omissions from, the information given.

Working on your car can be dangerous. This page shows just some of the potential risks and hazards, with the aim of creating a safety-conscious attitude.

General hazards

Scalding

• Don't remove the radiator or expansion tank cap while the engine is hot.
• Engine oil, automatic transmission fluid or power steering fluid may also be dangerously hot if the engine has recently been running.

Burning

• Beware of burns from the exhaust system and from any part of the engine. Brake discs and drums can also be extremely hot immediately after use.

Crushing

• When working under or near a raised vehicle, always supplement the jack with axle stands, or use drive-on ramps. *Never venture under a car which is only supported by a jack.*

• Take care if loosening or tightening high-torque nuts when the vehicle is on stands. Initial loosening and final tightening should be done with the wheels on the ground.

Fire

• Fuel is highly flammable; fuel vapour is explosive.
• Don't let fuel spill onto a hot engine.
• Do not smoke or allow naked lights (including pilot lights) anywhere near a vehicle being worked on. Also beware of creating sparks
(electrically or by use of tools).
• Fuel vapour is heavier than air, so don't work on the fuel system with the vehicle over an inspection pit.
• Another cause of fire is an electrical overload or short-circuit. Take care when repairing or modifying the vehicle wiring.
• Keep a fire extinguisher handy, of a type suitable for use on fuel and electrical fires.

Electric shock

• Ignition HT voltage can be dangerous, especially to people with heart problems or a pacemaker. Don't work on or near the ignition system with the engine running or the ignition switched on.

• Mains voltage is also dangerous. Make sure that any mains-operated equipment is correctly earthed. Mains power points should be protected by a residual current device (RCD) circuit breaker.

Fume or gas intoxication

• Exhaust fumes are poisonous; they often contain carbon monoxide, which is rapidly fatal if inhaled. Never run the engine in a confined space such as a garage with the doors shut.

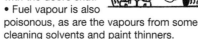

• Fuel vapour is also poisonous, as are the vapours from some cleaning solvents and paint thinners.

Poisonous or irritant substances

• Avoid skin contact with battery acid and with any fuel, fluid or lubricant, especially antifreeze, brake hydraulic fluid and Diesel fuel. Don't syphon them by mouth. If such a substance is swallowed or gets into the eyes, seek medical advice.
• Prolonged contact with used engine oil can cause skin cancer. Wear gloves or use a barrier cream if necessary. Change out of oil-soaked clothes and do not keep oily rags in your pocket.
• Air conditioning refrigerant forms a poisonous gas if exposed to a naked flame (including a cigarette). It can also cause skin burns on contact.

Asbestos

• Asbestos dust can cause cancer if inhaled or swallowed. Asbestos may be found in gaskets and in brake and clutch linings. When dealing with such components it is safest to assume that they contain asbestos.

Special hazards

Hydrofluoric acid

• This extremely corrosive acid is formed when certain types of synthetic rubber, found in some O-rings, oil seals, fuel hoses etc, are exposed to temperatures above 400°C. The rubber changes into a charred or sticky substance containing the acid. *Once formed, the acid remains dangerous for years. If it gets onto the skin, it may be necessary to amputate the limb concerned.*
• When dealing with a vehicle which has suffered a fire, or with components salvaged from such a vehicle, wear protective gloves and discard them after use.

The battery

• Batteries contain sulphuric acid, which attacks clothing, eyes and skin. Take care when topping-up or carrying the battery.
• The hydrogen gas given off by the battery is highly explosive. Never cause a spark or allow a naked light nearby. Be careful when connecting and disconnecting battery chargers or jump leads.

Air bags

• Air bags can cause injury if they go off accidentally. Take care when removing the steering wheel and/or facia. Special storage instructions may apply.

Diesel injection equipment

• Diesel injection pumps supply fuel at very high pressure. Take care when working on the fuel injectors and fuel pipes.

⚠ *Warning: Never expose the hands, face or any other part of the body to injector spray; the fuel can penetrate the skin with potentially fatal results.*

Remember...

DO

• Do use eye protection when using power tools, and when working under the vehicle.

• Do wear gloves or use barrier cream to protect your hands when necessary.

• Do get someone to check periodically that all is well when working alone on the vehicle.

• Do keep loose clothing and long hair well out of the way of moving mechanical parts.

• Do remove rings, wristwatch etc, before working on the vehicle – especially the electrical system.

• Do ensure that any lifting or jacking equipment has a safe working load rating adequate for the job.

DON'T

• Don't attempt to lift a heavy component which may be beyond your capability – get assistance.

• Don't rush to finish a job, or take unverified short cuts.

• Don't use ill-fitting tools which may slip and cause injury.

• Don't leave tools or parts lying around where someone can trip over them. Mop up oil and fuel spills at once.

• Don't allow children or pets to play in or near a vehicle being worked on.

Jacking and vehicle support

The jack supplied with the vehicle tool kit should only be used for changing the roadwheels - see "Wheel changing" later in this Section. When carrying out any other kind of work, raise the vehicle using a hydraulic jack, and always supplement the jack with axle stands positioned under the vehicle jacking points **(see illustration)**.

When using a hydraulic jack or axle stands, always position the jack head or axle stand head under one of the relevant jacking points.

To raise the front of the vehicle, position the jack with an interposed block of wood underneath the front section of the sill. Do not jack the vehicle under the sump or any of the steering or suspension components. To raise the rear of the vehicle, position the jack head underneath the rear section of the sill **(see illustration)**. Do not attempt to raise the vehicle with the jack positioned underneath the suspension components.

The jack supplied with the vehicle, locates in the jacking points in the ridge on the underside of the sill. Ensure that the jack head is correctly engaged before attempting to raise the vehicle.

Never work under, around, or near a raised vehicle, unless it is adequately supported in at least two places.

Sill jacking points - arrowed

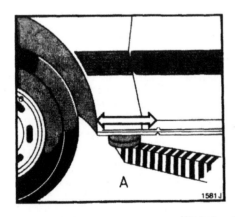 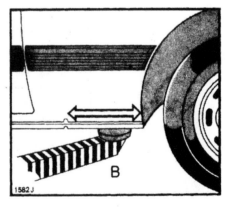

Workshop jack lifting points

A Front   *B Rear*

Towing

Towing eyes are fitted to the front and rear of the vehicle for attachment of a tow rope. The front towing eye is accessed through a slot in the bumper and the rear towing eye is located underneath the body **(see illustrations)**. Always turn the ignition key to position I when the vehicle is being towed, so that the steering lock is released, and that the direction indicator and brake lights will work.

Before being towed, release the handbrake and select neutral on the transmission. Note that greater-than-usual pedal pressure will be required to operate the brakes, since the vacuum servo unit is only operational with the engine running. Similarly, on models with power steering, greater-than-usual steering effort will be required.

On models with an automatic transmission to prevent the transmission being damaged, the vehicle should be towed with its front wheels off the ground. If the vehicle is being towed with its front wheels on the ground the car must not be towed for more than 70 miles (100 km) and should never be towed at speeds in excess of 50 mph (80 kmh).

Front towing hook

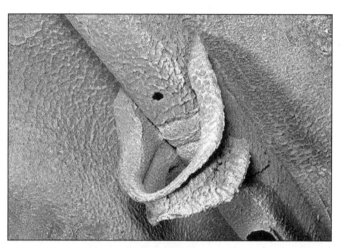

Rear towing hook

Wheel changing

The spare wheel, jack and wheel brace are located in the luggage compartment **(see illustration)**.

To change a wheel, remove the spare wheel, jack and wheel brace and proceed as follows.

Apply the handbrake, and place chocks at the front and rear of the wheel diagonally opposite the one to be changed. Select first or reverse gear and make sure that the vehicle is

located on firm, level ground. Prise off, and remove, the wheel trim (if applicable). Slightly loosen the wheel bolts with the brace provided. Locate the jack head in the jacking point nearest to the wheel to be changed, and raise the jack by turning the handle **(see illustration)**. On certain models, it may be necessary to unclip access covers to reveal the jacking points. When the wheel is clear of the ground, remove the bolts and lift off the

wheel. Fit the spare wheel and moderately tighten the bolts. Lower the vehicle, and then tighten the bolts fully in a diagonal sequence. Refit the wheel trim, where applicable. If possible, check the tyre pressure on the spare wheel. Remove the chocks and stow the jack, tools and the damaged wheel in the luggage compartment. Have the damaged tyre or wheel repaired, or renew it, as soon as possible.

Jack and spare wheel location

Tool kit jack in use

Identifying leaks

Puddles on the garage floor or drive, or obvious wetness under the bonnet or underneath the car, suggest a leak that needs investigating. It can sometimes be difficult to decide where the leak is coming from, especially if the engine bay is very dirty already. Leaking oil or fluid can also be blown rearwards by the passage of air under the car, giving a false impression of where the problem lies.

 Warning: Most automotive oils and fluids are poisonous. Wash them off skin, and change out of contaminated clothing, without delay.

 The smell of a fluid leaking from the car may provide a clue to what's leaking. Some fluids are distictively coloured. It may help to clean the car carefully and to park it over some clean paper overnight as an aid to locating the source of the leak.
Remember that some leaks may only occur while the engine is running.

Sump oil

Engine oil may leak from the drain plug...

Oil from filter

...or from the base of the oil filter.

Gearbox oil

Gearbox oil can leak from the seals at the inboard ends of the driveshafts.

Antifreeze

Leaking antifreeze often leaves a crystalline deposit like this.

Brake fluid

A leak occurring at a wheel is almost certainly brake fluid.

Power steering fluid

Power steering fluid may leak from the pipe connectors on the steering rack.

Booster battery (jump) starting

When jump-starting a car using a booster battery, observe the following precautions:

A) Before connecting the booster battery, make sure that the ignition is switched off.

B) Ensure that all electrical equipment (lights, heater, wipers, etc) is switched off.

C) Make sure that the booster battery is the same voltage as the discharged one in the vehicle.

D) If the battery is being jump-started from the battery in another vehicle, the two vehcles MUST NOT TOUCH each other.

E) Make sure that the transmission is in neutral (or PARK, in the case of automatic transmission).

HAYNES HiNT *Jump starting will get you out of trouble, but you must correct whatever made the battery go flat in the first place. There are three possibilities:*

1 *The battery has been drained by repeated attempts to start, or by leaving the lights on.*

2 *The charging system is not working properly (alternator drivebelt slack or broken, alternator wiring fault or alternator itself faulty).*

3 *The battery itself is at fault (electrolyte low, or battery worn out).*

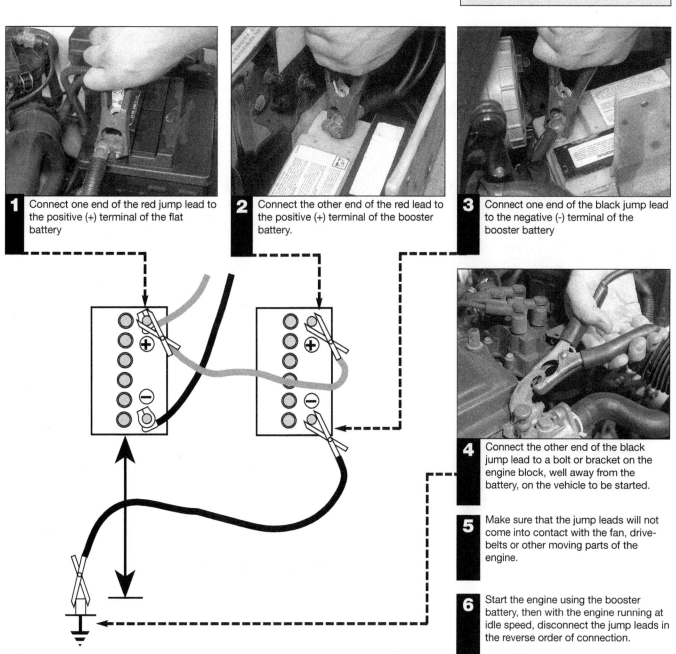

1 Connect one end of the red jump lead to the positive (+) terminal of the flat battery

2 Connect the other end of the red lead to the positive (+) terminal of the booster battery.

3 Connect one end of the black jump lead to the negative (-) terminal of the booster battery

4 Connect the other end of the black jump lead to a bolt or bracket on the engine block, well away from the battery, on the vehicle to be started.

5 Make sure that the jump leads will not come into contact with the fan, drive-belts or other moving parts of the engine.

6 Start the engine using the booster battery, then with the engine running at idle speed, disconnect the jump leads in the reverse order of connection.

Introduction

There are some very simple checks which need only take a few minutes to carry out, but which could save you a lot of inconvenience and expense.

These "Weekly checks" require no great skill or special tools, and the small amount of time they take to perform could prove to be very well spent, for example;

☐ Keeping an eye on tyre condition and pressures, will not only help to stop them wearing out prematurely, but could also save your life.

☐ Many breakdowns are caused by electrical problems. Battery-related faults are particularly common, and a quick check on a regular basis will often prevent the majority of these.

☐ If your car develops a brake fluid leak, the first time you might know about it is when your brakes don't work properly. Checking the level regularly will give advance warning of this kind of problem.

☐ If the oil or coolant levels run low, the cost of repairing any engine damage will be far greater than fixing the leak, for example.

Underbonnet check points

◀ **1.3 litre**

A *Engine oil level dipstick*

B *Engine oil filler cap*

C *Coolant expansion tank*

D *Brake fluid reservoir*

E *Screen washer fluid reservoir*

F *Battery*

◀ 1.8 litre (up to 1987)

A *Engine oil level dipstick*

B *Engine oil filler cap*

C *Coolant expansion tank*

D *Brake fluid reservoir*

E *Screen washer fluid reservoir*

F *Battery*

◀ 1.8 litre (from 1987-on)

A *Engine oil level dipstick*

B *Engine oil filler cap*

C *Coolant expansion tank*

D *Brake fluid reservoir*

E *Screen washer fluid reservoir*

F *Battery*

Engine oil level

Before you start

✔ Make sure that your car is on level ground.
✔ Check the oil level before the car is driven, or at least 5 minutes after the engine has been switched off.

 HAYNES HiNT *If the oil is checked immediately after driving the vehicle, some of the oil will remain in the upper engine components, resulting in an inaccurate reading on the dipstick!*

The correct oil

Modern engines place great demands on their oil. It is very important that the correct oil for your car is used (See "Lubricants and Fluids").

Car Care

● If you have to add oil frequently, you should check whether you have any oil leaks. Place some clean paper under the car overnight, and check for stains in the morning. If there are no leaks, the engine may be burning oil *(see "Fault Finding")*.

● Always maintain the level between the upper and lower dipstick marks (see photo 3). If the level is too low severe engine damage may occur. Oil seal failure may result if the engine is overfilled by adding too much oil.

1 The dipstick top is often brightly coloured for easy identification (see *"Underbonnet check points"* on page 0•10 for the exact location). Withdraw the dipstick.

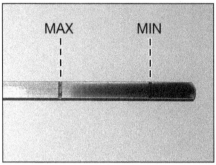

3 Note the oil level on the end of the dipstick, which should be between the upper ("MAX") mark and lower ("MIN") mark. Approximately 1.0 litre of oil will raise the level from the lower mark to the upper mark.

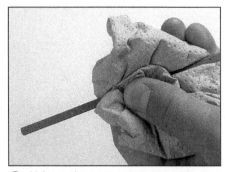

2 Using a clean rag or paper towel remove all oil from the dipstick. Insert the clean dipstick into the tube as far as it will go, then withdraw it again.

4 Oil is added through the filler cap. Unscrew the cap and top-up the level; a funnel may help to reduce spillage . Add the oil slowly, checking the level on the dipstick frequently. Avoid overfilling (see *"Car Care"*).

Coolant level

⚠ *Warning: DO NOT attempt to remove the expansion tank pressure cap when the engine is hot, as there is a very great risk of scalding. Do not leave open containers of coolant about, as it is poisonous.*

Car Care

● With a sealed-type cooling system, adding coolant should not be necessary on a regular basis. If frequent topping-up is required, it is likely there is a leak. Check the radiator, all hoses and joint faces for signs of staining or wetness, and rectify as necessary.

● It is important that antifreeze is used in the cooling system all year round, not just during the winter months. Don't top-up with water alone, as the antifreeze will become too diluted.

1 The coolant level varies with the temperature of the engine. When the engine is cold, the coolant level should be as shown. When the engine is hot, the level may rise slightly above the "COLD" mark.

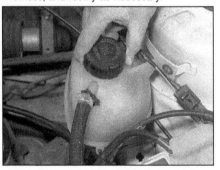

2 If topping-up is necessary, **wait until the engine is cold**. Slowly turn the expansion tank cap anti-clockwise to relieve the system pressure. Once any pressure is released, turn the cap anti-clockwise unti it can be lifted off.

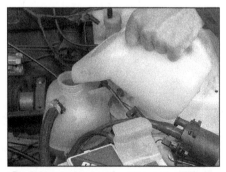

3 Add a mixture of water and antifreeze through the expansion tank filler neck until the coolant reaches the "COLD" level mark. Refit the cap, turning it clockwise as far as it will go until it is secure.

Screen washer fluid level

Screenwash additives not only keep the winscreen clean during foul weather, they also prevent the washer system freezing in cold weather - which is when you are likely to need it most. Don't top up using plain water as the screenwash will become too diluted, and will freeze during cold weather. On no account use engine antifreeze in the washer system - this could discolour or damage paintwork.

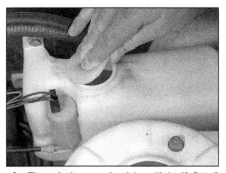

1 The windscreen (and headlight if fitted) washer fluid reservoir is located at the rear left-hand corner of the engine compartment.

2 On models fitted with a tailgate washer system, an additional reservoir is located in the luggage compartment; on Hatchback models it is at the rear, on Estate models it is on the right-hand side.

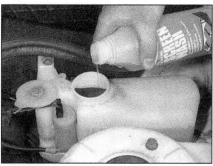

3 When topping-up the reservoir(s), a screenwash additive should be added in the quantities recommended on the bottle.

Brake fluid level

Warning:Brake hydraulic fluid can harm your eyes and damage painted surfaces, so use extreme caution when handling and pouring it.

● *Do not use fluid that has been standing open for some time, as it absorbs moisture from the air which can cause a dangerous loss of braking effectiveness.*

HAYNES HiNT
• Make sure that your car is on level ground.
• The fluid level in the master cylinder reservoir will drop slightly as the brake pads wear down, but the fluid level must never be allowed to drop below the 'MIN' mark.

Safety first

● If the reservoir requires repeated topping-up this is an indication of a fluid leak somewhere in the system, which should be investigated immediately.

● If a leak is suspected, the car should not be driven until the braking system has been checked. Never take any risks where brakes are concerned.

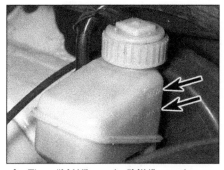

1 The "MAX" and "MIN" marks are indicated on the side of the reservoir. The fluid level must be kept between the marks.

3 When adding fluid, it's a good idea to inspect the reservoir. The system should be drained and refilled if dirt is seen in the fluid (see Chapter 9 for details).

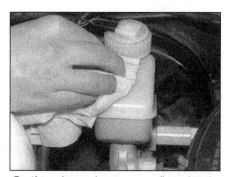

2 If topping-up is necessary, first wipe the area around the filler cap with a clean rag before removing the cap.

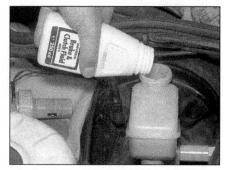

4 Carefully add fluid avoiding spilling it on surrounding paintwork. Use only the specified hydraulic fluid; mixing different types of fluid can cause damage to the system. After filling to the correct level, refit the cap securely, to prevent leaks and the entry of foreign matter. Wipe off any spilt fluid.

Power steering fluid level

Before you start:
✔ Park the vehicle on level ground.
✔ Set the steering wheel pointing straight-ahead.
✔ The engine should be turned off.

 For the check to be accurate the steering must not be turned once the engine has been stopped.

Safety First:
● The need for frequent topping-up indicates a leak, which should be investigated immediately.

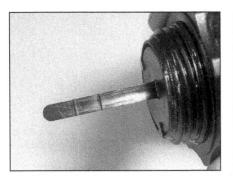

1 The fluid level is checked with a dipstick attached to the reservoir filler cap. The reservoir is located in the front left-hand corner of the engine compartment behind the headlight unit.

2 Clean the area around the reservoir. Remove the cap and wipe the dipstick with a clean rag. When the engine is cold, the fluid should come up to the lower ADD mark; when hot, it should come up to the FULL mark.

3 When topping-up, use the specified type of fluid. and do not overfill the reservoir. When the level is correct, refit the cap.

Electrical system

✔ Check all external lights and the horn. Refer to the appropriate Sections of Chapter 12 for details if any of the circuits are found to be inoperative.

✔ Visually check all wiring connectors, harnesses and retaining clips for security, and for signs of chafing or damage.

 If you need to check your brake lights and indicators unaided, back up to a wall or garage door and operate the lights. The reflected light should show if they are working properly.

1 If a single indicator light, brake light or headlight has failed it is likely that a bulb has blown and will need to be replaced. Refer to Chapter 12 for details.
If both brake lights have failed, it is possible that the brake light switch above the brake pedal needs adjusting. This simple operation is described in Chapter 9.

2 If more than one indicator light or headlight has failed it is likely that either a fuse has blown or that there is a fault in the circuit (refer to *"Electrical fault-finding"* in Chapter 12).
The fuses are mounted in a panel located at the lower right-hand corner of the facia under a removable cover.

3 To replace a blown fuse, simply pull it out. Fit a new fuse of the same rating, available from car accessory shops.
It is important that you find the reason that the fuse blew - a checking procedure is given in Chapter 12.

Battery

Caution: Before carrying out any work on the vehicle battery, read the precautions given in "Safety first" at the start of this manual.
✔ Make sure that the battery tray is in good condition, and that the clamp is tight. Corrosion on the tray, retaining clamp and the battery itself can be removed with a solution of water and baking soda. Thoroughly rinse all cleaned areas with water. Any metal parts damaged by corrosion should be covered with a zinc-based primer, then painted.
✔ Periodically (approximately every three months), check the charge condition of the battery as described in Chapter 5A.
✔ If the battery is flat, and you need to jump start your vehicle, see *"Roadside Repairs"*.

1 The battery is located on the left-hand side of the engine compartment. The exterior of the battery should be inspected periodically for damage such as a cracked case or cover.

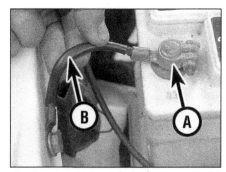

2 Check the tightness of battery clamps (A) to ensure good electrical connections. You should not be able to move them. Also check each cable (B) for cracks and frayed conductors.

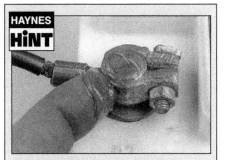

HAYNES HINT

Battery corrosion can be kept to a minimum by applying a layer of petroleum jelly to the clamps and terminals after they are reconnected.

3 If corrosion (white, fluffy deposits) is evident, remove the cables from the battery terminals, clean them with a small wire brush, then refit them. Accessory stores sell a useful tool for cleaning the battery post ...

4 ... as well as the battery cable clamps

Wiper blades

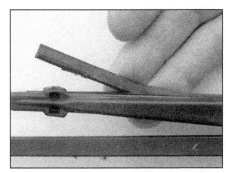

1 Check the condition of the wiper blades; if they are cracked or show any signs of deterioration, or if the glass swept area is smeared, renew them. For maximum clarity of vision, wiper blades should be renewed annually, as a matter of course.

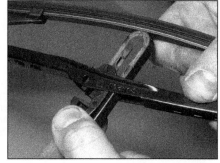

2 To remove a wiper blade, pull the arm fully away from the glass until it locks. Swivel the blade through 90°, press the locking tab(s) with your fingers, and slide the blade out of the arm's hooked end. On refitting, ensure that the blade locks securely into the arm.

Tyre condition and pressure

It is very important that tyres are in good condition, and at the correct pressure - having a tyre failure at any speed is highly dangerous. Tyre wear is influenced by driving style - harsh braking and acceleration, or fast cornering, will all produce more rapid tyre wear. As a general rule, the front tyres wear out faster than the rears. Interchanging the tyres from front to rear ("rotating" the tyres) may result in more even wear. However, if this is completely effective, you may have the expense of replacing all four tyres at once!

Remove any nails or stones embedded in the tread before they penetrate the tyre to cause deflation. If removal of a nail does reveal that the tyre has been punctured, refit the nail so that its point of penetration is marked. Then immediately change the wheel, and have the tyre repaired by a tyre dealer.

Regularly check the tyres for damage in the form of cuts or bulges, especially in the sidewalls. Periodically remove the wheels, and clean any dirt or mud from the inside and outside surfaces. Examine the wheel rims for signs of rusting, corrosion or other damage. Light alloy wheels are easily damaged by "kerbing" whilst parking; steel wheels may also become dented or buckled. A new wheel is very often the only way to overcome severe damage.

New tyres should be balanced when they are fitted, but it may become necessary to re-balance them as they wear, or if the balance weights fitted to the wheel rim should fall off. Unbalanced tyres will wear more quickly, as will the steering and suspension components. Wheel imbalance is normally signified by vibration, particularly at a certain speed (typically around 50 mph). If this vibration is felt only through the steering, then it is likely that just the front wheels need balancing. If, however, the vibration is felt through the whole car, the rear wheels could be out of balance. Wheel balancing should be carried out by a tyre dealer or garage.

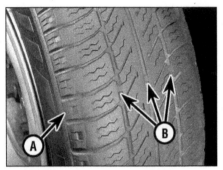

Tread Depth - visual check

1 The original tyres have tread wear safety bands (B), which will appear when the tread depth reaches approximately 1.6 mm. The band positions are indicated by a triangular mark on the tyre sidewall (A).

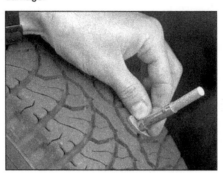

Tread Depth - manual check

2 Alternatively tread wear can be monitored with a simple, inexpensive device known as a tread depth indicator gauge.

Tyre Pressure Check

3 Check the tyre pressures regularly with the tyres cold. Do not adjust the tyre pressures immediately after the vehicle has been used, or an inaccurate setting will result. Tyre pressures are shown on the next page.

4 *Tyre tread wear patterns*

Shoulder Wear

Underinflation (wear on both sides)
Under-inflation will cause overheating of the tyre, because the tyre will flex too much, and the tread will not sit correctly on the road surface. This will cause a loss of grip and excessive wear, not to mention the danger of sudden tyre failure due to heat build-up.
Check and adjust pressures
Incorrect wheel camber (wear on one side)
Repair or renew suspension parts
Hard cornering
Reduce speed!

Centre Wear

Overinflation
Over-inflation will cause rapid wear of the centre part of the tyre tread, coupled with reduced grip, harsher ride, and the danger of shock damage occurring in the tyre casing.
Check and adjust pressures

If you sometimes have to inflate your car's tyres to the higher pressures specified for maximum load or sustained high speed, don't forget to reduce the pressures to normal afterwards.

Uneven Wear

Front tyres may wear unevenly as a result of wheel misalignment. Most tyre dealers and garages can check and adjust the wheel alignment (or "tracking") for a modest charge.
Incorrect camber or castor
Repair or renew suspension parts
Malfunctioning suspension
Repair or renew suspension parts
Unbalanced wheel
Balance tyres
Incorrect toe setting
Adjust front wheel alignment
Note: *The feathered edge of the tread which typifies toe wear is best checked by feel.*

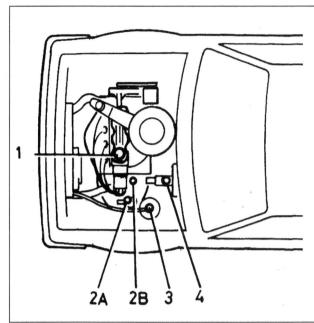

Lubricants and fluids

Component or system	Lubricant type/specification
1 Engine	Multigrade engine oil, viscosity range SAE 10W/40 to 20W/50, to API SF/CC, SF/CD, SG/CC or SG/CD
2A Manual transmission	SAE 80EP gear oil or GM gear oil 90 188 629
2B Automatic transmission	Dexron II type automatic transmission fluid
3 Cooling system	Ethylene glycol-based antifreeze
4 Braking system	Hydraulic fluid to DOT 4 or SAE J1703
Power steering fluid	Dexron II type automatic transmission fluid

Capacities

Engine oil
Capacity (all engines - oil change, including filter):
- 1.3 litre engine . . . . .3.0 litres
- 1.6 litre engine . . . . .3.5 litres
- 1.8 and 2.0 litre engine . . . . .4.0 litres
Difference between "MAX" and "MIN" dipstick marks . . . . . . .1.0 litre

Cooling system
Capacity (approximate)
- 1.3 litre engine . . . . .6.7 litres
- 1.6, 1.8 and 2.0 litre engines . . . . .7.5 litres

Manual gearbox
Capacity (approximate) . . . . .2.1 litres

Automatic transmission
Capacity (approximate):
- From dry . . . . .9.0 litres
- Drain and refill . . . . .7.0 litres

Fuel tank
Capacity models . . . . .61 litres

Tyre pressures

Pressures (tyres cold):	Front	Rear
1.3 litre models:		
155 x 13 tyres	2.0 bar (29 psi)	1.9 bar (28 psi)
165 x 13 tyres	1.9 bar (28 psi)	1.7 bar (25 psi)
1.6 litre models:		
Early (pre 1985) models:		
All models except SR	1.9 bar (28 psi)	1.7 bar (25 psi)
SR models	2.0 bar (29 psi)	2.0 bar (29 psi)
Later (1985 onwards) models:		
Base	2.0 bar (29 psi)	1.8 bar (26 psi)
L, GL and GLS	1.9 bar (28 psi)	1.7 bar (25 psi)
1.8 and 2.0 litre models:		
Early (pre 1984) models:		
185/70 x 13 tyres	1.9 bar (28 psi)	1.8 bar (26 psi)
195/60 x 14 tyres	2.0 bar (29 psi)	2.0 bar (29 psi)
Later (1985 onwards) models:		
185/70 x 13 tyres	2.0 bar (29 psi)	1.8 bar (26 psi)
195/60 x 14 tyres	2.1 bar (30 psi)	1.9 bar (28 psi)

Note: *Pressures apply only to original-equipment tyres, and may vary if any other make of tyre is fitted; check with the tyre manufacturer or supplier for correct pressures if necessary*
*Add 0.2 bar (3 psi) to both front and rear tyres for full-load operation or high speed driving.

Chapter 1
Routine maintenance and servicing

Contents

Air cleaner filter element renewal 31
Automatic transmission fluid level check 13
Automatic transmission fluid renewal 33
Auxiliary drivebelt check and renewal 8
Battery check 4
Brake fluid level check 3
Brake fluid renewal 27
Carburettor fuel inlet filter cleaning 24
Clutch adjustment check 26
Coolant level check 3
Coolant renewal 32
Driveshaft CV joint and gaiter check 19
Electrical system check 14
Engine oil and filter renewal 6
Engine oil level check 3
Exhaust system check 21
Front brake pad, caliper and disc check 17
Fuel filter renewal - fuel injection models 23
Fuel pump filter cleaning - carburettor models 11
Handbrake adjustment 28
Headlamp aim check 30
Hinge and lock lubrication 20
Hose and fluid leak check 7
Idle speed and mixture adjustments 10
Ignition system check 9
Introduction 2
Manual transmission oil level check 12
Power steering fluid level check 3
Rear brake shoe, wheel cylinder and drum check 18
Rear wheel bearing adjustment 29
Road test 22
Roadwheel bolt tightness check 16
Spark plug renewal 25
Tyre checks 5
Vauxhall Cavalier maintenance schedule 1
Washer fluid level check 3
Wiper blade check 15

Degrees of difficulty

Easy, suitable for novice with little experience	**Fairly easy,** suitable for beginner with some experience	**Fairly difficult,** suitable for competent DIY mechanic	**Difficult,** suitable for experienced DIY mechanic	**Very difficult,** suitable for expert DIY or professional

1 Vauxhall Cavalier maintenance schedule

The maintenance intervals in this manual are provided with the assumption that you, not the dealer, will be carrying out the work. These are the minimum maintenance intervals recommended by the manufacturer for vehicles driven daily. If you wish to keep your vehicle in peak condition at all times, you may wish to perform some of these procedures more often. We encourage frequent maintenance, because it enhances the efficiency, performance and resale value of your vehicle.

If the vehicle is driven in dusty areas, used to tow a trailer, or driven frequently at slow speeds (idling in traffic) or on short journeys, more frequent maintenance intervals are recommended.

When the vehicle is new, it should be serviced by a factory-authorised dealer service department, in order to preserve the factory warranty.

Models up to (and including) 1982

Every 250 miles (400 km) or weekly

☐ See Weekly checks

Every 9000 miles (15 000 km) or 6 months, whichever comes first

☐ Renew the engine oil and filter (Section 6)
☐ Check all underbonnet and underbody components, pipes and hoses for leaks (Section 7)
☐ Check the condition of the auxiliary drivebelt, and renew if necessary (Section 8)
☐ Check the ignition system components and renew the contact breaker points (Section 9)
☐ Check idle speed and mixture adjustments (Section 10)
☐ Clean the fuel pump filter (carburettor models) (Section 11)
☐ Check the throttle cable adjustment (Chapter 4)
☐ Check the manual transmission oil level (Section 12)
☐ Check the automatic transmission fluid level (Section 13)
☐ Check the operation of the horn, all lights, and the wipers and washers (Section 14)
☐ Check the condition of the wiper blades (Section 15)
☐ Check the tightness of the roadwheel bolts (Section 16)
☐ Check the condition of the front brake pads (renew if necessary), and the calipers and discs (Section 17)
☐ Check the condition of the rear brake shoes (renew if necessary), wheel cylinders and drums (Section 18)
☐ Check the driveshaft joints and gaiters for condition (Section 19)
☐ Lubricate locks and hinges (Section 20)
☐ Check the exhaust for condition and security (Section 21)
☐ Road test the vehicle (Section 22)

Every 18 000 miles (30 000 km) or 12 months, whichever comes first

In addition to all the items listed previously, carry out the following:
☐ Renew the fuel filter (fuel injection models) (Section 23)
☐ Clean the carburettor fuel inlet filter (Section 24)
☐ Renew the spark plugs (Section 25)
☐ Check the clutch adjustment (Section 26)
☐ Renew the brake fluid (Section 27)
☐ Check the handbrake adjustment (Section 28)
☐ Check the rear wheel bearings adjustment (Section 29)
☐ Check the headlamp alignment (Section 30)

Every 27 000 miles (45 000 km) or 18 months, whichever comes first

In addition to all the relevant items listed previously, carry out the following:
☐ Renew the air cleaner element (Section 31)

Every 36 000 miles

☐ Renew the camshaft toothed belt (Chapter 2)

Every 2 years (regardless of mileage)

☐ Renew the coolant (Section 32)

Every 54 000 miles (90 000 km) or 3 years, whichever comes first

In addition to all the relevant items listed previously, carry out the following:
☐ Renew the automatic transmission fluid (Section 33)

Models from 1983-on

Every 250 miles (400 km) or weekly

☐ See Weekly checks

Every 9000 miles (15 000 km) or 6 months, whichever comes first

☐ Renew the engine oil and filter (Section 6)

Every 9000 miles (15 000 km) or 12 months, whichever comes first

In addition to all the items listed previously, carry out the following:

☐ Check all underbonnet and underbody components, pipes and hoses for leaks (Section 7)
☐ Check the condition of the auxiliary drivebelt, and renew if necessary (Section 8)
☐ Check the ignition system components (Section 9)
☐ Check idle speed and mixture adjustments (Section 10)
☐ Check the throttle cable adjustment (Chapter 4)
☐ Check the manual transmission oil level (Section 12)
☐ Check the automatic transmission fluid level (Section 13)
☐ Check the operation of the horn, all lights, and the wipers and washers (Section 14)
☐ Check the condition of the wiper blades (Section 15)
☐ Check the tightness of the roadwheel bolts (Section 16)
☐ Check the condition of the front brake pads (renew if necessary), and the calipers and discs (Section 17)
☐ Check the condition of the rear brake shoes (renew if necessary), wheel cylinders and drums (Section 18)
☐ Check the driveshaft joints and gaiters for condition (Section 19)
☐ Lubricate locks and hinges (Section 20)
☐ Check the exhaust for condition and security (Section 21)
☐ Road test the vehicle (Section 22)
☐ Renew the spark plugs (Section 25)
☐ Check the clutch adjustment (Section 26)
☐ Renew the brake fluid (Section 27)
☐ Check the headlamp alignment (Section 30)

Every 18 000 miles (30 000 km) or 2 years, whichever comes first

In addition to all the items listed previously, carry out the following:

☐ Renew the fuel filter (fuel injection models) (Section 23)
☐ Clean the carburettor fuel inlet gauze filter (if applicable) (Section 24)
☐ Check the handbrake adjustment (Section 28)
☐ Renew the air cleaner element (Section 31)
☐ Renew the coolant (Section 32)

Every 36 000 miles (60 000 km) or 4 years, whichever comes first

In addition to all the items listed previously, carry out the following:

☐ Renew the camshaft toothed belt (Chapter 2)
☐ Renew the automatic transmission fluid (Section 33)

Underbonnet view of 1.3 litre model

1 Wiper motor
2 Heater blower motor
3 Suspension strut turret
4 Air cleaner
5 Brake servo/master cylinder
6 Washer fluid reservoir
7 Fuel pump
8 Alternator
9 Cooling system expansion bottle
10 Intake air temperature valve vacuum unit
11 Oil filler cap
12 Distributor
13 Battery
14 Radiator electric cooling fan
15 Bonnet support strut

Underbonnet view of an early (pre-1987) 1.8 litre model

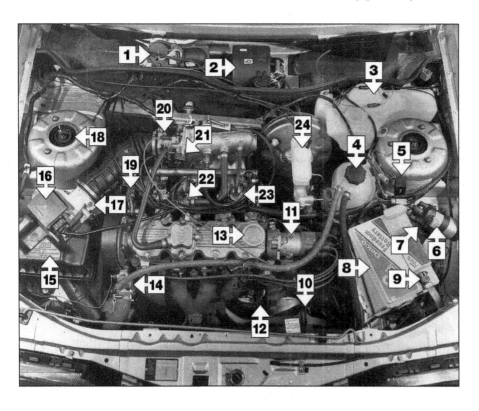

1 Wiper motor
2 Heater blower motor
3 Washer fluid reservoir
4 Cooling system expansion bottle
5 Fuel injection system control relay
6 Ignition coil
7 Electronic ignition control unit
8 Battery
9 Battery negative terminal
10 Radiator cooling fan
11 Distributor
12 Engine oil dipstick
13 Oil filler cap
14 Thermostat housing
15 Air cleaner
16 Airflow sensor
17 Idle mixture bypass screw
18 Suspension strut mounting
19 Alternator
20 Throttle valve housing
21 Throttle valve switch
22 Auxiliary air valve
23 Fuel pressure regulator
24 Brake master cylinder/fluid reservoir

Underbonnet view of a later (1987 onwards) 1.8 litre model

1 Wiper motor
2 Heater blower motor
3 Washer fluid reservoir
4 Cooling system expansion bottle
5 Fuel injection system control relay
6 Ignition coil
7 Battery
8 Distributor
9 Radiator cooling fan
10 Engine oil dipstick
11 Oil filler cap
12 Thermostat housing
13 Air cleaner
14 Airflow sensor
15 Suspension strut mounting
16 Ignition system control unit
17 Brake fluid reservoir
18 Brake vacuum servo unit
19 Throttle valve housing

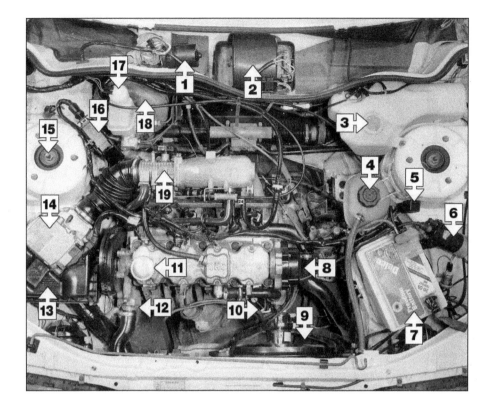

Front underbody view of a 1.3 litre model

1 Suspension control arm support
2 Exhaust pipe
3 Suspension control arm
4 Final drive cover plate
5 Driveshaft inboard joint
6 Engine/transmission mounting bracket
7 Flywheel housing cover plate
8 Sump
9 Radiator
10 Oil filter
11 Brake hose
12 Brake pipes
13 Fuel pipe
14 Anti-roll bar

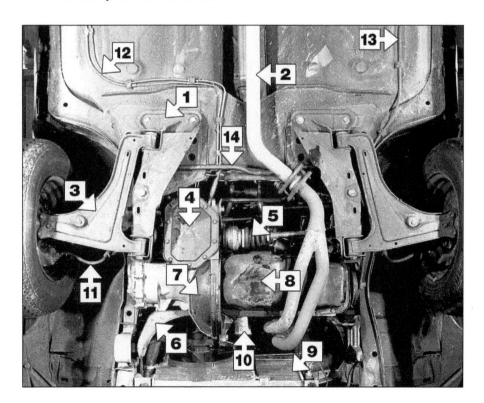

Front underbody view of a 1.8 litre model

1 Suspension control arm support
2 Exhaust pipe
3 Suspension control arm
4 Final drive cover plate
5 Driveshaft inboard joint
6 Sump
7 Flywheel housing cover plate
8 Brake pipes
9 Fuel pipes
10 Brake hose
11 Anti-roll bar

Rear underbody view of a 1.3 litre model

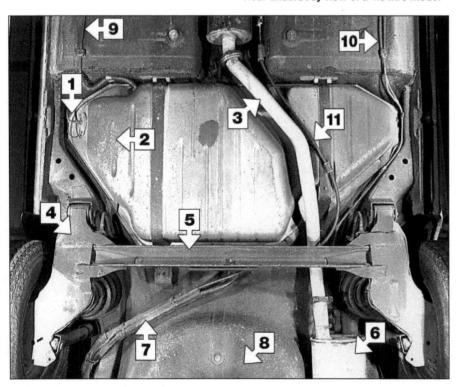

1 Fuel level sender unit
2 Fuel tank
3 Exhaust pipe
4 Rear suspension trailing arm
5 Rear axle member
6 Exhaust silencer
7 Fuel tank filler/breather hoses
8 Spare wheel recess
9 Fuel pipe
10 Brake pipes
11 Handbrake cable

Rear underbody view of a 1.8 litre model

1 Fuel tank
2 Exhaust expansion box
3 Spare wheel recess
4 Fuel level sender unit
5 Anti-roll bar
6 Fuel filler pipe
7 Rear axle member
8 Suspension trailing arm
9 Fuel filter
10 Electric fuel pump and regulator
11 Towing hook
12 Brake pipes
13 Handbrake cable
14 Fuel return pipe
15 Fuel delivery pipe

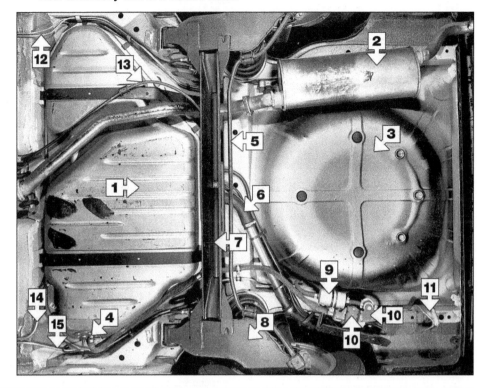

2 Introduction

General information

This Chapter is designed to help the home mechanic maintain his/her vehicle for safety, economy, long life and peak performance.

The Chapter contains a master maintenance schedule, followed by sections dealing specifically with each task on the schedule. Visual checks, adjustments, component renewal and other helpful items are included. Refer to the accompanying illustrations of the engine compartment and the underside of the vehicle for the locations of components.

Servicing of your vehicle in accordance with the mileage/time maintenance schedule and the following sections will provide a planned maintenance programme, which should result in a long and reliable service life. This is a comprehensive plan, so maintaining some items but not others at the specified service intervals, will not produce the same results.

As you service your vehicle, you will discover that many of the procedures can - and should - be grouped together, because of the particular procedure being performed, or because of the close proximity of two otherwise-unrelated components to one another. For example, if the vehicle is raised for any reason, the exhaust can be inspected at the same time as the suspension and steering components.

The first step in this maintenance programme is to prepare yourself before the actual work begins. Read through all the sections relevant to the work to be carried out, then make a list and gather together all the parts and tools required. If a problem is encountered, seek advice from a parts specialist, or a dealer service department.

Intensive maintenance

If, from the time the vehicle is new, the routine maintenance schedule is followed closely, and frequent checks are made of fluid levels and high-wear items, as suggested throughout this manual, the engine will be kept in relatively good running condition, and the need for additional work will be minimised.

It is possible that there will be times when the engine is running poorly due to the lack of regular maintenance. This is even more likely if a used vehicle, which has not received regular and frequent maintenance checks, is purchased. In such cases, additional work may need to be carried out, outside of the regular maintenance intervals.

If engine wear is suspected, a compression test (Chapter 2) will provide valuable information regarding the overall performance of the main internal components. Such a test can be used as a basis to decide on the extent of the work to be carried out. If for example a compression test indicates serious internal engine wear, conventional maintenance as described in this Chapter will not greatly improve the performance of the engine, and

may prove a waste of time and money, unless extensive overhaul work (Chapter 2) is carried out first.

The following series of operations are those most often required to improve the performance of a generally poor-running engine:

Primary operations

a) Clean, inspect and test the battery (Section 4).
b) Check all the engine-related fluids (Section 3).
c) Check the condition and tension of the auxiliary drivebelt (Section 8).
d) Renew the spark plugs (Section 25).
e) Inspect the ignition system components (Section 9).
f) Inspect the ignition HT leads (Section 9).
g) Check the condition of the air filter, and renew if necessary (Section 31).
h) Check the condition of all hoses, and check for fluid leaks (Section 7).

If the above operations do not prove fully effective, carry out the following secondary operations:

Secondary operations

All items listed under "Primary operations", plus the following:

a) Check the charging system (Chapter 5A).
b) Check the fuel system (Chapter 4A).
c) Renew the air filter (Section 31).
d) Renew the distributor cap and rotor arm (Section 9).
e) Renew the ignition HT leads (Section 9).

Every 250 miles or weekly

3 Fluid level checks

Refer to "Weekly checks"

4 Battery check

Refer to "Weekly checks"

5 Tyre checks

Refer to "Weekly checks"

Every 9000 miles

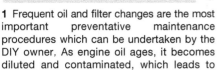

6 Engine oil and filter renewal

1 Frequent oil and filter changes are the most important preventative maintenance procedures which can be undertaken by the DIY owner, As engine oil ages, it becomes diluted and contaminated, which leads to premature engine wear.
2 Before starting this procedure, gather together all the necessary tools and materials. Also make sure that you have plenty of clean rags and newspapers handy, to mop up any spills. Ideally, the engine oil should be warm, as it will drain more easily, and more built-up sludge will be removed with it. Take care not to touch the exhaust or any other hot parts of the engine when working under the vehicle. To avoid any possibility of scalding, and to protect yourself from possible skin irritants and other harmful contaminants in used engine oils, it is advisable to wear gloves when carrying out this work. Access to the underside of the vehicle will be greatly improved if it can be raised on a lift, driven onto ramps, or jacked up and supported on axle stands (see *"Jacking and Vehicle Support"*). Whichever method is chosen, make sure that the vehicle remains level, or if it is at an angle, that the drain plug is at the lowest point. The drain plug is located at the rear of the sump.
3 Remove the oil filler cap from the camshaft cover (twist it through a quarter-turn anti-clockwise and withdraw it).

4 Using a spanner, or preferably a suitable socket and bar, slacken the drain plug about half a turn **(see illustration)**. Position the draining container under the drain plug, then remove the plug completely. If possible, try to keep the plug pressed into the sump while unscrewing it by hand the last couple of turns. As the plug releases from the threads, move it away sharply, so that the stream of oil from the sump runs into the container, not up your sleeve!
5 Allow some time for the oil to drain, noting that it may be necessary to reposition the container as the oil flow slows to a trickle.
6 After all the oil has drained, wipe the drain plug and the sealing washer with a clean rag. Examine the condition of the sealing washer, and renew it if it shows signs of scoring or other damage which may prevent an oil-tight seal. Clean the area around the drain plug opening, and refit the plug complete with the washer. Tighten the plug securely, preferably to the specified torque, using a torque wrench.
7 The oil filter is located at the right-hand end of the engine.
8 Move the container into position under the oil filter.
9 Use an oil filter removal tool to slacken the filter initially, then unscrew it by hand the rest of the way **(see illustration)**. Empty the oil from the old filter into the container.
10 Use a clean rag to remove all oil, dirt and sludge from the filter sealing area on the engine. Check the old filter to make sure that the rubber sealing ring has not stuck to the engine. If it has, carefully remove it.

11 Apply a light coating of clean oil to the sealing ring on the new filter, and screw the filter into position on the engine. Tighten the filter firmly by hand only - **do not** use any tools.
12 Remove the old oil and all tools from under the vehicle then, if applicable, lower the vehicle to the ground.
13 Fill the engine through the filler hole in the camshaft cover, using the correct grade and type of oil. Pour in half the specified quantity of oil first, then wait a few minutes for the oil to drain into the sump. Continue to add oil, a small quantity at a time, until the level is up to the lower mark on the dipstick. Adding a further 1.0 litre (approx.) will bring the level up to the upper mark on the dipstick.
14 Start the engine and run it for a few minutes, while checking for leaks around the oil filter seal and the sump drain plug. Note that there may be a delay of a few seconds before the low oil pressure warning light goes out when the engine is first started, as the oil circulates through the new oil filter and the engine oil galleries before the pressure builds up.
15 Stop the engine, and wait a few minutes for the oil to settle in the sump once more. With the new oil circulated and the filter now completely full, recheck the level on the dipstick, and add more oil as necessary.

OIL CARE

FOLLOW THE CODE

OIL BANK LINE
0800 66 33 66

Note: It is antisocial and illegal to dump oil down the drain. To find the location of your local oil recycling bank, call this number free.

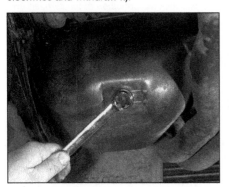

6.4 Removing the sump drain plug

6.9 Using an oil filter removal tool to unscrew the oil filter

7 Hose and fluid leak check

1 Visually inspect the engine joint faces, gaskets and seals for any signs of water or oil leaks. Pay particular attention to the areas around the camshaft cover, cylinder head, oil filter and sump joint faces. Bear in mind that, over a period of time, some very slight

seepage from these areas is to be expected; what you are really looking for is any indication of a serious leak. Should a leak be found, renew the offending gasket or oil seal by referring to the appropriate Chapters in this manual.

2 Also check the security and condition of all the engine-related pipes and hoses. Ensure that all cable-ties or securing clips are in place, and in good condition. Clips which are broken or missing can lead to chafing of the hoses pipes or wiring, which could cause more serious problems in the future.

3 Carefully check the radiator hoses and heater hoses along their entire length. Renew any hose which is cracked, swollen or deteriorated. Cracks will show up better if the hose is squeezed. Pay close attention to the hose clips that secure the hoses to the cooling system components. Hose clips can pinch and puncture hoses, resulting in cooling system leaks. If wire-type hose clips are used, it may be a good idea to replace them with screw-type clips.

4 Inspect all the cooling system components (hoses, joint faces etc.) for leaks. Where any problems of this nature are found on system components, renew the component or gasket with reference to Chapter 3.

A leak in the cooling system will usually show up as white- or rust-coloured deposits on the area adjoining the leak.

5 Where applicable, inspect the automatic transmission fluid cooler hoses for leaks or deterioration.

6 With the vehicle raised, inspect the petrol tank and filler neck for punctures, cracks and other damage. The connection between the filler neck and tank is especially critical. Sometimes, a rubber filler neck or connecting hose will leak due to loose retaining clamps or deteriorated rubber.

7 Carefully check all rubber hoses and metal fuel lines leading away from the petrol tank. Check for loose connections, deteriorated hoses, crimped lines and other damage. Pay particular attention to the vent pipes and hoses, which often loop up around the filler neck and can become blocked or crimped. Follow the lines to the front of the vehicle, carefully inspecting them all the way. Renew damaged sections as necessary.

8 From within the engine compartment, check the security of all fuel hose attachments and pipe unions, and inspect the fuel hoses and vacuum hoses for kinks, chafing and deterioration.

9 Where applicable, check the condition of the power steering fluid hoses and pipes.

8 Auxiliary drivebelt check and renewal

Alternator drivebelt

Checking and adjustment

1 Correct tensioning of the auxiliary drivebelt will ensure that it has a long life. Beware, however, of overtightening, as this can cause excessive wear in the alternator.

2 The belt should be inspected along its entire length, and if it is found to be worn, frayed or cracked, it should be renewed as a precaution against breakage in service. It is advisable to carry a spare drivebelt of the correct type in the vehicle at all times.

3 Although special tools are available for measuring the belt tension, a good approximation can be achieved if the belt is tensioned so that there is approximately 13.0 mm of free movement under firm thumb pressure at the mid-point of the longest run between pulleys. If in doubt, err on the slack side, as an excessively-tight belt may cause damage to the alternator or other components.

4 If adjustment is required, loosen the alternator upper mounting nut and bolt - use two spanners, one to counterhold the bolt. Lever the alternator away from the engine using a wooden lever at the mounting bracket until the correct tension is achieved, then tighten the bolt securing the adjuster bracket, and the alternator mounting nuts and bolts. On no account lever at the free end of the alternator, as serious internal damage could be caused to the alternator.

Removal, renewal and refitting

5 To remove the belt, simply loosen the mounting nuts and bolts, and the bolt securing the adjuster bracket, as described previously, and slacken the belt sufficiently to slip it from the pulleys. On models with power steering it will first be necessary to remove the power steering pump drivebelt as described below.

6 Refit the belt, and tension it as described previously. Note that when a new belt has been fitted it will probably stretch slightly to start with and the tension should be re-checked, and if necessary adjusted, after about 5 minutes running.

Power steering pump drivebelt

Checking and adjustment

7 Refer to the information given in paragraphs 1 to 3, noting that there should be approximately 8 mm of free movement in the belt.

8 If adjustment is required, slacken the adjuster bolt locknut (situated on the base of the pump) and rotate the adjuster nut as necessary to tension the belt. Once the belt tension is correct, securely tighten the locknut.

Removal, renewal and refitting

9 To remove the belt, simply loosen the locknut and fully slacken the adjuster nut sufficiently to slip the drivebelt from the pulleys.

10 Refit the belt, and tension it as described previously. Note that when a new belt has been fitted it will probably stretch slightly to start with and the tension should be re-checked, and if necessary adjusted, after about 5 minutes running.

9 Ignition system check

Models with contact breaker ignition system

1 Renew the contact breaker points and adjust the gap and dwell angle as described in Chapter 5B. After adjustment put one or two drops of engine oil into the centre of the cam recess where appropriate and smear the surfaces of the cam itself with petroleum jelly. Do not over-lubricate as any excess could get onto the contact point surfaces and cause ignition difficulties.

2 The spark plug (HT) leads should also be checked.

3 Ensure that the leads are numbered before removing them, if not make identification marks to avoid confusion when refitting. Pull the leads from the plugs by gripping the end fitting, not the lead, otherwise the lead connection may be fractured.

4 Check inside the end fitting for signs of corrosion, which will look like a white crusty powder. Push the end fitting back onto the spark plug ensuring that it is a tight fit on the plug. If not, remove the lead again and use pliers to carefully crimp the metal connector inside the end fitting until it fits securely on the end of the spark plug.

5 Using a clean rag, wipe the entire length of the lead to remove any built-up dirt and grease. Once the lead is clean, check for burns, cracks and other damage. Do not bend the lead excessively or pull the lead lengthwise - the conductor inside might break.

6 Disconnect the other end of the lead from the distributor cap. Again, pull only on the end fitting. Check for corrosion and a tight fit in the same manner as the spark plug end. If an ohmmeter is available, check the resistance of the lead by connecting the meter between the spark plug end of the lead and the segment inside the distributor cap. Refit the lead securely on completion.

7 Check the remaining leads one at a time, in the same way.

8 If new spark plug (HT) leads are required, purchase a set for your specific car and engine.

9 Remove the distributor cap, wipe it clean and carefully inspect it inside and out for signs of cracks, carbon tracks (tracking) and worn, burned or loose contacts; check that the cap's carbon brush is unworn, free to move against spring pressure and making good contact with the rotor arm. Also inspect the cap seal for signs of wear or damage and renew if necessary. Remove and inspect the rotor arm **(see illustrations)**. It is common practice to renew the cap and rotor arm whenever new spark plug (HT) leads are fitted. On refitting ensure that the arm is securely pressed onto the shaft and the cap is securely fitted.

 When fitting a new cap, remove the leads from the old cap one at a time and fit them to the new cap in the exact same location - do not simultaneously remove all the leads from the old cap or firing order confusion may occur.

10 Even with the ignition system in first class condition, some engines may still occasionally experience poor starting attributable to damp ignition components, in which case, a moisture dispersant can be used.

Models with an electronic ignition system

 Voltages produced by an electronic ignition system are considerably higher than those produced by conventional ignition systems. Extreme care must be taken when working on the system with the ignition switched on. Persons with surgically-implanted cardiac pacemaker devices should keep well clear of the ignition circuits, components and test equipment.

11 Check the condition of the HT leads and distributor components as described above in paragraphs 3 to 10.
12 Check the ignition timing (Chapter 5C).

10 Idle speed and mixture adjustments

1 Before checking the idle speed and mixture setting, always check first the following.
a) *Check that the ignition timing is accurate (Chapter 5B or 5C).*

9.9a Remove the distributor cap . . .

b) *Check that the spark plugs are in good condition and correctly gapped (Section 25).*
c) *Check that the accelerator cable and, on carburettor models, the choke cable (where fitted) is correctly adjusted (see relevant Part of Chapter 4).*
d) *Check that the crankcase breather hoses are secure with no leaks or kinks (Chapter 2).*
e) *Check that the air cleaner filter element is clean (Section 31).*
f) *Check that the exhaust system is in good condition (see relevant Part of Chapter 4).*
g) *If the engine is running very roughly, check the compression pressures as described in Chapter 2.*

2 Take the car on a journey of sufficient length to warm it up to normal operating temperature. Proceed as described under the relevant sub-heading.
Note: *Adjustment should be completed within two minutes of return, without stopping the engine. If this cannot be achieved, or if the radiator electric cooling fan operates, wait for the cooling fan to stop and clear any excess fuel from the inlet manifold by racing the engine two or three times to between 2000 and 3000 rpm, then allow it to idle again.*

Carburettor models

GM Varajet carburettor

3 The carburettor throttle stop screw and mixture adjusting screws are set during production and are fitted with tamperproof caps **(see illustrations)**.
4 An additional mixture adjusting screw

9.9b . . . and pull off the rotor arm from the distributor shaft (1.6 litre model shown)

(bypass) is provided. This is not fitted with a tamperproof cap as it is the means by which the engine idle speed is adjusted.
5 Connect a tachometer in accordance with the manufacturer's instructions.
6 If the idle speed is outside the specified tolerance (see Specifications), turn the additional mixture (bypass) screw as necessary. This will not alter the CO content of the exhaust gas to any extent.
7 If an exhaust gas analyser is available, check the exhaust gas CO content as follows.
8 Remove the tamperproof caps from the mixture adjustment screw. Satisfy yourself that you are not breaking any local or national laws by so doing.
9 With the engine at normal operating temperature, check the CO content of the exhaust gas. If it is outside the permitted tolerance, turn the mixture adjusting screw as necessary to correct it. To reduce the CO content, turn the screw clockwise; to increase it, turn the screw anti-clockwise.
10 When the adjustments are correct, fit a new tamperproof cap to the screw. These are blue in colour and are obtainable from your Vauxhall/Opel dealer.

Pierburg 2E3 carburettor

11 Connect a tachometer to the engine in accordance with their makers' instructions.
12 Start the engine and allow it to idle. If the idle speed is outside the specified limits, adjust by means of the throttle stop screw **(see illustration)**.

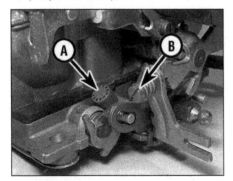

10.3a Throttle stop (A) and fast idle adjustment (B) screws - GM Varajet carburettor

10.3b Additional mixture (bypass) screw (C) and mixture screw (D) - GM Varajet carburettor

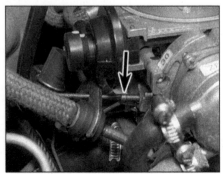

10.12 Throttle stop screw (arrowed) - Pierburg 2E3 carburettor

10.13 Mixture adjustment screw (arrowed) behind the tamperproof cap - Pierburg 2E3

13 When the idle speed is correct, if an exhaust gas analyser is available check the CO level in the exhaust gas. If it is outside the specified limits, adjust by means of the idle mixture adjustment screw. In production the screw is covered by a tamperproof plug; satisfy yourself that you are not breaking any local or national laws before removing the plug (see illustration).

14 With the idle mixture correct, readjust the idle speed if necessary.

15 When both speed and mixture are correct, stop the engine and disconnect the test equipment. Fit a new tamperproof plug to the idle mixture adjustment screw where this is required by law.

Fuel-injected models

1.8 litre models

16 With the engine at normal operating temperature, connect a tachometer using its manufacturer's instructions.

17 Allow the engine to idle, and compare the idle speed with that given in the Specifications. If adjustment is necessary, slacken the locknut and turn the idle speed adjusting screw until the specified speed is obtained. The adjusting screw is situated on the throttle valve housing. Tighten the locknut on completion.

18 If an exhaust gas analyser is available, check the mixture (CO level) as follows.

19 With the engine idling at the specified speed, read the CO level and compare it with that specified.

10.20 On 1.8 litre fuel-injected models the mixture adjustment screw is located underneath the tamperproof cap on the airflow sensor

20 If adjustment is necessary, remove the tamperproof cap from the mixture adjusting screw on the airflow sensor (see illustration). Turn the screw clockwise to enrich the mixture, and anti-clockwise to weaken it.

21 On completion, re-adjust the idle speed if necessary. Note that failure to bring the CO level within the specified range indicates a fault in the injection system, or a worn engine.

2.0 litre models

22 On 2.0 litre models both the idle speed and mixture CO content are automatically controlled by the control unit and cannot be manually adjusted (See Chapter 4B). If necessary, they can be checked by if they are found to be incorrect then a fault is present in the fuel injection/ignition system.

11 Fuel pump filter cleaning - carburettor models

⚠️ *Warning: Before carrying out the following operation refer to the precautions given in Safety first! at the beginning of this Manual and follow them implicitly. Petrol is a highly dangerous and volatile liquid and the precautions necessary when handling it cannot be overstressed*

Note: *On some models the fuel pump may be a sealed unit, in which case this procedure is not necessary.*

1 Place a wad of rag underneath the fuel

11.2 Removing the fuel pump cover, filter and rubber seal - carburettor models

pump to catch the fuel which will be spilt.

2 Undo the retaining screw and remove the end cover from the fuel pump. Recover the rubber seal (see illustration).

3 Remove the filter from the cover and wash it fresh fuel to remove any debris from it. Inspect the filter for signs of clogging or splitting and renew it if necessary.

4 Refitting is the reverse of removal. On completion, start the engine and check for signs of fuel leakage.

12 Manual transmission oil level check

1 Ensure that the vehicle is standing on level ground and the handbrake applied.

2 Working underneath the vehicle, unscrew the transmission oil level plug (see illustration). The level plug is located beside the driveshaft inner CV joint; on 1.3 litre models the plug is on the left-hand side of the transmission, and on larger-engine models it is on the right-hand side.

3 The oil level should be up to the lower edge of the level plug hole.

4 If necessary, top-up with oil through the breather/filler orifice in the gear selector cover. Unscrew the breather/filler plug, and top-up with the specified grade of oil, until oil just begins to run from the level plug hole. A funnel may be helpful, to avoid spillage (see illustrations). Do not overfill - if too much oil is added, wait until the excess has run out of the level plug hole. Refit the level plug and the breather/filler plug on completion.

12.2 Removing the manual transmission level plug - 1.6 litre model shown

12.4a To top up the fluid level, unscrew the breather/filler plug from the top of the transmission . . .

12.4b . . . then top up via the breather/filler plug orifice

13 Automatic transmission fluid level check

1 To check the fluid level, the vehicle must be parked on level ground. Apply the handbrake.
2 If the transmission fluid is cold (ie, if the engine is cold), the level check must be completed with the engine idling, within one minute of the engine being started.
3 With the engine idling, fully depress the brake pedal, and move the gear selector lever smoothly through all positions, finishing in position "P".
4 With the engine still idling, withdraw the transmission fluid level dipstick (located at the left-hand side of the engine compartment, next to the engine oil level dipstick). Pull up the lever on the top of the dipstick to release it from the tube. Wipe the dipstick clean with a lint-free rag, re-insert it and withdraw it again.
5 If the transmission fluid was cold at the beginning of the procedure, the fluid level should be on the "MAX" mark on the side of the dipstick marked "+20ºC". Note that 0.4 litres of fluid is required to raise the level from the "MIN" to the "MAX" mark.
6 If the transmission fluid was at operating temperature at the beginning of the procedure (ie, if the vehicle had been driven for at least 12 miles/20 km), the fluid level should be between the "MIN" and "MAX" marks on the side of the dipstick marked "+94ºC". Note that 0.2 litres of fluid is required to raise the level from the "MIN" to the "MAX" mark.
7 If topping-up is necessary, stop the engine, and top-up with the specified type of fluid through the transmission dipstick tube.
8 Re-check the level, and refit the dipstick on completion.

14 Electrical system check

1 Check the operation of all the electrical equipment, ie lights, direction indicators, horn, etc. Refer to the appropriate sections of Chapter 12 for details if any of the circuits are found to be inoperative.
2 Note that stop-light switch adjustment is described in Chapter 9.
3 Check all accessible wiring connectors, harnesses and retaining clips for security, and for signs of chafing or damage. Rectify any faults found.

15 Wiper blade check

Check the condition of the wiper blades. If they are cracked, or show any signs of deterioration, or if they fail to clean the glass effectively, renew the blades. Ideally, the wiper blades should be renewed annually as a matter of course.

To remove a wiper blade, pull the arm away

from the glass until it locks. Swivel the blade through 90º, then squeeze the locking clip, and detach the blade from the arm. When fitting the new blade, make sure that the blade locks securely into the arm, and that the blade is orientated correctly.

16 Roadwheel bolt tightness check

Using a torque wrench on each wheel bolt in turn, ensure that the bolts are tightened to the specified torque.

17 Front brake pad, caliper and disc check

1 Apply the handbrake, then jack up the front of the vehicle and support securely on axle stands; remove the roadwheels (see "*Jacking and Vehicle Support*").
2 If any pad is worn to the specified minimum thickness or less, all four pads must be renewed (see Chapter 9).
3 For a comprehensive check, the brake pads should be removed and cleaned. This will allow the operation of the caliper to be checked, and the condition of the brake disc itself to be fully examined on both sides (see Chapter 9).

18 Rear brake shoe, wheel cylinder and drum check

1 Chock the front wheels, then jack up the rear of the vehicle, and support it securely on axle stands (see "*Jacking and Vehicle Support*").
2 For a quick check, the thickness of friction material remaining on one of the brake shoes can be observed through the hole in the brake backplate which is exposed by prising out the sealing grommet **(see illustration)**. If a rod of the same diameter as the specified minimum friction material thickness is placed against the shoe friction material, the amount of wear can be assessed. A torch or inspection light will probably be required. If the friction material on

18.2 Removing the sealing grommet from the inspection hole in the rear brake backplate

For a quick check, the thickness of friction material remaining on each pad can be measured through the slot in the front of the caliper body.

any shoe is worn down to the specified minimum thickness or less, all four shoes must be renewed as a set.
3 For a comprehensive check, the brake drum should be removed and cleaned. This will allow the wheel cylinders to be checked, and the condition of the brake drum itself to be fully examined (see Chapter 9).

19 Driveshaft CV joint and gaiter check

Refer to Chapter 8, Section 5.

20 Hinge and lock lubrication

Lubricate the hinges of the bonnet, doors and tailgate with a light general-purpose oil. Similarly, lubricate all latches, locks and lock strikers. At the same time, check the security and operation of all the locks, adjusting them if necessary (see Chapter 11).

Lightly lubricate the bonnet release mechanism and cable with a suitable grease.

21 Exhaust system check

1 With the engine cold (at least an hour after the vehicle has been driven), check the complete exhaust system from the engine to the end of the tailpipe. The exhaust system is most easily checked with the vehicle raised on a hoist, or suitably supported on axle stands, so that the exhaust components are readily visible and accessible.
2 Check the exhaust pipes and connections for evidence of leaks, severe corrosion and damage. Make sure that all brackets and mountings are in good condition, and that all relevant nuts and bolts are tight. Leakage at any of the joints or in other parts of the system will usually show up as a black sooty stain in the vicinity of the leak.
3 Rattles and other noises can often be traced to the exhaust system, especially the brackets

and mountings. Try to move the pipes and silencers. If the components are able to come into contact with the body or suspension parts, secure the system with new mountings. Otherwise separate the joints (if possible) and twist the pipes as necessary to provide additional clearance.

22 Road test

Instruments and electrical equipment

1 Check the operation of all instruments and electrical equipment.
2 Ensure that all instruments read correctly, and switch on all electrical equipment in turn, to check that it functions properly.

Steering and suspension

3 Check for any abnormalities in the steering, suspension, handling or road "feel".
4 Drive the vehicle, and check that there are no unusual vibrations or noises.
5 Check that the steering feels positive, with no excessive "sloppiness", or roughness, and check for any suspension noises when cornering and driving over bumps.

Drivetrain

6 Check the performance of the engine, clutch (if applicable), gearbox/transmission and driveshafts.
7 Listen for any unusual noises from the engine, clutch and gearbox/transmission.
8 Make sure that the engine runs smoothly when idling, and that there is no hesitation when accelerating.
9 Check that, where applicable, the clutch action is smooth and progressive, that the drive is taken up smoothly, and that the pedal travel is not excessive. Also listen for any noises when the clutch pedal is depressed.
10 On manual gearbox models, check that all gears can be engaged smoothly without noise, and that the gear lever action is not abnormally vague or "notchy".
11 On automatic transmission models, make sure that all gearchanges occur smoothly, without snatching, and without an increase in engine speed between changes. Check that all the gear positions can be selected with the vehicle at rest. If any problems are found, they should be referred to a Vauxhall/Opel dealer.
12 Listen for a metallic clicking sound from the front of the vehicle, as the vehicle is driven slowly in a circle with the steering on full-lock. Carry out this check in both directions. If a

clicking noise is heard, this indicates wear in a driveshaft joint, in which case renew the joint .

Check the operation and performance of the braking system

13 Make sure that the vehicle does not pull to one side when braking, and that the wheels do not lock prematurely when braking hard.
14 Check that there is no vibration through the steering when braking.
15 Check that the handbrake operates correctly without excessive movement of the lever, and that it holds the vehicle stationary on a slope.
16 Test the operation of the brake servo unit as follows. With the engine off, depress the footbrake four or five times to exhaust the vacuum. Hold the brake pedal depressed, then start the engine. As the engine starts, there should be a noticeable "give" in the brake pedal as vacuum builds up. Allow the engine to run for at least two minutes, and then switch it off. If the brake pedal is depressed now, it should be possible to detect a hiss from the servo as the pedal is depressed. After about four or five applications, no further hissing should be heard, and the pedal should feel considerably harder.

Every 18 000 miles

23 Fuel filter renewal - fuel injection models

 Warning: Before carrying out the following operation refer to the precautions given in Safety first! at the beginning of this Manual and follow them implicitly. Petrol is a highly dangerous and volatile liquid and the precautions necessary when handling it cannot be overstressed

1 The fuel filter is located under the rear of the vehicle, next to the fuel pump. Chock the front wheels, then jack up the rear of the vehicle, and support securely on axle stands (see "Jacking and Vehicle Support").
2 Disconnect the battery negative lead and position a suitable container below the fuel filter, to catch spilt fuel.
3 Slacken the retaining clips and, bearing in mind the information given in Chapter 4B on depressurising the fuel system, disconnect both hoses. To minimise fuel loss clamp the hoses either side of the filter or be prepared to plug the hose ends as they are disconnected (see illustration).
4 Loosen the clamp bolt, and withdraw the filter. Note the orientation of the fuel flow indicator on the filter. This will be in the form of an arrow which points in the direction of the

fuel flow, or the filter will have AUS (out) stamped on its outlet side **(see illustration)**.
5 Recover the mounting rubber from the old filter, and transfer it to the new filter.
6 Fit the new filter making sure its fuel flow direction indicator is facing the right way.
7 Reconnect the hose and securely tighten their retaining clips.
8 Start the engine and check the disturbed hose connections for signs of leakage.

24 Carburettor fuel inlet filter cleaning

 Refer to the Warning at the beginning of Section 23 concerning the precautions required when handling petrol

1 Disconnect the battery negative lead.
2 Disconnect the fuel hose from the carburettor and plug the hose.
3 On the GM Varajet carburettor, unscrew the fuel inlet union from the carburettor and remove the filter. On the Pierburg 2E3 carburettor withdraw the filter from the fuel inlet union (see Chapter 4A).
4 Wash with it fresh fuel to remove any debris. Inspect the filter for signs of clogging or splitting and renew it if necessary.
5 Refit the filter and reconnect the fuel hose.

23.3 Fuel filter showing mounting and hose connections

23.4 Fuel filter directional marking

25.5 Removing a spark plug

25.10a Measuring a spark plug electrode gap using a feeler blade

25 Spark plug renewal

Note: *This operation is required at 9000 miles (or 12 months) on models from 1983-on.*

1 The correct functioning of the spark plugs is vital for the correct running and efficiency of the engine. It is essential that the plugs fitted are appropriate for the engine, the suitable type being specified at the end of this Chapter. If the correct type of plug is used and the engine is in good condition, the spark plugs should not need attention between scheduled renewal intervals, except for adjustment of their gaps. Spark plug cleaning is rarely necessary, and should not be attempted unless specialised equipment is available, as damage can easily be caused to the firing ends.

2 To remove the plugs, first open the bonnet, then proceed as follows.

3 If necessary, mark the HT leads 1 to 4, to correspond to the cylinder the lead serves (No 1 cylinder is nearest the timing belt end of the engine). Pull the HT leads from the plugs by gripping the end connectors, not the leads, otherwise the lead connections may be fractured.

4 It is advisable to remove any dirt from the spark plug recesses using a clean brush, vacuum cleaner or compressed air, before removing the plugs, to prevent the dirt dropping into the cylinders.

5 Unscrew the plugs using a spark plug spanner, a box spanner, or a deep socket and

extension bar **(see illustration)**. Keep the socket in alignment with the spark plugs, otherwise if it is forcibly moved to either side, the porcelain top of the spark plug may be broken off.

6 Examination of the spark plugs will give a good indication of the condition of the engine. If the insulator nose of the spark plug is clean and white, with no deposits, this is indicative of a weak mixture or too hot a plug (a hot plug transfers heat away from the electrode slowly, while a cold plug transfers heat away quickly).

7 If the tip and insulator nose are covered with hard black-looking deposits, then this is indicative that the idle mixture is too rich. Should the plug be black and oily, then it is likely that the engine is fairly worn, as well as the mixture being too rich.

8 If the insulator nose is covered with light-tan to greyish-brown deposits, then the mixture is correct and it is likely that the engine is in good condition.

9 The spark plug gap is of considerable importance as, if it is too large or too small, the size of the spark and its efficiency will be seriously impaired. For the best results, the spark plug gap should be set in accordance with the Specifications at the end of this Chapter.

10 To set the spark plug gap, measure the gap between the electrodes with a feeler blade, and then bend open, or close, the outer plug electrode until the correct gap is achieved **(see illustrations)**. The centre electrode should never be bent, as this may crack the insulation and cause plug failure, if nothing worse.

11 Special spark plug electrode gap adjusting tools are available from most motor accessory shops **(see illustration)**.

12 Before fitting the new spark plugs, check that the threaded connector sleeves on the top of the plug are tight, and that the plug exterior surfaces and threads are clean.

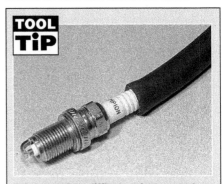

TOOL TiP

It is very often difficult to insert spark plugs into their holes without cross-threading them. To avoid this, fit a short length of 5/16-inch internal diameter hose over the end of the spark plug. The flexible hose acts as a universal joint to help align the plug with the plug hole. Should the plug begin to cross-thread, the hose will slip on the spark plug, preventing thread damage to the aluminium cylinder head.

13 Screw in the spark plugs by hand where possible, then tighten them to the specified torque. Take extra care to enter the plug threads correctly, as the cylinder head is of light alloy construction.

14 Reconnect the HT leads in the correct order.

26 Clutch adjustment check

Note: *This operation is required at 9000 miles (or 12 months) on models from 1983-on.*
  Refer to Chapter 6

27 Brake fluid renewal

⚠ *Warning: Brake hydraulic fluid can harm your eyes and damage painted surfaces, so use extreme caution when handling and pouring it. Do not use fluid that has been standing open for some time as it absorbs moisture from the air. Excess moisture can cause a dangerous loss of braking effectiveness.*

Note: *This operation is required at 9000 miles (or 12 months) on models from 1983-on.*

1 The procedure is similar to that for the bleeding of the hydraulic system as described in Chapter 9, except that the brake fluid reservoir should be emptied by siphoning, using a clean poultry baster or similar before

25.10b Measuring a spark plug electrode gap using a wire gauge

25.11 Adjusting a spark plug electrode gap

starting, and allowance should be made for the old fluid to be expelled when bleeding a section of the circuit.

2 Working as described in Chapter 9, open the first bleed screw in the sequence and pump the brake pedal gently until nearly all the old fluid has been emptied from the master cylinder reservoir. Top-up to the `MAX' level with new fluid and continue pumping until only the new fluid remains in the reservoir and new fluid can be seen emerging from the bleed screw. Tighten the screw and top the reservoir level up to the `MAX' level line.

HAYNES HINT *Old hydraulic fluid is invariably much darker in colour than the new, making it easy to distinguish the two.*

3 Work through the remaining bleed screws in the sequence until new fluid can be seen at all of them. Be careful to keep the master cylinder reservoir topped up to above the `MIN' level at all times or air may enter the system and greatly increase the length of the task.

4 When the operation is complete, check that all bleed screws are securely tightened and that their dust caps are refitted. Wash off all traces of spilt fluid and recheck the master cylinder reservoir fluid level.

5 Check the operation of the brakes before taking the car on the road.

Every 27 000 miles

28 Handbrake adjustment

Note: *This operation is required at 18000 miles (or 2 years) on models from 1983-on.*

1 The handbrake should be kept in correct adjustment by the routine adjustment of the rear shoes. However, due to cable stretch over a period of time, the travel of the handbrake lever may become excessive and the following operations should be carried out.

2 On early (pre 1984) models with adjustable brakes, ensure that the brake shoes are fully adjusted by means of their backplate adjusters (see Chapter 9, Section 7).

3 Raise the rear of the vehicle so that the rear roadwheels are free to turn.

4 Pull the handbrake control lever onto its first notch.

5 Using two spanners, adjust the cable by turning the nuts on the threaded part of the cable end fitting. This is located on or above the rear axle beam. After adjusting, the brake linings should just be heard to rub when the rear wheels are turned by hand in the normal rotational direction **(see illustration)**.

6 Fully release the handbrake lever and check that both wheels are free to rotate easily.

7 Adjustment is now correct. Keep the threads of the cable end fitting smeared with grease to prevent corrosion.

8 Lower the vehicle to the ground.

28.5 The handbrake cable adjuster nut (arrowed) is located on the top of the axle

29 Rear wheel bearing adjustment

Refer to Chapter 10, Section 10.

30 Headlamp aim check

Note: *This operation is required at 9000 miles (or 12 months) on models from 1983-on.*

1 Accurate adjustment of the headlight beam is only possible using optical beam-setting equipment, and this work should therefore be carried out by a Vauxhall/Opel dealer or service station with the necessary facilities.

2 Basic adjustments can be carried out in an emergency; further details are in Chapter 12.

31 Air cleaner filter element renewal

Note: *This operation is required at 18000 miles (or 2 years) on models from 1983-on.*

Carburettor models

1 To remove the air cleaner element, remove the air cleaner cover. This is secured by a centre nut or bolt, or by three screws. Additionally, release the spring clips around the edge of the cover or, if spring clips are not fitted, carefully prise around the lower edge of the cover with your fingers to release the retaining lugs **(see illustrations)**.

2 With the cover removed, lift out the element **(see illustrations)**.

3 Wipe inside the air cleaner, being careful not to introduce dirt into the carburettor throat. It is preferable to remove the air cleaner completely. Remember to clean the inside of the air cleaner cover.

4 Fit the new element, then refit and secure the cover. Observe any cover-to-body alignment lugs or slots.

Fuel injection models

5 The air cleaner on these models is contained within the airflow sensor housing.

31.1a On carburettor models, undo the retaining nut (or screws) . . .

31.1b . . . and release the retaining clips . . .

31.2a . . . then lift off the air cleaner lid . . .

31.2b . . . and withdraw the filter element

31.6 On fuel-injected models disconnect the airflow sensor wiring connector . . .

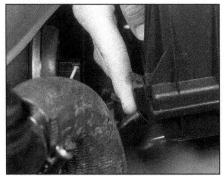

31.7a . . . then release the retaining clips . . .

31.7b . . . and remove the housing cover, complete with the filter element

6 Release the locking clip, and disconnect the plug from the airflow sensor **(see illustration)**. Disconnect the air trunking.
7 Release the spring clips, and lift off the air cleaner cover with airflow sensor attached. The element will probably come away with the cover **(see illustrations)**. Do not drop or jar the airflow sensor.

8 Wipe clean the inside of the air cleaner and fit a new element to the cover, engaging the seal in the cover recess **(see illustration)**. Refit and secure the cover, then reconnect the airflow sensor plug. Refit the air trunking.

31.8 On fitting, ensure the element is correctly seated in the cover groove

Every 2 Years

32 Coolant renewal

⚠️ *Warning: Wait until the engine is cold before starting this procedure. Do not allow antifreeze to come in contact with your skin or painted surfaces of the vehicle. Rinse off spills immediately with plenty of water. Never leave antifreeze lying around in an open container or in a puddle in the driveway or on the garage floor. Children and pets are attracted by its sweet smell. Antifreeze is fatal if ingested.*

Cooling system draining

Note: *This operation is required at 18000 miles (or 2 years) on models from 1983-on.*
1 To drain the cooling system, remove the expansion tank filler cap. Turn the cap anti-clockwise until it reaches the first stop. Wait until any pressure remaining in the system is released then push the cap down, turn it anti-clockwise to the second stop and lift off.
2 Position a suitable container beneath the radiator bottom hose union.
3 Slacken the hose clip and ease the hose from the radiator stub. If the hose joint has not been disturbed for some time, it will be necessary to gently manipulate the hose to break the joint. Do not use excessive force, or the radiator stub could be damaged. Allow the coolant to drain into the container.
4 As no cylinder block drain plug is fitted and the radiator bottom hose union may be situated halfway up the radiator, this may not fully drain the cooling system.
5 If the coolant has been drained for a reason other than renewal, then provided it is clean and less than two years old, it can be re-used.
6 Reconnect the hose and securely tighten its retaining clip on completion of draining.

Cooling system flushing

7 If coolant renewal has been neglected, or if the antifreeze mixture has become diluted, then in time, the cooling system may gradually lose efficiency, as the coolant passages become restricted due to rust, scale deposits, and other sediment.
8 The cooling system efficiency can be restored by flushing the system clean.
9 The radiator should be flushed independently of the engine to avoid unnecessary contamination.

Radiator flushing

10 To flush the radiator, drain the cooling system then proceed as follows.
11 Slacken the retaining clips and disconnect the top and bottom hoses from the radiator.
12 Insert a garden hose into the radiator top inlet. Direct a flow of clean water through the radiator, and continue flushing until clean water emerges from the radiator bottom outlet.
13 If after a reasonable period, the water still does not run clear, the radiator can be flushed with a good proprietary cleaning agent. It is important that the manufacturers instructions are followed carefully. If the contamination is particularly bad, insert the hose in the radiator bottom outlet, and flush the radiator in reverse.

Engine flushing

14 To flush the engine, remove the thermostat as described in Chapter 3, then temporarily refit the thermostat cover.
15 With the top and bottom hoses disconnected from the radiator, insert a garden hose into the radiator top hose. Direct a clean flow of water through the engine, and continue flushing until clean water emerges from the radiator bottom hose.
16 On completion of flushing, refit the thermostat and reconnect the hoses with reference to Chapter 3.

Cooling system filling

17 Before attempting to fill the cooling system, make sure that all hoses and clips are in good condition, and that the clips are tight.

Note that an antifreeze mixture must be used all year round, to prevent corrosion of the engine components (see following sub-Section).

18 Remove the expansion tank filler cap.

19 On 1.3 litre engines models, disconnect the wire and unscrew the coolant temperature sender from the inlet manifold. On larger-engine models, unscrew the bleed screw which is situated in the thermostat housing cover.

20 Fill the system by slowly pouring the coolant into the expansion tank to prevent airlocks from forming.

21 If the coolant is being renewed, begin by pouring in a couple of litres of water, followed by the correct quantity of antifreeze, then top-up with more water.

22 When coolant free of air bubbles emerges from the orifice, refit the coolant temperature sender and tighten it securely (1.3 litre engines), or refit the bleed screw and tighten it securely (larger engines).

23 Top-up the coolant level to the "KALT" (or "COLD") mark on the expansion tank, then refit the expansion tank cap.

24 Start the engine and run it until it reaches normal operating temperature, then stop the engine and allow it to cool.

25 Check for leaks, particularly around disturbed components. Check the coolant level in the expansion tank, and top-up if necessary. Note that the system must be cold before an accurate level is indicated in the expansion tank. If the expansion tank cap is removed while the engine is still warm, cover the cap with a thick cloth, and unscrew the cap slowly to gradually relieve the system pressure (a hissing sound will normally be heard). Wait until any pressure remaining in the system is released, then continue to turn the cap until it can be removed.

Antifreeze mixture

26 The antifreeze should always be renewed at the specified intervals. This is necessary not only to maintain the antifreeze properties, but also to prevent corrosion which would otherwise occur as the corrosion inhibitors become progressively less effective.

27 Always use an ethylene-glycol based antifreeze which is suitable for use in mixed metal cooling systems. The quantity of antifreeze and levels of protection are indicated in the Specifications.

28 Before adding antifreeze the cooling system should be completely drained, preferably flushed, and all hoses checked for condition and security.

29 After filling with antifreeze, a label should be attached to the expansion tank stating the type and concentration of antifreeze used and the date installed. Any subsequent topping up should be made with the same type and concentration of antifreeze.

 Do not use engine antifreeze in the screen washer system, as it will cause damage to the vehicle paintwork. A screen wash should be added to the washer system in the recommended quantities.

Specifications

Cooling system

Antifreeze mixtures:
Protection down to -15ºC	28% antifreeze
Protection down to -30ºC	50% antifreeze

Note: *Refer to antifreeze manufacturer for latest recommendation*

Fuel system

Idle speed:
Carburettor models:	
Manual transmission	900 to 950 rpm
Automatic transmission	800 to 850 rpm
Fuel-injected models:	
1.8 litre models:	
Early (pre-1987) models:	
Manual transmission	900 to 950 rpm
Automatic transmission	800 to 850 rpm
Later (1987 onwards) models	800 to 900 rpm
2.0 litre models	720 to 780 rpm*
Idle mixture CO content:	
Carburettor models	1.0 to 1.5%
Fuel-injected models	Less than 1.0%*

On 2.0 litre models both the idle speed and exhaust gas CO content are regulated by the control unit and are not adjustable

Ignition system

Spark plugs:
Type	Champion RN9YCC or RN9YC
Electrode gap:	
RN9YCC plugs	0.8 mm
RN9YC plugs	0.7 mm

The spark plug gap quoted is that recommended by Champion for their specified plugs listed above. If spark plugs of any other type are to be fitted, refer to their manufacturer's spark plug gap recommendations.

Braking system

Brake pad minimum thickness (including backing plate)	7.0 mm
Rear brake shoe minimum friction material-to-rivet head depth	0.5 mm

Torque wrench settings

	Nm	lbf ft
Sump drain plug	45	33
Spark plugs	20	15
Roadwheel bolts	90	66

Every 54 000 miles

33 Automatic transmission fluid renewal

Note: *This operation is required at 36000 miles (or 4 years) on models from 1983-on.*

1 Allow the transmission to cool down before draining, as the fluid: can be very hot indeed.

2 Remove all the fluid pan screws except one which should be unscrewed through several turns.

3 Release the fluid pan from its gasket and as the end of the pan tilts downwards, catch the fluid in a suitable container.

4 Remove the remaining screw and the pan. Peel off the gasket (where fitted) or remove all traces of sealant (as applicable).

5 Pull the filter mesh from its securing clips and recover its sealing ring. Clean the filter in a high flash-point solvent and allow it to dry. If the filter is clogged or split it must be renewed.

6 Fit a new O-ring and refit the filter securely.

7 Ensure that the fluid pan and transmission mating surfaces are clean and dry and bolt on the fluid pan using a new gasket. Where no gasket is fitted, apply a bead of sealant about 5.0 mm thick to clean surfaces. The fluid pan which is fitted with a gasket can be identified by the strengthening ribs on the pan flanges. The pan for use with silicone sealant has plain flanges.

8 Fill the transmission with the specified quantity of fluid and then check the level as described in Section 13.

Chapter 2
Engine

Contents

Camshaft - renewal (engine in car) 7
Camshaft front oil seal - renewal (engine in car) 6
Camshaft housing and camshaft - dismantling and reassembly 9
Camshaft toothed belt - removal and refitting 5
Compression test description and interpretation 2
Crankshaft front (pulley end) oil seal - renewal 14
Crankshaft rear (flywheel end) oil seal - renewal 15
Cylinder head - overhaul 30
Cylinder head - removal and refitting 8
Engine - complete dismantling 26
Engine - complete reassembly 34
Engine - examination and renovation information 31
Engine - initial start-up after overhaul 41
Engine - methods of removal 17
Engine - refitting (automatic transmission still in the vehicle) 38
Engine - refitting (complete with automatic transmission) 40
Engine - refitting (complete with manual transmission) 37
Engine - refitting (manual transmission still in the vehicle) 35
Engine - removal (complete with automatic transmission) 22
Engine - removal (complete with manual transmission) 19
Engine - removal (leaving automatic transmission in the vehicle) . .21
Engine - removal (leaving manual transmission in the vehicle) 18
Engine ancillary components - removal 25
Engine components - examination and renovation 32
Engine dismantling - general 24
Engine lubrication and crankcase ventilation systems - description . .27
Engine oil and filter renewal .See Chapter 1
Engine oil level check . . . . .See Weekly checks
Engine reassembly - general information 33
Engine/automatic transmission - reconnection before refitting 39
Engine/automatic transmission - separation after removal 23
Engine/manual transmission - reconnection before refitting 36
Engine/manual transmission - separation after removal 20
Engine/transmission mountings - renewal .16
Flywheel - removal and refitting 13
General description 1
General engine checks . . . . .See Chapter 1
Oil filter relief valve - renewal 28
Oil pressure regulator valve - removal and refitting 4
Oil pump - overhaul 29
Oil pump - removal and refitting 11
Operations possible without removing the engine 3
Pistons/connecting rods - removal and refitting 12
Sump - removal and refitting 10

Degrees of difficulty

| **Easy,** suitable for novice with little experience | | **Fairly easy,** suitable for beginner with some experience | | **Fairly difficult,** suitable for competent DIY mechanic | | **Difficult,** suitable for experienced DIY mechanic | | **Very difficult,** suitable for expert DIY or professional | |

Specifications

General

Type . . . . Four-cylinder, in-line, water-cooled, single overhead camshaft, transversely mounted

Engine codes:
  1.3 litre engine 13S
  1.6 litre engine.
    Early (pre 1987 models) 16S
    Later (1987 onwards models) 16SH
  1.8 litre models:
    Early (pre 1987 models) 18E
    Later (1987 onwards models) 18SE
  2.0 litre models . . . . 20NE or 20SEH
Note: *The engine code forms the first digits of the engine number*
Engine
  1.3 litre engine . . . .
  1.6 litre engine . . . .
  1.8 litre engine . . . .
  2.0 litre engine . . . .
Firing order . . . .
Crankshaft rotation . . . .

Capacity	Bore	Stroke
1297 cc	75.0 mm	73.4 mm
1598 cc	80.0 mm	79.5 mm
1796 cc	84.8 mm	79.5 mm
1998 cc	86.0 mm	86.0 mm

1-3-4-2 (No.1 cylinder at timing belt end)
Clockwise

Compression ratio:
1.3 litre engine	9.2:1
1.6 litre engine	9.2:1
1.8 litre engine	9.5:1

2.0 litre engine:
20NE engine	9.2:1
20SEH engine	10.0:1
Cylinder block (crankcase) material	Cast-iron
Maximum cylinder bore out of round	0.013 mm
Maximum permissible taper	0.013 mm
Maximum rebore oversize	0.5 mm

Crankshaft

Number of main bearings	5

Main bearing journal diameter:
1.3 litre engine	54.972 to 54.985 mm
1.6, 1.8 and 2.0 litre engines	57.982 to 57.995 mm

Crankpin diameter:
1.3 litre engine	42.971 to 42.987 mm
1.6, 1.8 and 2.0 litre engines	48.971 to 48.987 mm
Undersizes	0.25 and 0.50 mm

Crankshaft endfloat:
1.3 litre engine	0.1 to 2.0 mm
1.6, 1.8 and 2.0 litre engines	0.07 to 0.3 mm

Main bearing running clearance:
1.3 litre engine	0.025 to 0.05 mm
1.6, 1.8 and 2.0 litre engines	0.015 to 0.04 mm

Big-end running clearance:
1.3 litre engine	0.019 to 0.071 mm
1.6 and 1.8 litre engines	0.019 to 0.063 mm
2.0 litre engine	0.006 to 0.031 mm

Big-end side-play:
1.3 litre engine	0.11 to 0.24 mm
1.6, 1.8 and 2.0 litre engines	0.07 to 0.24 mm

Bearing shell identification:
Top shells:
Main bearings, standard	Brown
Main bearings, 0.25 mm undersize	Brown/blue
Main bearings, 0.5 mm undersize	Brown/white
Big-end bearings, standard	None
Big-end bearings, 0.25 mm undersize	Blue
Big-end bearings, 0.5 mm undersize	White

Bottom shells:
Main bearings, standard	Green
Main bearings, 0.25 mm undersize	Green/blue
Main bearings, 0.5 mm undersize	Green/white
Big-end bearings, standard	None
Big-end bearings, 0.25 mm undersize	Blue
Big-end bearings, 0.5 mm undersize	White

Camshaft

Identification code:
1.3 litre engine	B
1.6 litre engine	A

1.8 litre engine:
18E	B
18SE	E

2.0 litre engine:
20NE	J
20SEH	K
Endfloat	0.09 to 0.21 mm

Camshaft journal diameters:
1.3 litre engines:
No 1	39.435 to 39.450 mm
No 2	39.685 to 39.700 mm
No 3	39.935 to 39.950 mm
No 4	40.125 to 40.200 mm
No 5	40.435 to 40.450 mm

Camshaft journal diameters (continued):
  1.6, 1.8 and 2.0 litre engines:
    No 1 . . . . 42.455 to 42.470 mm
    No 2 . . . . 42.705 to 42.720 mm
    No 3 . . . . 42.955 to 42.970 mm
    No 4 . . . . 43.205 to 43.220 mm
    No 5 . . . . 43.455 to 43.470 mm
Camshaft bearing (direct in housing) diameters:
  1.3 litre engine:
    No 1 . . . . 39.500 to 39.525 mm
    No 2 . . . . 39.750 to 39.775 mm
    No 3 . . . . 40.000 to 40.025 mm
    No 4 . . . . 40.250 to 40.275 mm
    No 5 . . . . 40.550 to 40.525 mm
  1.6, 1.8 and 2.0 litre engine:
    No 1 . . . . 42.500 to 42.525 mm
    No 2 . . . . 42.750 to 42.775 mm
    No 3 . . . . 43.000 to 43.025 mm
    No 4 . . . . 43.250 to 43.275 mm
    No 5 . . . . 43.500 to 43.525 mm

Pistons and rings

Type . . . . Alloy, recessed head
Number of piston rings . . . . 2 compression, 1 oil control
Ring end gap:
  Compression . . . . 0.3 to 0.5 mm
  Oil control (rail) . . . . 0.40 to 1.40 mm
Ring gap offset (to gap of adjacent ring) . . . . 180°
Gudgeon pin-to-piston clearance:
  1.3 litre engine . . . . 0.007 to 0.010 mm
  1.6, 1.8 and 2.0 litre engines . . . . 0.011 to 0.014 mm
Piston diameter (nominal):
  1.3 litre engine . . . . 74.98 mm
  1.6 litre engine . . . . 79.99 mm
  1.8 litre engine . . . . 84.79 mm
  2.0 litre engine . . . . 85.98 mm
  Oversize . . . . 0.5 mm
Piston-to-bore clearance:
  New engine . . . . 0.02 mm
  After rebore:
    1.3 litre engine . . . . 0.01 to 0.03 mm
    1.6 litre engine . . . . 0.02 to 0.04 mm
    1.8 litre engine:
      18E engine . . . . 0.02 to 0.04 mm
      18SE engine . . . . 0.01 to 0.03 mm
    2.0 litre engine . . . . 0.01 to 0.03 mm

Cylinder head

Material . . . . Light alloy
Maximum permissible distortion of sealing face . . . . 0.025 mm
Overall height of cylinder head:
  1.3 litre engine . . . . 95.9 to 96.1 mm
  1.6, 1.8 and 2.0 litre engines . . . . 95.75 to 96.25 mm
Valve seat width:
  Inlet:
    1.3 and 1.6 litre engines . . . . 1.3 to 1.4 mm
    1.8 litre engine:
      18E engine . . . . 1.3 to 1.4 mm
      18SE engine . . . . 1.0 to 1.5 mm
    2.0 litre engine . . . . 1.0 to 1.5 mm
  Exhaust:
    1.3 and 1.6 litre engines . . . . 1.7 to 1.8 mm
    1.8 litre engine:
      18E engine . . . . 1.7 to 1.8 mm
      18SE engine . . . . 1.7 to 2.2 mm
    2.0 litre engine . . . . 1.7 to 2.2 mm

Valves

Valve clearance	Automatic by hydraulic valve lifters (cam followers)

Valve stem-to-guide clearance:

Inlet:

1.3 litre engine	0.02 to 0.05 mm
1.6 litre engine	0.015 to 0.042 mm

1.8 litre engine:

18E engine	0.015 to 0.042 mm
18SE engine	0.018 to 0.052 mm
2.0 litre engine	0.018 to 0.052 mm

Exhaust:

1.3 litre engine	0.04 to 0.07 mm
1.6 litre engine	0.03 to 0.06 mm

1.8 litre engine:

18E engine	0.03 to 0.06 mm
18SE engine	0.04 to 0.07 mm
2.0 litre engine	0.04 to 0.07 mm
Valve seat angle	44°

Valve guide installed height:

1.3 litre engine	80.85 to 81.25 mm
1.6 litre engine	80.95 to 81.85 mm

1.8 litre engine:

18E engine	80.95 to 81.85 mm
18SE engine	83.50 to 83.80 mm
2.0 litre engine	83.50 to 83.80 mm

Valve stem diameter:

Inlet:

1.3 litre engine	7.000 to 7.010 mm
1.6 litre engine	7.795 to 7.970 mm

1.8 litre engine:

18E engine	7.795 to 7.970 mm
18SE engine	6.998 to 7.012 mm
2.0 litre engine	6.998 to 7.012 mm

Exhaust:

1.3 litre engine	6.980 to 6.990 mm
1.6 litre engine	7.957 to 7.970 mm

1.8 litre engine:

18E engine	7.957 to 7.970 mm
18SE engine	6.978 to 6.992 mm
2.0 litre engine	6.978 to 6.992 mm
Oversizes	0.075, 0.150, 0.250 mm

Valve guide bore diameter:

1.3 litre engine	7.030 to 7.050 mm
1.6, 1.8 and 2.0 litre engine	8.000 to 8.017 mm

Flywheel

Maximum thickness reduction at driven plate and pressure plate cover contact surfaces	0.3 mm

Lubrication

Oil pump:

Tooth play (gear to gear)	0.1 to 0.2 mm

Gear-to-housing clearance (endfloat):

1.3	0.08 to 0.15 mm
1.6 and 1.8	0.03 to 0.10 mm
Oil pressure at idle (engine at operating temperature)	1.5 bar

Torque wrench settings

	Nm	lbf ft
Flywheel to crankshaft:		
1.3 litre engine	60	44
1.6, 1.8 and 2.0 litre engines:		
Stage 1	50	37
Stage 2	Angle tighten a further 25 to 35°	
Driveplate to crankshaft	60	44
Main bearing cap bolts	65	48
Oil pump mounting bolts	6	4
Oil pump relief valve cap	30	22
Oil filter to engine	15	11

Torque wrench settings (continued)

	Nm	lbf ft
Oil pressure switch	30	22
Oil pump bolts	6	4
Oil drain plug	45	33
Sump pan bolts	5	4
Big-end cap bolts:		
1.3 litre engine	28	21
1.6, 1.8 and 2.0 litre engines:		
Stage 1	35	26
Stage 2	Angle tighten a further 45°	
Cylinder head bolts:		
1.3 and 1.6 litre engines:		
Stage 1	25	18
Stage 2	Angle tighten a further 60°	
Stage 3	Angle tighten a further 60°	
Stage 4	Angle tighten a further 60°	
1.8 and 2.0 litre engines:		
Stage 1	25	18
Stage 2	Turn bolt through 90°	
Stage 3	Turn bolt through 90°	
Stage 4	Turn bolt through 90°	
Camshaft sprocket bolt	45	33
Crankshaft pulley bolt:		
1.3 litre engine	55	41
1.6, 1.8 and 2.0 litre engine	20	15
Crankshaft sprocket bolt - 1.6, 1.8 and 2.0 litre engines:		
Stage 1	130	96
Stage 2	Angle tighten a further 40° to 50°	
Starter motor bolts:		
1.3 litre engine	25	18
1.6, 1.8 and 2.0 litre engines	45	33
Engine mounting bracket to crankcase	50	37
Engine mounting bracket to transmission	30	22
Engine mountings to bodyframe	40	30
Alternator bracket to block	40	30
Fuel pump to camshaft housing	18	13

1 General description

The engine is of four-cylinder, in-line, overhead camshaft type, mounted transversely at the front of the car.

The crankshaft is supported in five shell-type main bearings. Thrustwashers are incorporated in the centre main bearing, to control crankshaft endfloat.

The connecting rods are attached to the crankshaft by horizontally-split shell-type big-end bearings, and to the pistons by gudgeon pins, which are an interference fit in the connecting rod small-end bore. The aluminium alloy pistons are fitted with three piston rings: two compression rings and an oil control ring.

The camshaft is driven by a toothed composite rubber belt from the crankshaft, and operates the valves via rocker arms. The rocker arms are supported at their pivot end by hydraulic self-adjusting valve lifters (tappets) which automatically take up any clearance between the camshaft, rocker arm and valve stems. The inlet and exhaust valves are each closed by a single spring, and operate in guides pressed into the cylinder head.

Engine lubrication is by a gear-type pump, located in a housing attached to the front of the cylinder block. The oil pump is driven by the crankshaft, while the fuel pump (on carburettor models) and the distributor are driven by the camshaft.

2 Compression test - description and interpretation

1 When engine performance is down, or if misfiring occurs which cannot be attributed to the ignition or fuel systems, a compression test can provide diagnostic clues as to the engine's condition. If the test is performed regularly, it can give warning of trouble before any other symptoms become apparent.

2 The engine must be fully warmed-up to normal operating temperature, the battery must be fully charged, and all the spark plugs must be removed (Chapter 1). The aid of an assistant will also be required.

3 Disable the ignition system by disconnecting the ignition HT coil lead from the distributor cap and earthing it on the cylinder block. Use a jumper lead or similar wire to make a good connection.

4 Fit a compression tester to the No 1 cylinder spark plug hole - the type of tester which screws into the plug thread is to be preferred.

5 Have the assistant hold the throttle wide open, and crank the engine on the starter motor; after one or two revolutions, the compression pressure should build up to a maximum figure, and then stabilise. Record the highest reading obtained.

6 Repeat the test on the remaining cylinders, recording the pressure in each.

7 All cylinders should produce very similar pressures; a difference of more than 2 bars between any two cylinders indicates a fault. Note that the compression should build up quickly in a healthy engine; low compression on the first stroke, followed by gradually-increasing pressure on successive strokes, indicates worn piston rings. A low compression reading on the first stroke, which does not build up during successive strokes, indicates leaking valves or a blown head gasket (a cracked head could also be the cause). Deposits on the undersides of the valve heads can also cause low compression.

8 Although Vauxhall do not specify exact compression pressures, as a guide, any cylinder pressure of below 10 bars can be considered as less than healthy. Refer to a dealer or other specialist if in doubt as to whether a particular reading is acceptable.

9 If the pressure in any cylinder is low, carry out the following test to isolate the cause. Introduce a teaspoonful of clean oil into that cylinder through its spark plug hole, and repeat the test.

10 If the addition of oil temporarily improves the compression pressure, this indicates that bore or piston wear is responsible for the pressure loss. No improvement suggests that leaking or burnt valves, or a blown head gasket, may be to blame.

11 A low reading from two adjacent cylinders is almost certainly due to the head gasket having blown between them; the presence of coolant in the engine oil will confirm this.

12 If one cylinder is about 20 percent lower than the others and the engine has a slightly rough idle, a worn camshaft lobe could be the cause.

13 If the compression reading is unusually high, the combustion chambers are probably coated with carbon deposits. If this is the case, the cylinder head should be removed and decarbonised.

14 On completion of the test, refit the spark plugs and reconnect the ignition system.

3 Operations possible without removing engine

The following operations may be carried out without having to remove the engine from the vehicle:

a) Removal and refitting of oil pressure regulator valve.
b) Renewal of camshaft toothed belt.
c) Removal and refitting of cylinder head.
d) Removal and refitting of camshaft housing.
e) Removal and refitting of camshaft.
f) Removal and refitting of sump.
g) Removal and refitting of oil pump.
h) Removal and refitting of pistons/connecting rods.
j) Removal and refitting of flywheel.
k) Renewal of crankshaft front oil seal.
l) Renewal of crankshaft rear oil seal.
m) Renewal of engine/transmission mountings.
n) Removal and refitting of ancillary components (coolant pump, fuel pump, manifolds, distributor, carburettor or fuel injection components (as applicable) - refer to appropriate Chapters).

4 Oil pressure regulator valve - removal and refitting

Removal

1 From just to the rear of the crankshaft pulley, unscrew the pressure regulator valve plug and extract the spring and plunger.

2 Renew the spring if it is distorted or weak (compare it with a new one if possible).

3 If the plunger is scored, renew it.

Refitting

4 Refitting is the reverse of removal, ensuring all components are clean. Use a new plug sealing washer on 1.3 litre engines.

5 Camshaft toothed belt - removal and refitting

1.3 litre engines and early 1.6 (16S) and 1.8 (18E) litre engines

Removal

1 Release the alternator adjustment link and mounting bolts, push the alternator in towards the engine and slip the drivebelt from the pulleys.

2 Unscrew the bolts and remove the timing belt cover. Remove the air cleaner unit for improved access on fuel injection models (Chapter 4B).

3 Using a socket spanner on the crankshaft pulley bolt, turn the crankshaft until No 1 piston is rising on its compression stroke. To check that this is the compression stroke, either remove No 1 spark plug and place a finger over the plug hole to feel the compression being generated or remove the distributor cap and check that the rotor is aligned with No 1 spark plug contact in the cap. The notch in the rim of the crankshaft pulley should be aligned with the timing pointer, and represents ignition timing at the specified degrees BTDC **not** TDC which is not marked on these engines. The camshaft sprocket mark will be in alignment with the mark on the belt cover backplate **(see illustration)**.

4 On 1.3 litre engines, unscrew the crankshaft pulley bolt without disturbing the previously set position of the crankshaft. On larger engine models, undo and remove the four bolts which secure the pulley to the crankshaft drive sprocket. To prevent the crankshaft rotating as the bolt(s) are removed, either engage a gear and apply the handbrake fully, or remove the flywheel housing lower cover and jam the flywheel ring gear with a suitable tool. Withdraw the pulley from the crankshaft or drive sprocket (as applicable) **(see illustration)**.

5 Drain the cooling system (Chapter 1).

6 Release the coolant pump mounting bolts just enough to be able to swivel the pump and

5.3 Camshaft sprocket timing marks

to release the tension of the toothed belt. Flats are provided on the pump body behind the sprocket, and if necessary a large thin spanner can be used to turn the eccentrically-mounted pump. Alternatively, working under the car, the pump can be turned by carefully tapping it with a hammer and long drift.

7 If the toothed belt is to be used again, note its running direction before removing it.

Refitting

8 Fit the new belt without moving the set position of the camshaft or crankshaft.

9 Engage the new belt over the sprockets and apply some tension by moving the coolant pump.

10 Refit the crankshaft pulley into position and then check that the pulley notch is still in alignment with the timing pointer and that the camshaft sprocket mark is aligned with the groove in the plate behind it. If not, release the belt tension and readjust the position of the sprockets as necessary.

11 The belt tension should now be adjusted in the following way if the official tool is not available. Partially tighten the clamping screws on the coolant pump and, using the thumb and forefinger, twist the belt through 90°. If, with moderate effort, the belt twists too easily or will not reach the full 90°, increase or decrease the tension as necessary by moving the coolant pump. If the belt is overtightened, it will usually be heard to hum when the engine is running. Fully tighten the coolant pump bolts **(see illustrations)**,

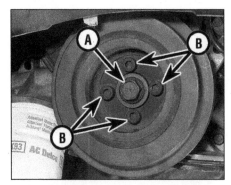

5.4 Crankshaft pulley on a 1.6 engine

A Torsional damper and crankshaft sprocket retaining bolt
B Pulley retaining bolts (fillister type)

5.11a Checking the timing belt tension

5.11b Adjusting the timing belt tension

5.11c Tightening the coolant pump bolt after tightening the timing belt

5.17 Alternator adjustment link bolt (arrowed)

12 Remove the crankshaft pulley, then fit the timing belt cover into position.
13 Refit the crankshaft pulley.
14 Refit the alternator drivebelt and adjust the tension as described in Chapter 1.

Later 1.6 (16SH) and 1.8 (18SE) litre engines and all 2.0 litre engines

Note: *Accurate adjustment of the toothed belt entails the use of a tension checking gauge, which is a Vauxhall special tool. An approximate setting can be achieved using the method described in this Section, but ideally, the tension should be checked by a dealer on completion.*

Removal

15 Disconnect the battery earth lead, and for improved access, remove the air cleaner assembly, as described in Chapter 4.
16 Drain the cooling system, (Chapter 1).
17 Slacken the alternator adjustment link and mounting bolts **(see illustration)**, push the alternator in towards the engine, and slip the drivebelt off the pulleys.
18 Release the retaining clips, and remove the toothed belt upper cover **(see illustration)**.
19 Using a socket or spanner on the crankshaft pulley bolt, turn the crankshaft until No 1 piston is at its firing point. This is indicated by the notch in the crankshaft pulley being in line with the pointer on the oil pump housing, and the notch on the camshaft sprocket being in line with the pip on the inner circumference of the toothed belt inner cover **(see illustrations)**.

20 Raise and support the front of the car, then remove the right-hand front roadwheel.
21 Using a suitable Allen key, unscrew four bolts securing the crankshaft pulley to the toothed belt sprocket, and remove the pulley **(see illustrations)**.
22 Release the retaining clips, and remove the toothed belt intermediate cover from the vicinity of the coolant pump **(see illustration)**.
23 Using a suitable Allen key or socket bit, slacken the three coolant pump securing bolts, then swivel the pump to release the tension on the toothed belt. The pump can be moved using the cast projection on the side of the pump body **(see illustrations)**.
24 If the belt is to be re-used, mark its running direction using chalk, then ease the belt off the three sprockets **(see illustration)**.

5.18 Removing the toothed belt upper cover

5.19a Align the timing notch on the camshaft sprocket (arrowed) . . .

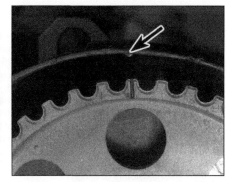

5.19b . . . with the pip on the toothed belt inner cover (arrowed)

5.21a Unscrew the four crankshaft pulley retaining bolts . . .

5.21b . . . and remove the pulley

5.22 Removing the toothed belt intermediate cover

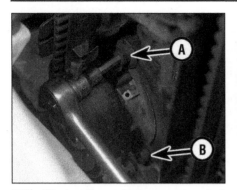

5.23a Slacken the coolant pump upper bolt (A), front bolt (B) . . .

5.23b . . . and rear bolt (C), then move the pump by means of the cast projection (D)

5.24 Slip the toothed belt off the sprockets

25 Inspect the condition of the belt, and renew it if there is any sign of cracking, splitting, oil contamination or general deterioration.

Refitting

26 Without disturbing the set position of the crankshaft and camshaft, locate the new belt over the sprockets. Apply some tension to the belt by moving the coolant pump, then temporarily tighten the coolant pump bolts.

27 Place the crankshaft pulley in position (without the retaining bolts), and check that the timing marks are still aligned as described in paragraph 19. Now turn the crankshaft through two complete revolutions, in the normal direction of rotation, and check that the marks can be re-aligned with their respective pointers. If not, release the belt tension, and alter the position of the belt on the camshaft sprocket until the marks can be correctly aligned.

28 Slacken the coolant pump bolts, and move the pump to tension the belt. The tension will be approximately correct when it is just possible to twist the belt through 90° by hand, at a point midway between the camshaft and crankshaft sprockets on the straight side of the belt. When the adjustment is correct, tighten the coolant pump bolts, turn the crankshaft through one full turn, and check the tension again. Repeat this procedure until the correct tension is obtained.

29 Refit the toothed belt intermediate cover to the coolant pump.

30 Refit the crankshaft pulley, and secure with the four bolts tightened to the specified torque.

31 Place the toothed belt upper cover in position, and secure with the retaining clips.

32 Refit the alternator drivebelt and adjust its tension as described in Chapter 1.

33 Refit the roadwheel and lower the car to the ground.

34 Refit the air cleaner as described in Chapter 4, refill the cooling system as described in Chapter 3, then reconnect the battery earth lead.

6 Camshaft front oil seal - renewal (engine in car)

1.3 litre engines and early 1.6 (16S) and 1.8 (18E) litre engines

1 The camshaft front oil seal may be renewed without removing the camshaft. Proceed as follows.

2 Remove the camshaft toothed belt, as described in Section 5.

3 Hold the camshaft stationary using a spanner on the flats provided. Unscrew the camshaft sprocket retaining bolt and pull off the sprocket.

4 Punch or drill a small hole in the centre of the oil seal. Screw in a self-tapping screw and pull on the screw with pliers to extract the seal.

5 Clean out the oil seal seat with a wooden or

plastic scraper. Grease the lips of the new seal and fit it, lips inwards, using a piece of tube and a mallet to drive it home. Take care not to damage the seal lips during fitting; if a protective sleeve is supplied with the new seal, use it.

6 Refit the camshaft sprocket and tighten its securing bolt to the specified torque (see Specifications).

7 Refit and tension the camshaft toothed belt, as described in Section 5. Renew the belt if the old one was contaminated with oil.

Later 1.6 (16SH) and 1.8 (18SE) litre engines and all 2.0 litre engines

8 Remove the camshaft toothed belt as described in Section 5.

9 Where applicable, detach the breather hose, then undo the bolts and remove the camshaft cover. Note the position of the cable clips under the retaining bolts to aid reassembly. Remove the cover gasket.

10 Undo the centre retaining bolt, and remove the sprocket from the camshaft **(see illustration)**. To prevent the camshaft turning while the bolt is undone, engage a spanner with the flats provided between Nos 3 and 4 camshaft lobes.

11 Undo the crankshaft sprocket central bolt without disturbing the set position of the crankshaft. To prevent the crankshaft turning as the bolt is undone, it may be sufficient to engage a gear and apply the footbrake (manual gearbox only); a better way is to

6.10 Removing the sprocket from the camshaft

6.12a Use a puller, if necessary, to release the crankshaft sprocket . . .

6.12b . . . then remove the sprocket from the crankshaft

6.13a Remove the Woodruff key (arrowed) . . .

6.13b . . . followed by the spacer

6.14a Toothed belt rear cover lower retaining bolts (arrowed)

remove the flywheel bottom cover plate, and lock the ring gear with a large screwdriver or tyre lever.

12 Withdraw the sprocket from the crankshaft. If it is tight, refit the bolt two or three turns, and draw the sprocket off using a two-legged puller **(see illustrations)**.

13 Carefully ease out the Woodruff key, then remove the spacer(s) behind the key **(see illustrations)**.

14 Undo the two upper bolts securing the toothed belt rear cover to the camshaft housing, and release the electrical lead from the upper retaining clip. Undo the two lower bolts securing the rear cover to the oil pump housing, and remove the cover from below **(see illustrations)**.

15 Punch or drill a small hole in the centre of the oil seal. Screw in a self-tapping screw, and pull on the screw with pliers to extract the seal.

16 Clean out the oil seal seat in the camshaft housing, then lubricate the lips and side surfaces of the new seal with engine oil.

17 Fit the seal with its sealing lips inwards, and use a piece of tube and a mallet to drive it home. Take care not to damage the seal lips during fitting; if a protective sleeve is supplied with the new seal, it should be used.

18 Refit the toothed belt rear cover, and secure it with the four bolts.

19 Place the spacer(s) over the crankshaft, refit the Woodruff key and the toothed belt sprocket. Refit the sprocket retaining bolt, and tighten it to the specified torque **(see illustration)**.

20 Refit the camshaft sprocket, and secure it with the retaining bolt, tightened to the specified torque.

21 Using a new gasket if necessary, refit the camshaft cover. Tighten the retaining bolts progressively and in a diagonal sequence, to the specified torque. Reconnect the breather hose.

22 Fit and adjust the camshaft toothed belt, using the procedure described in Section 5.

7 Camshaft - renewal (engine in car)

1 The procedure for camshaft renewal is given in Sections 8 and 9. While it is not strictly necessary to remove the cylinder head, there is no doubt that it is good practice to renew the head gasket since the joint may be disturbed during removal of the camshaft housing.

2 When fitting the new camshaft, coat the cam lobes and followers with molybdenum disulphide paste, or with special cam lube if supplied with the camshaft.

3 When the engine is first started after camshaft renewal, observe the following running-in schedule:
  a) 1 minute at 2000 rpm
  b) 1 minute at 1500 rpm
  c) 1 minute at 3000 rpm
  d) 1 minute at 2000 rpm

4 Change the engine oil (but not the filter) after 600 miles (1000 km).

8 Cylinder head - removal and refitting

Note: *The cylinder head can be removed together with the inlet/exhaust manifolds and associated fuel system components or, if preferred, these items can be detached prior to the removal of the cylinder head itself. The method to be employed should be considered prior to starting and is dependent on the extent to which the cylinder head is to be dismantled once removed from the car. The following text (and photos) describes the removal and refitting of the cylinder head on a carburettor engine model For more detailed procedures concerning the removal of such items as the fuel injection components, refer to the appropriate Sections in Chapter 4.*

1.3 litre engines and early 1.6 (16S) and 1.8 (18E) litre engines

Removal

1 The cylinder head should only be removed from an engine that has completely cooled off. Removal from a warm engine could cause distortion.

2 Disconnect the battery earth lead.

3 Drain the coolant (Chapter 1) and retain it for further use if required.

4 On carburettor models, remove the air cleaner unit. On fuel injection models disconnect the air inlet duct at the throttle housing.

5 Disconnect the fuel supply lines to the fuel pump (carburettor models) or the fuel manifold and pressure regulator (fuel injection models) as applicable. Be prepared for fuel spillage.

6 Disconnect the control cables and electrical leads from the carburettor or throttle housing as applicable.

7 Disconnect the heater hoses and vacuum pipe from the inlet manifold.

8 Disconnect the lead from the temperature sensor on the inlet manifold or throttle housing as applicable **(see illustration)**.

9 Remove the alternator drivebelt (Chapter 1).

10 Remove the cover from the camshaft belt then set No 1 piston on the firing stroke as described in Section 5.

6.14b Removing the toothed belt rear cover

6.19 Tighten the sprocket retaining bolt to the specified torque

8.8 Coolant temperature switch leads (1.3)

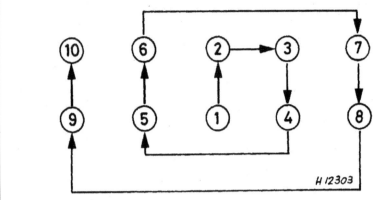

8.26a Cylinder head bolt tightening sequence - work in the spiral shown

11 Remove the distributor or disconnect the cap and low tension lead harness connector. On later fuel injection models, detach the HT cable at the coil to remove the distributor with the cylinder head.

12 Remove the camshaft cover.

13 Check that the mark on the camshaft sprocket is in alignment with the one on the camshaft housing.

14 Disconnect the exhaust downpipe from the manifold.

15 Release the coolant pump bolts, move the pump to relieve the tension on the toothed belt and slip the belt from the sprockets.

16 Remove the cylinder head bolts in the reverse sequence to that shown in **illustration 8.26a**; loosening all the bolts first by a quarter-turn each, and then by half-turn increments, still using the same sequence, until all tension is removed from the bolts. This procedure is important to avoid distortion of the cylinder head or camshaft housing. Discard the original bolts and obtain new ones.

17 Lift off the camshaft housing. This is located on dowels. Lift straight upwards.

18 Lift off the cylinder head. If it is stuck, tap it gently with a plastic-faced hammer.

19 Peel away the cylinder head gasket and discard it.

20 Remove the rocker arms and thrust pads from the cylinder head. Withdraw the hydraulic valve lifters and immerse them in a container of clean engine oil to avoid any possibility of them draining. Keep all components in their original order. If full dismantling and valve grinding is to be carried out, refer to Section 30. Check the head for distortion.

Refitting

21 Clean the cylinder block and the cylinder head free from carbon and old pieces of gasket by careful scraping. Take care not to damage the cylinder head, which is made of light alloy and is easily scored. Cover the coolant passages and other openings with masking tape or rag to prevent dirt and carbon falling in. Mop out oil from the bolt holes; hydraulic pressure could crack the block when the bolts are screwed in if oil is left in the holes.

22 When all is clean, put a new gasket on the block so that the word OBEN is uppermost.

23 Refit the hydraulic lifters, thrust pads and rocker arms to the cylinder head in their original order. If new hydraulic lifters are being used, initially immerse each one in a container of clean engine oil and compress it (by hand) several times to charge it.

24 With the mating surfaces scrupulously clean, locate the cylinder head on the block so that the positioning dowels engage in their holes.

25 Apply jointing compound to the mating flanges of the cylinder head and the camshaft housing and refit the camshaft housing to the cylinder head (camshaft sprocket marks in alignment).

26 Fit the new cylinder head bolts, and tighten them in a spiral pattern, as shown in **illustration 8.26a**, following the stages given in the Specifications. Note that the bolts are tightened initially to the stage 1 torque wrench setting, and then to an angular measurement in four further stages. The required angular measurement can be marked on a card, and then placed over the bolt as a guide to the movement of the bolt. Alternatively, an angular torque gauge can be used to accurately determine the required movement **(see illustrations)**. Gauges of this type are readily available from motor factors at modest cost, or it may be possible to hire one from larger DIY outlets.

27 Fit and tension the toothed belt as described in Section 5; refit the belt cover.

28 Fit the camshaft cover, using a new gasket **(see illustration)**.

29 Fit and tension the alternator drivebelt (Chapter 1).

30 The remainder of the refitting details are a reversal of the removal procedures. On completion, refill the cooling system and bleed it as described in Chapter 1.

31 When the engine is restarted check for signs of fuel and cooling system leaks. Once the engine is warmed up to its normal operating temperature, check and if necessary adjust the idle speed with reference to Chapter 1, and carry out the final stage of tightening the head bolts (see Specifications).

Later 1.6 (16SH) and 1.8 (18SE) litre engines and all 2.0 litre engines

Note: *The following procedure describes the removal and refitting of the cylinder head, complete with manifolds, on fuel-injected engines. The operations also apply to carburettor engines, but where necessary, refer to Chapter 4 for details of fuel and electrical connections at the carburettor and inlet manifold*

Removal

32 The cylinder head must only be removed when the engine is cold, otherwise there is a risk of distortion.

33 Disconnect the battery earth lead.

34 Remove the air cleaner assembly as described in Chapter 4.

8.26b Using an angular torque gauge to measure cylinder head bolt rotation

8.28 Spark plug lead clip on camshaft housing cover

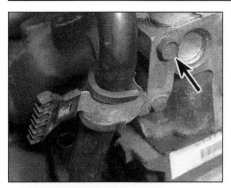

8.38 Undo the crankcase breather pipe retaining bolt (arrowed)

8.39a Detach the breather pipe connecting hose at the camshaft housing

8.39b Removing the breather pipe assembly

35 Drain the cooling system (see Chapter 1).
36 Disconnect the radiator and heater hoses from the cylinder head and inlet manifold.
37 Disconnect the spark plug HT leads, identifying them if necessary, then remove the distributor cap. On 1.6 engines, remove the distributor as described in Chapter 5.
38 Undo the bolt securing the crankcase breather pipe to the side of the cylinder head **(see illustration)**.
39 Slacken the breather pipe connecting hose at the camshaft housing, withdraw the engine oil dipstick, and undo the two breather pipe retaining bolts on the block. Detach the hose, and remove the breather pipe assembly **(see illustrations)**.
40 Disconnect the throttle cable at the carburettor or throttle housing as applicable.

41 Disconnect the electrical leads and wiring multi-plugs from the carburettor, fuel injection system components, manifold and cylinder head as applicable. Label all the wiring as it is removed, to avoid confusion when reassembling; where necessary, refer to Chapter 4 for further information. With all the wiring disconnected, it should be possible to move the complete engine wiring loom to one side, clear of the engine.
42 Disconnect and plug the fuel lines from the carburettor and fuel injection system as applicable. Also on carburettor models, remove the fuel pump.
43 Disconnect the brake servo vacuum hose at the inlet manifold **(see illustration)**.
44 Disconnect the exhaust downpipe from the manifold.

45 Disconnect the hoses at the auxiliary air valve **(see illustration)** then remove the valve from the camshaft housing.
46 Undo the bolts and remove the camshaft cover **(see illustration)**. Recover the gasket.
47 Slacken the alternator adjustment link and mounting bolts, push the alternator in towards the engine, and slip the drivebelt off the pulleys.
48 Remove the toothed belt covers, and slacken the belt tension as described in Section 5.
49 Slip the toothed belt off the camshaft sprocket, then undo the centre retaining bolt and remove the sprocket from the camshaft. To prevent the camshaft turning while the bolt is undone, engage a spanner with the flats provided between Nos 3 and 4 camshaft lobes.
50 Undo the two bolts securing the toothed belt rear cover to the camshaft housing **(see illustration)**.
51 Remove the cylinder head bolts in the reverse order to that shown in **illustration 8.26a**; slacken all the bolts by a quarter-turn each, and then by half-turn increments, still using the same sequence, until all tension is removed from the bolts. This procedure is important to avoid distortion of the cylinder head or camshaft housing. Discard the original bolts and obtain new ones.
52 Ease the toothed belt rear cover away from the camshaft housing, then lift the housing upwards and off the locating dowels **(see illustration)**.

8.43 Brake servo vacuum hose connection at the manifold (arrowed)

8.45 Hose connections at the auxiliary air valve

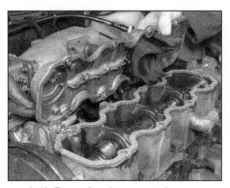

8.46 Removing the camshaft cover

8.50 Toothed belt rear cover-to-camshaft housing retaining bolts

8.52 Removing the camshaft housing from the cylinder head

8.53a Remove the rocker arms . . .

8.53b . . . followed by the thrust pads . . .

8.53c . . . then withdraw the valve lifters

53 Remove the rocker arms and thrust pads from the cylinder head. Withdraw the hydraulic valve lifters, and immerse them in a container of clean engine oil to avoid any possibility of them draining. Keep all components in their original order **(see illustrations)**.

54 Lift off the cylinder head **(see illustration)**. If it is stuck, tap it gently upwards with a hide or plastic mallet. Remove the cylinder head gasket.

55 If further dismantling of the cylinder head is to be carried out, refer to the relevant Sections of this Chapter.

Refitting

56 Clean the cylinder head and cylinder block free from carbon by careful scraping. Cover the coolant passages and other openings with masking tape or rag, to prevent dirt and carbon falling in. Mop out oil from the bolt holes; hydraulic pressure could crack the block when the bolts are screwed in if oil is left in the holes.

57 When all is clean, locate a new cylinder head gasket on the block so that the word "OBEN" can be read from above **(see illustration)**.

58 If the crankshaft has been turned whilst the cylinder head was removed, re-position the crankshaft so that No 1 piston is at its firing point.

59 With the mating surfaces scrupulously clean, locate the cylinder head on the block, so that the locating dowels engage in their holes.

60 Refit the hydraulic lifters, thrust pads and rocker arms to the cylinder head, in their original order. If new hydraulic lifters are being used, initially immerse each one in a container of clean engine oil, and compress it (by hand) several times to charge it.

61 Temporarily refit the camshaft sprocket to the camshaft, and check that the timing mark on the sprocket is at the 12 o'clock position. Re-position the camshaft if necessary, then remove the sprocket.

62 Apply jointing compound to the mating faces of the cylinder head and camshaft housing, and refit the housing to the cylinder head.

63 Fit the new cylinder head bolts and tighten them in a spiral pattern, as shown in **illustration 8.26a** to the stages given in the

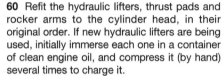

8.54 Removing the cylinder head

Specifications. Note that the bolts are tightened initially to the Stage 1 torque wrench setting, and then to an angular measurement in four further stages. The required angular measurement can be marked on a card, and then placed over the bolt as a guide to the movement of the bolt. Alternatively, an angular torque gauge can be used to accurately determine the required movement **(see illustrations)**. Gauges of this type are readily available from motor factors at modest cost, or it may be possible to hire one from larger DIY outlets.

64 Refit the two bolts securing the toothed belt rear cover to the camshaft housing.

65 Refit the camshaft sprocket, and secure with the centre retaining bolt, tightened to the specified torque **(see illustration)**.

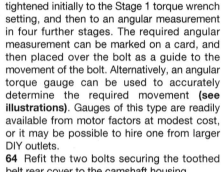

8.57 Fit the new gasket with the word "OBEN" uppermost

8.63a Tighten the bolts initially to the Stage 1 torque wrench setting . . .

8.63b . . . then to an angular measurement in four further stages

8.65 Hold the camshaft, and tighten the sprocket bolt to the specified torque

66 Check that the camshaft sprocket and crankshaft pulley timing marks are still in the correct positions as described earlier, then refit and tension the toothed belt (Section 5).
67 Fit the camshaft cover, using a new gasket.
68 Fit and tension the alternator drivebelt as described in Chapter 1.
69 The remainder of the refitting details are a reversal of the removal procedures. On completion, refill the cooling system, as described in Chapter 1.
70 When the engine is started and has reached normal operating temperature, check and if necessary adjust the idle speed (where applicable), and carry out the final stage of tightening the head bolts (see Specifications).

9 Camshaft housing and camshaft - dismantling and reassembly

Dismantling

1 With the camshaft housing removed from the cylinder head, as described in Section 8, remove any ancillary items such as the fuel pump, distributor, injector rail etc, according to model. Fit an open-ended spanner to the flats on the camshaft. Hold the camshaft from turning and unscrew the camshaft sprocket retaining bolt. Pull off the sprocket.
2 At the opposite end of the camshaft housing, use an Allen key to unscrew the two screws which retain the camshaft lockplate.
3 Withdraw the lockplate.
4 Remove the camshaft carefully out of the distributor end of the camshaft housing taking care not to damage the camshaft bearing surfaces.

Reassembly

5 Before refitting the camshaft, oil the bearings.
6 Fit the camshaft retaining plate with fixing screws and then check the camshaft endfloat. If it exceeds the specified limit, renew the retaining plate.
7 Renew the seal in its retainer **(see illustration)**.
8 Hold the camshaft from rotating while the sprocket bolt is tightened to specified torque.

9.7 Camshaft bearing retainer housing oil seal

10 Sump - removal and refitting

1.3 litre engines and early 1.6 (16S) and 1.8 (18E) litre engines

Removal

1 Unscrew the drain plug and allow the engine oil to drain from the sump into a container. Refit and tighten the drain plug.
2 On 1.3 litre engines, unbolt and remove the sump guard plate, where fitted.
3 Disconnect the exhaust downpipes from the manifold and at the ball coupling, and remove the front exhaust section from the vehicle.
4 Unscrew and remove the sump fixing bolts and lower the sump. Scrape off the old gasket and clean the mating surfaces.

Refitting

5 To refit the sump, apply jointing compound to the seams in the crankcase jointing face and stick the gasket in position after having applied a thin film of compound to both sides of the gasket.
6 Offer up the sump and screw in the fixing bolts, which should have jointing compound applied to their threads **(see illustration)**.
7 Refit the exhaust pipe, using a new gasket at the manifold/downpipe flange joint.
8 Fill the engine with oil.
9 Refit the guard plate (if applicable).

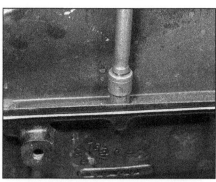

10.6 Tightening a sump bolt (engine inverted)

Later 1.6 (16SH) and 1.8 (18SE) litre engines and all 2.0 litre engines

Removal

10 Unscrew the drain plug, and allow the engine oil to drain into a suitable container. Refit the plug after draining.
11 Raise and support the front of the car.
12 Disconnect the exhaust downpipes from the manifold and at the ball coupling, and remove the front exhaust section from the vehicle.
13 Undo the bolts and remove the flywheel cover plate **(see illustration)**.
14 Progressively slacken, then remove the sump fixing bolts.
15 Lower the sump from under the vehicle **(see illustration)**.
16 If the sump is being removed for access to the crankshaft and bearings, remove the oil pick-up pipe and sump baffle plate as follows.
17 Undo the two bolts securing the pick-up pipe to the oil pump housing **(see illustration)**, and undo the bolt securing the support bracket to the edge of the crankcase.
18 Withdraw the oil pick-up pipe, followed by the baffle plate **(see illustration)**.
19 Remove the double-sided rubber gasket from the baffle plate **(see illustration)**.

Refitting

20 Thoroughly clean the sump, and obtain a new gasket if the old one shows any signs of deterioration. The O-ring seal on the oil pick-

10.13 Removing the flywheel cover plate

10.15 Removing the sump

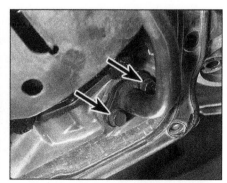

10.17 Oil pick-up pipe retaining bolts (arrowed)

10.18 Removing the baffle plate

10.19 Removing the double-sided rubber gasket from the baffle plate

10.20 Oil pick-up pipe O-ring seal

up pipe should be renewed as a matter of course (see illustration).

21 Fit the gasket to the baffle plate, then locate the plate in position, using two sump bolts to hold it in place temporarily.

22 Refit the oil pick-up pipe, and secure it with the two flange bolts and the support bracket bolt. Remove the two temporary retaining bolts from the baffle plate, then offer up the sump. Fit the bolts, and tighten them progressively, and in a diagonal sequence, to the specified torque.

23 Refit the flywheel cover plate and the exhaust front section.

24 Lower the car to the ground, and fill the engine with oil.

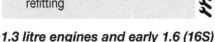

11 Oil pump - removal and refitting

1.3 litre engines and early 1.6 (16S) and 1.8 (18E) litre engines

Removal

1 Remove the camshaft toothed belt as described in Section 5. Remove the belt cover backplate.

2 Remove the crankshaft sprocket centre bolt, where applicable. Using two screwdrivers as levers, prise off the belt sprocket from the front end of the crankshaft. Remove the Woodruff key.

3 Remove the sump as described in Section 10.

4 Remove the oil pump pick-up pipe and strainer.

5 Unbolt the oil pump from the cylinder block and remove it.

6 Refer to Section 29 for details of oil pump overhaul.

Refitting

7 Before refitting the oil pump, steps must be taken to protect the seal lips from damage or turning back on the shoulder at the front end of the crankshaft. To do this, grease the seal lips and then bind tape around the crankshaft to form a gentle taper. Locate a new gasket.

8 Refit the oil pump and unwind and remove the tape.

9 Tighten the bolts to the specified torque and fit the belt sprocket.

10 Refit the pick-up pipe and strainer, the sump and the timing belt and its cover as previously described.

11 Refit the crankshaft pulley and the drivebelt and fill the engine with oil.

Later 1.6 (16SH) and 1.8 (18SE) litre engines and all 2.0 litre engines

Removal

12 Remove the camshaft toothed belt and belt covers as described in Section 5.

13 Remove the sump, as described in Section 10.

14 Remove the oil filter, and disconnect the oil pressure switch wire from the oil pump housing (see illustration).

15 Undo the retaining bolts and withdraw the oil pump housing from the locating dowels on the cylinder block (see illustrations). Remove the gasket.

16 If further dismantling of the oil pump is to be undertaken, refer to Section 29.

Refitting

17 Clean away all traces of old gasket from the pump housing and cylinder block mating faces.

18 Apply jointing compound to the new gasket, and position it over the cylinder block dowels (see illustration).

19 To protect the oil seal lips when refitting

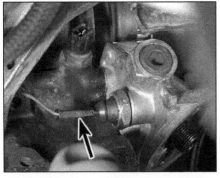

11.14 Oil pressure switch wire connection (arrowed)

11.15a Undo the oil pump housing retaining bolts (arrowed) . . .

11.15b . . . and withdraw the housing

11.18 Position a new housing gasket over the locating dowels

the pump housing, wrap some tape around the step in the crankshaft, and grease the seal lips thoroughly.

20 Carefully place the housing in position and unwind the tape.

21 Refit the retaining bolts, and tighten them to the specified torque.

22 Fit a new oil filter, and reconnect the oil pressure switch wire.

23 Refit the sump as described in Section 10.

24 Refit the toothed belt as described in Section 5.

12 Pistons/connecting rods - removal and refitting

Removal

1 Remove the cylinder head (Section 8).

2 Remove the sump (Section 10).

3 Remove the oil pump pick-up pipe and filter screen.

4 Check that the rods and caps are marked with their position in the crankcase. If they are not, centre-punch them at adjacent points either side of the cap/rod joint. Note to which side of the engine the marks face.

5 Unscrew the big-end cap bolts from the first rod and remove the cap. If the bearing shells are to be used again, tape the cap and shell together.

6 Check the top of the cylinder bores for a wear ridge. If evident, carefully scrape it away with a ridge reaming tool, otherwise as the piston is pushed out of the block, the piston top ring may jam against it.

7 Place the wooden handle of a hammer against the bottom of the connecting rod and push the piston/rod assembly up and out of the cylinder bore.

8 Remove the remaining three assemblies in a similar way. Rotate the crankshaft as necessary to bring the big-end bolts to the most accessible position.

9 If the piston must be separated from its rod, leave this job to your dealer as special tools and a press will be required.

Refitting

10 Commence reassembly by laying the piston/connecting rod assemblies out in their

12.13 Identifying contour on underside of piston

correct order, complete with bearing shells, ready for refitting into their respective bores in the cylinder block. Make sure that the seats for the shells are absolutely clean and then fit the shells into the seats.

11 Wipe out the bores and oil them. Oil the piston rings liberally. Ensure that the ring gaps are correctly positioned (see Section 34).

12 Fit a piston ring compressor to the first assembly to be installed.

13 Insert the rod and piston into the top of the bore so that the base of the compressor stands on the block. Check that the rod markings are towards the side of the engine as noted before dismantling. Although there are no marks on the piston crowns, different contours on their undersides can be used to identify which way round they are fitted **(see illustration)**.

14 Apply the wooden handle of a hammer to the piston crown and tap the assembly into the bore, at the same time releasing the compressor **(see illustration)**.

15 Guide the big-end of the connecting rod near to the crankpin and then pull it firmly onto the crankpin which should have been oiled liberally.

16 Fit the cap and bolts and tighten to the specified torque.

17 Repeat the operations on the other pistons/rods.

18 Refit the cylinder head, the pick-up pipe and filter and the sump, all as described in earlier Sections of this Chapter.

13 Flywheel - removal and refitting

Removal

1 Refer to Chapter 6 and remove the clutch.

2 Although the flywheel bolt holes are offset so that it can only be fitted one way, it will make fitting easier if its relationship to the crankshaft flange is marked before removal.

3 Remove the clutch release bearing and guide sleeve, again referring to Chapter 6.

4 Jam the flywheel starter ring gear and using a ring spanner or socket, unscrew the bolts from the flywheel. As the heads of these bolts are very shallow, if a chamfered type of socket

12.14 Fitting a piston to cylinder block

is being used it is best to grind it flat to ensure more positive engagement.

5 Remove the flywheel.

Refitting

6 Refit by reversing the removal operations, but apply thread locking compound to the bolts.

14 Crankshaft front (pulley end) oil seal - renewal

1.3 litre engines and early 1.6 (16S) and 1.8 (18E) litre engines

1 It is possible to renew the oil seal without the need to remove the oil pump.

2 Remove the toothed belt as described in Section 5.

3 On 1.6 and 1.8 litre models, undo the torsional damper/sprocket retaining bolt. Remove the bolt and damper.

4 Using two screwdrivers as levers, prise the sprocket from the crankshaft. Remove the Woodruff key.

5 Punch or drill a small hole in the metal face of the oil seal and screw in a self-tapping screw. Use the head of the screw to lever out the seal.

6 Fill the lips of the new seal with grease and tape the step on the crankshaft as described in Section 11.

7 Using a piece of tubing, tap the oil seal into position. Refit the Woodruff key.

8 Refit the crankshaft sprocket.

9 Refit the toothed belt as described in Section 5.

Later 1.6 (16SH) and 1.8 (18SE) litre engines and all 2.0 litre engines

10 Remove the camshaft toothed belt and belt covers, as described in Section 5.

11 Punch or drill a small hole in the front face of the oil seal, and screw in a self-tapping screw. Pull on the screw with pliers to extract the seal.

12 Apply some tape over the step in the crankshaft, and grease the seal lips thoroughly.

13 Using a piece of tubing and a mallet, tap the seal into position.

14 Refit the toothed belt as described in Section 5.

15 Crankshaft rear (flywheel end) oil seal - renewal

1 Remove the clutch (Chapter 6).

2 Remove the flywheel (Section 13).

3 The defective rear oil seal can now be prised off the crankshaft using a suitably hooked tool.

4 Grease the lips of the new seal before installing it. As there is very little space to tap the seal into position, it is better to use a bolt with a thick nut and a piece of tubing inserted between the outer face of the seal and the clutch release bearing guide. If the nut is then unscrewed to effectively increase the overall length of the bolt, the seal will be pressed into its seat.

5 Refit the flywheel and clutch by reversing the removal operations.

16 Engine/transmission mountings - renewal

1 The engine/transmission flexible mountings can be renewed if they have hardened or been compressed. Take the weight of the engine/transmission on either a hoist or a jack and a wooden block used as an insulator.

2 Unbolt the mounting brackets from the crankcase or transmission casing and the body frame member and separate the brackets from the flexible member.

3 Refit the mountings with the new flexible components, but have the bolts only "nipped up" initially.

4 Once the hoist or jack has been removed, tighten all bolts to the specified torque with the weight of the engine/transmission on the mountings.

17 Engine - methods of removal

It is possible to remove the engine on its own or to remove it complete with transmission.

It is much easier to remove the engine independently and this should be done if overhaul of the transmission is not required at the same time.

Both methods are described in the following Sections.

18 Engine - removal (leaving manual transmission in the vehicle)

1 Disconnect the battery earth lead.

2 With the help of an assistant, unbolt and remove the bonnet (Chapter 11).

3 Remove the air cleaner and preheater ducting (carburettor models). On fuel injection models, disconnect the air inlet trunking between the air cleaner unit and the airflow manifold.

4 Remove the radiator (Chapter 3).

5 Disconnect the brake servo vacuum hose from the inlet manifold.

6 Disconnect the throttle linkage from the carburettor also the choke operating cable or automatic choke electrical lead. On versions equipped with fuel injection disconnect the wiring harness plugs and the brake servo pipe from the throttle housing. Pull off the distributor vacuum pipe and disconnect the fuel pipes noting that the one with the white band is attached to the distribution pipe stub nearest the alternator. Disconnect the crankcase

18.8 Engine oil pressure switch lead

ventilation hose and the throttle housing coolant hoses. Disconnect the injector wiring harness (No 4 nearest clutch bellhousing). Remove the throttle housing/inlet manifold assembly after reference to Chapter 4.

7 Disconnect the fuel supply hose to the fuel pump (carburettor models) or the fuel rail manifold. Similarly detach the fuel return pipes and plug them to prevent fuel leakage. Be prepared for fuel spillage.

8 Disconnect the electrical leads from:
 a) The alternator.
 b) The starter motor.
 c) The distributor.
 d) The coolant temperature sensor.
 e) The oil pressure switch (see illustration).
 f) The inductive pulse sensor (fuel injection models).
 g) The injector nozzles.
Unclip and move the leads out of the way.

9 Raise and support the front end of the vehicle securely or position it over an inspection pit.

10 Disconnect the exhaust downpipe from the manifold, also disconnect the pipe at the spring-loaded ball coupling.

11 Unscrew the threaded plug from the transmission casing end cover.

12 Remove the retaining circlip now exposed.

13 A screw will now be observed which has a splined recess in its head. A twelve-point splined key will be required to unscrew it. Accessory shops can supply a socket adapter, or sometimes an Allen key will do the job.

14 Unscrew and remove the screw.

15 As described in more detail in Chapter 6, the input shaft can be slid out of engagement with the clutch driven plate. To do this, the vehicle makers supply a special tool (KM449-1 and 22-1), but a substitute can be used by borrowing one of the four bolts which secure the gearchange mechanism cover to the top of the transmission casing. Screw this bolt into the end of the input shaft. Grip the head of the bolt and pull the shaft out of engagement with the splined hub of the clutch driven plate. Don't forget to refit the bolt to the gearchange mechanism cover. The foregoing substitute method of withdrawing the input shaft may not always be possible with 5-speed transmissions as the shaft is often very tight

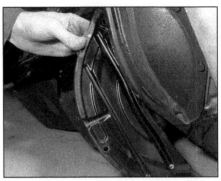

18.22 Flywheel housing front cover plate

requiring the use of the special tool or even a slide hammer.

16 Connect a hoist to the engine and just take its weight. Support the transmission on a jack.

17 Remove the alternator and its bracket in order to provide access to the right rear engine mounting bracket.

18 Disconnect the right front engine mounting bracket from both the engine and the flexible member of the mounting.

19 Remove the right rear engine mounting bracket from both the engine and the flexible member of the mounting. This engine bracket incorporates the alternator mounting lugs.

20 Unbolt and remove the starter motor.

21 On 1.6, 1.8 litre and 2.0 litre engines remove the pulley from the front end of the crankshaft (four bolts). The engine will have to be locked in order to unscrew these four bolts. In order to do this, jam the starter ring gear by inserting a lever into the starter motor aperture.

22 Unbolt and remove the cover plate from the bottom of the flywheel housing. This is the plate which faces towards the timing belt end of the engine (see illustration).

23 Support the transmission on a jack.

24 Unscrew all the engine to transmission connecting bolts from the flywheel housing flange. Note the clips for the starter motor and clutch cables held by the two upper bolts.

25 Disconnect the engine earth strap.

26 Pull the engine from the transmission just enough to clear the positioning dowels, turn the unit slightly so that the timing belt cover moves towards the engine compartment rear bulkhead.

27 Lift the engine straight up, taking care not to damage adjacent components and remove it from the engine compartment.

19 Engine - removal (complete with manual transmission)

1 Proceed as described in paragraphs 1 to 8 inclusive in Section 18, then as follows.

2 Disconnect the gearchange rod from the transmission (Chapter 7A).

3 Disconnect the clutch operating cable.

4 Disconnect the speedometer cable from the transmission, also the reverse lamp switch leads.

19.17 Engine-to-underbody earth strap

19.18 Right rear engine mounting

5 The front end of the vehicle should now be raised and safely supported to provide sufficient clearance under the front to be able to withdraw the engine transmission once it has been lowered to the floor (see paragraph 22).

6 Connect a suitable hoist to the engine and just take the weight of the engine and transmission.

7 Disconnect the exhaust downpipe from the manifold, also disconnect the pipe at its spring-loaded balljoint coupling.

8 Mark the fitted position of the front left-hand roadwheel on its hub. This is necessary to prevent altering the wheel balance which will have been carried out on the car during production. Marking can be done by applying a dab of paint to one wheel bolt hole and to the corresponding bolt hole on the hub.

9 Remove the left-hand front roadwheel.

10 Remove the nut lock or split pin from the driveshaft hub castellated nut and unscrew the nut. To prevent the hub from rotating, use a length of flat steel as a lever, either bolting it to the hub after having drilled two holes, or simply by screwing in two roadwheel bolts and passing the lever between them. Take care not to damage the threads of the roadwheel bolts.

11 The suspension control arm and support must now be disconnected (see Chapter 10).

12 Make sure that the body is well supported under the jacking points with the suspension hanging free before starting operations.

13 Press the driveshaft from the hub. This can usually be done using hand pressure. If

tight, use a plastic-faced hammer or engage a two or three-legged puller and use its centre screw as a press.

14 Release the left-hand driveshaft from the transmission as described in Chapter 8, then pull the hub/stub axle carrier with suspension lower arm outwards until the shaft can be removed from the vehicle.

15 Unbolt the right rear engine mounting bracket from its flexible member.

16 Unbolt the left rear mounting bracket from its flexible member.

17 Disconnect the earth straps from the transmission casing also the engine crankcase **(see illustration)**.

18 Unbolt the right rear engine mounting from the bodyframe side member **(see illustration)**.

19 Unbolt the engine/transmission front mountings **(see illustrations)**.

20 Check that the engine/transmission is now hanging free on the hoist with all leads, hoses and controls disconnected.

21 Carefully lower the engine/transmission at the same time swivelling it so that the right-hand driveshaft can be released from the transmission. Do not allow the shaft to drop to the floor.

22 With the engine/transmission on the floor, disconnect the hoist and use it to raise the front end of the vehicle, if necessary, to provide room for the assembly to be withdrawn from under the vehicle. Alternatively, use a jack and axle stands (see *"Jacking and Vehicle Support"*). placed under the bodyframe side-members.

20 Engine/manual transmission - separation after removal

1 With the combined assembly removed from the vehicle, clean away external dirt using paraffin or a water soluble solvent, and a stiff brush.

2 Unbolt and remove the starter motor.

3 Unbolt and remove the clutch cover plate.

4 Support the transmission and unbolt the engine/transmission connecting bolts.

5 Withdraw the transmission from the engine without allowing the weight of the transmission to hang upon the input shaft while it is in engagement with the clutch driven plate.

21 Engine - removal (leaving automatic transmission in the vehicle)

1 Carry out the operations described in Section 18 for engine removal leaving manual transmission in vehicle (paragraphs 1 to 8).

2 Disconnect the kickdown cable from the carburettor/throttle housing as applicable.

3 Unbolt and withdraw the starter motor.

4 Unscrew and remove the torque converter cover plate. On 1.6, 1.8 and 2.0 litre engines, unbolt and remove the torsional damper from the crankshaft.

5 Unbolt the engine driveplate from the torque converter. Hold the driveplate from rotating by jamming the starter ring gear with a heavy screwdriver blade. New connecting bolts must be used at reconnection.

6 Support the transmission on a jack.

7 Attach a suitable hoist to the engine and just take its weight.

8 Unbolt the engine from the transmission.

9 Disconnect the engine mountings.

10 Separate the engine and transmission just enough to clear the positioning dowels and then turn the engine slightly until it can be lifted from the engine compartment.

22 Engine - removal (complete with automatic transmission)

1 Carry out the operations described in paragraphs 1 to 8 of Section 18.

2 Disconnect the kickdown cable from the carburettor (or throttle housing as applicable) and the transmission.

3 Disconnect the speed selector lever cable (see Chapter 7B).

4 Disconnect the speedometer drive cable from the transmission, also the reverse lamp switch leads.

5 Withdraw the oil level dipstick and oil filler tube.

6 Disconnect the anti-roll bar from the suspension lower control arm (Chapter 10).

7 Disconnect the oil cooler hoses and plug them.

19.19a Right front engine mounting bracket

19.19b Left front transmission mounting bracket

8 Carry out the operations described in Section 19, paragraphs 5 and 6.

9 Disconnect the exhaust downpipe from the manifold, also disconnect its bracket from the transmission. Swing the bracket upwards.

10 Carry out the operations described in Section 19, paragraphs 8 to 14.

11 Disconnect the engine and transmission mountings, noting that the left-hand rear mounting is accessible from below.

12 Disconnect the transmission earth strap.

13 Check that the engine and transmission are now free with all leads, hoses and controls disconnected and then lower the complete assembly to the floor. Swivel the unit as it is lowered so that the right-hand driveshaft can be released from the transmission. Do not allow the shaft to drop to the floor.

14 With the engine/transmission on the floor, disconnect the hoist and use it to raise the front end of the vehicle if necessary to provide room for the assembly to be withdrawn from under the vehicle.

15 Alternatively, use a jack and axle stands placed under the bodyframe side members.

23 Engine/automatic transmission - separation after removal

1 With the combined assembly removed from the vehicle, clean away external dirt using paraffin or a water soluble solvent, and a stiff brush.

2 Unbolt and remove the starter motor.

3 Unscrew and remove the torque converter cover plate.

4 Unbolt the driveplate from the torque converter. To prevent the driveplate from rotating as the bolts are unscrewed, jam the starter ring gear with a heavy screwdriver blade. New connecting bolts must be used at reassembly.

5 Unscrew and remove the engine-to-transmission connecting bolts.

6 Withdraw the transmission from the engine, at the same time retaining the torque converter fully within its housing.

24 Engine dismantling - general

1 It is best to mount the engine on a dismantling stand, but if this is not available, stand the engine on a strong bench at a comfortable working height. Failing this, it will have to be stripped down on the floor.

2 During the dismantling process, the greatest care should be taken to keep the exposed parts free from dirt. As an aid to achieving this thoroughly clean down the outside of the engine, first removing all traces of oil and congealed dirt.

3 A good grease solvent will make the job much easier, for, after the solvent has been applied and allowed to stand for a time, a vigorous jet of water will wash off the solvent and grease with it. If the dirt is thick and

deeply embedded, work the solvent into it with a strong stiff brush.

4 Finally, wipe down the exterior of the engine with a rag and only then, when it is quite clean, should the dismantling process begin. As the engine is stripped, clean each part in a bath of paraffin.

5 Never immerse parts with oilways in paraffin (eg crankshaft and camshaft). To clean these parts, wipe down carefully with a paraffin-dampened rag. Oilways can be cleaned out with wire. If an air line is available, all parts can be blown dry and the oilways blown through as an added precaution.

6 Re-use of old gaskets is false economy. To avoid the possibility of trouble after the engine has been reassembled **always** use new gaskets throughout.

7 Do not throw away the old gaskets, for sometimes it happens that an immediate replacement cannot be found and the old gasket is then very useful as a template.

8 To strip the engine, it is best to work from the top down. When the stage is reached where the crankshaft must be removed, the engine can be turned on its side and all other work carried out with it in this position.

9 Wherever possible, refit nuts, bolts and washers finger tight from wherever they were removed. This helps to avoid loss and muddle. If they cannot be fitted then arrange them in a sequence that ensures correct reassembly.

10 Make sure that you have a valve grinding tool and a valve spring compressor.

25 Engine ancillary components - removal

1 Before engine dismantling begins, it is necessary to remove the following ancillary components:
  a) Alternator (Chapter 5A).
  b) Fuel pump - carburettor models (Chapter 4A).
  c) Thermostat (Chapter 3).
  d) Inlet manifold and carburettor (Chapter 4A).
  e) Throttle housing, injectors and associated fuel injection system components (Chapter 4B).
  f) Distributor (Chapter 5B or 5C).
  g) Coolant pump (Chapter 3).
  h) Exhaust manifold (Chapter 4A).
  Refer to the Chapters concerned for the removal procedures of the items listed.

26 Engine - complete dismantling

1 With the engine removed from the vehicle and suitably positioned on a solid working surface, carry out the following sequence of operations.

2 Refer to earlier Sections of this Chapter and remove the following:
  a) Camshaft toothed belt.
  b) Cylinder head.

26.4 A main bearing cap showing identification number

  c) Sump.
  d) Oil pump and oil pick-up pipe.
  e) Pistons, connecting rods.
  f) Clutch and flywheel.

3 Invert the engine so that it is standing on the top surface of the cylinder block.

4 The main bearing caps are numbered 1 to 4 from the timing belt end of the engine. The rear (flywheel end) cap is not marked. To ensure that the caps are refitted the correct way round, note that the numbers are read from the coolant pump side when the crankcase is inverted **(see illustration)**.

5 Unscrew and remove the main bearing cap bolts and tap off the caps. If the bearing shells are to be used again, keep them with their respective caps. The original shells are colour-coded and if used again must be returned to their original locations.

6 Note that the centre bearing shell incorporates thrust flanges to control crankshaft endfloat.

7 Lift the crankshaft from the crankcase. Extract the upper half shells and again identify their position in the crankcase if they are to be used again.

8 Refer to Section 30 for details of dismantling and decarbonising the cylinder head and pistons, and to Section 9 for removal of the camshaft.

9 Unbolt and remove the timing belt cover backing plate.

10 The rubber plug located adjacent to the bellhousing flange on the crankcase covers the aperture for installation of a TDC sensor. This sensor when connected to a suitable monitoring unit, indicates TDC from the position of the contact pins set in the crankshaft counterbalance weight.

27 Engine lubrication and crankcase ventilation systems - description

1 Oil pressure for all moving components is provided by a gear type oil pump which is driven from the front end of the crankshaft. The crankshaft has flats for this purpose.

2 The pump draws oil from the sump through a pick-up pipe and strainer and pumps it through the oil filter and oil galleries to the engine friction surfaces.

27.3 Oil pressure switch and washer (1.3 litre engine)

27.5 Cylinder head oil pressure regulating valve (arrowed)

27.7 Crankcase vent system oil separator

27.8 Crankcase ventilation hose attached to camshaft cover (1.6 litre engine)

29.2a Checking the oil pump gear tooth clearance

29.2b Checking oil pump gear endfloat

29.3 Oil pump gear positioning mark (arrowed)

29.4 Exploded view of oil pump pressure regulator valve (1.3 litre engine)

3 A pressure regulator valve is screwed into the body of the oil pump. A relief valve, located in the oil filter mounting base opens should the filter block due to clogging caused by neglected servicing. An oil pressure switch is screwed into the pump casing (see illustration).

4 The cylinder bores are lubricated by oil splash from the sump.

5 The hydraulic valve lifters are pressurised with oil to maintain optimum valve clearance at all times, and this pressure is stabilised on 1.6, 1.8 and 2.0 litre engines by an oil pressure regulating valve in the cylinder head (see illustration).

6 The crankcase ventilation system is designed to draw oil fumes and blow-by gas (combustion gas which has passed the piston rings) from the crankcase into the air cleaner, whence they are drawn into the engine and burnt during the normal combustion cycles.

7 On 1.3 litre engines, the ventilation system incorporates an oil separator bolted to the block. Although it is not a specified maintenance task, the separator can be removed for cleaning (see illustration).

8 On 1.6, 1.8 and 2.0 litre engines, one of the crankcase ventilation hoses is attached to the camshaft cover (see illustration). Inside the cover is a filter, which should be cleaned in paraffin periodically.

28 Oil filter relief valve - renewal

1 Drain the oil and remove the oil filter (Chapter 1).

2 The oil filter relief valve is located under the oil filter, in the oil filter mounting block. Screw an M10 tap into it and extract the valve.

3 The new valve should be driven into position up to its stop, using a drift, approximately 15 mm in diameter.

4 Fit a new oil filter and fill the engine with fresh oil (Chapter 1).

29 Oil pump - overhaul

1 With the oil pump removed from the vehicle, withdraw the rear cover. The cross-head fixing screws are very tight and an impact driver will be required to remove them.

2 Check the clearance between the inner and outer gear teeth, and the endfloat between the gear edges and the housing (see illustrations).

3 If any of the clearances are outside the specified tolerance, renew the components as necessary. Note that the outer gear face is marked for position (see illustration).

4 The pressure regulator valve can be unscrewed from the oil pump housing and the components cleaned and examined (see illustration).

29.6 Oil pump seal

5 Note that the valve components are not identical for both engines. The copper washer used on the 1.3 valve must be renewed when reassembling.

6 Always renew the oil seal; a socket is useful to remove and install it **(see illustration)**.

30 Cylinder head - overhaul

1 With the cylinder head removed, clean away external dirt.

2 To remove the valves, the springs will have to be compressed to allow the split collets to be released from the groove in the upper section of the valve stems. A valve spring compressor will therefore be necessary.

3 Locate the compressor to enable the forked end of the arm to be positioned over the valve spring collar whilst the screw part of the clamp is situated squarely on the face of the valve.

4 Screw up the clamp to compress the spring and release the pressure of the collar acting on the collets. If the collar sticks, support the head and clamp frame and give the end of the clamp a light tap with a hammer to help release it.

5 Extract the two collets and then release the tension of the clamp. Remove the clamp, withdraw the collar and spring and extract the valve.

6 As they are released and removed, keep the valves in order so that if they are to be refitted they will be replaced in their original positions in the cylinder head. A piece of stiff card with eight holes punched in it is a sure method of keeping the valves in order.

7 Bearing in mind that the cylinder head is of light alloy construction and is easily damaged, use a blunt scraper or rotary wire brush to clean all traces of carbon deposits from the combustion spaces and the ports. The valve head stems and valve guides should also be freed from any carbon deposits. Wash the combustion spaces and ports down with paraffin and scrape the cylinder head surface free of any foreign matter with the side of a steel rule, or a similar article.

8 If the engine is installed in the car, clean the pistons and the top of the cylinder bores. If the pistons are still in the block, then it is essential that great care is taken to ensure that no carbon gets into the cylinder bores as this could scratch the cylinder walls or cause damage to the pistons and rings. To ensure this does not happen, first turn the crankshaft so that two of the pistons are at the top of their bores. Stuff rag into the other two bores or seal them off with paper and masking tape. The waterways should also be covered with small pieces of masking tape to prevent particles of carbon entering the cooling system and damaging the coolant pump.

9 Press a little grease into the gap between the cylinder walls and the two pistons which are to be worked on. With a blunt scraper carefully scrape away the carbon from the piston crown, taking great care not to scratch the aluminium. Also scrape away the carbon from the surrounding lip of the cylinder wall. When all carbon has been removed, scrape away the grease which will now be contaminated with carbon particles, taking care not to press any into the bores. To assist prevention of carbon build-up the piston crown can be polished with a metal polish. Remove the rags or masking tape from the other two cylinders and turn the crankshaft so that the two pistons which were at the bottom are now at the top. Place rag or masking tape in the cylinders which have been decarbonised, and proceed as just described.

10 Examine the head of the valves for pitting and burning, especially the heads of the exhaust valves. The valve seatings should be examined at the same time. If the pitting on the valve and seat is very slight, the marks can be removed by grinding the seats and valves together with coarse, and then fine, valve grinding paste.

11 Where bad pitting has occurred to the valve seats it will be necessary to recut them and fit new valves. This latter job should be entrusted to the local agent or engineering works. In practice it is very seldom that the seats are so badly worn for refitting. Normally it is the valve that is too badly worn for refitting, and the owner can easily purchase a new set of valves and match them to the seats by valve grinding.

12 Valve grinding is carried out as follows. Smear a trace of coarse carborundum paste on the seat face and apply a suction grinder tool to the valve head. With a semi-rotary motion, grind the valve head to its seat, lifting the valve occasionally to redistribute the grinding paste. When a dull matt even surface is produced on both the valve seat and the valve, wipe off the paste and repeat the process with fine carborundum paste, lifting and turning the valve to redistribute the paste as before. A light spring placed under the valve head will greatly ease this operation. When a smooth unbroken ring of light grey matt finish is produced, on both valve and valve seat faces, the grinding operation is complete. Carefully clean away every trace of grinding compound, taking great care to leave none in the ports or in the valve guides. Clean the valves and valve seats with a paraffin-soaked rag, then with a clean rag, and finally, if an air line is available, blow the valves, valve guides and valve ports clean.

13 Check that all valve springs are intact. If any one is broken, all should be renewed. Check the free height of the springs against new ones. If some springs are not long enough, replace them all. Springs suffer from fatigue and it is a good idea to renew them even if they look serviceable.

14 The cylinder head can be checked for warping either by placing it on a piece of plate glass or using a straight-edge and feeler blades. If there is any doubt or if its block face is corroded, have it re-faced by your dealer or motor engineering works.

15 On 1.6, 1.8 and 2.0 litre models, always renew the sealing ring between the cylinder head and the thermostat housing when the head is removed for overhaul. Reference to Chapter 3 will show that a considerable amount of work is involved if it is wished to renew the sealing ring with the cylinder head installed.

16 If the oil pressure regulating valve in the cylinder head is to be renewed, access is gained via the circular plug covering the end of the valve. The old valve must be crushed, then its remains extracted, and a thread (M10) cut in the valve seat to allow removal using a suitable bolt. A new valve and plug can then be driven into position. In view of the intricacies of this operation, it is probably best to have the valve renewed by a GM dealer if necessary.

31 Engine - examination and renovation information

With the engine stripped and all parts thoroughly cleaned, every component should be examined for wear. The items listed in the following Sections should receive particular attention and where necessary be renewed or renovated.

So many measurements of engine components require accuracies down to tenths of a thousandth of an inch. It is advisable therefore to check your micrometer against a standard gauge occasionally to ensure that the instrument zero is set correctly.

If in doubt as to whether or not a particular component must be renewed, take into account not only the cost of the component, but the time and effort which will be required to renew it if it subsequently fails at an early date.

32 Engine components - examination and renovation

Crankshaft

1 Examine the crankpin and main journal surfaces for signs of scoring or scratches, and check the ovality and taper of the crankpins and main journals. If the bearing surface dimensions do not fall within the tolerance ranges given in the Specifications at the beginning of this Chapter, the crankpins and/or main journals will have to be reground.

2 Big-end and crankpin wear is accompanied by distinct metallic knocking, particularly noticeable when the engine is pulling from low revs, and some loss of oil pressure.

3 Main bearing and main journal wear is accompanied by severe engine vibration rumble - getting progressively worse as engine revs increase - and again by loss of oil pressure.

4 If the crankshaft requires regrinding take it to an engine reconditioning specialist, who will machine it for you and supply the correct undersize bearing shells.

Big-end and main bearing shells

5 Inspect the big-end and main bearing shells for signs of general wear, scoring, pitting and scratches. The bearings should be matt grey in colour. With lead-indium bearings, should a trace of copper colour be noticed, the bearings are badly worn as the lead bearing material has worn away to expose the indium underlay. Renew the bearings if they are in this condition or if there are any signs of scoring or pitting. **You are strongly advised to renew the bearings - regardless of their condition at time of major overhaul. Refitting used bearings is a false economy.**

6 The undersizes available are designed to correspond with crankshaft regrind sizes. The bearings are in fact, slightly more than the stated undersize as running clearances have been allowed for during their manufacture.

7 Main and big-end bearing shells can be identified as to size by the marking on the back of the shell. Standard size shell bearings are marked STD or.00, undersize shells are marked with the undersize such as 0.020 u/s. This marking method applies only to replacement bearing shells and not to those used during production.

Cylinder bores

8 The cylinder bores must be examined for taper, ovality, scoring and scratches. Start by carefully examining the top of the cylinder bores. If they are at all worn a very slight ridge will be found on the thrust side. This marks the top of the piston ring travel. The owner will have a good indication of the bore wear prior to dismantling the engine, or removing the cylinder head. Excessive oil consumption accompanied by blue smoke from the exhaust is a sure sign of worn cylinder bores and piston rings.

9 Measure the bore diameter across the block and just below any ridge. This can be done with an internal micrometer or a dial gauge. Compare this with the diameter of the bottom of the bore, which is not subject to wear. If no measuring instruments are available, use a piston from which the rings have been removed and measure the gap between it and the cylinder wall with a feeler blade. Refer to the Specifications. If the cylinder wear exceeds the permitted tolerances then the cylinders will need reboring, in which case note the following points:

a) *Piston and cylinder bores are closely matched in production. The actual diameter of the piston is indicated by numbers on its crown; the same numbers stamped on the crankcase indicate the bore diameter.*

b) *After reboring has taken place, the cylinder bores should be measured accurately and oversize pistons selected from the grades available to give the specified piston-to-bore clearance.*

c) *For grading purposes, the piston diameter is measured across the bottom of the skirt.*

10 If the wear is marginal and within the tolerances given, new special piston rings can be fitted to offset the wear.

Connecting rods

11 Examine the mating faces of the big-end caps to see if they have ever been filed in a mistaken attempt to take up wear. If so, the offending rods must be renewed.

12 Check the alignment of the rods visually, and if all is not well, take the rods to your local agent for checking on a special jig.

13 The gudgeon pins are an interference (shrink) fit in the connecting rod small end. As previously explained, removal and refitting of pistons to rods is a job for your dealer, as would be any remedial action required if the gudgeon pin is no longer an interference fit in the rod.

Pistons and piston rings

14 If the pistons and/or rings are to be re-used, remove the rings from the pistons. Three strips of tin or 0.38 mm feeler blades should be prepared and the top ring then sprung open just sufficiently to allow them to be slipped behind the ring. The ring can then be slid off the piston upwards without scoring or scratching the piston lands.

15 Repeat the process for the second and third rings.

16 Mark the ring or keep them in order so they may be refitted in their original location. The top ring may be fitted either way up. The second ring is marked TOP on its upper facing side.

17 Inspect the pistons to ensure that they are suitable for re-use. Check for cracks, damage to the piston ring grooves and lands, and scores or signs of picking-up on the piston walls.

18 Clean the ring grooves using a piece of old piston ring ground to a suitable width and scrape the deposits out of the grooves, taking care not to remove any metal or score the piston lands. Protect your fingers - piston rings are sharp **(see illustration)**.

19 Check the rings in their respective bores.

Press the ring down to the unworn lower section of the bore (use a piston to do this, and keep the ring square in the bore). Measure the ring end gap and check that it is within the tolerance allowed (see Specifications). If this measurement exceeds the specified tolerance the rings will have to be renewed, and if the ring grooves in the pistons are worn new pistons may be needed.

20 If genuine spares are used, new pistons and rings are not supplied separately; however, if the pistons are in good condition, new rings can be obtained from specialist suppliers who will also undertake any machining work necessary to modify the pistons to suit the new rings.

21 If new rings (or pistons and rings) are to be fitted to an existing bore the top ring must be stepped to clear the wear ridge at the top of the bore, or the bore must be de-ridged.

22 Check the end gap of any new rings as described in paragraph 19. If a ring is slightly tight in its groove it may be rubbed down using an oilstone or a sheet of carborundum paper laid on a sheet of glass. If the end gap is inadequate the ring can be carefully ground until the specified clearance is achieved.

23 If new pistons are to be installed they will be selected from the grades available, after measuring the bores as described in paragraph 9. Normally the appropriate oversize pistons are supplied by the repairer when the block is rebored. Whenever new piston rings are being installed, the glaze on original cylinder bores should be "broken" using either abrasive paper or a glaze removing tool in an electric drill. If abrasive paper is used, use strokes at 60° to the bore centre line to create a cross hatching effect.

Flywheel

24 If the teeth on the flywheel starter ring are badly worn, or if some are missing, then it will be necessary to remove the ring and fit a new one.

25 The old ring can be split with a cold chisel after making a cut with a hacksaw blade between two gear teeth. Take great care not to damage the flywheel during this operation, and use eye protectors at all times. Once the ring has been split, it will spread apart and can be lifted from the flywheel.

32.18 Cleaning a piston ring groove

26 The new ring gear must be heated to 180 to 230°C and unless facilities for heating by oven or flame are available, leave the fitting to your dealer or motor engineering works. The new ring gear must not be overheated during this work or the temper of the metal will be altered.

27 The ring should be tapped gently down onto its register and left to cool naturally when the contraction of the metal on cooling will ensure that it is a secure and permanent fit.

28 If the driven plate contact surface of the flywheel is scored or on close inspection shows evidence of small hair cracks, caused by overheating, it may be possible to have the flywheel surface ground provided the overall thickness of the flywheel is not reduced too much. Consult your specialist engine repairer and if it is not possible, renew the flywheel complete.

29 If the needle bearing in the centre of the crankshaft flange is worn, fill it with grease and tap in a close-fitting rod. Hydraulic pressure will remove it. Alternatively, a very small extractor having a claw type leg may be used. When tapping the new bearing into position, make sure that the chamfered side of the bearing enters first. After Engine No. 14089444 the crankshaft does not incorporate a needle bearing.

Driveplate (automatic transmission)

30 Should the starter ring gear on the driveplate require renewal, renew the driveplate complete.

Camshaft

31 With the camshaft removed, examine the bearings for signs of obvious wear and pitting. If evident, a new camshaft housing will probably be required.

32 The camshaft itself should show no marks or scoring on the journal or cam lobe surfaces. If evident, renew the camshaft. Where the camshaft has to be renewed then the camshaft housing should be modified (if an early production model - 1.3 and 1.6 litre engine) to improve lubrication. To do this, temporarily fit the old camshaft into the housing without its retaining plate. Centre punch the housing at the point shown on the circumference of the camshaft journal according to the engine type (1.3 or 1.6 litre engine). Now drill a hole 16.0 mm deep using a 3.0 mm diameter drill into the housing. On no account drill deeper than specified depth **(see illustrations)**.

33 The retaining plate should appear unworn and without grooves. In any event, check the camshaft endfloat and fit a new plate where necessary.

34 The housing front oil seal should always be renewed at major overhaul. A filter is incorporated in the camshaft housing cover on 1.6, 1.8 and 2.0 litre engines. Remove it and wash thoroughly in petrol and allow to dry.

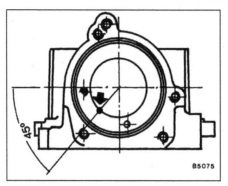

32.32a Camshaft housing drilling point - 1.3 litre engine

Camshaft toothed belt

35 Closely inspect the belt for cracking, fraying or tooth deformation. Where evident, renew the belt.

36 If the belt has been in use for 30 000 miles (48 000 km) or more, it is recommended that it is renewed even if it appears in good condition.

37 Whenever the original belt is to be removed, but is going to be used again, always note its running direction before removing it. It is even worthwhile marking the tooth engagement points on each sprocket. As the belt will have worn in a set position, refitting it in exactly the same way will prevent any increase in noise which might otherwise occur when the engine is running.

Valve lifters, rockers and thrust pads

38 Any signs of wear in a hydraulic valve lifter can only be rectified by renewal.

39 Inspect the rockers and thrust pads for wear or grooving. Again, renew if evident.

Cylinder block and core plugs

40 Ensure that the cylinder block is thoroughly cleaned inside and out. Check the core plugs for signs of corrosion. If the engine has covered a high mileage it is advisable to renew them irrespective of their condition.

41 To remove the old core plugs, drill them through then insert a suitable rod and prise them out using the rod as a lever.

42 Clean the plug orifice thoroughly then carefully drive the new plug into position taking care not to distort it. Apply some suitable sealant around the periphery of the plug when fitting to ensure a good seal. Use aluminium coated plugs where possible.

33 Engine reassembly - general information

To ensure maximum life with minimum trouble from a rebuilt engine, not only must everything be correctly assembled, but everything must be spotlessly clean, all the oilways must be clear, locking washers and spring washers must always be fitted where

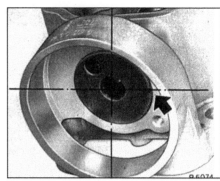

32.32b Camshaft housing drilling point - 1.6 litre engine

indicated and all bearing and other working surfaces must be thoroughly lubricated during assembly.

Before assembly begins renew any bolts or studs, the threads of which are in any way damaged, and whenever possible use new spring washers.

Apart from your normal tools, a supply of clean rag, an oil can filled with engine oil (an empty plastic detergent bottle thoroughly cleaned and washed out, will do just as well), a new supply of assorted spring washers, a set of new gaskets, and a torque wrench, should be collected together.

34 Engine - complete reassembly

Crankshaft and main bearings

1 Ensure that the crankcase and crankshaft are thoroughly clean and that all oilways are clear. If possible blow the drillings out with compressed air, and then inject clean engine oil through them to ensure that they are clear.

2 Wipe the shell seats in the crankcase and bearing caps clean and then fit the upper halves of the main bearing shells into their seats.

3 Note that there is a tab on the back of each bearing which engages with a groove in the shell seating (in both crankcase and bearing cap).

4 Wipe away all traces of protective grease on the new shells.

34.5a Centre main bearing shell showing thrust flanges

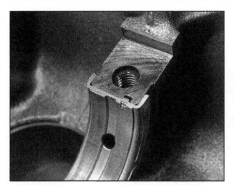

34.5b Main bearing shell locating notch

34.8a Lowering the crankshaft into position

34.8b Crankshaft rear oil seal

5 The central bearing shell also takes up the crankshaft endfloat. Note that the half-shells fitted to the cylinder block all have oil duct holes **(see illustrations)**.

6 When the shells are fully located in the crankcase and bearing caps, lubricate them with clean engine oil.

7 Fill the lips of a new crankshaft oil seal with grease and fit it to the end of the crankshaft.

8 Carefully install the crankshaft into position in the crankcase **(see illustrations)**.

9 Lubricate the crankshaft main bearing journals and then refit the centre and intermediate main bearing caps. Tighten the retaining bolts to the specified torque wrench setting **(see illustrations)**.

10 Clean the grooves of the rear main bearing cap free from old sealant, then coat the inner

surfaces of the cap with sealant to GM spec 90297970 (This sealant is available in 200 ml tubes from GM parts departments.) Fill the side grooves of the bearing cap with RTV jointing compound, then after fitting the bearing cap and tightening its securing bolts, inject further RTV jointing compound into the side grooves until it is certain that they are full. Wipe clean any excess jointing compound **(see illustrations)**.

11 Fit the front main bearing cap but before fitting the retaining bolts, smear them with sealant, and then tighten to the specified torque wrench setting. Check that the bearing cap is exactly flush with the end face of the crankcase as it is tightened.

12 Now rotate the crankshaft and check that it turns freely, and shows no signs of binding

or tight spots. Check that the crankshaft endfloat is within the limits specified. Alternative centre bearing shells are available if necessary to adjust the endfloat. The endfloat can be checked using a dial gauge or with feeler blades inserted between the flange of the centre bearing shell and the machined surface of the crankshaft. Before measuring, make sure that the crankshaft has been forced fully towards one end of the crankcase to give the widest gap at the measuring location **(see illustration)**.

Piston rings

13 Check that the piston ring grooves are thoroughly clear. Always move the rings into position from the top of the piston.

14 The easiest method of fitting piston rings is to use feeler blades (or similar) around the top of the piston and move the rings into position over the feelers. This sequence is a reversal of the removal procedure detailed earlier in this Chapter.

15 Follow the manufacturer's instructions carefully when fitting rings to ensure that they are correctly fitted. Several variations of compression and oil control rings are available and it is of the utmost importance that they be located correctly in their grooves **(see illustration)**.

16 When the rings are in position, check that the compression rings are free to expand and contract in their grooves. Certain types of multi-segment oil control rings are a light interference fit in their grooves and this may

34.9a Fitting main bearing cap

34.9b Tightening main bearing cap bolt

34.10a Fitting rear main bearing cap

34.10b Injecting RTV sealer into rear main bearing cap grooves

34.12 Checking the crankshaft endfloat using feeler blade method

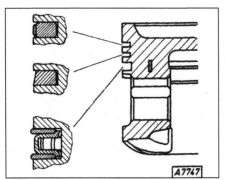

34.15 Piston ring fitting diagram

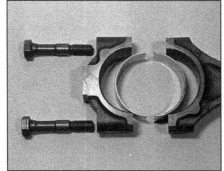

34.23a Connecting rod big-end components

34.23b Fitting a big-end cap

not therefore apply to them. When all the rings are in position on the pistons move them around to bring each ring gap to be some 180° away from the gap on the adjacent ring(s). When the oil control ring consists of two rails and a spacer, offset the upper rail gap 25 to 50 mm to the left of the spacer gap; offset the lower rail gap a similar distance to the right.

Piston/connecting rods

17 As previously described, removing and refitting pistons on the connecting rod is a job for your dealer or specialist repairer. Press equipment and a means of accurately heating the connecting rod will be required for removal and insertion of the gudgeon pin.
18 Commence reassembly by laying the piston/connecting rod assemblies out in their correct order, complete with bearing shells,

ready for refitting into their respective bores in the cylinder block.
19 Wipe out the bores and oil them. Oil the piston rings liberally.
20 Fit a piston ring compressor to the first assembly to be installed.
21 Insert the rod and piston into the top of the bore so that the base of the compressor stands on the block. Check that the rod markings are towards the side of the engine as noted before dismantling. This is very important as the piston crowns do not have front directional marks.
22 Apply the wooden handle of a hammer to the piston crown and tap the assembly into the bore. The compressor will be left standing on top of the block.
23 Guide the big-end of the connecting rod near to the crankpin. Fit and oil the bearing

shells, then fit the cap and bolts (see illustrations).

Oil pump

24 Before refitting the oil pump, steps must be taken to protect the seal lips from damage or turning back on the shoulder at the front end of the crankshaft. To do this, grease the seal lips and then bind tape around the crankshaft to form a gentle taper. Locate a new gasket (see illustrations).
25 Refit the oil pump and unwind and remove the tape.
26 Tighten the bolts to the specified torque.
27 Refit the oil pick-up pipe and strainer (see illustrations).
28 Refit the sump (Section 10) (see illustration).

34.23c Tightening a big-end cap bolt

34.24a Crankshaft step taped

34.24b Fitting oil pump and gasket

34.27a Oil pick-up pipe connecting flange

34.27b Oil pick-up pipe support bracket

34.28 Fitting the sump and gasket

34.29 Fitting Woodruff key to crankshaft

34.30 Flywheel correctly located

34.32 Tightening a flywheel bolt

29 Fit the Woodruff key to the front end of the crankshaft and then stand the engine on the sump **(see illustration)**.

Flywheel

30 Offer the flywheel to the crankshaft rear mounting flange, align the bolt holes which are offset, so that the flywheel can only be fitted in one position **(see illustration)**.
31 Apply thread locking compound to the bolt threads and screw in the bolts.
32 Jam the starter ring gear teeth and tighten the bolts to the specified torque **(see illustration)**.

Cylinder head and camshaft housing

33 Ensure that all valves and springs are clean and free from carbon deposits and that the ports and valve guides in the cylinder head

have no carbon dust or valve grinding paste left in them.
34 Starting at one end of the cylinder head, fit the valve components as follows.
35 Insert the appropriate valve into its guide, making sure that the valve stem is well lubricated. The valves must be installed into the seats into which they have been ground, which, in the case of the original valves, will mean that their original sequence of fitting is retained **(see illustration)**.
36 If working on an inlet valve, fit the spring seat. If working on an exhaust valve, fit the valve rotator **(see illustrations)**.
37 Hold the valve in position, and gently push the valve stem oil seal over the valve stem and onto the valve guide, using finger pressure only, until the bead on the seal slips into the groove in the guide. Do not push the seal beyond the groove, or the sealing properties

will be lost. Note that the oil seals for 1.6 and 1.8 litre engines have been modified **(see illustration)**. New type seals can be fitted to old (pre-modification) engines.
38 Place the valve spring in position over the valve.
39 Place the cap over the spring, with the recessed part inside the coil of the spring **(see illustration)**.
40 Place the end of the spring compressor over the cap and valve stem and with the screw head of the compressor over the valve head, screw up the clamp until the spring is compressed past the groove in the valve stem. Then put a little grease round the groove.
41 Place the two halves of the split collets into the groove with the narrow ends pointing towards the spring. The grease will hold them in the groove **(see illustration)**.

34.35 Fitting a valve to the cylinder head

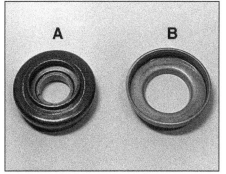
34.36a Exhaust valve rotator (A) and inlet valve spring seat (B)

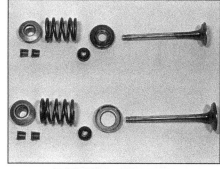
34.36b Valve components
Upper - Exhaust   Lower - Inlet

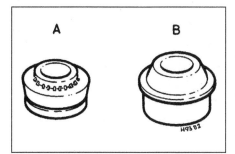
34.37 Valve stem oil seal types
A Early type seal   B Late type seal

34.39 Fitting a valve spring cap

34.41 Fitting valve split collets

34.43 Fitting a hydraulic valve lifter to cylinder head

34.44a Fitting a thrust pad

34.44b Fitting a rocker

34.45 Tightening a thermostat housing bolt

34.46 Timing belt cover backplate (1.3 litre engine)

34.47 Inserting the camshaft

34.48a Camshaft retaining plate (arrowed)

34.48b Checking camshaft endfloat

34.49 Tightening camshaft sprocket bolt

34.51 Cylinder head gasket top marking

34.52 Lowering cylinder head onto block

34.53 Fitting camshaft housing

34.54 Tightening a cylinder head bolt

34.55 Fitting coolant pump

34.56 Fitting timing belt cover backplate

42 Release the clamp slowly and carefully, making sure that the collets are not dislodged. When the clamp is fully released the top edges of the collets should be in line with each other. Give the top of each spring a smart tap with a soft-faced mallet when assembly is complete to ensure that the collets are properly settled.
43 Lubricate the hydraulic valve lifters (valve lash adjuster) and insert them into their bores in the head **(see illustration)**. If new hydraulic lifters are being used, immerse each one in a container of clean engine oil and compress it (by hand) several times to charge it.
44 Fit the rockers and the thrust pads, also new spark plugs of the specified type **(see illustrations)**.
45 Fit the thermostat into its seat, use a new sealing ring and fit the thermostat housing cover. Screw in the bolts **(see illustration)**.
46 On 1.3 litre models, fit the timing belt

cover backplate to the front end of the camshaft cover **(see illustration)**.
47 Lubricate the camshaft bearings and carefully insert the camshaft into its housing **(see illustration)**.
48 Fit the retaining plate and fixing screws and then check the camshaft endfloat **(see illustrations)**.
49 Fit a new seal into the seal retainer (if not already done), then hold the camshaft still with an open-ended spanner while the sprocket and its bolt are fitted and the bolt tightened to the specified torque **(see illustration)**.
50 Thoroughly clean the mating faces of the cylinder head and block.
51 Locate a new cylinder head gasket on the block so that the word OBEN can be read from above **(see illustration)**.
52 Locate the cylinder head on the block so that the positioning dowels engage in their

holes **(see illustration)**.
53 Apply jointing compound to the mating flanges of the cylinder head and the camshaft housing and refit the camshaft housing to the cylinder head (camshaft sprocket marks in alignment) **(see illustration)**.
54 Screw in the cylinder head bolts, and tighten them in the sequence shown in **illustration 8.26a** (Page 2•10). The bolts must be tightened in the five stages given in the Specifications, and described in detail in Section 8 **(see illustration)**.
55 Fit the coolant pump as described in Chapter 3, but leave the bolts finger tight pending adjustment of the timing belt **(see illustration)**.
56 Bolt on the belt cover backplate **(see illustration)**.
57 Fit the belt sprocket to the front end of the crankshaft so that the raised key on the sprocket will engage in the pulley slot when it is fitted **(see illustration)**.
58 Refit the crankshaft sprocket bolt and tighten to the specified torque (see Specifications).
59 Fit and tension the timing belt as described in Section 5.
60 Fit the timing belt cover. On early models, note that the upper screw can only be screwed in after the camshaft housing cover has been fitted using a new gasket **(see illustrations)**.
61 Using new gaskets, bolt on the inlet and exhaust manifolds. Do not forget the lifting lugs **(see illustrations)**.

34.57 Crankshaft sprocket

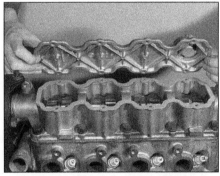

34.60a Fitting camshaft housing cover

34.60b Timing belt cover connecting link to camshaft housing cover

34.61a Engine lifting lug location on inlet manifold stud

34.61b Engine lifting lug location on exhaust manifold stud

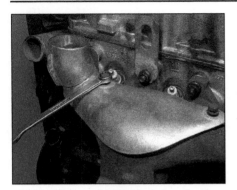

34.62 Exhaust manifold hot air collecting shield

62 Fit the hot air shroud to the exhaust manifold (1.3 and 1.6 litre engines) **(see illustration)**.

63 Fit the ancillary components by reference to the appropriate Chapters, but do not fit the alternator or drivebelt until the engine is installed otherwise access to the right-hand rear mounting will be restricted. Do not fit the starter motor until the engine is installed.

64 On 1.8 and 2.0 litre engines, reconnect the fuel injection system (Chapter 4B).

35 Engine - refitting (manual transmission still in the vehicle)

1 If the clutch has been disturbed, the driven plate (friction disc) must be centralised before the engine can be coupled to the transmission, otherwise the input shaft will not pass through the hub to the plate.

2 To do this, locate the driven plate against the flywheel so that the greater projecting hub of the plate is away from the flywheel.

3 Bolt on the cover, aligning the marks made before dismantling, but only screw in the bolts finger tight.

4 An alignment tool will now be required to pass through the hub of the driven plate and to engage in the bearing in the end of the crankshaft in order to align the plate. A stepped rod, or one of the clutch alignment tools available at motor stores, should be used to do this.

5 When the plate is aligned, tighten the cover bolts to the specified torque and withdraw the tool.

6 Lower the engine into the engine compartment at an angle so that it can be coupled to the flywheel housing.

7 Screw in the upper connecting bolts.

8 Refit the clutch cover plate.

9 With the weight of engine and transmission now taken on the hoist, remove the jack which has been supporting the transmission.

10 Fit the alternator and its mounting bracket.

11 Reconnect the right rear engine mounting.

12 Reconnect the right front engine mounting and the two left-hand engine mountings.

13 Remove the hoist.

14 Refit the crankshaft pulley and where applicable (1.6, 1.8 and 2.0 litre engines) refit the torsional damper. Tighten the securing bolt(s) to the specified torque wrench setting whilst holding the crankshaft from rotating by jamming the starter ring gear with a large screwdriver inserted through the starter motor aperture.

15 Refit the starter motor and the alternator.

16 Reconnect the input shaft to the clutch driven plate (friction disc) and the flywheel by reversing the withdrawal operations described in Section 18, paragraphs 9 to 13.

17 Reconnect the exhaust downpipe to the manifold and the exhaust rear section coupling.

18 Lower the front end of the vehicle.

19 Reconnect the supply and return fuel hoses.

20 Fit the auxiliary drivebelt and tension it as described in Chapter 1.

21 Reconnect the electrical leads to the terminals indicated in Section 18, paragraph 8.

22 Reconnect the carburettor controls. On fuel injection models, reconnect and refit wiring plugs and components and other items mentioned in Section 18, paragraph 6.

23 Refit the radiator.

24 Reconnect the coolant and heater hoses.

25 Reconnect the distributor and brake servo vacuum hoses.

26 Fit the air cleaner and inlet duct (carburettor models). On fuel injection models reconnect the air inlet duct.

27 Refit the bonnet.

28 Fill the cooling system (Chapter 1).

29 Fill the engine and transmission with oil.

30 Connect the battery.

36 Engine/manual transmission - reconnection before refitting

1 If the clutch has been disturbed, centralise the driven plate as described in Section 35.

2 Offer the transmission to the engine without allowing its weight to hang upon the input shaft while the latter is engaged in the hub of the driven plate.

3 Locate the bellhousing flange on the dowels and then insert and tighten the connecting bolts.

4 Refit the clutch cover plate.

5 Refit the starter motor.

37 Engine - refitting (complete with manual transmission)

1 With the front end of the vehicle raised and safely supported on stands, position the engine/transmission on the floor under the engine compartment **(see illustration)**.

2 Hoist the assembly upwards and turn it slightly until the right-hand driveshaft can be engaged in the transmission final drive side gear.

3 Connect the engine front mountings.

4 Connect the engine rear mountings.

5 Leave all mounting bolts and nuts finger tight until the weight of the power unit is lowered onto the mountings. This will allow the unit to take up its correct alignment. This is provided for by means of the elongated holes in the left-hand front mounting bracket.

6 Connect the transmission earth strap.

7 Reconnect the left-hand driveshaft, the suspension control arm and anti-roll bar by reversing the removal operations.

8 Refer to Chapter 10 for details of control arm support bolt fitting which is very important.

9 Refit the roadwheel. The tightening of the driveshaft nut can wait until the vehicle is lowered onto its roadwheels.

10 Remove the engine lifting hoist.

11 With the weight of the engine now on its mountings, tighten all mounting nuts and bolts to the specified torque.

12 Check that all suspension, hub and steering nuts and bolts have been tightened to the specified torque.

13 Refit the roadwheels and lower the vehicle to the floor.

14 Reconnect the speedometer cable to the transmission.

15 Reconnect the reverse lamp switch wires to the transmission.

16 Reconnect the clutch operating cable.

17 Reconnect the gearchange rod.

18 Check the clutch cable adjustment (Chapter 6) and the gearchange linkage adjustment (Chapter 7A).

19 Reconnect the fuel hoses.

20 Reconnect the electrical leads to all the components listed in Section 18, paragraph 8.

21 Reconnect the controls to the carburettor. On fuel injection engines reconnect all the items mentioned in Section 16, paragraph 6 and refit the system components (Chapter 4B).

22 Connect the vacuum hoses to the brake servo and the distributor.

23 Reconnect the heater and radiator coolant hoses.

24 Refit the air cleaner and pre-heater ducting (carburettor models). On fuel injection models reconnect the air inlet ducting.

25 Refit the bonnet.

26 Fill the engine with oil and coolant.

27 Refill or top-up the transmission.

28 Reconnect the battery.

37.1 Engine/transmission ready for installation

38 Engine - refitting (automatic transmission still in the vehicle)

1 Using a hoist, lower the engine into its compartment and engage it on the transmission locating dowels.
2 Connect the engine mountings.
3 Fit and tighten the bellhousing to engine bolts.
4 Remove the hoist and transmission jack.
5 Align the white spot on the driveplate with the coloured spot on the torque converter and screw in new bolts. Tighten the bolts to the specified torque while preventing the torque converter from rotating by jamming the starter ring gear.
6 Fit the torque converter cover plate.
7 Bolt on the starter motor.
8 Reconnect the kickdown cable.
9 Carry out the operations described in Section 35, paragraphs 17 to 30.
10 Refit the crankshaft pulley and the torsional damper (1.6, 1.8 and 2.0 litre engines), see Section 35, paragraph 14.
11 Adjust the kickdown cable as described in Chapter 7B.

39 Engine/automatic transmission - reconnection before refitting

1 Check that the torque converter is fully inserted into the bellhousing (see Chapter 7B).
2 Offer the transmission to the engine so that the white spot on the driveplate is aligned with the coloured spot on the torque converter.
3 Screw in the bellhousing bolts.
4 Screw in new driveplate-to-torque converter connecting bolts and while jamming the starter ring gear, tighten the bolts to the specified torque.
5 Bolt on the torque converter cover plate.
6 Fit the starter motor.

40 Engine - refitting (complete with automatic transmission)

1 Position the engine/transmission on the floor under the engine compartment.
2 Hoist the assembly into position, twisting it

in order to be able to engage the right-hand driveshaft in the transmission side gear.
3 Connect the mountings, but leave the mounting nuts and bolts finger tight until the weight of the power unit is lowered onto the mountings. This will allow the unit to take up its correct alignment. This is provided for by means of the elongated holes in the left-hand front mounting bracket.
4 Connect the transmission earth strap.
5 Reconnect the left-hand driveshaft, the suspension lower arm and the anti-roll bar by reversing the removal operations (refer to Chapter 10).
6 Lock the driveshafts into the transmission side gears by applying a drift to the weld bead on the inboard joint and striking it hard to engage the driveshaft circlip in its groove.
7 Reconnect the exhaust downpipe to the manifold, also at its spring-loaded balljoint coupling.
8 Tighten the driveshaft to hub nuts to the specified torque preventing the hub from rotating by locking it as described at dismantling.
9 Fit the nut lock or split pin.
10 Fit the roadwheel.
11 Reconnect the oil cooler fluid lines.
12 Refit the fluid level dipstick and filler tube to the transmission.
13 Reconnect the speedometer drive cable.
14 Reconnect the speed selector lever.
15 Reconnect the kickdown cable.
16 Reconnect the fuel hoses to the fuel pump.
17 Reconnect the electrical leads to all accessories and components.
18 Connect the carburettor controls. On fuel injection models, reconnect all the items mentioned in Section 18, paragraph 6.
19 Reconnect the brake vacuum hose.
20 Reconnect the heater and radiator coolant hoses.
21 Refit the air cleaner and pre-heater duct.
22 Refit the bonnet.
23 Reconnect the battery.
24 Fill the cooling system (Chapter 1).
25 Fill the engine and transmission with oil.
26 Check the adjustment of the kickdown cable and the speed selector control linkage (refer to Chapter 7B).

41 Engine - initial start-up after overhaul

1 Make sure the battery is fully charged and that all lubricants, coolant and fuel are replenished.
2 If the fuel system has been dismantled it will require several revolutions of the engine on the starter motor to pump the petrol up to the carburettor.
3 As soon as the engine fires and runs, keep it going at a fast tickover only (no faster), and bring it up to the normal working temperature. Expect some initial noise from the hydraulic valve lifters until they are properly pressurized with oil.
4 As the engine warms up there will be odd smells and some smoke from parts getting hot and burning off oil deposits. The signs to look for are leaks of water or oil which will be obvious if serious. Check also the exhaust pipe and manifold connections, as these do not always "find" their exact gastight position until the warmth and vibration have acted on them, and it is almost certain that they will need tightening further. This should be done, of course, with the engine stopped.
5 When normal running temperature has been reached adjust the engine idling speed, as described in Chapter 1, and check the ignition timing as described in Chapter 5 (where necessary). With the engine stopped, also carry out the final stage of cylinder head bolt tightening, if applicable (see Specifications and Section 8).
6 Stop the engine and wait a few minutes to see if any lubricant or coolant is dripping out when the engine is stationary.
7 Road test the car to check that the timing is correct and that the engine is giving the necessary smoothness and power. Do not race the engine - if new bearings and/or pistons have been fitted it should be treated as a new engine and run in at a reduced speed for the first 500 miles (800 km). Some valve clatter is to be expected until the hydraulic valve lifters fill with oil.
8 On vehicles equipped with automatic transmission, pay particular attention to checking the fluid level as described in *Weekly checks*.

Chapter 3
Cooling and heating systems

Contents

Antifreeze mixture ....See Chapter 1
Coolant level check ....See Weekly checks
Coolant pump - removal and refitting 5
Cooling system - draining ....See Chapter 1
Cooling system - filling ....See Chapter 1
Cooling system - flushing ....See Chapter 1
Cooling system electrical switches - testing, removal and refitting ..7
Cooling system hoses - disconnection and renewal 2
General information and precautions 1
Heater components - removal and refitting 9
Heater/ventilation system - general information 8
Radiator - removal, inspection and refitting 3
Radiator electric cooling fan - testing, removal and refitting 6
Thermostat - removal, testing and refitting 4
Vents and grilles - removal and refitting 10

Degrees of difficulty

Easy, suitable for novice with little experience		Fairly easy, suitable for beginner with some experience		Fairly difficult, suitable for competent DIY mechanic		Difficult, suitable for experienced DIY mechanic		Very difficult, suitable for expert DIY or professional	

Specifications

Thermostat

Opening temperature:
1.3 litre models	91°C
1.6, 1.8 and 2.0 litre models	92°C

Fully open temperature:
1.3 litre models	103°C
1.6, 1.8 and 2.0 litre models	107°C

Expansion tank cap

Colour	Blue or yellow

Opening pressure:
Blue	1.20 to 1.35 bar
Yellow	1.02 to 1.15 bar

Fan thermoswitch (all models)
Switches on at	97°C
Switches off at	93°C

Torque wrench settings

	Nm	lbf ft
Coolant pump bolts:		
1.3 litre models	8	6
1.6, 1.8 and 2.0 litre models	25	18
Thermostat housing bolts:		
1.3 litre models	10	7
1.6, 1.8 and 2.0 litre models	15	11
Temperature sender in manifold	10	7
Temperature sender in thermostat housing	8	6

1 General information and precautions

General information

The cooling system is of pressurised type, comprising of a pump driven by the timing belt, an aluminium crossflow radiator, electric cooling fan, and a thermostat. The system functions as follows. Cold coolant from the radiator passes through the hose to the coolant pump where it is pumped around the cylinder block and head passages. After cooling the cylinder bores, combustion surfaces and valve seats, the coolant reaches the underside of the thermostat, which is initially closed. The coolant passes through the heater and is returned via the cylinder block to the coolant pump.

When the engine is cold the coolant circulates only through the cylinder block, cylinder head, expansion tank and heater. When the coolant reaches a predetermined temperature, the thermostat opens and the coolant passes through to the radiator. As the coolant circulates through the radiator it is cooled by the inrush of air when the car is in forward motion. Airflow is supplemented by the action of the electric cooling fan when necessary. Upon reaching the radiator, the coolant is now cooled and the cycle is repeated.

The electric cooling fan mounted on the rear of the radiator is controlled by a thermostatic switch. At a predetermined coolant temperature the switch actuates the fan.

Precautions

⚠️ *Warning: Do not attempt to remove the expansion tank filler cap or disturb any part of the cooling system while the engine is hot, as there is a high risk of scalding. If the expansion tank filler cap must be removed before the engine and radiator have fully cooled (even though this is not recommended) the pressure in the cooling system must first be relieved. Cover the cap with a thick layer of cloth, to avoid scalding, and slowly unscrew the filler cap until a hissing sound can be heard. When the hissing has stopped, indicating that the pressure has reduced, slowly unscrew the filler cap until it can be removed; if more hissing sounds are heard, wait until they have stopped before unscrewing the cap completely. At all times keep well away from the filler cap opening.*

⚠️ *Warning: Do not allow antifreeze to come into contact with skin or painted surfaces of the vehicle. Rinse off spills immediately with plenty of water. Never leave antifreeze lying around in an open container or in a puddle in the driveway or on the garage floor. Children and pets are attracted by its sweet smell. Antifreeze can be fatal if ingested.*

⚠️ *Warning: If the engine is hot, the electric cooling fan may start rotating even if the engine is not running, so be careful to keep hands, hair and loose clothing well clear when working in the engine compartment.*

2 Cooling system hoses - disconnection and renewal

Note: *Refer to the warnings given in Section 1 of this Chapter before proceeding.*

1 If the checks described in Chapter 1 reveal a faulty hose, it must be renewed as follows.
2 First drain the cooling system (see Chapter 1). If the coolant is not due for renewal, it may be re-used.
3 To disconnect a hose, use a screwdriver to slacken the clips, then move them along the hose, clear of the relevant inlet/outlet union.

Carefully work the hose free. While the hoses can be removed with relative ease when new, or when hot, **do not** attempt to disconnect any part of the system while it is still hot.
4 Note that the radiator inlet and outlet unions are fragile; do not use excessive force when attempting to remove the hoses. Try to release it by rotating the hose ends before attempting to free it. If all else fails, cut the hose with a sharp knife, then slit it so that it can be peeled off in two pieces. Although this may prove expensive if the hose is otherwise undamaged, it is preferable to buying a new radiator.
5 When fitting a hose, first slide the clips onto the hose, then work the hose into position. If clamp type clips were originally fitted, it is a good idea to replace them with screw type clips when refitting the hose. If the hose is stiff, use a little soapy water as a lubricant, or soften the hose by soaking it in hot water.
6 Work the hose into position, checking that it is correctly routed, then slide each clip along the hose until it passes over the flared end of the relevant inlet/outlet union, before tightening the clips securely.
7 Refill the cooling system (Chapter 1).
8 Check for leaks as soon as possible after disturbing any part of the cooling system.

3 Radiator - removal, inspection and refitting

HAYNES HiNT *If leakage is the reason for wanting to remove the radiator, bear in mind that minor leaks can be often be cured using a radiator sealant with the radiator in situ.*

Removal

1 The radiator can be removed complete with the electrically-driven cooling fan if there is no need to disturb the fan.
2 Drain the system as described in Chapter 1, and disconnect and remove the battery.
3 Detach the radiator top and bottom hoses, and also the small diameter vent hose between the top of the radiator and the expansion tank **(see illustration)**. On automatic transmission models it will also be necessary to disconnect the fluid cooler hoses

from the radiator and suitably plug them to avoid loss of automatic transmission fluid.
4 Disconnect the electric wiring from the switch in the radiator at the lower right-hand side. Disconnect the fan motor leads at the connector near the front of the battery.
5 Remove the two clips which secure the radiator located at the top left and right corners of the radiator. Pull the top of the radiator back to free it from the top mountings and then lift it out of the bottom mountings and clear of the car **(see illustrations)**.

Inspection

6 If the radiator has been removed due to suspected blockage, reverse flush it as described in Chapter 1. Clean dirt and debris from the radiator fins, using an air line (wear eye protection!) or a soft brush. Be careful, as the fins are easily damaged, and are sharp.
7 If necessary, a radiator specialist can perform a 'flow test' on the radiator, to establish whether an internal blockage exists.
8 A leaking radiator must be referred to a specialist for permanent repair. Do not attempt to weld or solder a leaking radiator, as damage may result.
9 In an emergency, minor leaks from the radiator can be cured by using a radiator sealant in accordance with the manufacturers instructions with the radiator *in situ*.
10 If the radiator is to be sent for repair or renewed, remove the cooling fan switch.
11 Inspect the condition of the radiator mounting rubbers, and renew them if necessary.

Refitting

12 Refitting the radiator is the reverse of the removal procedure. Check that the rubber mountings are in good condition and ensure that the bottom location pegs fit correctly on installation. Refill the cooling system as described in Chapter 1. On automatic transmission models check and top-up the transmission fluid level as necessary.

4 Thermostat - removal, testing and refitting

Removal

1 Disconnect the battery negative terminal.
2 Drain the cooling system (Chapter 1).

3.3 Radiator top hose

3.5a Radiator clip

3.5b Removing the radiator

**4.4a Removing the thermostat housing
(1.3 litre model)**

**4.4b Extracting the thermostat and seal
(1.3 litre model)**

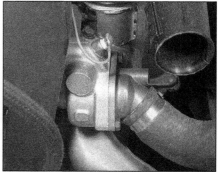

**4.5 Thermostat housing and cover
(1.6 litre model)**

1.3 litre models

3 Undo the securing bolts and remove the timing belt cover. Disconnect the radiator upper hose at its connection on the engine, which is the thermostat housing.

4 Undo the two securing bolts and remove the housing to reveal the thermostat in the cylinder head. Remove the thermostat, noting how it fits in the recesses in the aperture **(see illustrations)**.

1.6, 1.8 and 2.0 litres

5 The procedure for removing, testing and refitting of the thermostat on these models is basically the same as that given for the 1.3 model. However, the thermostat is located in a housing which is located externally to the toothed belt cover allowing easier access **(see illustration)**. On carburettor models, remove the air cleaner unit for improved access to the thermostat housing cover.

6 If the thermostat housing is to be removed, first remove the camshaft toothed belt and the belt rear cover from the engine (Chapter 2).

7 Disconnect all hoses from the thermostat housing, noting their position for subsequent reconnection (if still attached).

8 Remove the two bolts securing the thermostat housing and lift off the housing. Extract the sealing ring.

Testing

9 A rough test of the thermostat may be made by suspending it with a piece of string in a container full of water. Heat the water to bring it to the boil - the thermostat must open by the time the water boils. If not, renew it.

10 If a thermometer is available, the precise opening temperature may be determined, and compared with the figures given in the Specifications. The opening temperature is marked on the thermostat **(see illustrations)**.

11 A thermostat which fails to close as the water cools must also be renewed.

Refitting

1.3 litre models

12 Refitting the thermostat is the reverse procedure to removal, but fit a new rubber seal to the thermostat and install it to locate in the two recesses noted during removal **(see illustrations)**. Tighten the thermostat housing bolts to the specified torque and refill the cooling system as described in Chapter 1.

1.6, 1.8 and 2.0 litre models

13 Refitting is the reverse of removal using a new cover seal and, where necessary, a new housing sealing ring. On completion refill the cooling system as described in Chapter 1.

5 Coolant pump - removal and refitting

Removal

1 Drain the cooling system as described in Chapter 1.

2 Remove the camshaft toothed belt as described in Chapter 2.

3 On early models unbolt and remove toothed belt cover backplate from the block.

4 Unbolt and remove the coolant pump from the engine block. On later modes, to separate the pump and plate, apply sideways pressure to it whilst rotating it around the pump body **(see illustrations)**.

5 Although the pump can be dismantled and reassembled, a press and several special tools are necessary and it is considered that the work is outside the scope of the home mechanic. For this reason a defective pump should be renewed.

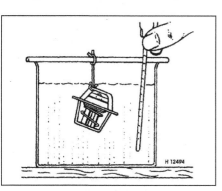

**4.10a Testing the thermostat opening
temperature**

**4.10b Opening temperature is marked on
thermostat**

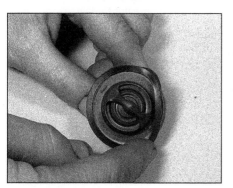

4.12a Fitting a new thermostat seal

**4.12b Fitting the thermostat to the cylinder
head (1.3 litre model)**

5.4a Removing the coolant pump (early model)

5.4b On later models, remove the toothed belt cover from the pump as described

5.6 Coolant pump O-ring seal

Refitting

6 Before fitting the coolant pump, clean its mounting in the engine block and fit a new O-ring seal to the pump body **(see illustration)**. Apply silicone grease to the seal, and to the sealing surface in the block. On later models, if necessary, refit the toothed belt backplate to the pump body, making sure it is fitted the correct way around.

7 Install the pump in the block and fit the three retaining bolts and washers, but only hand tighten them at this stage. The cut-out in the pump flange must be positioned as shown to act as the toothed belt adjustment limit stop when the pump is rotated to tension the timing belt **(see illustration)**. On early models, refit the belt cover backplate.

8 Refit the camshaft toothed belt as described in Chapter 2 and tighten the pump securing bolts to the specified torque.

9 Refill the cooling system as described in Chapter 1

6 Radiator electric cooling fan - testing, removal and refitting

Testing

1 The cooling fan is supplied with current via the ignition switch, relay and a fuse (see Chapter 12). The circuit is completed by the cooling fan thermostatic switch, which is mounted in the right-hand end of the radiator.

2 If a fan does not appear to work, run the

engine until normal operating temperature is reached, then allow it to idle. If the fan does not cut in within a few minutes, switch off the ignition and disconnect the wiring plug from the cooling fan switch. Bridge the two contacts in the wiring plug using a length of spare wire, and switch on the ignition. If the fan now operates, the switch is probably faulty and should be renewed.

3 If the fan still fails to operate, check that full battery voltage is available at the feed wire to the switch; if not, then there is a fault in the feed wire (possibly due to a fault in the fan motor, or a blown fuse). If there is no problem with the feed, check that there is continuity between the switch earth terminal and a good earth point on the body; if not, then the earth connection is faulty and must be re-made.

4 If the switch and the wiring are in good condition, the fault must lie in the motor itself. The motor can be checked by disconnecting the motor wiring connector and connecting a 12 volt supply directly to the motor terminals. If the motor is faulty, it must be renewed, as no spares are available.

Removal

5 Disconnect the battery negative terminal.

6 Disconnect the fan motor leads at the connecting plug.

7 Unbolt the fan/shroud assembly from the radiator and withdraw it upwards **(see illustration)**.

8 To separate the fan motor from the shroud, unscrew the three nuts.

Refitting

9 Reassembly, if the unit was dismantled, and refitting to the car are the reverse of the dismantling and removal sequences. On completion run the engine up to normal operating temperature and check the fan for correct functioning.

7 Cooling system electrical switches - testing, removal and refitting

Electric cooling fan thermostatic switch

Testing

1 Testing of the switch is described as part of the cooling fan test procedure (Section 6).

Removal

2 The switch is located in the right-hand side of the radiator. The engine and radiator should be cold before removing the switch.

3 Disconnect the battery negative lead. If necessary, firmly apply the handbrake then jack up the front of the vehicle and support it on axle stands (see *"Jacking and Vehicle Support"*).. Access to the switch can then be gained from underneath the vehicle.

4 Either drain the cooling system to below the level of the switch (as described in Chapter 1), or have ready a suitable plug which can be used to plug the switch aperture in the radiator whilst the switch is removed. If a plug is used, take great care not to damage the radiator, and do not use anything which will allow foreign matter to enter the radiator.

5 Disconnect the wiring plug from the switch **(see illustration)**.

6 Carefully unscrew the switch from the radiator and recover the sealing ring/washer.

Refitting

7 Refitting is a reversal of removal using a new sealing ring/washer. Securely tighten the switch and top-up/refill the cooling system as described in Chapter 1.

8 On completion, start the engine and run it until it reaches normal operating temperature, then continue to run the engine and check that the cooling fan cuts in and functions correctly.

5.7 Coolant pump correctly fitted with rotational stops arrowed

6.7 Radiator/fan shroud assembly - early models. Two securing bolts are arrowed

7.5 Radiator thermostat switch

Coolant temperature gauge sender

Testing

9 The coolant temperature gauge, mounted in the instrument panel, is fed with a stabilised voltage supply from the instrument panel feed (via the ignition switch and a fuse), and its earth is controlled by the sender.

10 The sender is screwed into the inlet manifold on 1.3 litre engines, and into the thermostat housing on all other engines **(see illustration)**. The sender contains a thermistor, which consists of an electronic component whose electrical resistance decreases at a predetermined rate as its temperature rises. When the coolant is cold, the sender resistance is high, current flow through the gauge is reduced, and the gauge needle points towards the 'cold' end of the scale. If the sender is faulty, it must be renewed.

11 If the gauge develops a fault, first check the other instruments; if they do not work at all, check the instrument panel electrical feed. If the readings are erratic, there may be a fault in the voltage stabiliser, which will necessitate renewal of the stabiliser (see Chapter 12). If the fault lies in the temperature gauge alone, check it as follows.

12 If the gauge needle remains at the 'cold' end of the scale, disconnect the sender wire, and earth it to the cylinder head. If the needle then deflects when the ignition is switched on, the sender unit is proved faulty, and should be renewed. If the needle still does not move,

7.10 Coolant temperature sender (1.3 litre model)

remove the instrument panel (Chapter 12) and check the continuity of the wiring between the sender unit and the gauge, and the feed to the gauge unit. If continuity is shown, and the fault still exists, then the gauge is faulty, and the gauge unit should be renewed.

13 If the gauge needle remains at the 'hot' end of the scale, disconnect the sender wire. If the needle then returns to the 'cold' end of the scale when the ignition is switched on, the sender unit is proved faulty and should be renewed. If the needle still does not move, check the remainder of the circuit as described previously.

Removal

14 Either partially drain the cooling system to just below the level of the sender (as described in Chapter 1), or have ready a suitable plug which can be used to plug the sender aperture whilst it is removed. If a plug is used, take great care not to damage the sender unit threads, and do not use anything which will allow foreign matter to enter the cooling system.

15 Disconnect the battery negative lead.

16 Disconnect the wiring from the sender, then unscrew the unit from its location.

Refitting

17 Ensure that the sender threads are clean and apply a smear of suitable sealant to them.

18 Refit the sender, tightening it securely, and reconnect the wiring.

19 Top-up the cooling system as described in Chapter 1.

20 On completion, start the engine and check the operation of the temperature gauge. Also check for coolant leaks.

Fuel injection system coolant temperature sensor

21 Refer to Chapter 4.

8 Heater/ventilation system - general information

The heater system depends upon fresh air being drawn into the grille at the base of the windscreen and passed through a matrix which is heated from the engine cooling system.

Temperature regulation is controlled by mixing cold inlet air with warm air, using flap valves both for this function and for the direction of air to the interior, windscreen or side air outlets.

An electric booster fan is mounted within the engine compartment to supplement the normal ram effect provided when the vehicle is in forward motion.

An independent fresh air ventilation system provides a supply of unheated fresh air at the nozzles on the instrument panel.

Stale air is exhausted from the vehicle interior through the slots just to the rear of the rear side windows on Saloon models, or from vents at the rear pillar on other models.

9 Heater components - removal and refitting

Control unit

1 Remove the panel from the bottom of the facia **(see illustration)**.

2 Prise off the four retaining clips and remove the cover from the heater matrix housing.

3 Extract the self-tapping screws and remove the switch plate from the facia panel. As the switch plate is withdrawn, disconnect the plugs from the rear of the switches. Where a centre console is fitted, this must first be removed or displaced to gain access to the lower screws. The upper securing screws are located in the heated rear window switch recess and in the choke control recess.

4 Note the position of the heater control rods in their clamps and clips. Use quick-drying paint if necessary to mark the rods, then disconnect them from the heater housing and from the operating arms of the flap valves in the air distribution housing.

5 Extract the two self-tapping screws which secure the heater control assembly and remove it.

6 Refitting is a reversal of removal, but reconnect the control rods in the following sequence:
 a) *Short rod to upper heat distribution valve arm*
 b) *Intermediate rod to lower heat distribution valve arm*
 c) *Long rod to air mix flap*

Blower motor

7 Open the bonnet and prop it open.

8 Remove the water deflector (if fitted) from the opening on the top of the engine compartment rear bulkhead.

9 Disconnect the wiring harness from the blower motor at the multi-pin plug **(see illustration)**.

10 Prise off the clips which retain the cover over the motor and remove it.

11 Unscrew the two motor mounting screws and lift the motor from its location.

12 Refitting is a reversal of removal.

Heater matrix

13 Clamp the heater hoses close to the engine compartment rear bulkhead. Self-locking grips will serve for this purpose.

14 Disconnect the heater hoses from the matrix pipe stubs.

15 Plug the pipe stubs to prevent coolant spillage during removal of the matrix.

16 Extract the two screws and remove the centre console.

17 Remove the lower left panel from under the facia, then remove the right-hand one (refer to Chapter 11).

18 Prise off the four retaining clips and remove the cover from the base of the matrix housing.

19 Extract the four screws and one nut which

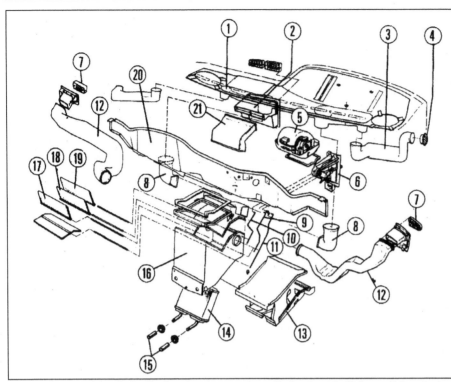

9.1 Exploded view of heater

1 Facia padding
2 Fresh air duct
3 Side window demister duct
4 Side window demister nozzle
5 Blower motor
6 Control unit
7 Heater side vent
8 Windscreen demister hose
9 Control rod (air distributor valve)
10 Control rod (air mix)
11 Control rod (upper distributor valve)
12 Heater vent hose
13 Matrix housing
14 Matrix
15 Coolant flow and return hoses
16 Air distribution housing
17 Upper distributor valve
18 Air mix flap
19 Lower distributor valve
20 Bulkhead
21 Centre duct

hold the flanges of the air distribution chamber and the matrix housing together.

20 Disconnect the control rod for the air mix flap valve.

21 Release the air mix control rod on the right-hand side.

22 Extract the matrix mounting screws and withdraw the matrix from the heater housing. In order to reach the upper mounting screws, position the flap valve in a vertical position. As the matrix is withdrawn, ease the pipe stubs and their sealing grommets through the bulkhead. Be prepared for some coolant spillage.

23 If the matrix is blocked, try reverse flushing as described for the radiator (see Chapter 1). If this fails, try a radiator cleansing agent, but use it strictly in accordance with the manufacturer's instructions.

24 If the matrix is leaking, have it professionally repaired by a radiator repairer, or purchase a new one. Temporary repairs are

9.9 Heater blower motor

not worth the trouble if the unit has to be removed again after a short period of service.

25 Refitting is a reversal of removal.

26 Top-up the cooling system as described in "Weekly checks".

Air distribution housing

27 Remove the heater matrix as described in paragraphs 13 to 22.

28 Extract the screws and remove the glove compartment.

29 Extract the securing screws from the switch plate. Pull the plate forwards until the switch plugs can be disconnected and the assembly removed.

30 Extract the two mounting screws and remove the heater control lever assembly.

31 Extract the two screws which retain the centre fresh air nozzle housing and then pull the housing down and out of the facia panel.

32 Where applicable, disconnect the leads for the radio and clock.

33 Pull off the air distribution ducts for the heater side vents, also the hose from the air distribution housing.

34 Loosen (but do not remove) the two instrument panel fasteners and pull the instrument panel slightly away from the bulkhead.

35 Disconnect the air distribution housing at the top from the bulkhead, and at the base from the facia panel.

36 Remove the air distribution housing.

37 Refitting is a reversal of removal, but make sure that the foam sealing strip is in good condition. Reconnect the control rods as described in paragraph 6. On completion, top-up/refill the cooling system as described in "Weekly checks".

10 Vents and grilles - removal and refitting

Removal

Door window demister nozzle

1 Carefully remove the nozzle by prising it from the facia panel padding with a screwdriver.

Side heater vent

2 Remove the swivelling insert by tilting it downwards and carefully depressing one side of it to disengage the locating pivot lug.

3 According to which side the vent is being removed from, either remove the glove compartment or the lighting switch and strip.

4 Extract the two self-tapping screws and pull the vent housing from the facia panel.

Centre fresh air nozzle

5 The swivelling vent is removed in exactly the same way as described for the side vent in paragraph 2.

Stale air exhaust grille

6 Carefully lever off the grille from its fixing grommets.

Refitting

7 Refitting of all components is a reversal of removal, but apply sealing compound around the fixing grommets when engaging the grille lugs in order to make a good weatherproof seal.

Chapter 4 Part A:
Fuel and exhaust system - carburettor models

Contents

Air cleaner air temperature control system - general information and
    testing 3
Air cleaner filter element renewal . . . . .See Chapter 1
Air cleaner housing - removal and refitting 2
Carburettor - general information 11
Carburettor - removal and refitting 12
Choke cable - removal, refitting and adjustment 10
Exhaust manifold - removal and refitting .16
Exhaust system - removal and refitting 17
Fuel filter renewal . . . . .See Chapter 1
Fuel pump - testing, removal and refitting 5
Fuel tank - removal and refitting 7
Fuel tank sender unit - removal and refitting 6

Fuel tank vent chamber - general information, removal and
    refitting 8
General fuel system checks .See Chapter 1
General information 1
GM Varajet carburettor - fault diagnosis, overhaul and
    adjustments 13
Idle speed and mixture adjustment . . . . .See Chapter 1
Inlet manifold - removal and refitting 15
Pierburg 2E3 carburettor - fault diagnosis, overhaul and
    adjustments 14
Throttle control cable - removal, refitting and adjustment 9
Unleaded petrol - general information and usage 4

Degrees of difficulty

Easy, suitable for novice with little experience	**Fairly easy,** suitable for beginner with some experience	**Fairly difficult,** suitable for competent DIY mechanic	**Difficult,** suitable for experienced DIY mechanic	**Very difficult,** suitable for expert DIY or professional

Specifications

Fuel pump

Operation	Mechanical from camshaft
Pressure	0.25 to 0.36 bar

GM Varajet II Carburettor

Throttle valve diameter:	
Stage 1	35.0 mm
Stage 2	46.0 mm
Venturi diameter	28.0 mm
Main jet:	
1.3 litre models	201
1.6 litre models	204
Partial load needle	1.51
Float weight	5.6g
Float setting (top surface to flange)	4.5 to 6.5 mm
Automatic choke valve gaps (see text):	
A (pull-down)	2.8 to 3.4 mm
B (fast idle)	2.3 to 2.8 mm
C (full throttle)	9.5 to 10.5 mm
Manual choke valve gap	2.8 to 3.4 mm
Accelerator pump plunger adjustment	7.8 to 8.2 mm
Air valve lever free play at rod	0.1 to 0.3 mm

Pierburg 2E3 carburettor - 1.3 litre models

	Primary	Secondary
Venturi diameter	20 mm	24 mm
Main jet	X97.5	X112.5
Air correction jet	X80	X100
Emulsion tube code number	88	60
Partial load enrichment orifice	0.5 mm	-
Pre-atomizer diameter	8 mm	7 mm
Mixture outlet orifice	2.5 mm	3.0 mm
Idle fuel jet	37.5	-
Idle air jet	130	-
Fuel enrichment jet	-	105 to 125
Float needle valve diameter	1.5 mm	-
Float level	28 to 30 mm	-
Pull-down unit code	55	-
Pull-down unit code	59	-
Throttle valve fast idle gap:		
Manual transmission	0.8 to 0.9 mm	-
Automatic transmission	1.1 to 1.2 mm	-
Choke valve gap:		
Manual transmission	1.7 to 2.1 mm	-
Automatic transmission	2.1 to 2.5 mm	-
Accelerator pump delivery (cc per stroke):		
Manual transmission	0.38 to 0.62	-
Automatic transmission	0.18 to 0.42	-

Pierburg 2E3 carburettor - 1.6 litre models

	Primary	Secondary
Venturi diameter	20 mm	24 mm
Main jet	X95	X105
Air correction jet	X110	X80
Emulsion tube code number	88	51
Partial load enrichment orifice	0.55	-
Pre-atomizer diameter	8 mm	7 mm
Mixture outlet orifice	2.5 mm	3.0 mm
Idle fuel jet	42.5	-
Idle air jet	132.5	-
Fuel enrichment jet	-	85 to 105
Float needle valve diameter	1.5 mm	-
Float level	28 to 30 mm	-
Throttle valve fast idle gap:		
Manual transmission	0.8 to 0.9 mm	-
Automatic transmission	1.1 to 1.2 mm	-
Choke valve gap:		
Manual transmission	1.7 to 2.1 mm	-
Automatic transmission	2.1 to 2.5 mm	-
Accelerator pump delivery (cc per stroke):		
Manual transmission	0.38 to 0.62	-
Automatic transmission	0.18 to 0.42	-

Adjustment data

	Manual transmission	Automatic transmission
Idle speed	900 to 950 rpm	800 to 850 rpm
Fast idle speed:		
Varajet II:		
1.3 litre models:		
Models with automatic choke	2150 to 2250 rpm	2550 to 2650 rpm
Models with manual choke	2500 rpm	2600 rpm
1.6 litre models	2050 to 2150 rpm	2250 to 2350 rpm
Pierburg 2E3	2100 to 2500 rpm	2400 to 2800 rpm
Exhaust gas CO content at idle	1.0 to 1.5%	1.0 to 1.5%

Recommended fuel

Minimum octane rating .... 98 RON leaded (4-star) or unleaded (Super unleaded)*
*If the ignition timing is retarded by 3°, 95 RON unleaded (unleaded premium) petrol can be used (see Chapter 5 for details)

Torque wrench settings

	Nm	lbf ft
Fuel pump nuts:		
1.3 litre models	20	15
1.6 litre models	15	11
Carburettor mounting nuts:		
1.3 litre models	20	15
1.6 litre models	15	11

1 General information

The fuel system consists of a fuel tank mounted under the rear of the car, a mechanical fuel pump and a carburettor. The fuel pump is operated by an eccentric on the camshaft and is mounted on the rear of the cylinder head. The air cleaner contains a disposable paper filter element and incorporates a flap valve air temperature control system which allows cold air from the outside of the car and warm air from the exhaust manifold to enter the air cleaner in the correct proportions.

The fuel pump lifts fuel from the fuel tank via a filter and supplies it to the carburettor. Excess fuel is returned from the anti-percolation chamber to the fuel tank.

⚠ *Warning: Many of the procedures in this Chapter require the removal of fuel lines and connections which may result in some fuel spillage. Before carrying out any operation on the fuel system refer to the precautions given in Safety first! at the beginning of this Manual and follow them implicitly. Petrol is a highly dangerous and volatile liquid and the precautions necessary when handling it cannot be overstressed.*

2 Air cleaner housing - removal and refitting

Removal

Remove the centre retaining nut or bolt or the three screws from the air cleaner cover.

Lift the air cleaner off the carburettor, disengaging the hot air pick-up from the manifold shroud, together with the breather and vacuum hoses **(see illustrations)**.

Refitting

Refit by reversing the removal operations, making sure that the gasket or sealing ring is in place on the carburettor.

3 Air cleaner air temperature control system - general information and testing

General information

1 The air cleaner on all models provides clean air for combustion, excluding airborne dust and dirt which could damage the engine, carburettor or fuel injection system.
2 On carburettor models, a thermostatically-controlled air cleaner is used to regulate the temperature of the air entering the carburettor, according to ambient temperatures and engine load. The air cleaner has two sources of supply, through the normal inlet spout (cold air) or from a hot air box mounted on the exhaust manifold (hot air).

2.2a Disconnect the breather hose at the air cleaner . . .

3 The airflow through the air cleaner is controlled by a flap valve in the air cleaner spout, which covers or exposes the hot or cold air ports according to temperature and manifold vacuum.
4 A vacuum motor operates the flap valve, and holds it fully open when the temperature in the air cleaner is below a predetermined level. As the air inlet temperature rises, the vacuum motor opens or closes the flap valve dependent entirely on manifold vacuum. Thus, during light or constant throttle applications, the flap valve will remain open, supplying the carburettor with hot air, and will close under heavy throttle applications, so that only cold air enters the carburettor.
5 As the temperature in the air cleaner rises still further, the vacuum motor closes the flap valve, therefore allowing only cold air to enter the carburettor under all operating conditions.
6 The vacuum motor is operated by vacuum created in the inlet manifold, and is controlled by a temperature-sensing unit located inside the air cleaner.

Testing

7 Should the operation of the temperature-regulating components be suspect, their operation can be tested as follows.
8 Remove the air cleaner as described in Section 2.
9 Apply warm air to the hot air inlet port from an external source, such as a hair dryer. At the same time apply vacuum (suction by mouth) to the vacuum hose. Observe the operation of

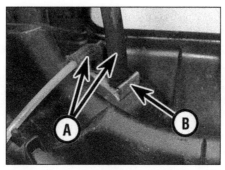

3.10a Air cleaner temperature sensing unit vacuum hose connections (A) and retaining plate (B) (1.6 litre model)

2.2b . . . and the vacuum hose (arrowed) at the carburettor

the flap valve, with reference to the previous operating description, as the heat source and suction are applied and removed.
10 If the flap valve fails to respond as described, make sure that the vacuum hoses and connections are sound, and if so, a fault in one of the temperature regulating components is indicated. On 1.6 models, it is possible to renew the temperature-sensing unit after prising off the retaining plate, and also the vacuum motor and inlet spout assembly after prising the spout out of the air cleaner body **(see illustrations)**. On 1.3 models, none of the parts are available separately, and a complete air cleaner must be obtained. In all cases, consult with a dealer concerning parts availability before disturbing any of the components.

4 Unleaded petrol - general information and usage

Note: *The information given in this Chapter is correct at the time of writing and applies only to petrols currently available in the UK. If updated information is thought to be required check with a Vauxhall dealer. If travelling abroad consult one of the motoring organisations (or a similar authority) for advice on the petrols available and their suitability for your vehicle.*

1 The fuel recommended by Vauxhall is given in the Specifications Section of this Chapter, followed by the equivalent petrol currently on sale in the UK.

3.10b Removing the inlet spout from the air cleaner body (1.6 litre model)

2 RON and MON are testing standards; RON stands for Research Octane Number, while MON stands for Motor Octane Number.

3 All Vauxhall Cavalier carburettor models are designed to run on 98 (RON) octane leaded or unleaded petrol (see Specifications). If the vehicle is to be run on 95 (RON) unleaded petrol, the ignition timing **must** be retarded by 3° (see Chapter 5 for details); this is necessary to avoid detenation (knocking and pinking) which could lead to possible engine damage. **Do not** use 95 (RON) unleaded petrol if the ignition timing has not been retarded.

5 Fuel pump - testing, removal and refitting

Note: *Refer to the warning note in Section 1 before proceeding.*

Testing

1 To test the fuel pump on the engine, disconnect the outlet pipe which leads to the carburettor, and hold a wad of rag over the pump outlet while an assistant spins the engine on the starter. *Keep the hands away from the electric cooling fan.* Regular spurts of fuel should be ejected as the engine turns.

2 The pump can also be tested by removing it. With the pump outlet pipe disconnected but the inlet pipe still connected, hold the wad of rag by the outlet. Operate the pump lever by hand, moving it in and out; if the pump is in good condition, the lever should move and return smoothly and a strong jet of fuel should be ejected.

Removal

3 Mark the pump inlet and outlet hoses, for identification purposes then slacken both retaining clips **(see illustration)**. Place wads of rag beneath the hose unions to catch any spilled fuel; disconnect both hoses from the pump and plug the hoses to minimise fuel loss.

4 Unscrew and remove the pump mounting bolts and withdraw the pump from the camshaft housing.

Refitting

5 Refitting is a reversal of removal, but use new flange joint gaskets.

5.3 Fuel pump hoses

6 Fuel tank sender unit - removal and refitting

Note: *Refer to the warning note in Section 1 before proceeding.*

Removal

1 Disconnect the battery negative lead. Siphon the fuel from the tank into a clean metal container which can be sealed. Alternatively, working under the car, disconnect an accessible fuel line connection at the tank, and drain the fuel into a suitable container.

2 Disconnect the leads from the sender unit terminals **(see illustration)**. On later models also disconnect the fuel line to the pump. Clamp the hose to prevent fuel leakage.

3 To remove the sender unit, either engage a flat piece of steel as a lever between two of the raised tabs on the sender unit and turn it anti-clockwise to release it, or undo the retaining bolts (as applicable).

4 Remove the unit carefully to avoid bending the float arm.

5 Take out the sealing ring.

Refitting

6 Refit by reversing the removal operations, but make sure that the sealing ring is in good condition and seats correctly.

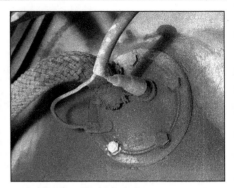

6.2 Fuel tank sender unit - sender unit retained by bolts

7 Fuel tank - removal and refitting

Note: *Refer to the warning note in Section 1 before proceeding.*

Removal

1 Disconnect the battery and then siphon the fuel from the tank into a clean metal container which can be sealed. Alternatively, working under the car, disconnect an accessible fuel line connection at the tank, and drain the fuel into a suitable container.

2 Measure the exposed part of the threads on the short handbrake cable at the equaliser for ease of resetting, then disconnect the cable.

3 Refer to Section 17 and remove the exhaust system to provide adequate clearance for removal of the tank.

4 Disconnect the longer handbrake cable from the pullrod.

5 Bend the bracket under the fuel tank upwards and to the rear.

6 Disconnect and clamp the fuel outlet hose from the fuel tank **(see illustration)**. Note that on fuel injection models, this is connected to the sender unit **(see illustration 6.2)**.

7 Disconnect the leads from the sender unit terminals.

8 Release the clips and disconnect the filler and short vent hoses from the tank **(see illustrations)**.

9 Support the weight of the fuel tank on a jack with a block of wood as an insulator.

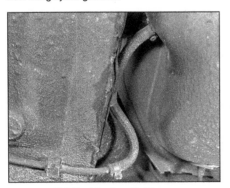

7.6 Fuel tank outlet hose

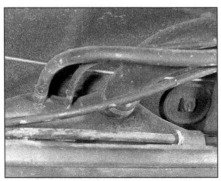

7.8a Fuel tank filler/vent hose connections

7.8b Filler/vent hose routing under rear wing

7.10 Fuel tank mounting strap

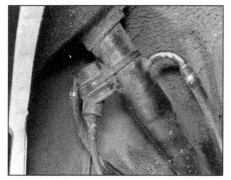

8.1a Fuel tank vent chamber - early type

8.1b Fuel tank vent chamber - later type

10 Release the tank mounting straps **(see illustration)** and then lower the tank sufficiently to be able to disconnect the long vent hose and fuel feed hose (where applicable) from it.

11 Remove the fuel tank from the vehicle.

12 If the tank contains sediment or water, it may be cleaned out using two or three rinses with paraffin. Shake vigorously using several changes of paraffin, but before doing so remove the sender unit (see Section 6). Allow the tank to drain thoroughly.

13 If removal of the tank was carried out in order to mend a leak, have it repaired professionally; radiator repairers will usually do this. To remove all trace of vapour requires several hours of steaming out.

Refitting

14 Refitting the fuel tank is a reversal of removal, but observe the following points:
  a) Use new hose clips.
  b) Make sure that the rubber buffers are in position on the left-hand mounting strap.
  c) Check the handbrake adjustment as described in Chapter 1.

8 Fuel tank vent chamber - general information, removal and refitting

General information

1 The vent line from the fuel tank incorporates a vent chamber. This chamber acts as an expansion tank for any increase in the volume of fuel which may occur due to a rise in temperature **(see illustrations)**.

2 The chamber incorporates three individual cells which are interconnected by holes.

3 When filling the fuel tank, it is worth remembering the significance of the following if the tank capacity is to be fully utilised.

4 When fuel reaches the end of the tank vent pipe, the fuel dispensing pump on the garage forecourt will cut off. This indicates that the tank is 95% full. More fuel may be added slowly for a further 30 seconds. After this period, no more fuel should be added, otherwise there will be no space left to allow for fuel expansion, and fuel could be lost through the vent pipe under conditions of rising temperature.

5 The vent chamber also acts as a housing for the fuel cut-off valve. This valve is designed to prevent fuel from escaping from the tank through the vent chamber should the vehicle turn over after an accident.

Removal

6 To remove the vent chamber, remove the clips and pull the hoses from it.

7 The hose clips should be levered off with a screwdriver and then discarded as they cannot be used again. Purchase new clips of a suitable type.

8 To check the functioning of the valve, invert the chamber. Pour some fuel into nozzle A and check that fuel is not seen to leak from nozzle B **(see illustration)**.

Refitting

9 Refitting is a reversal of removal. Make sure that the hoses are correctly connected and use new hose clips.

9 Throttle control cable - removal, refitting and adjustment

Removal

1 Slacken off all adjustment by removing the E-clip from the groove in the outer cable end fitting then remove the retaining clip and free the inner cable ball end fitting from the throttle linkage **(see illustrations)**.

2 Working back along the length of the cable, free it from any relevant retaining clips or ties whilst noting its correct routing.

3 From in the vehicle, reach up behind the facia; release the cable from the slot in the pedal.

4 Free the end of the outer cable and tie a length of string to the end of the inner cable.

5 In the engine compartment, release the outer cable retainer from the bulkhead. Withdraw the cable from the bulkhead until the end of the cable appears; untie the string and leave it in position. The string can be used to draw the cable back into position on refitting.

Refitting

6 Tie the string to the end of the cable then use the string to draw the cable into position through the bulkhead. Once the cable end is visible, untie the string.

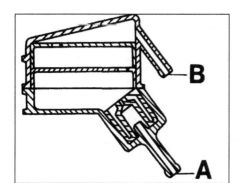

8.8 Fuel tank vent chamber
A Vent line from tank   B To atmosphere

9.1a Throttle cable bracket and clip at carburettor

9.1b Throttle link balljoint with retaining clip released

9.12 Throttle pedal stop screw

7 Clip the outer cable into position and hook the inner cable onto the pedal, making sure it is securely retained.

8 From within the engine compartment, ensure that the outer cable is correctly seated in the bulkhead grommet. Work along the cable, securing it in position with all the relevant retaining clips and ties, whilst ensuring that it is correctly routed.

9 Pass the cable through its mounting bracket grommet and reconnect the inner cable to the throttle linkage. Secure the ball end fitting in position with the retaining clip.

Adjustment

10 Remove the E-clip from the accelerator outer cable then, ensuring that the throttle cam is fully against its stop, gently pull the cable out of its grommet until all free play is removed from the inner cable.

11.1a GM Varajet carburettor - float chamber side

11.1b GM Varajet carburettor - vacuum capsule side

11 With the cable held in this position, fit the E-clip so that there is only a small amount of freeplay in the inner cable.

12 Have an assistant depress the accelerator pedal and check that the throttle cam opens fully and returns smoothly to its stop. If necessary, the pedal travel can be adjusted slightly using the throttle pedal screw **(see illustration)**.

10 Choke cable - removal, refitting and adjustment

Removal

1 Disconnect the battery earth lead.

2 Tap out the small pin which secures the choke control knob to the cable end fitting. Unscrew and remove the knob.

3 Undo the retaining ring or nut which secures the choke control to the facia. Push the control into the facia and disconnect the warning light switch (when fitted).

4 Remove the air cleaner.

5 Disconnect the choke inner and outer cable from the carburettor. On some carburettors the inner cable is secured by a grub screw which must be undone with an Allen key **(see illustration)**.

6 Release the bulkhead grommet and remove the cable.

Refitting

7 Refit in the reverse order to removal, adjusting the cable as follows.

Adjustment

8 Release the clamp screws on the inner and outer choke cables.

9 Push the choke control arm to the fully off position, when the control arm should be engaged with the spring metal retaining clip.

10 Position the outer cable comfortably in its clamp and tighten the retaining screw.

11 Now tighten the clamp screw on the inner cable.

12 Check the operation of the choke for full and free movement, and that it returns to the fully off position in contact with the spring metal retaining clip **(see illustration)**.

11.1c GM Varajet carburettor - automatic choke side

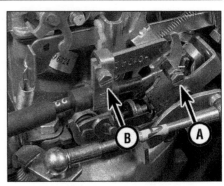

10.5 Choke cable connections at carburettor

A Inner cable clamp   B Outer cable clamp

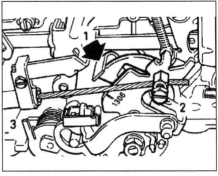

10.12 Choke cable adjustment

1 Spring retaining clip   3 Outer cable clamp
2 Inner cable clamp

11 Carburettor - general information

GM Varajet carburettor

1 The GM Varajet II carburettor is of dual barrel downdraught design **(see illustrations)**.

2 On all 1.6 models, and on 1.3 models built before August 1982, an automatic electrically-heated choke is fitted.

3 As from engine numbers 0832150 (manual) and 0858780 (automatic), 1.3 models are fitted with a manual choke Varajet carburettor.

11.1d GM Varajet carburettor - manual choke type

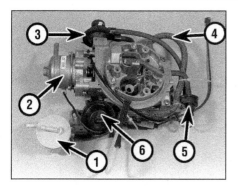

11.8a Top view of Pierburg carburettor

1 Vapour separator
2 Choke cover
3 Choke pull-down
  unit
4 Fuel hose
5 Vacuum switch
6 Secondary throttle
  vacuum unit

4 The carburettors are very similar except for the choke (cold start) arrangement.

5 On later versions of the 1.3 automatic choke carburettor, a damping valve was introduced in order to overcome a tendency to misfire during hard acceleration between 2700 and 3500 rpm. This valve (Part No 96009298) may be fitted to earlier model carburettors.

6 Enrichment and compensation systems are incorporated to provide optimum performance under all operating and load conditions, and a mechanically-operated accelerator pump is fitted.

7 The new 1.3 manual choke carburettor has a weakening (choke pull-down) feature in which the choke valve plate is opened according to inlet vacuum immediately after starting, to prevent over-rich mixtures during the warming-up period.

Pierburg 2E3 carburettor

8 The Pierburg 2E3 carburettor is a dual barrel downdraught instrument with automatic choke. It is fitted to vehicles with the 1.6 engine and the 1.3 engine made from 1985 **(see illustrations)**.

9 The automatic choke is of the usual strangler type, controlled by a bi-metallic spring; the choke cover is heated electrically

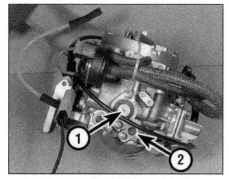

11.8d Pierburg carburettor - side view showing part load enrichment valve (1) and accelerator pump cam (2)

11.8b Pierburg carburettor - showing side view choke cover

and by coolant, ensuring a rapid response to changing engine and ambient temperature. Over-choking is avoided by the eccentric mounting of the choke valve plate, by a vacuum pull-down system and by a mechanical linkage with the throttle mechanism **(see illustration)**.

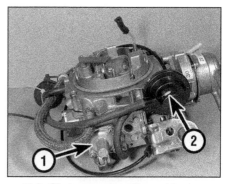

11.8c Pierburg carburettor - side view showing accelerator pump (1) and choke pull-down unit (2)

10 With the engine at operating temperature, idling mixture is supplied via a bypass system. Although an idle cut-off valve is shown in some of the illustrations, no such valve was found on the carburettor examined. Unusually, idle speed adjustment takes place at the throttle stop screw.

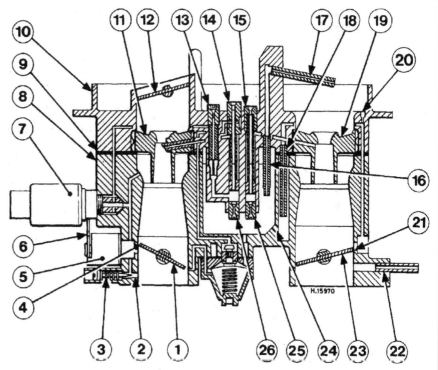

11.9 Sectional view of the Pierburg 2E3 carburettor

1 Primary throttle valve
2 Idle mixture outlet
3 Idle mixture adjustment
  screw
4 Transition louvre
5 Not on Cavalier
6 Not on Cavalier
7 Not on Cavalier
8 Carburettor body
9 Gasket
10 Carburettor cover
11 Primary pre-atomizer

12 Choke valve
13 Idle fuel and air jet
14 Primary air correction jet
  and emulsion tube
15 Secondary air correction
  jet and emulsion tube
16 Riser tube (secondary full
  load enrichment)
17 Discharge beak (secondary
  full load enrichment)
18 Riser tube (secondary
  transition)

19 Secondary pre-atomizer
20 Secondary transition vent
21 Secondary transition
  louvre
22 Choke pull-down vacuum
  take - off
23 Secondary throttle valve
24 Secondary transition jet
25 Secondary main jet
26 Primary main jet

11 Opening of the throttle valves is sequential. The primary throttle valve is opened mechanically; the secondary throttle valve is opened by vacuum developed in both venturis, but is prevented from so doing until the primary valve is at least half open. For safety reasons both throttle valves are closed mechanically.

12 Efficient operation under all speed and load conditions is ensured by a part load enrichment valve and by primary and secondary transition systems. An accelerator pump provides extra fuel needed for rapid acceleration **(see illustration)**.

12 Carburettor - removal and refitting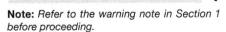

Note: *Refer to the warning note in Section 1 before proceeding.*

Removal

1 Disconnect the battery negative terminal then remove the air cleaner as described in Section 2 and proceed as described under the relevant sub-heading.

GM Varajet carburettor

2 Disconnect the fuel hose from the carburettor and plug the hose.

3 Disconnect the electrical lead from the automatic choke, or disconnect the manual choke cable.

4 Disconnect the throttle control linkage at the balljoint. Disconnect the distributor vacuum hose, also the one to the air cleaner.

5 Clamp the coolant hoses to the rear of the throttle body, these being the warm-up feed and return hoses.

6 Unscrew and remove the four mounting nuts from the carburettor flange and remove the carburettor from the manifold.

Pierburg 2E3 carburettor

7 Disconnect and plug the coolant hoses from the automatic choke, noting which hose goes to which connection. Be prepared for some coolant spillage.

8 Disconnect and plug the fuel return hose from the top of the vapour separator and the fuel supply hose from the side of the vapour separator. Be prepared for some fuel spillage.

9 Disconnect the throttle cable outer by pulling it out of its bracket. Unhook the inner cable from the throttle operating plate.

10 Disconnect the distributor vacuum hose at the distributor.

11 Disconnect the carburettor electrical supply at the wiring harness connector near the bulkhead.

12 Remove the three nuts from the top of the carburettor and lift the carburettor off its studs.

Refitting

13 Refit in the reverse order to removal. Use a new carburettor-to-manifold gasket if the old one was damaged. On the Pierburg

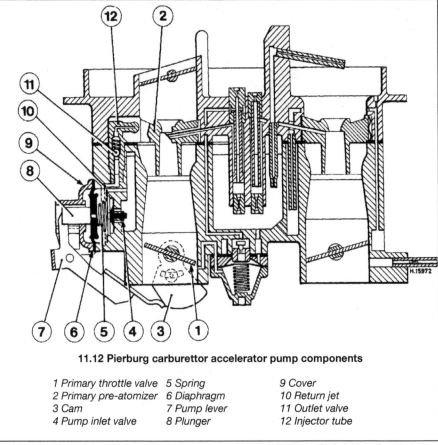

11.12 Pierburg carburettor accelerator pump components

1 Primary throttle valve	5 Spring	9 Cover
2 Primary pre-atomizer	6 Diaphragm	10 Return jet
3 Cam	7 Pump lever	11 Outlet valve
4 Pump inlet valve	8 Plunger	12 Injector tube

carburettor, if much coolant was lost, check the coolant level after the engine has been run and top-up if necessary (see Chapter 1).

13 GM Varajet carburettor - fault diagnosis, overhaul and adjustments

Diagnosis

1 If a carburettor fault is suspected, always check first that the ignition timing is accurate and the spark plugs are in good condition and correctly gapped, that the accelerator and choke cables are correctly adjusted, and that the air cleaner filter element is clean; see the relevant Sections of Chapter 1 or of this Chapter. If the engine is running very roughly, first check the compression pressures as described in Chapter 2.

2 If careful checking of all of the above produces no improvement, the carburettor must be removed for cleaning and overhaul.

3 Note that in the rare event of a complete carburettor overhaul being necessary, it may prove more economical to renew the carburettor as a complete unit. Check the price and availability of a replacement carburettor and of its component parts before starting work; note that most sealing washers, screws and gaskets are available in kits, as are some of the major sub-assemblies. In most

cases it will be sufficient to dismantle the carburettor and to clean the jets and passages.

Overhaul

Note: *Refer to the warning note in Section 1 before proceeding.*

4 Remove the carburettor from the vehicle as described in Section 12. The following text is written for the automatic choke carburettor. If work is being carried out on a manual choke carburettor, ignore all references to the automatic choke mechanism **(see illustration)**.

5 With the carburettor removed and external dirt cleaned away, pull off the vacuum hose from the choke vacuum unit. Extract the three screws from the automatic choke retaining ring and withdraw the assembly. Extract the split pin and disconnect the accelerator pump rod from the lever.

6 Unscrew the fuel inlet nozzle and extract the gauze filter from inside it **(see illustration)**.

7 Extract the retaining clip and disconnect the choke connecting rod from the cam.

8 Extract the three short and four long carburettor cover retaining bolts **(see illustration)**.

9 Remove the cover, making sure that, as it is withdrawn, the gasket remains behind on the flange of the float chamber. Remember that the accelerator pump plunger is under spring tension.

13.4 Exploded view of the GM Varajet carburettor

1 Cover
2 Gasket
3 Packing piece
4 Float pin
5 Accelerator pump plunger
6 Spring
7 Float
8 Fuel inlet needle valve
9 Check ball (accelerator pump)
10 Fuel filter union
11 Fuel filter
12 Bypass screw
13 Link rod
14 Mixture screw
15 Throttle valve block
16 Fast idle screw and spring
17 Gasket
18 Fast idle cam
19 Fast idle link rod
20 Vacuum hose
21 Part load needle valve and piston
22 Spring
23 Suction valve and check ball
24 Choke vacuum unit
25 Choke housing cover
26 Cover retainer
27 Choke valve plate (primary barrel)
28 Baffle flap (secondary barrel)
29 Full load needle valve

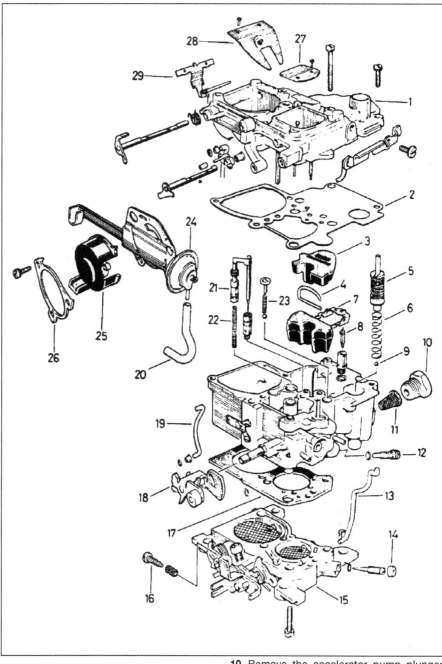

13.6 Fuel inlet union and gauze

13.8 Varajet carburettor top cover

13.10 Removing the accelerator pump plunger and spring

10 Remove the accelerator pump plunger and spring and carefully peel off the cover gasket **(see illustration)**. Extract the pump suction valve spring retainer from the body using a pair of pliers.

11 Pull or twist out the vacuum piston spring and needle of the carburettor first stage. Take care not to bend the retaining bracket or partial load needle.

12 If necessary, the partial load plunger may be withdrawn by gripping its rod with a pair of pliers.

13 Remove the packing piece, float and needle from the float chamber. Empty the fuel from the chamber **(see illustration)**.

14 Note their location and unscrew the jets.

15 Extract the four retaining screws and remove the throttle valve plate block.

16 Further dismantling is not recommended.

17 Clean all components and renew any that are worn or damaged. If the throttle valve plate spindle is worn then the complete throttle block must be renewed. Clean jets and passages with air pressure only; never probe with wire or their calibration will be ruined.

18 Obtain a repair kit which will contain all the necessary renewable items including gaskets.

19 Reassembly is a reversal of dismantling, but observe the following points.

a) *When assembling the accelerator pump, ensure the check ball is correctly located.*

b) *Make sure that the needle valve spring is correctly located against the float.*

c) *When installing the cover to the carburettor body, ensure the accelerator pump plunger does not become wedged.*

d) *Make sure that the breather screen is in position.*

e) *Make sure that the bi-metallic spring of the automatic choke engages positively with the choke valve plate spindle arm on refitting.*

f) *Check the operation of the throttle valve plate lever. Remember that the secondary valve plate does not open until the primary valve plate has opened by two-thirds of its travel. The secondary throttle valve plate will not open until the choke valve plate is fully open after the engine has reached operating temperature.*

g) *Carry out those checks and adjustments described under the following sub-heading which can be done with the carburettor on the bench.*

h) *When the carburettor has been refitted to the engine, adjust the idle speed and the fuel/air mixture (CO content of exhaust gas) as described in Chapter 1. Also carry out the remainder of the adjustments described under the following sub-heading.*

Adjustments

Note: *If the adjustments are being carried out with the carburettor removed, ignore any preliminary dismantling information given.*

13.13 Float and fuel inlet valve

Automatic choke type carburettor

Fast idle speed

20 First make sure that the engine idle speed is correct as described in Chapter 1.

21 Remove the air cleaner and then plug the end of the vacuum hose which normally connects with the vacuum capsule in the air cleaner.

22 Switch off the ignition.

23 Slightly open the throttle valve plate so that the fast idle screw can be positioned on the second highest step of the cam **(see illustration)**.

24 Without touching the accelerator, start the engine. The engine speed should be as specified. If it is not, turn the fast idle screw as necessary.

Choke valve flap pull-down setting (gap A)

25 In order to be able to carry out this adjustment, a suitable vacuum pump must be available. It is possible to create sufficient vacuum using a modified hand pump or by making a connection with a rubber hose or plastic tube between the choke vacuum unit of the carburettor and the inlet manifold of another vehicle (engine running).

26 Remove the air cleaner.

27 Position the fast idle screw on the uppermost step of the cam. Check that the choke valve plate is fully closed. This may not be the case if the choke cover is still warm, in which case use a rubber band to close it.

28 Apply vacuum to the choke vacuum unit as described in paragraph 25.

13.23 Carburettor fast idle screw (arrowed) set on second highest cam step (2)

29 Refer to **illustration 13.29**, Measure the gap A between the edge of the choke valve plate and the wall of the carburettor. Measure at the flatter side of the valve plate. A twist drill or similar should be used as a gauge. The gap should be as specified.

30 If necessary, turn the screw B to bring the gap to the specified clearance. If the gap was found to be too small, it will probably be necessary to bend the pullrod slightly to provide sufficient clearance for movement of the adjustment screw.

31 On completion of adjustment, lock the adjustment screw with a drop of suitable sealant.

32 Now check the play between the baffle flap lever and the pullrod with the vacuum source still connected so that the pullrod is in the fully extended position **(see illustration)**. The clearance A must be as shown. Where necessary, bend the end of the pullrod to bring the clearance within tolerance.

Choke valve flap fast idle setting (gap B)

33 Close the choke valve with a rubber band.

34 Open the throttle and position the fast idle screw on the second highest step of the fast idle cam **(see illustration 13.23)**. Release the throttle and check that the screw stays on the step.

35 Open the choke valve slightly and release it in order to let it find its correct position. Check the choke valve gap B by the same method as when checking the pull-down gap.

36 If adjustment is necessary, remove the

13.29 Checking valve plate-to-carburettor gap

A See Specifications

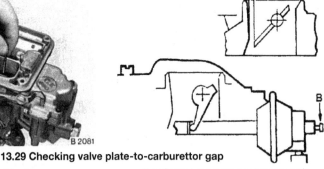

B Adjustment screw on vacuum unit

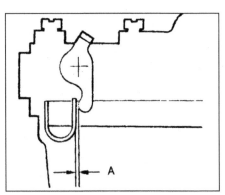

13.32 Baffle flap-to-pullrod clearance
A = 0.1 to 0.3 mm

13.39 Varajet carburettor adjustment: bend
tag G to adjust the choke valve gap

13.44 Accelerator lever-to-rod setting
A = 7.8 to 8.2 mm

13.47 Measuring float setting

carburettor and take off the choke cover. Bend
the rod which connects the fast idle cam to
the choke valve lever until the gap is correct.

37 If adjustment has been necessary, recheck
the pull-down gap after refitting the
carburettor.

Choke valve flap full throttle setting (gap C)

38 Close the choke valve with a rubber band.
Open the throttle fully and hold it open while
measuring the choke valve gap.

39 If adjustment is necessary, bend that part
of the linkage shown in **illustration 13.39**.
Bend the tag to the right to increase the gap,
to the left to decrease it.

Automatic choke cover

40 The pointer on the choke housing cover
should be set in the central position. If there is
any tendency to stall or hesitate during warm-
up, it is permissible to turn the cover through
one or two divisions towards R (rich).

41 When starting the engine from cold, it
should take between two and three minutes
for the choke valve plate to reach the fully
open position. If a longer time is required,
renew the choke cover and check the valve
plate for free movement.

Accelerator pump

42 With the air cleaner removed, check that,
with the engine at normal operating
temperature, the throttle valve plate lever is in
the idle position. Stop the engine.

43 With the fingers, open the throttle valve
plate smoothly to the full throttle position, at
the same time observing the fuel being ejected
from the accelerator pump nozzle. The fuel

stream must be continuous without
interruption over the complete pump stroke. If
it is not, the pump must be dismantled and
worn seals renewed.

44 Using a screwdriver, depress the
accelerator pump pushrod to its stop and then
measure the clearance between the end of the
lever and the rod **(see illustration)**. This
should be within the specified limits. If it is not,
bend the pump lever.

Float level

45 Remove the carburettor cover.

46 Using moderate finger pressure, hold the
fuel inlet needle valve closed by applying
pressure to the float arms and pivot clip.

47 The top surface of the float should be the
specified distance below the carburettor top
flange **(see illustration)**.

48 Where necessary, bend the arms of the
float equally at the points indicated **(see
illustration)**.

**Throttle linkage damper - automatic
transmission models**

49 Automatic transmission models may be
equipped with a throttle linkage damper, the
purpose of which is to stop the throttle
snapping shut suddenly when the pedal is
released.

50 Correct adjustment of the damper is
carried out as follows. Release the damper

locknut and unscrew the damper until the
damper pin is only just touching the throttle
lever. From this position, screw the damper
back in between 3 and 4 complete turns, then
secure with the locknut **(see illustration)**.

Part load regulator screw

51 Conditions such as jerking or hesitation at
light throttle openings, or excessive fuel
consumption despite moderate driving habits,
may be due to incorrect adjustment of the part
load regulator screw.

52 It is emphasised that this adjustment
should not be attempted until all other
possible causes of the problems mentioned
have been investigated.

53 Remove the carburettor from the vehicle.

54 Prise out the metal plug covering the part
load regulator screw (adjacent to the fuel inlet
union).

55 If stalling or hesitation is the reason for
adjustment - ie the mixture is too weak - turn
the screw one-quarter turn anti-clockwise.

56 If excessive fuel consumption is the
problem - ie the mixture is too rich - turn the
screw one-quarter turn clockwise.

57 Refit the carburettor and test drive the
vehicle to see if any improvement has
occurred. If necessary a further adjustment can
be made, but do not deviate from the original
setting by more than half a turn of the screw.

58 Fit a new metal plug on completion, where
this is required by law.

Manual choke type carburettor

Choke valve flap pull-down

59 Remove the air cleaner.

60 Pull the choke control until the mark on the
cam is aligned with the centre of the fast idle
screw.

61 An outside vacuum source must now be
applied to the carburettor vacuum unit. To do
this, either use a hand-operated suction
pump, or connect a tube to the inlet manifold
of another vehicle which has its engine idling.

62 Check the gap between the edge of the
choke valve plate and the carburettor throat
wall. The gap should be measured with a twist
drill of suitable diameter (see Specifications).

63 Where adjustment is required, turn the
adjusting screw **(see illustration 13.29)**.
Should it be found that the gap is too small for
correction, bend the rod end fitting.

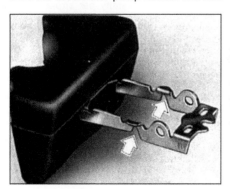

13.48 Float level adjustment
Bend at points arrowed

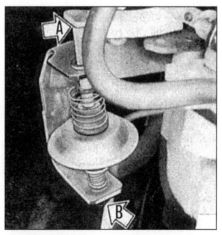

13.50 Varajet carburettor throttle damper

A Damper pin   B Locknut

Fast idle speed

64 With the engine at normal operating temperature, stop the engine and remove the air cleaner.

65 Plug the end of the small bore hose which was disconnected from the air cleaner and runs to the carburettor.

66 Pull the choke control cable until the mark on the cam is aligned with the centre of the fast idle screw.

67 Hold the choke valve plate fully open using the fingers or a rubber band.

68 Start the engine and check that the fast idle speed is as given in the Specifications. The vehicle tachometer can be used for this, but if one is not fitted, then a suitable instrument will have to be temporarily connected in accordance with the manufacturer's instructions.

69 If adjustment is required then the fast idle screw should be turned in or out as necessary.

Accelerator pump

70 Refer to paragraphs 42 to 44.

Float level

71 Refer to paragraphs 45 to 48.

Throttle linkage damper - automatic transmission models

72 Refer to paragraphs 49 and 50.

Part load regulator screw

73 Refer to paragraphs 51 to 56.

---

14 Pierburg 2E3 carburettor - fault diagnosis, overhaul and adjustments

Fault diagnosis

1 See Section 13.

Overhaul

Note: *Refer to the warning note in Section 1 before proceeding.*

2 Clean the outside of the carburettor then remove the hoses and wires from the carburettor, making identifying marks or notes to avoid confusion on reassembly.

3 Access to the jets and float chamber is obtained by removing the top half of the carburettor, which is secured by five screws. Blow through the jets and drillings with compressed air, or air from a foot pump - do not probe them with wire. If it is wished to remove the jets, unscrew them carefully with well-fitting tools.

4 Remove the fuel strainer from the inlet pipe by hooking it out with a small screwdriver, or by snaring it with a long thin screw. Renew the strainer **(see illustration)**.

5 Clean any foreign matter from the float chamber. Renew the inlet needle valve and seat if wear is evident, or if a high mileage has been covered. Renew the float if it is punctured or otherwise damaged.

6 No procedure has been specified for float level adjustment; in any case the tolerance allowed is so wide that precision setting is clearly unnecessary. Simply check that the

14.4 Removing fuel strainer from inlet pipes

inlet needle valve is closed completely before the float reaches the top of its stroke.

7 Renew the diaphragms in the part load enrichment valve and in the accelerator pump. If additional pump or valve parts are supplied in the overhaul kit, renew these parts also.

8 Further dismantling is not recommended. Pay particular attention to the throttle opening mechanism if it is decided to dismantle it; the interlocking arrangement is important.

9 Reassemble in the reverse order to dismantling. Use new gaskets and seals throughout, lubricate linkages with a smear of molybdenum-based grease.

10 Before refitting the carburettor, carry out the checks and adjustments described in the following Section.

Adjustments

Adjustments with the carburettor removed

Fast idle cam position

11 The choke pull-down adjustment, described in paragraphs 26 to 31, must be correct.

12 If not already done, remove the choke cover.

13 Open the throttle, then close the choke valve by light finger pressure on the choke drive lever. Release the throttle.

14 Check that the fast idle adjustment screw is resting on the second highest step of the fast idle cam, in the position shown in **illustration 14.14**. If not, first check that the

14.21 Accelerator pump delivery adjustment (+ to increase, - to decrease)

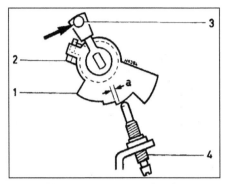

14.14 Pierburg carburettor: fast idle cam adjustment

1 Fast idle cam
2 Adjustment lever
3 Choke drive lever (press in direction arrowed)
4 Fast idle adjustment screw
a = 0.2 to 0.8 mm

choke return spring is correctly positioned, then adjust by bending the lever 2.

15 Refit and secure the choke cover, observing the alignment marks.

Throttle valve fast idle gap

16 Position the fast idle adjustment screw on the highest step of the fast idle cam.

17 Use a gauge rod or twist drill of the specified diameter to measure the opening of the primary throttle screw. Adjust if necessary at the fast idle adjustment screw. (This is a preliminary adjustment; final adjustment of the fast idle speed should take place with the engine running.)

Accelerator pump delivery

18 It will be necessary to feed the float chamber with fuel from a small reservoir during this test. Take all necessary fire precautions when dealing with fuel and fuel vapour.

19 Position the primary barrel over an accurate measuring glass. Fully open and close the throttle ten times, taking approximately one second for each opening and pausing for three seconds after each return stroke. Make sure that the fast idle cam is not restricting throttle travel at either end.

20 Measure the quantity of fuel delivered and divide by ten to obtain the quantity per stroke. Compare the quantity per stroke with the specified value.

21 If adjustment is necessary, release the clamp screw and turn the cam plate in the desired direction **(see illustration)**. Tighten the clamp screw and recheck the pump delivery.

Adjustments with the carburettor in position on vehicle

Fast idle speed

22 The engine must be at operating temperature and the idle speed and mixture must be correctly adjusted. Remove the air cleaner to improve access.

23 Position the fast idle adjustment screw on the second highest step of the fast idle cam.

14.24 Fast idle adjustment screw (arrowed) - carburettor removed for clarity

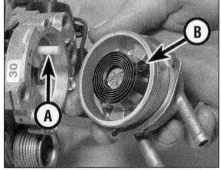

14.27 Choke drive lever (A) engages loop (B)

14.29 Checking the choke pull-down gap with a twist drill. Apply vacuum to hose arrowed

Connect a tachometer to the engine. Make sure that the choke plate is fully open.
24 Start the engine without touching the throttle pedal and compare the engine speed with that given in Specifications. If adjustment is necessary, remove the tamperproof cap from the head of the fast idle screw by crushing it with pliers and adjust by means of the screw **(see illustration)**.
25 When adjustment is correct, stop the engine and disconnect the tachometer. Fit a new tamperproof cap when required by law.
Choke pull-down
26 Remove the air cleaner.
27 Remove the choke cover by removing the three screws and the securing ring. There is no need to disconnect the coolant hoses, just move the cover aside. Notice how the loop in the end of the bi-metallic spring engages in the choke drive lever **(see illustration)**.
28 Move the choke drive lever to close the choke valve completely. Position the fast idle screw on the highest step of the cam.
29 Apply vacuum to the choke pull-down unit (at the hose nearest the carburettor body) using a modified bicycle pump or similar item. Apply light pressure to the choke drive lever in a clockwise direction (as if to close the choke valve) and check the choke valve gap by inserting a gauge rod or twist drill of the specified size **(see illustration)**.
30 If adjustment is necessary, turn the adjusting screw on the side of the choke housing **(see illustration)**.

31 Refit the choke cover, making sure that the spring loop engages in the choke drive lever. Align the notches in the choke cover and choke housing when tightening the screws **(see illustration)**.
Vacuum units - checking for leaks
32 If a vacuum source incorporating a gauge is available, apply approx 300 mbar (9 in Hg) to the choke pull-down unit at the hose nearest the carburettor body. Close off the vacuum source and check that the vacuum is held. If there is a leak, rectify or renew the leaking component.
33 Similarly check the secondary throttle vacuum unit.
34 If a suitable vacuum source is not available, testing of suspect vacuum units must be by substitution of a known good item.

15 Inlet manifold - removal and refitting

Note: *Refer to the warning note in Section 1 before proceeding.*

Removal
1 Disconnect the battery negative terminal.
2 Before the inlet manifold can be removed, the cooling system must be drained and the coolant hoses disconnected from it.
3 On 1.3 models, disconnect the lead from the coolant temperature sender switch.
4 Disconnect the brake vacuum hose.

5 The manifold may be removed complete with carburettor or independently.
6 To remove the carburettor first, refer to Section 12.
7 To remove the manifold complete with carburettor, refer to the appropriate carburettor removal Section and disconnect the associated items from the carburettor, but leave the carburettor-to-manifold retaining nuts.
8 Unscrew the manifold nuts and lift the assembly from the cylinder head **(see illustration)**.
9 Remove and discard the flange gasket.

Refitting
10 Refitting is a reversal of removal. Use a new flange gasket. On completion, refill and bleed the cooling system as described in Chapter 1.

16 Exhaust manifold - removal and refitting

Removal
1 Disconnect the battery negative lead.
2 Unbolt the heat shield (warm air collector) from the manifold.
3 Disconnect the manifold from the downpipes by removing the nuts at the connecting flange **(see illustration)**.
4 Unscrew and remove the exhaust manifold

14.30 Choke pull-down adjusting screw

14.31 Choke cover alignment marks (arrowed)

15.8 Inlet manifold removal (complete with carburettor)

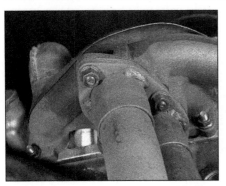

16.3 Exhaust downpipe flanges at manifold

16.4 Removing the exhaust manifold

17.8a Exhaust system coupling joint and mounting

nuts and lift the manifold from the cylinder head **(see illustration)**.

5 Remove the flange gaskets.

Refitting

6 Refitting is a reversal of removal. Use new gaskets. Should a gas leak occur at the downpipe flange on the exhaust manifold, two gaskets may be used to remedy the leak.

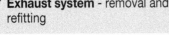

17 Exhaust system - removal and refitting

Removal

1 The exhaust system comprises a dual downpipe, a front silencer and a rear expansion box with a tailpipe.

2 The exhaust system fitted at the factory, and any Vauxhall replacement system, is of heavy duty aluminised construction. Under normal operating conditions this should be found to last a considerable time before removal is necessary.

3 Holts Flexiwrap and Holts Gun Gum exhaust repair systems can be used for effective repairs to exhaust pipes and silencer boxes, including ends and bends. Holts Flexiwrap is an MOT approved permanent exhaust repair.

4 The system fitted in production is of three-piece construction. Sections may therefore be renewed individually if necessary.

5 If the complete system is to be renewed, position the vehicle over an inspection pit. If this is not possible, jack the vehicle up as high as possible and secure it on axle stands (see *"Jacking and Vehicle Support"*).

6 When renewing the complete system, cutting through the connecting pipes will probably make removal in sections easier than attempting to dismantle corroded joints.

7 If only one section is to be renewed, and this section is to be cut to remove it, make quite sure that an adequate overlap of the original pipe is left to fit the new section. Failure to do this will prevent a gas tight joint being achieved.

8 The exhaust system is flexibly mounted. Remove any mounting components which are deformed or have deteriorated. Always renew clamps **(see illustrations)**.

Refitting

9 Refitting is the reverse of removal noting the following points.
   a) *When connecting a new section of pipe, expansion box or silencer, remove burrs from the socket joints and apply a little grease before connecting. Fit the clamps only finger tight at first until the alignment of the system has been checked and adjusted.*
   b) *Make sure that no component of the system is likely to touch adjacent parts of the bodyframe or suspension when deflected within the full extent of movement of its flexible mounting.*
   c) *Application of some graphite grease to the contact surfaces of the spring-loaded ball coupling before bolting up will prevent it seizing due to rust* **(see illustration)**.

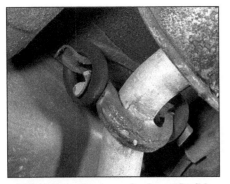

17.8b Alternative type of exhaust flexible mounting

17.8c Exhaust flexible mounting

17.9 Exhaust spring-loaded ball coupling

Chapter 4 Part B:
Fuel and exhaust systems - fuel-injected models

Contents

Air cleaner filter element renewal . . . . .See Chapter 1
Air cleaner housing - removal and refitting 2
Exhaust manifold - removal and refitting 13
Exhaust system - removal and refitting .14
Exhaust system check . . . . .See Chapter 1
Fuel filter renewal . . . . .See Chapter 1
Fuel gauge sender unit - removal and refitting 8
Fuel injection system - general information 5
Fuel injection system - testing and adjustment 10
Fuel injection system components - removal and refitting 11

Fuel pump - removal and refitting 7
Fuel system - depressurisation 6
Fuel tank - removal and refitting 9
General fuel system checks . . . . .See Chapter 1
General information and precautions 1
Idle speed and mixture adjustment information . . . . . .See Chapter 1
Inlet manifold - removal and refitting .12
Throttle control cable - removal, refitting and adjustment 3
Unleaded petrol - general information and usage 4

Degrees of difficulty

Easy, suitable for novice with little experience		Fairly easy, suitable for beginner with some experience		Fairly difficult, suitable for competent DIY mechanic		Difficult, suitable for experienced DIY mechanic		Very difficult, suitable for expert DIY or professional	

Specifications

System type

1.8 litre models:	
Early (pre 1987) models	Bosch LE Jetronic
Later (1987 onwards) models	Bosch L3 Jetronic
2.0 litre models	Bosch Motronic

Fuel pump

Type	Electric
Pressure	2.5 bar

Adjustment data

Idle speed:	
1.8 litre models:	
Early (pre-1987) models:	
Manual transmission	900 to 950 rpm
Automatic transmission	800 to 850 rpm
Later (1987-on) models	800 to 900 rpm
2.0 litre models	720 to 780 rpm*
Exhaust gas CO content (at idle)	Less than 1.0%*

*On 2.0 litre models both the idle speed and exhaust gas CO content are regulated by the the control unit and are not adjustable

Recommended fuel

Minimum octane rating	98 RON leaded (4-star) or unleaded (Super unleaded)*

*If the necessary precautions are taken, 95 RON unleaded (unleaded premium) petrol can be used (see Section 4 for details)

Torque wrench setting

	Nm	lbf ft
Fuel injectors	32	24

1 General information and precautions

1 The fuel system consists of a fuel tank mounted under the rear of the car with an electric fuel pump immersed in it, a fuel filter, fuel feed and return lines. The fuel pump supplies fuel to the fuel rail which acts as a reservoir for the four fuel injectors which inject fuel into the inlet tracts. A fuel filter is incorporated in the feed line from the pump to the fuel rail to ensure that the fuel supplied to the injectors is clean.
2 Refer to Section 5 for further information on the operation of the fuel injection system.

 Warning: Many of the procedures in this Chapter require the removal of fuel lines and connections which may result in some fuel spillage. Before carrying out any operation on the fuel system refer to the precautions given in Safety first! at the beginning of this Manual and follow them implicitly. Petrol is a highly dangerous and volatile liquid and the precautions necessary when handling it cannot be overstressed.

Note: *Residual pressure will remain in the fuel lines long after the vehicle was last used, when disconnecting any fuel line, depressurise the fuel system as described in Section 7.*

2 Air cleaner housing - removal and refitting

Removal

Remove the air cleaner element as described in Chapter 1.

Disconnect the air inlet tube then undo the retaining screws and remove the housing from the engine compartment.

Refitting

Refit by reversing the removal operations.

4.5 Fuel octane rating adjustment plug - later 1.8 and 2. litre models

3 Throttle control cable - removal, refitting and adjustment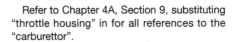

Refer to Chapter 4A, Section 9, substituting "throttle housing" in for all references to the "carburettor".

4 Unleaded petrol - general information and usage

Note: *The information given in this Chapter is correct at the time of writing and applies only to petrols currently available in the UK. If updated information is thought to be required check with a Vauxhall dealer. If travelling abroad consult one of the motoring organisations (or a similar authority) for advice on the petrols available and their suitability for your vehicle.*

1 The fuel recommended by Vauxhall is given in the Specifications Section of this Chapter, followed by the equivalent petrol currently on sale in the UK.
2 RON and MON are different testing standards; RON stands for Research Octane Number, while MON stands for Motor Octane Number.
3 All models are designed to run on 98 (RON) octane leaded or unleaded petrol (see Specifications). If it is wished to run the vehicle on 95 (RON) unleaded petrol the following operations **must** first be carried out; this is necessary to avoid detenation (knocking and pinking) which could lead to possible engine damage

Early (pre 1987) 1.8 litre models

4 On these models (fitted with Bosch LE Jetronic system), to allow the vehicle to run on 95 (RON) unleaded petrol, the ignition timing **must** be retarded by 3∞ (see Chapter 5 for details). **Do not** use 95 (RON) unleaded petrol if the ignition timing has not been retarded.

Later (1987 onwards) 1.8 litre and 2.0 litre models

5 On later 1.8 litre models (with Bosch L3 Jetronic system) and all 2.0 litre models (with Bosch Motronic system) have a fuel octane rating coding plug in the ignition system wiring harness **(see illustration)**. The plug which is located on the right-hand side of the engine compartment, is set during production to give optimum engine output and efficency when run on 98 (RON) fuel.
6 To run the vehicle on 95 (RON) unleaded fuel, the plug position can be reset to modify the timing characteristics of the ignition system. To reset the plug, release its locking clip then remove the plug and rotate it through half a turn (180°) before reconnecting it. **Note**: *If after making the adjustment, the octane rating of the fuel used is found to be so low that excessive knocking still occurs, seek the advice of your Vauxhall dealer.*

5 Fuel injection system - general information

Early (pre 1987) 1.8 litre models

1 A Bosch LE Jetronic fuel injection system is fitted to all early (pre 1987) 1.8 litre models.
2 By means of electronic control, the fuel injection system supplies the precise amount of fuel for optimum engine performance with minimum exhaust emission levels. This is achieved by continuously monitoring the engine using various sensors, whose data is input to an electronic control unit in the form of electrical signals. Based on this constantly-changing data, the control unit determines the fuel necessary to suit all engine speed and load conditions, which is then injected directly into the inlet manifold.
3 The main components of the system are:
a) *Control unit - the signals delivered by the various sensors are processed in the control unit, and from these signals, the appropriate control impulses for the fuel injectors are generated Additional circuitry within the control unit operates an overrun fuel cut-off to reduce fuel consumption, and a cold start booster for cold starting fuel enrichment.*
b) *Control relay - this comprises an electronic timing element and a switch relay, which cuts off the fuel supply immediately after the engine stops.*
c) *Airflow sensor - the amount of air drawn in by the engine is measured by the airflow sensor to determine the engine load condition. This is achieved by using a flap valve attached to a spindle, which is free to pivot within the airflow sensor bore, and is deflected by the passage of inlet air. Attached to the flap valve spindle is a potentiometer, which transforms the angular position of the flap valve into a voltage, which is then sent to the control unit. Airflow passing through the sensor is one of the main variables used by the control unit to determine the precise fuel requirement for the engine at any given time.*
d) *Fuel injectors - each fuel injector consists of a solenoid-operated needle valve, which opens under commands from the control unit. Fuel from the fuel distribution pipe is then delivered through the injector nozzle into the inlet manifold. All four fuel injectors operate simultaneously; once for each turn of the crankshaft regardless of inlet valve position. Therefore, each injector will operate once with the inlet valve closed, and once with it open, for each cycle of the engine. The fuel injectors always open at the same time relative to crankshaft position, but the length of time in which they stay open, eg the injector duration, is governed by other variables, and is determined by the control unit. For a given volume of air passing through the airflow sensor, the control unit can enrich the air/fuel mixture ratio by*

increasing the injector duration, or weaken it by decreasing the duration.

e) *Fuel pump* - the fuel pump is an electric self-priming roller cell unit, located at the rear of the car. Fuel from the tank is delivered by the pump, at a predetermined pressure, through the fuel filter to the fuel distribution pipe. From the fuel distribution pipe, the fuel is supplied to the four fuel injectors the excess being returned to the fuel tank via the fuel pressure regulator. A greater volume of fuel is circulated through the system than will be needed, even under the most extreme operating conditions, and this continual flow ensures that a low fuel temperature is maintained. This reduces the possibility of vapour lock, and ensures good hot starting characteristics.

f) *Fuel pressure regulator* - the fuel pressure regulator Is fitted to the fuel distribution pipe, and controls the operating pressure in the fuel system. The unit consists of a metal housing, divided into two chambers by a diaphragm. Fuel from the fuel distribution pipe fills one chamber of the regulator, whilst the other chamber contains a compression spring, and is subject to inlet manifold vacuum via a hose connected to the manifold, downstream of the throttle valve. A valve attached to the diaphragm opens a fuel return port in the fuel chamber of the regulator as the diaphragm deflects. When the fuel pressure in the regulator exceeds a certain value, the diaphragm is deflected, and fuel returns to the tank through the now open return port. This also occurs when the port is opened by the deflection of the diaphragm under the influence of manifold vacuum. Therefore, as manifold vacuum increases, the regulated fuel pressure is reduced in direct proportion.

g) *Throttle valve switch* - the throttle valve switch is attached to the throttle spindle on the throttle valve housing. As the throttle spindle turns in response to movement of the accelerator pedal, contacts within the switch are closed at the two extremes of shaft movement. One contact closes in the idle position, and one in the full-throttle position. These signals are then processed by the control unit to determine throttle valve position.

h) *Auxiliary air valve* - this device comprises a large-bore air channel, connected by hoses to the throttle housing and inlet manifold, and allowing inlet air to bypass the throttle valve. In the centre of the air channel is a blocking plate attached to a bi-metal strip. When the engine is cold, the blocking plate is withdrawn from the air channel, allowing air to pass through the valve. As the engine warms up, a current is supplied to the valve, heating the bi-metal strip and causing the blocking plate to begin closing the air channel until, as engine temperature increases, the channel is closed completely. The additional air passing through the valve is measured by the airflow sensor, which

compensates by increasing the injector duration to provide additional fuel. Therefore, the engine receives a greater air/fuel mixture during cold driveaway and warm-up conditions.

i) *Temperature sensors* - information on engine (coolant) temperature and inlet air temperatures are measured by sensors, one located in the coolant jacket and the other in the inlet air stream. The sensors consist of resistors whose resistance decreases as temperature increases. The change in electrical resistance of the sensors is measured by the control unit, and this information is used to modify injector duration accordingly.

Later (1987 onwards) 1.8 litre models

4 A Bosch L3 Jetronic fuel injection system is fitted to all later (1987-on) 1.8 litre models.
5 The system is based on the LE system used previously, but it has a digital control system, rather than the analogue system used on the LE type. The L3 system control unit is housed within the engine compartment as part of the airflow sensor assembly, and the system wiring layout differs to suit.

2.0 litre models

6 A Bosch Motronic fuel injection system is fitted to all 2.0 models.
7 The system is a further development of the LE Jetronic system used on earlier 1.8 litre models, but differs in that it also controls the ignition firing point and spark advance. By combining the control of the fuel and ignition systems, the engine performance is improved in terms of power, economy and reliability. Other advantages are that the system is maintenance-free, and incorporates a self-diagnosis system in which any faults that may occur will be registered and indicated for identification by a flashing code signal from the instrument panel (when activated by a service mechanic). In this way, any system faults can be quickly diagnosed and repaired.
8 Since the Motronic control unit also regulates the ignition spark advance, the conventional mechanical and vacuum advance control items are not required, and the ignition distributor is used only as a high voltage distribution unit. The ignition point on Motronic models is controlled in accordance with the engine temperature, the air inlet temperature, the throttle opening, and the engine speed.
9 An inductive pulse sensor is fitted to the side of the cylinder block, and a sensor disc is attached to the crankshaft. As the teeth of the sensor disc pass the pulse sensor during engine rotation, the air gap between them alternates in accordance with the engine speed, and this signal is then transmitted to the control unit The information transmitted from the pulse sensor, together with the engine temperature sensor, also serves to enable the control unit to regulate the ignition advance angle.

10 The Motronic system also incorporates an idle speed adjuster device. This unit is mounted between the camshaft cover and the throttle housing, and its function is to provide an electrically-operated airflow control system past the throttle valve when it is in the idle position. The airflow is regulated as required by means of an electric motor driving a rotary spool. The idle speed adjuster is regulated automatically as required, in accordance with signals received from the control unit. No manual adjustment of the idle speed is possible.

6 Fuel system - depressurisation

Note: *Refer to the warning note in Section 1 before proceeding.*

 Warning: The following procedure will merely relieve the pressure in the fuel system - remember that fuel will still be present in the system components and take precautions accordingly before disconnecting any of them.

1 The fuel system referred to in this Section is defined as the tank-mounted fuel pump, the fuel filter, the fuel injectors, the fuel rail and the pressure regulator, and the metal pipes and flexible hoses of the fuel lines between these components. All these contain fuel which will be under pressure while the engine is running and/or while the ignition is switched on. The pressure will remain for some time after the ignition has been switched off and must be relieved before any of these components are disturbed for servicing work.
2 Disconnect the battery negative terminal.
3 Place a suitable container beneath the relevant connection/union to be disconnected, and have a large rag ready to soak up any escaping fuel not being caught by the container.
4 Slowly loosen the connection or union nut (as applicable) to avoid a sudden release of pressure and position the rag around the connection to catch any fuel spray which may be expelled. Once the pressure is released, disconnect the fuel line and insert plugs to minimise fuel loss and prevent the entry of dirt into the fuel system.

7 Fuel pump - removal and refitting

Note: *Refer to the warning note in Section 1 before proceeding.*

Removal

1 The fuel pump is located at the rear of the fuel tank on the right-hand side. Before removing the pump or associated components, detach the battery earth lead.
2 Clamp the fuel hoses on either side of the pump to prevent loss of fuel when they are

7.3a Fuel pump mounting bolt

7.3b Fuel pump and damper diaphragm unit mounting

disconnected. Self-locking grips are useful for this. Disconnect the hoses, bearing in mind the information given in Section 6.

3 Unscrew the pump mounting clamp bolts and withdraw the pump from its flexible insulator. Disconnect the electrical plug as the pump is withdrawn **(see illustrations)**.

4 Alternatively, the pump can be removed complete with filter and damper diaphragm unit if the mounting strap nuts are unscrewed and the assembly removed from its flexible mountings.

Refitting

5 Refitting is the reverse of removal, ensuring that the hose clips are securely tightened. On completion, start the engine and check the hoses for signs of leakage.

8 Fuel gauge sender unit - removal and refitting

Refer to Chapter 4 Part A, Section 6.

9 Fuel tank - removal and refitting

Refer to Chapter 4 Part A, Section 7.

10 Fuel injection system - testing and adjustment

Testing

1 If a fault appears in the fuel injection system first ensure that all the system wiring connectors are securely connected and free of corrosion. Then ensure that the fault is not due to poor maintenance; ie, check that the air cleaner filter element is clean, the spark plugs are in good condition and correctly gapped, the cylinder compression pressures are correct, the ignition timing is correct and the engine breather hoses are clear and undamaged, referring to Chapters 1, 2 and 5 for further information.

2 If these checks fail to reveal the cause of the problem the vehicle should be taken to a suitably equipped Vauxhall dealer for testing. Your dealer has access to special electronic diagnostic equipment which will locate the

fault quickly and simply, alleviating the need to test all the system components individually (a time consuming operation that carries a high risk of damaging the control unit).

Adjustment

3 On 1.8 litre models, both the idle speed and idle mixture (exhaust gas CO level) are adjustable. Refer to Chapter 1 for information on the adjustment procedure.

4 On 2.0 litre models, whilst experienced home mechanics with a considerable amount of skill and equipment (including a good-quality tachometer and a good-quality, carefully-calibrated exhaust gas analyser) may be able to check the exhaust CO level and the idle speed, if these are found to be in need of adjustment the car **must** be taken to a suitably-equipped Vauxhall dealer for testing. Neither the mixture (exhaust gas CO level) or idle speed are adjustable, and should either be incorrect then a fault must be present in the fuel injection system.

11 Fuel injection system components - removal and refitting

1 Disconnect the battery negative lead and proceed as described under the relevant sub-heading.

Early (pre 1987) 1.8 litre models

Throttle valve housing

2 Disconnect the distributor vacuum hose from the throttle housing **(see illustration)**.

3 Disconnect the crankcase ventilation hose **(see illustration)**.

4 Disconnect the coolant (preheat) hoses from the housing connection **(see illustration)**. Clamp the hoses to prevent the loss of coolant. If the engine is still warm when this work is being carried out then the system pressure must be released before disconnecting the hoses. Do this by gently unscrewing the expansion bottle cap.

5 Release the securing clips and disconnect the flexible ducting which connects the throttle valve housing with the airflow sensor **(see illustration)**.

11.2 Disconnect the distributor vacuum hose from the throttle valve housing

11.3 Disconnect the crankcase ventilation hose from the throttle housing

11.4 Disconnect the throttle housing coolant hoses. The other hose is on the underside

11.5 Separate the duct from the throttle housing

11.9 Throttle valve switch and plug

11.10 Release the throttle valve switch
mounting screws

11.13 Slackening a fuel distribution pipe
hose clamp

6 Disconnect the wiring plug from the throttle valve switch.

7 Separate the throttle linkage by disengaging at the balljoint, then undo the retaining nuts and withdraw the throttle housing from the inlet manifold.

8 Refitting is a reversal of removal, but note the wiring harness connections. Number 4 fuel injector is nearest the flywheel housing.

Throttle valve switch

9 Disconnect the three-pin wiring plug (see illustration).

10 Unscrew the two mounting screws and pull the switch from the throttle valve spindle (see illustration).

11 Refitting is a reversal of removal, but

adjust the switch as follows. Release the switch mounting screws and rotate the switch in an anti-clockwise direction until resistance is felt. Tighten the screws. Have an assistant open the throttle valve slightly by depressing the accelerator pedal. A click should be heard from the switch. A click should also be heard when the pedal is released.

Fuel injectors

12 Make sure that the engine is cool to eliminate the danger of fuel igniting. Do not smoke, and guard against external sources of ignition (eg pilot lights).

13 Bearing in mind the information given in Section 6, release the hose clamps and pull the fuel distribution pipe from the hoses of the

injectors (see illustration). Catch as much fuel as possible.

14 Disconnect the wiring plug (see illustration).

15 Unscrew the retaining bolts and withdraw the injector from its holder, taking care not to damage the needle valve (see illustration).

16 Refitting is a reversal of removal, but renew the sealing rings if there is any doubt about their condition.

Airflow sensor

17 The airflow sensor is located between the air cleaner and the throttle valve housing.

18 Pull the wiring harness plug from the airflow sensor. Release the securing band and remove the rubber trunking (see illustrations).

19 Release the toggle locks and remove the airflow sensor with the upper part of the air cleaner housing.

20 Unbolt the airflow sensor from the air cleaner housing (see illustration).

21 Check the airflow sensor flap valve for free movement, without any jerkiness.

Control unit

22 The control unit is located at the side of the front footwell.

23 Remove the trim panel from the side of the front footwell on the passenger side (see illustrations).

24 Pull the wiring plug from the control unit by pressing aside the retaining spring.

25 Extract the three screws and remove the control unit.

11.14 Fuel injector wiring plug

11.15 Fuel injector removal

11.18a Airflow sensor wiring plug

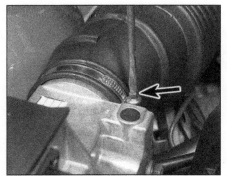

11.18b Disconnecting the airflow sensor
rubber trunking

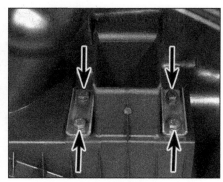

11.20 Airflow sensor securing bolts
(arrowed)

11.23a Footwell side trim panel removal gives access to the . . .

11.23b . . . control unit

11.28 Coolant temperature sensor wiring plug

Coolant temperature sensor

26 The sensor is located next to the alternator. The engine and radiator should be cold before removing the switch.

27 Either drain the cooling system to below the level of the sensor (as described in Chapter 1), or have ready a suitable plug which can be used to plug the sensor aperture whilst it is removed. If a plug is used, take great care not to damage the threads, and do not use anything which will allow foreign matter to enter the cooling system.

28 Disconnect the wiring plug from the sensor **(see illustration)**.

29 Carefully unscrew the sensor and remove it from the engine along with its sealing washer.

30 Refitting is a reversal of removal using a new sealing washer. Securely tighten the sensor and top-up/refill the cooling system as described in "Weekly checks".

Auxiliary air valve

31 This valve is located on the side of the camshaft housing.

32 Pull the connecting plug from the valve **(see illustration)**.

33 Disconnect the hoses. Unscrew the two mounting bolts and remove the valve.

34 A check can be made on the serviceability of the valve by observing the blocking plate. With the valve cold, the plate should be open; with the valve hot (by connection to a 12V battery) the plate should be closed.

35 Refitting is a reversal of removal.

Control relay

36 The relay is located on the front suspension strut turret.

37 Unscrew the mounting bolt, disconnect the wiring plug and remove the relay **(see illustrations)**.

38 Refitting is a reversal of removal.

Fuel pressure regulator

39 The fuel pressure regulator is located between injectors 3 and 4 **(see illustration)**.

40 Clamp the fuel hoses to prevent loss of fuel. Self-locking grips are useful for this.

41 Disconnect the fuel hoses and the vacuum hose from the pressure regulator.

42 Refitting is a reversal of removal.

Later (1987 onwards) 1.8 litre and 2.0 litre models

Throttle valve housing

43 Using a small screwdriver, extract the retaining clip, and release the throttle cable end fitting from the throttle housing linkage.

44 Slacken the hose clips, and disconnect the flexible ducting between the throttle valve housing and the airflow sensor.

45 Disconnect the auxiliary air valve hose, or idle speed adjuster hose as applicable, the crankcase ventilation hose, and the coolant hoses at the throttle valve housing connections **(see illustration)**. If the engine is warm, release the cooling system pressure by

11.32 Disconnecting the auxiliary air valve wiring plug

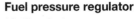

11.37a Unscrew the control relay mounting bolt . . .

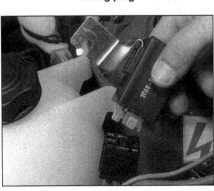

11.37b . . . and disconnect the wiring plug

11.39 Pressure regulator

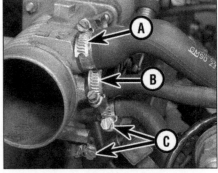

11.45 Disconnect the auxiliary air valve hose (A), the crankcase ventilation hose (B) and the coolant hoses (C)

11.49 Throttle valve switch - 2. litre models

11.53 Disconnect the fuel injector wiring connector

11.54 Prise out the fuel distribution pipe securing clips (arrowed)

carefully removing the expansion tank cap before disconnecting the coolant hoses. Plug the hoses after removal, to minimise coolant loss.

46 Disconnect the wiring plug from the throttle valve switch at the rear of the housing.

47 Undo the four nuts and remove the housing from the manifold.

48 Refitting is a reversal of removal, but use new gaskets and top-up the cooling system on completion.

Throttle valve switch

49 Refer to paragraphs 9 to 11 of this Section, noting that the switch is located on the opposite side of the throttle valve housing, nearest to the engine compartment bulkhead **(see illustration)**.

Fuel injectors

50 Disconnect the battery earth lead, and perform the following operations with the engine cold, and in a well-ventilated area.

51 Undo the two bolts securing the throttle cable support bracket to the manifold.

52 Disconnect the brake servo vacuum hose and auxiliary air valve hose at the manifold.

53 Disconnect the wiring plugs from the fuel injectors **(see illustration)**.

54 Using a small screwdriver, prise out the clips securing the fuel distribution pipe to the injectors **(see illustration)**.

55 Undo the four fuel distribution pipe retaining bolts, and pull the pipe squarely upwards and off the injectors.

56 Withdraw the fuel injectors from their locations in the manifold.

57 Refitting is the reversal of removal, but renew the injector sealing O-rings if they show any signs of deterioration.

Airflow sensor

58 Refer to paragraphs 17 to 21 of this Section.

Control unit

1.8 litre models

59 Remove the airflow sensor, (Chapter 3).

60 Undo the four bolts and lift off the control unit cover.

61 Remove the cover insert, and lift out the control unit.

62 Refitting is the reversal of removal.

2.0 litre models

63 Remove the trim panel from the side of the front footwell on the driver's side.

64 Disconnect the wiring plug from the control unit by pressing aside the retaining spring.

65 Undo the three screws and remove the control unit.

66 Refitting is the reversal of removal.

Coolant temperature sensor

67 Refer to paragraphs 26 to 30 of this Section.

Auxiliary air valve

68 Refer to paragraphs 31 to 35 of this Section.

Control relay

69 Refer to paragraphs 36 to 38 of this Section.

Fuel pressure regulator

70 Refer to paragraphs 39 to 42 of this Section.

Idle speed adjuster (2.0 litre models)

71 Disconnect the wiring plug from the end of the idle speed adjuster **(see illustration)**.

72 Slacken the hose clips, detach the air hoses, and remove the adjuster.

73 Refitting is the reversal of removal.

12 Inlet manifold - removal and refitting

Note: *Refer to the warning given in Section 1.*

Removal

Early (pre 1987) 1.8 litre models

1 Remove the throttle housing as described in Section 11.

2 Disconnect the brake servo hose and the auxiliary air hose from the manifold **(see illustration)**.

3 Disconnect and plug the fuel hoses from the distribution tube pipe stubs. Note that the hose with the white band is located nearer the alternator **(see illustration)**. Do not connect these hoses incorrectly.

4 Release the wiring harness by

11.71 Idle speed adjuster showing wiring plug location

12.2 Disconnect the brake servo hose (A) and the auxiliary air hose (B)

12.3 Fuel hoses in engine compartment

12.4 Cam cover earthing point

12.7 Removing the inlet manifold

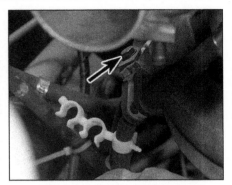

12.10 Fuel hose clip retaining bolt (arrowed)

disconnecting all the plugs and the earth connections. These include:
a) *Airflow sensor plug.*
b) *Coolant temperature sensor.*
c) *Fuel injectors.*
d) *Throttle valve switch.*
e) *Auxiliary air valve.*
f) *Cam cover earth screw* **(see illustration)**.

5 Disconnect the throttle cable from the throttle valve housing. The ball coupling on the end of the cable is retained by a wire clip. The outer cable end fitting is retained in its bracket by an E-clip locating in a groove in the end fitting. This arrangement provides the adjustment for tensioninq the cable.

6 Unscrew the inlet manifold fixing nuts. The lower ones are difficult to reach, but present no problems to remove if a small socket or ring spanner is used.

7 Lift the manifold away from the engine and peel off the flange gasket; renew it on reassembly **(see illustrations)**.

Later (1987 onwards) 1.8 and 2.0 litre models

8 Remove the throttle valve housing as described in Section 11.

9 Disconnect the brake servo hose and the auxiliary air valve hose from the manifold.

10 Disconnect and plug the fuel hoses from the fuel distribution pipe. Also undo the bolt and release the fuel hose clip from beneath the throttle valve housing **(see illustration)**.

11 Disconnect the throttle cable from the support bracket by releasing the E-clip from the groove in the outer cable.

12 Release the wiring loom by disconnecting all the additional plugs and earth connections. These include:
a) *Airflow sensor.*
b) *Coolant temperature sensor.*
c) *Fuel injectors.*
d) *Auxiliary air valve.*
e) *Idle speed adjuster (2.0 litre model).*
f) *Camshaft cover earth connection.*

13 Unscrew the inlet manifold fixing nuts, and lift off the throttle housing and manifold as a complete assembly. Recover the manifold gasket.

Refitting

14 Refitting is a reversal of removal ensuring all wiring harness and hose connections are correctly and securely made.

13 Exhaust manifold - removal and refitting

Refer to Chapter 4A, Section 16.

14 Exhaust system - removal and refitting

Refer to Chapter 4A, Section 17.

Chapter 5 Part A:
Starting and charging systems

Contents

Alternator - removal and refitting 7
Alternator - testing and overhaul 8
Alternator drivebelt - removal, refitting and tensioning 6
Battery - removal and refitting 4
Battery - testing and charging 3
Battery check ....See "Weekly checks"
Charging system - testing 5
Electrical fault finding - general information 2
Electrical system check ....See Chapter 1
General information and precautions 1
Ignition switch - removal and refitting 12
Oil pressure warning light switch - removal and refitting 13
Starter motor - removal and refitting 10
Starter motor - testing and overhaul 11
Starting system - testing 9

Degrees of difficulty

Easy, suitable for novice with little experience	**Fairly easy,** suitable for beginner with some experience	**Fairly difficult,** suitable for competent DIY mechanic	**Difficult,** suitable for experienced DIY mechanic	**Very difficult,** suitable for expert DIY or professional

Specifications

System type .... 12V negative earth

Battery
Capacity .... 36 or 44Ah
Charge condition:
  Poor .... 12.5 volts
  Normal .... 12.6 volts
  Good .... 12.7 volts

Alternator
Type .... Bosch or Delco
Output .... 45, 55 or 65A (depending upon model)

Starter motor
Type .... Pre-engaged Bosch or Delco

Torque wrench settings	**Nm**	**lbf ft**
Alternator pulley nut:		
Bosch	40	30
Delco	70	52
Alternator mounting bracket bolts	40	30
Alternator pivot and adjustment bolts	34	25
Starter motor mounting bolts:		
1.3 litre models	25	18
1.6, 1.8 and 2.0 litre models	45	33

1 General information and precautions

General information

The engine electrical system consists mainly of the charging and starting systems. Because of their engine-related functions, these components are covered separately from the body electrical devices such as the lights, instruments, etc (which are covered in Chapter 12). Refer to Part B or C for information on the ignition system.

The electrical system is of the 12-volt negative earth type.

The battery is of the low maintenance or "maintenance-free" (sealed for life) type and is charged by the alternator, which is belt-driven from the crankshaft pulley.

The starter motor is of the pre-engaged type incorporating an integral solenoid. On starting, the solenoid moves the drive pinion into engagement with the flywheel ring gear before the starter motor is energised. Once the engine has started, a one-way clutch prevents the motor armature being driven by the engine until the pinion disengages from the flywheel.

Precautions

Further details of the various systems are given in the relevant Sections of this Chapter. While some repair procedures are given, the usual course of action is to renew the component concerned. The owner whose interest extends beyond mere component renewal should obtain a copy of the *"Automobile Electrical & Electronic Systems Manual"*, available from the publishers of this manual.

It is necessary to take extra care when working on the electrical system to avoid damage to semi-conductor devices (diodes and transistors), and to avoid the risk of personal injury. In addition to the precautions given in the *"Safety first!"* Section in this manual, observe the following when working on the system:

Always remove rings, watches, etc before working on the electrical system. Even with the battery disconnected, capacitive discharge could occur if a component's live terminal is earthed through a metal object. This could cause a shock or nasty burn.

Do not reverse the battery connections. Components such as the alternator, electronic control units, or any other omponents having semi-conductor circuitry could be damaged.

If the engine is being started using jump leads and a slave battery, connect the batteries *positive-to-positive* and *negative-to-negative* (see *"Booster battery (jump) starting"*). This also applies when connecting a battery charger.

Never disconnect the battery terminals, the alternator, any electrical wiring or any test instruments when the engine is running.

Do not allow the engine to turn the alternator when the alternator is disconnected.

Never "test" for alternator output by `flashing' the output lead to earth.

Never use an ohmmeter of the type incorporating a hand-cranked generator for circuit or continuity testing.

Always ensure that the battery negative lead is disconnected when working on the electrical system.

Before using electric-arc welding equipment on the car, disconnect the battery, alternator and components such as the fuel injection/ignition electronic control unit to protect them from the risk of damage.

2 Electrical fault finding - general information

Refer to Chapter 12.

3 Battery - testing and charging

Standard and low maintenance battery - testing

1 If the vehicle covers a small annual mileage it is worthwhile checking the specific gravity of the electrolyte every three months to determine the state of charge of the battery. Use a hydrometer to make the check and compare the results with the following table. Note that the specific gravity readings assume an electrolyte temperature of 15°C (60°F); for every 10°C (18°F) below 15°C (60°F) subtract 0.007. For every 10°C (18°F) above 15°C (60°F) add 0.007.

Ambient temperature

	Above 25°C (77°F)	Below 25°C(77°F)
Fully-charged	1.210 to 1.230	1.270 to 1.290
70% charged	1.170 to 1.190	1.230 to 1.250
Discharged	1.050 to 1.070	1.110 to 1.130

2 If the battery condition is suspect, first check the specific gravity of electrolyte in each cell. A variation of 0.040 or more between any cells indicates loss of electrolyte or deterioration of the internal plates.

3 If the specific gravity variation is 0.040 or more, the battery should be renewed. If the cell variation is satisfactory but the battery is discharged, it should be charged as described later in this Section.

Maintenance-free battery - testing

4 In cases where a "sealed for life" maintenance-free battery is fitted, topping-up and testing of the electrolyte in each cell is not possible. The condition of the battery can therefore only be tested using a battery condition indicator or a voltmeter.

5 Wher a Delco type maintenance-free battery, with a built-in charge condition indicator. The indicator is located in the top of the battery casing, and indicates the condition of the battery from its colour. If the indicator shows green, then the battery is in a good state of charge. If the indicator turns darker, eventually to black, then the battery requires charging, as described later in this Section. If the indicator shows clear/yellow, then the electrolyte level in the battery is too low to allow further use, and the battery should be renewed. **Do not** attempt to charge, load or jump start a battery when the indicator shows clear/yellow **(see illustrations)**.

6 If testing the battery using a voltmeter, connect the voltmeter across the battery and compare the result with those given in the Specifications under "charge condition". The test is only accurate if the battery has not been subjected to any kind of charge for the previous six hours. If this is not the case, switch on the headlights for 30 seconds, then wait four to five minutes before testing the battery after switching off the headlights. All other electrical circuits must be switched off, so check that the doors and tailgate are fully shut when making the test.

7 If the voltage reading is less than 12.2 volts, then the battery is discharged, whilst a reading of 12.2 to 12.4 volts indicates a partially discharged condition.

3.5a Delco type maintenance-free type battery

8 If the battery is to be charged, remove it from the vehicle (Section 4) and charge it as described later in this Section.

Standard and low maintenance battery - charging

Note: *The following is intended as a guide only. Always refer to the manufacturer's recommendations (often printed on a label attached to the battery) before charging a battery.*

9 Charge the battery at a rate of 3.5 to 4 amps and continue to charge the battery at this rate until no further rise in specific gravity is noted over a four hour period.

10 Alternatively, a trickle charger charging at the rate of 1.5 amps can safely be used overnight.

11 Specially rapid `boost' charges which are claimed to restore the power of the battery in 1 to 2 hours are not recommended, as they can cause serious damage to the battery plates through overheating.

12 While charging the battery, note that the temperature of the electrolyte should never exceed 37.8°C (100°F).

Maintenance-free battery - charging

Note: *The following is intended as a guide only. Always refer to the manufacturer's recommendations (often printed on a label attached to the battery) before charging a battery.*

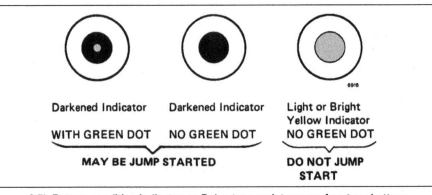

3.5b Battery condition indicator on Delco type maintenance-free type battery

13 This battery type takes considerably longer to fully recharge than the standard type, the time taken dependent on the extent of discharge, but it can take up to three days.

14 A constant voltage type charger is required, to be set, when connected, to 13.9 to 14.9 volts with a charger current below 25 amps. Using this method, the battery should be usable within three hours, giving a voltage reading of 12.5 volts, but this is for a partially discharged battery and, as mentioned, full charging can take considerably longer.

15 If the battery is to be charged from a fully discharged state (condition reading less than 12.2 volts), have it recharged by your Vauxhall dealer or local automotive electrician, as the charge rate is higher and constant supervision during charging is necessary.

4 Battery - removal and refitting

Removal

1 The battery is located on a support plate fitted to the left-hand wing valance in the engine compartment. Disconnect the negative and then the positive leads from the battery terminals after slackening the securing nuts and bolts.

2 Release the battery clamp plate and carefully lift the battery from the support plate. Hold it vertically to ensure that none of the electrolyte is spilled **(see illustration)**.

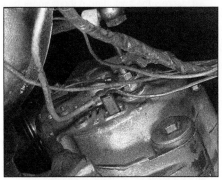

7.2 Alternator connections

Refitting

3 Refitting is a direct reversal of this procedure. Reconnect the positive lead before the negative lead and smear the terminals with petroleum jelly to prevent corrosion; never use ordinary grease. Do not overtighten the terminal securing bolts, nor hammer the fittings on. The terminals are made of lead and are easily damaged.

5 Charging system - testing

Note: *Refer to the warnings given in "Safety first!" and in Section 1 of this Chapter before starting work.*

1 If the ignition warning light fails to illuminate when the ignition is switched on, first check the alternator wiring connections for security. If satisfactory, check that the warning light bulb has not blown, and that the bulbholder is secure in its location in the instrument panel. If the light still fails to illuminate, check the continuity of the warning light feed wire from the alternator to the bulbholder. If all is satisfactory, the alternator is at fault and should be renewed or taken to an auto-electrician for testing and repair.

2 If the ignition warning light illuminates when the engine is running, stop the engine and check that the drivebelt is correctly tensioned (see Chapter 1) and that the alternator connections are secure. If all is so far satisfactory, have the alternator checked by an auto-electrician for testing and repair.

3 If the alternator output is suspect even though the warning light functions correctly, the regulated voltage may be checked as follows.

4 Connect a voltmeter across the battery terminals and start the engine.

5 Increase the engine speed until the voltmeter reading remains steady; the reading should be approximately 12 to 13 volts, and no more than 14 volts.

6 Switch on as many electrical accessories (eg, the headlights, heated rear window and heater blower) as possible, and check that the alternator maintains the regulated voltage at around 13 to 14 volts.

4.2 Battery fixing clamp

7 If the regulated voltage is not as stated, the fault may be due to worn brushes, weak brush springs, a faulty voltage regulator, a faulty diode, a severed phase winding or worn or damaged slip rings. The alternator should be renewed or taken to an auto-electrician for testing and repair.

6 Alternator drivebelt - removal, refitting and tensioning

Refer to the procedure given for the auxiliary drivebelt(s) in Chapter 1.

7 Alternator - removal and refitting

Removal

1 Disconnect the battery leads.

2 Note the terminal connections at the rear of the alternator and disconnect the plug, multi-pin connector or terminals as appropriate **(see illustration)**.

3 Undo and remove the alternator adjustment arm bolt, note the short earth wire. Slacken the lower pivot bolt and swing the alternator in towards the engine. Lift the drivebelt off the alternator pulley **(see illustrations)**.

4 Remove the lower pivot bolt and lift the alternator away from the engine. Take care not to drop or knock the alternator as this can cause irreparable damage **(see illustration)**.

7.3a Alternator adjustment link and earth cable

7.3b Alternator pivot mounting and adjustment link bolt

7.4 Alternator/engine mounting bracket

Refitting

5 Refitting the alternator is the reverse of the removal sequence. Tension the drivebelt as described in Chapter 1.

8 Alternator - testing and overhaul

If the alternator is thought to be suspect, it should be removed from the vehicle and taken to an auto-electrician for testing. Most auto-electricians will be able to supply and fit brushes at a reasonable cost. However, check on the cost of repairs before proceeding as it may prove more economical to obtain a new or exchange alternator.

9 Starting system - testing

Note: *Refer to the precautions given in "Safety first!" and in Section 1 of this Chapter before starting work.*

1 If the starter motor fails to operate when the ignition key is turned to the appropriate position, the following possible causes may be to blame.
 a) *The battery is faulty.*
 b) *The electrical connections between the switch, solenoid, battery and starter motor are somewhere failing to pass the necessary current from the battery through the starter to earth.*
 c) *The solenoid is faulty.*
 d) *The starter motor is mechanically or electrically defective.*
2 To check the battery, switch on the headlights. If they dim after a few seconds, this indicates that the battery is discharged - recharge (see Section 3) or renew the battery. If the headlights glow brightly, operate the ignition switch and observe the lights. If they dim, then this indicates that current is reaching the starter motor, therefore the fault must lie in the starter motor. If the lights continue to glow brightly (and no clicking sound can be heard from the starter motor solenoid), this indicates that there is a fault in the circuit or solenoid - see following paragraphs. If the starter motor turns slowly when operated, but the battery is in good condition, then this indicates that either the starter motor is faulty, or there is considerable resistance somewhere in the circuit.
3 If a fault in the circuit is suspected, disconnect the battery leads (including the earth connection to the body), the starter/solenoid wiring and the engine/transmission earth strap. Thoroughly clean the connections, and reconnect the leads and wiring, then use a voltmeter or test lamp to check that full battery voltage is available at the battery positive lead connection to the solenoid, and that the earth is sound. Smear petroleum jelly around the battery terminals to prevent corrosion -

corroded connections are amongst the most frequent causes of electrical system faults.
4 If the battery and all connections are in good condition, check the circuit by disconnecting the wire from the solenoid blade terminal. Connect a voltmeter or test lamp between the wire end and a good earth (such as the battery negative terminal), and check that the wire is live when the ignition switch is turned to the `start' position. If it is, then the circuit is sound - if not the circuit wiring can be checked as described in Chapter 12.
5 The solenoid contacts can be checked by connecting a voltmeter or test lamp between the battery positive feed connection on the starter side of the solenoid, and earth. When the ignition switch is turned to the `start' position, there should be a reading or lighted bulb, as applicable. If there is no reading or lighted bulb, the solenoid is faulty and should be renewed.
6 If the circuit and solenoid are proved sound, the fault must lie in the starter motor. In this event, it may be possible to have the starter motor overhauled by a specialist, but check on the cost of spares before proceeding, as it may prove more economical to obtain a new or exchange motor.

10 Starter motor - removal and refitting

Removal

1 With the engine installed in the car it is easier to get to the starter motor from underneath as it is located low on the rear side of the engine. If you prefer not to work under the car then it will be essential to remove the air cleaner to gain access to the starter.
2 Start by disconnecting the battery earth lead and then disconnect the solenoid and starter electrical leads. Take note of their respective locations to ensure correct reassembly **(see illustration)**.
3 Unscrew and remove the starter motor unit retaining bolts and withdraw the unit from the clutch housing **(see illustration)**. Note that on some models, there is an additional support

bracket at the commutator end of the starter, which must be unbolted from the engine.

Refitting

4 Refitting the starter motor assembly is a direct reversal of the removal procedure.

11 Starter motor - testing and overhaul

If the starter motor is thought to be suspect, it should be removed from the vehicle and taken to an auto-electrician for testing. Most auto-electricians will be able to supply and fit brushes at a reasonable cost. However, check on the cost of repairs before proceeding as it may prove more economical to obtain a new or exchange motor.

12 Ignition switch - removal and refitting

Refer to Chapter 10.

13 Oil pressure warning light switch - removal and refitting

Removal

1 The switch is screwed into the cylinder block.
2 Disconnect the battery negative lead and disconnect the wiring from the switch.
3 Unscrew the switch from the cylinder block, and recover the sealing washer. Be prepared for oil spillage, and if the switch is to be left removed from the engine for any length of time, plug the hole in the cylinder block.

Refitting

4 Examine the sealing washer for signs of damage or deterioration and if necessary renew.
5 Refit the switch, complete with washer, and tighten it securely. Reconnect the wiring connector.
6 Check and, if necessary, top-up the engine oil as described in *"Weekly checks"*.

10.2 Starter solenoid connections

10.3 Starter motor mounting bolts - early models (arrowed)

Chapter 5 Part B:
Contact breaker ignition system

Contents

Condenser - testing, removal and refitting .5
Contact breaker points - gap and dwell angle adjustment 3
Contact breaker points - removal and refitting 4
Distributor - overhaul 7
Distributor - removal and refitting 6
General information 1
Ignition HT coil - removal, testing and refitting 9
Ignition system - testing 2
Ignition system check . . . . .See Chapter 1
Ignition timing - adjustment 8

Degrees of difficulty

Easy, suitable for novice with little experience	Fairly easy, suitable for beginner with some experience	Fairly difficult, suitable for competent DIY mechanic	Difficult, suitable for experienced DIY mechanic	Very difficult, suitable for expert DIY or professional

Specifications

General

Type	Camshaft driven distributor with mechanical contact breaker points
Firing order	1-3-4-2 (No 1 at timing belt end of engine)

Distributor

Rotational direction of rotor	Anti-clockwise (viewed from cap)
Contact breaker points gap	0.4 mm (0.016 in)
Dwell angle	47 to 53°
Timing*	10° BTDC (crankshaft pulley notch and oil pump housing pulley pointer in alignment) - vacuum pipe disconnected

*Refer to text for information on usage of unleaded petrol

Ignition coil

Primary winding resistance (approximate)	1.2 to 1.6 ohm
Secondary winding resistance (approximate)	7k ohms

Torque wrench settings

	Nm	lbf ft
Spark plugs	20	15
Distributor clamp nuts	22	16

1 General information

In order that the engine can run correctly it is necessary for an electrical spark to ignite the fuel/air mixture in the combustion chamber at exactly the right moment in relation to engine speed and load. The ignition system is based on feeding low tension voltage from the battery to the coil where it is converted to high tension voltage. The high tension voltage is powerful enough to jump the spark plug gap in the cylinders many times a second under high compression, providing that the system is in good condition and that all adjustments are correct.

The ignition system is divided into two circuits, low tension and high tension.

The low tension circuit (sometimes known as the primary) consists of the battery, lead to the ignition switch, lead from the ignition switch to the low tension or primary coil windings, and the lead from the low tension coil windings to the contact breaker points and condenser in the distributor.

The high tension circuit consists of the high tension or secondary coil winding, the heavy ignition lead from the centre of the coil to the centre of the distributor cap, the rotor arm, and the spark plug leads and spark plugs.

The system functions in the following manner. Low tension voltage is changed in the coil into high tension voltage by the opening and closing of the contact breaker points in the low tension circuit. High tension voltage is then fed via the carbon brush in the centre of the distributor cap to the rotor arm of the

distributor cap, and each time it comes in line with one of the four metal segments in the cap, which are connected to the spark plug leads, the opening and closing of the contact breaker points causes the high tension voltage to build up, jump the gap from the rotor arm to the appropriate metal segment and so via the spark plug lead to the spark plug, where it finally jumps the spark plug gap before going to earth.

The ignition is advanced and retarded automatically, to ensure that the spark occurs at just the right instant for the particular load at the prevailing engine speed.

The ignition advance is controlled both mechanically and by a vacuum-operated system. The mechanical governor comprises two weights, which move out from the distributor shaft as the engine speed rises due to centrifugal force. As they move outwards they rotate the cam relative to the distributor shaft, and so advance the spark. The weights are held in position by two light springs and it is the tension of the springs which is largely responsible for correct spark advancement.

The vacuum control consists of a diaphragm, one side of which is connected via a small bore tube to the carburettor, and the other side to the contact breaker plate. Depression in the inlet manifold and carburettor, which varies with engine speed and throttle opening, causes the diaphragm to move, so moving the contact breaker plate, and advancing or retarding the spark.

A resistance wire in the low tension feed to the coil keeps the coil voltage down to 6V during normal running. This wire is bypassed when the starter motor is operating, to compensate for reduced battery voltage.

2 Ignition system - testing

1 By far the majority of breakdown and running troubles are caused by faults in the ignition system either in the low tension or high tension circuits.
2 There are two main symptoms indicating faults. Either the engine will not start or fire, or the engine is difficult to start and misfires. If it is a regular misfire, (ie the engine is running on only two or three cylinders), the fault is almost sure to be in the secondary or high tension circuit. If the misfiring is intermittent the fault could be in either the high or low tension circuits. If the car stops suddenly, or will not start at all, it is likely that the fault is in the low tension circuit. Loss of power and overheating, apart from faulty carburation settings, are normally due to faults in the distributor or to incorrect ignition timing.

Engine fails to start

3 If the engine fails to start and the car was running normally when it was last used, first check that there is fuel in the petrol tank. If the engine turns over normally on the starter motor and the battery is evidently well charged, then the fault may be in either the high or low tension circuits. First check the HT circuit.
4 One of the commonest reasons for bad starting is wet or damp spark plug leads and distributor. Remove the distributor cap. If condensation is visible internally dry the cap with a rag and also wipe over the leads. Refit the cap. If the engine fails to start due to either damp HT leads or distributor cap, a moisture dispersant can be very effective.
5 If the engine still fails to start, check that voltage is reaching the plugs by disconnecting each plug lead in turn at the spark plug end, and holding the end of the cable with rubber or an insulated tool about 6 mm away from the cylinder block. Spin the engine on the starter motor. **Note** *Do not operate the starter system*

with the plug leads disconnected in any other way to that described, or damage to system components may result.
6 Sparking between the end of the cable and the block should be fairly strong with a regular blue spark. If voltage is reaching the plugs, then remove them and clean and regap them. The engine should now start.
7 If there is no spark at the plug leads, take off the HT lead from the centre of the distributor cap and hold it to the block as before. Spin the engine on the starter once more. A rapid succession of blue sparks between the end of the lead and the block indicates that the coil is in order and that the distributor cap is cracked, the rotor arm is faulty or the carbon brush in the top of the distributor cap is not making good contact with the spring on the rotor arm.
8 If there are no sparks from the end of the lead from the coil, check the connections at the coil end of the lead. If it is in order start checking the low tension circuit. Possibly, the points are in bad condition. Clean and reset them as described in this Chapter, Section 3.
9 Use a 12V voltmeter or a 12V bulb and two lengths of wire. With the ignition switched on and the points open, test between the low tension wire to the coil and earth. No reading indicates a break in the supply from the ignition switch. Check the connections at the switch to see if any are loose. Refit them and the engine should run. A reading shows a faulty coil or condenser, or broken lead between the coil and the distributor.
10 Take the condenser wire off the points assembly and with the points open test between the moving point and earth. If there is now a reading then the fault is in the condenser. Fit a new one and the fault is cleared.
11 With no reading from the moving point to earth, take a reading between earth and the distributor terminal of the coil A reading here shows a broken wire which will need to be replaced between the coil and the distributor. No reading confirms that the coil has failed and must be renewed, after which the engine will run once more. Remember to refit the condenser wire to the points assembly. For these tests it is sufficient to separate the points with a piece of dry paper while testing with the points open.

Engine misfires

12 If the engine misfires regularly, run it at a fast idling speed. Pull off each of the plug caps in turn and listen to the note of the engine. Hold the plug cap in a dry cloth or with a rubber glove as additional protection against a shock from the HT supply.
13 No difference in engine running will be noticed when the lead from the defective circuit is removed. Removing the lead from one of the good cylinders will accentuate the misfire.
14 Remove the plug lead from the plug which is not firing and hold it about 6 mm away from

the block. Restart the engine. If the sparking is fairly strong and regular, the fault must lie in the spark plug.
15 The plug may be loose, the insulation may be cracked, or the points may have burnt away giving too wide a gap for the spark to jump. Worse still, one of the points may have broken off. Either renew the plug, or clean it, reset the gap, and then test it.
16 If there is no spark at the end of the plug lead, or if it is weak and intermittent, check the ignition lead from the distributor to the plug. If the insulation is cracked or perished, renew the lead. Check the connections at the distributor cap.
17 If there is still no spark, examine the distributor cap carefully for tracking. This can be recognised by a very thin black line running between two or more electrodes, or between an electrode and some other part of the distributor. These lines are paths which now conduct electricity across the cap thus letting it run to earth. The only answer is a new distributor cap.
18 Apart from the ignition timing being incorrect, other causes of misfiring have already been dealt with under the Section dealing with the failure of the engine to start. To recap, these are that:
a) *The coil may be faulty giving an intermittent misfire.*
b) *There may be a damaged wire or loose connection in the low tension circuit.*
c) *The condenser may be faulty.*
d) *There may be a mechanical fault in the distributor (broken driving spindle or contact breaker spring).*
19 If the ignition timing is too far retarded, it should be noted that the engine will tend to overheat, and there will be a quite noticeable drop in power. If the engine is overheating and the power is down, and the ignition timing is correct, then the carburettor should be checked, as it is likely that this is where the fault lies.
20 If the ballast resistor wire is broken or disconnected, the engine will fire when the starter motor is operating but will refuse to run. Renewal of the resistor wire will cure the problem. Do not bypass the resistor wire with ordinary wire, or overheating of the coil will occur.

3 Contact breaker points - gap and dwell angle adjustment

1 Prise the distributor cap weatherproof cover apart (if fitted) and remove it **(see illustration)**.
2 Unclip the distributor cap and lift the cap clear.
3 Wipe the inside and outside of the cap clean with a dry cloth. Scrape away any small deposits from the four studs and inspect the cover for cracks or surface deterioration. Check the brush in the centre of the cap, it should protrude about 6 mm. Renew the cap if cracked or if any of the HT studs are corroded,

3.1 Removing the distributor cap cover

3.3 Interior of distributor cap

3.4 Removing the rotor arm

worn away or cracked **(see illustration)**.

4 Lift the distributor rotor arm from the central shaft and wipe the metal tip clean **(see illustration)**.

5 Remove the plastic cover which protects the contact breaker and prevents condensation from settling on the mechanism and reducing its effectiveness. Do not remove the upper bearing plate **(see illustration)**.

6 Now that the contact breaker points are exposed, gently prise the contacts apart and examine the condition of their faces. If they are rough, pitted or dirty, it will be necessary to remove them for new points to be fitted.

7 Presuming the points are satisfactory, or they have been cleaned or replaced, measure the gap between the points by turning the engine until the contact breaker arm is on the peak of one of the four cam lobes. Refer to the Specifications for the size of the feeler blade

3.5 Removing distributor plastic cover

to use when measuring the gap. Take care not to contaminate the point faces with oil **(see illustration)**.

8 If the points are too close or too far apart, slacken the contact breaker mounting screw. Move the stationary point until the correct gap has been achieved and then secure by tightening the setscrew in the breaker set mounting plate.

9 Check the gap once again to ensure that the adjustment was not disturbed when the setscrew was tightened.

10 Refit the plastic cover, then the rotor arm and finally the distributor cap with its cover.

11 On modern engines, setting the contact breaker gap in the distributor using feeler blades must be regarded as a basic adjustment only. For optimum engine performance, the dwell angle must be checked. The dwell angle is the number of degrees through which the distributor cam turns during the period between the instants of closure and opening of the contact breaker points. Checking the dwell angle not only gives a more accurate setting of the contact breaker gap but also evens out any variations in the gap which could be caused by wear in the distributor shaft or its bushes, or difference in height of any of the cam peaks.

12 The angle should be checked with a dwell meter connected in accordance with the maker's instructions. Refer to the Specifications for the correct dwell angle. If the dwell angle is too large, increase the points gap, if too small, reduce the points gap.

13 The dwell angle should always be adjusted before checking and adjusting the ignition timing.

4 Contact breaker points - removal and refitting

Removal

1 If the contact breaker points are burned, pitted or badly worn, they must be removed and renewed.

2 Remove the distributor cover, the cap, rotor arm, and contact breaker mechanism cover.

3 Remove the rotor shaft upper bearing plate **(see illustrations)**.

4 Pull off the LT spade connector, then remove the setscrew which retains the contact breaker mechanism and lift out the breaker assembly.

5 Lift off the moving contact arm and spring followed by the fixed contact plate.

6 It is possible to reface the contact points using a fine carborundum stone or emery paper. However, if the points show signs of burning or pitting, it is strongly recommended that they are replaced with a new set. Clean the faces of new points with methylated spirit before fitting.

Refitting

7 Refitting of the points follows the reverse sequence to removal, adjusting the gap and dwell angle as described in Section 3.

3.7 Checking the contact breaker gap

4.3a Rotor shaft upper bearing plate

4.3b Contact breaker/baseplate assembly

5.2 Distributor condenser and clamp plate

6.5a Ignition timing mark . . .

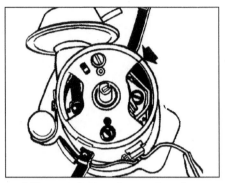

6.5b . . . and rotor alignment mark on distributor rim

5 Condenser - testing, removal and refitting

Testing

1 The purpose of the condenser (sometimes known as the capacitor) is to ensure that when the contact breaker points open there is no sparking across them which would waste voltage and cause wear.

2 On the Bosch distributor the condenser is mounted on the outside of the distributor body. If it develops a short-circuit it will cause ignition failure as the points will be prevented from interrupting the low tension circuit (see illustration).

3 If the engine becomes very difficult to start, or begins to miss after several miles running, and the points show signs of excessive burning, then the condition of the condenser must be suspect. A further test can be made by separating the points by hand with the ignition switched on. If this is accompanied by a strong blue flash it is indicative that the condenser has failed in the open circuit mode.

4 Without special equipment the only sure way to diagnose condenser trouble is to replace a suspected unit with a new one and note if there is any improvement.

Removal

5 To remove the condenser from the distributor take off the distributor cap, rotor arm and cover.

6 Remove the bearing plates, then pull off the contact points LT lead from the spade terminal located inside the distributor casing.

7 Remove the LT lead connecting the coil to the distributor, from the ignition coil.

8 Undo and remove the screw securing the condenser and LT lead assembly to the distributor case. Note that the condenser is supplied complete with the LT lead to the coil and the LT spade tag and mounting grommet.

Refitting

9 Refitting of the condenser follows the reverse procedure to removal.

6 Distributor - removal and refitting

Removal

1 Disconnect the battery earth terminal.

2 Remove the distributor cap and place it aside and out of the way.

3 If the cap and leads are to be dismantled then number the leads by putting tags on them to avoid mixing them up on reassembly.

4 Remove the spark plugs and check that the transmission is in neutral. This will enable the engine to be turned over by hand without resistance from compression.

5 Rotate the crankshaft by means of the pulley bolt until No 1 piston can be felt to be rising on its compression stroke (finger over spark plug hole). Continue turning until the notch in the crankshaft pulley is aligned with the pointer on the belt cover (see illustrations). The cut-out in the top of the distributor shaft should now be aligned with the mark on the rim of the distributor housing.

6 Once the engine has been set in this position ensure that the engine is not disturbed from this position whilst the distributor is removed. This will make the installation task easier.

7 Detach the LT lead from the coil.

8 Disconnect the vacuum advance tube from the distributor.

9 Unscrew and remove the distributor clamp plate. Withdraw the distributor from the engine (see illustration).

6.11a Fitting distributor O-ring seal

6.9 Releasing distributor clamp

Refitting

10 Refitting the distributor is a direct reversal of the removal sequence. Check that the engine has not been disturbed from any position set before removal. If the engine was turned over for any reason reset it to the position given in paragraph 5.

11 Fit a new O-ring seal to the distributor flange and then align the cut-out in the distributor shaft with the mark on the rim of the distributor body. Check that the distributor drive dog is in the correct relative position to engage in the camshaft drive slots, and push the distributor into position (see illustrations).

12 Turn the distributor body as necessary to align the distributor shaft cut-out with the mark on the rim of the distributor body again.

6.11b Fit the distributor . . .

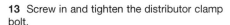

6.11c . . . aligning it with the offset drive slots in camshaft

7.6 Extract vacuum rod circlip

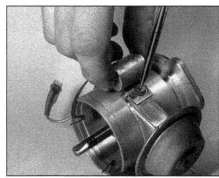

7.7a Condenser/vacuum unit fixing screw

13 Screw in and tighten the distributor clamp bolt.

14 Reconnect the LT lead to the coil and the vacuum tube to the vacuum unit. Refit the cap, leads, plugs and battery earth terminal to complete.

15 Check the timing using a stroboscope as described in Section 8.

7 Distributor - overhaul

1 Before overhauling the distributor, check on the availability of parts which may be necessary. If the distributor has seen a lot of service then the chances are that it is generally worn and should be renewed.

7.7b Unhooking vacuum unit control rod

2 If the distributor is to be dismantled, the work should be carried out on a clean workbench where the respective components can be laid out in order as they are removed.

3 If it has not already been removed, disconnect the distributor cap and cover, together with the leads (see Section 3). Withdraw the rotor arm and damp proof cover.

4 Remove the contact breaker set as described in Section 4.

5 Remove the condenser (Section 5).

6 Prise the circlip from the vacuum control rod-to-timing plate spindle **(see illustration)**.

7 Unscrew the vacuum control unit retaining screws and, remove the unit, unhooking the control rod **(see illustrations)**.

8 Unscrew and lift out the baseplate **(see illustrations)**.

9 The centrifugal weights and springs can now be inspected and removed if required, but take note of the respective spring and weight positions **(see illustration)**.

10 To withdraw the spindle, the drivegear or drive dog must be removed. Use a small punch and drive out the retaining pin and then extract the spindle upwards.

11 Clean all parts in an oil and grease solvent and wipe/blow dry ready for inspection.

12 Inspect all components for obvious signs of excessive wear or damage. Check the spindle play and drivegear teeth or drive dog faces for wear. Renew any parts which are defective or suspect.

13 Prior to reassembly smear all sliding parts and the centrifugal weight springs with a small amount of medium grease.

14 Slide the spindle into position and relocate the drivegear or dog. Drive a new retaining pin into position to secure the gear or dog.

15 Reassemble the centrifugal weights and springs, ensuring that they are securely located.

16 Refit the contact plates and tighten screws to secure.

17 Refit the vacuum control unit, relocating the control rod and tightening the screws to secure. Relocate the circlip to retain the rod on the plate spindle. Apply a little grease to the plate spindle.

18 Refit the condenser as described in Section 5.

19 Refit the contact breaker set as described in Section 4 and readjust the contact gap in accordance with Section 3.

20 Lubricate the sliding parts of the contact breaker base plate assembly with some clean oil and smear a small amount of high melting-point grease onto the cam surface.

21 Check the spindle for freedom of rotation and the contact points for correct operation. Support the gear and apply finger pressure to the rotor arm in the reverse direction to that in which it operates. It should spring back freely to its static position.

22 The distributor is now ready for refitting.

7.8a Releasing baseplate/clip fixing screw

7.8b Removing baseplate

7.9 Centrifugal weights and springs

8 Ignition timing - adjustment

Models using leaded (4-star) petrol

1 It is necessary to time the ignition when it has been upset due to overhauling or dismantling. Also, if maladjustments have affected the engine performance it is very desirable, although not always essential, to reset the timing starting from scratch. In the following procedures it is assumed that the intention is to obtain standard performance from the standard engine which is in reasonable condition. It is also assumed that the recommended fuel octane rating is used.

2 Set the transmission to neutral and remove all four spark plugs.

3 Place a thumb over No 1 cylinder spark plug hole and rotate the engine clockwise by means of the crankshaft pulley bolt until pressure is felt building up in No 1 cylinder. This indicates that the No 1 cylinder piston is approaching top dead centre (TDC) on the firing stroke.

4 Continue to rotate the crankshaft until the notch in the pulley is directly opposite the timing cover mark or the pointer as appropriate **(see illustration)**.

5 In this position, the timing is set at the specified BTDC number of degrees not TDC.

6 Slacken the distributor clamp bolt or nut and rotate the distributor body until the contact breaker points are just opening and then tighten the clamp bolt or nut.

7 Difficulty is sometimes experienced in determining exactly when the contact breaker points open. This can be ascertained most accurately by connecting a 12V bulb in parallel with the contact breaker points (one lead to earth and the other from the distributor low tension terminal). Switch on the ignition and turn the distributor body until the bulb lights up, indicating that the points have just opened.

8 If it was found impossible to align the rotor arm correctly the distributor cam assembly has been incorrectly fitted on the driveshaft. To rectify this, it will be necessary to partially dismantle the distributor and check the position of the cam assembly on the centrifugal advance mechanism; it may be 180° out of position.

9 As a final check on the ignition timing the best method is to use a strobe lamp.

10 Put a spot of white paint on the notch in the crankshaft pulley and the timing mark or the pointer and connect the strobe light into the No 1 cylinder HT circuit following the maker's instructions. Disconnect the vacuum pipe from the distributor vacuum unit.

11 Run the engine at idling speed and point the strobe lamp at the timing marks. At idling

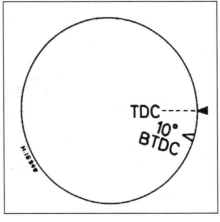

8.4 TDC and 10° BTDC ignition timing markings

speed the white paint marks should appear to be immediately opposite each other; open the throttle slightly and check that as the engine revolutions rise the spot on the crankshaft will move away from the pointer. This indicates the centrifugal advance mechanism is operating correctly.

12 If the timing marks do not line up under the strobe light, slightly slacken the distributor clamp bolt and carefully turn the distributor in its location to bring the marks into line and retighten the clamp bolt.

Models using unleaded petrol

13 The engines used in Vauxhall Cavalier models are designed to run on unleaded, but the manufacturers state that the ignition should be retarded by 3° to 7° BTDC.

14 The crankshaft pulley only has one timing mark (10° BTDC), so it will be necessary to make additional marks to accurately retard the ignition.

15 Turn the engine by means of the crankshaft pulley bolt, or by engaging top gear and pulling the car forward, until No 1 piston is at TDC on the firing stroke. This can be felt by removing No 1 spark plug and feeling for compression with your fingers as the engine is turned. The precise TDC point will have to be determined using a blunt probe (such as a knitting needle) inserted through No 1 spark plug hole.

16 Make a mark on the crankshaft pulley in alignment with the timing mark, or pointer, on the engine.

17 The original pulley mark indicates 10° BTDC, and the new mark TDC. Using these two markings, measure out and make a third mark on the pulley in the 7° BTDC position.

18 Using the new timing mark, adjust the ignition timing as described in paragraphs 11 and 12. If detonation occurs, it may be necessary to retard the ignition timing even further; some experimentation may be worthwhile to achieve satisfactory running.

9.2 The AC Delco coil

9 Ignition HT coil - removal, testing and refitting

Removal

1 Disconnect the battery leads.

2 Disconnect the LT wiring connectors from the coil, noting there correct fitted positions **(see illustration)**.

3 Disconnect the HT lead from the coil.

4 Undo the retaining bolts and remove the coil from the car.

Testing

5 Testing of the coil consists of using a multimeter set to its resistance function, to check the primary (LT '+' to '-' terminals) and secondary (LT '+' to HT lead terminal) windings for continuity, bearing in mind that on the four output, static type HT coil there are two sets of each windings. Compare the results obtained to those given in the Specifications at the start of this Chapter. Note the resistance of the coil windings will vary slightly according to the coil temperature, the results in the Specifications are approximate values for when the coil is at 20°C.

6 Check that there is no continuity between the HT lead terminal and the coil body/mounting bracket.

7 If the coil is thought to be faulty, have your findings confirmed by a Vauxhall dealer before renewing the coil.

Refitting

8 Refitting is a reversal of the relevant removal procedure ensuring that the wiring connectors are correctly and securely reconnected.

Chapter 5 Part C:
Electronic (breakerless) ignition system

Contents

Distributor - overhaul 4
Distributor - removal and refitting 3
General information 1
Ignition HT coil - removal, testing and refitting 6

Ignition module (control unit) - removal and refitting 7
Ignition system check . . . . .See Chapter 1
Ignition system - testing 2
Ignition timing - adjustment 5

Degrees of difficulty

Easy, suitable for novice with little experience		**Fairly easy,** suitable for beginner with some experience		**Fairly difficult,** suitable for competent DIY mechanic		**Difficult,** suitable for experienced DIY mechanic		**Very difficult,** suitable for expert DIY or professional	

Specifications

General

Type	Breakerless electronic ignition system
System type:	
1.3 litre models	AC Delco system
1.6 litre models and early (pre 1987) 1.8 litre models	Bosch (Hall effect) system
Later (1987 onwards) 1.8 litre models	EZ61 Microprocessor spark timing system
2.0 litre models	Bosch Motronic system
Firing order	1-3-4-2 (No 1 at timing belt end of engine)
Rotational direction of distributor rotor arm	Anti-clockwise (viewed from cap)

Ignition timing

At idle (with vacuum pipe disconnected - early models only	10° BTDC (crankshaft pulley notch and oil pump housing pulley pointer in alignment)

Ignition coil

Primary winding resistance (approximate)	1.2 to 1.6 ohm
Secondary winding resistance (approximate)	7k ohms

Torque wrench settings

	Nm	lbf ft
Spark plugs	20	15
Distributor clamp nuts	22	16

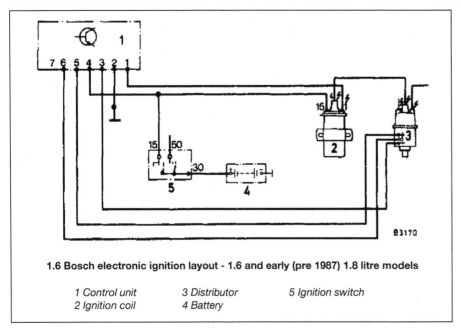

1.6 Bosch electronic ignition layout - 1.6 and early (pre 1987) 1.8 litre models

| 1 Control unit | 3 Distributor | 5 Ignition switch |
| 2 Ignition coil | 4 Battery | |

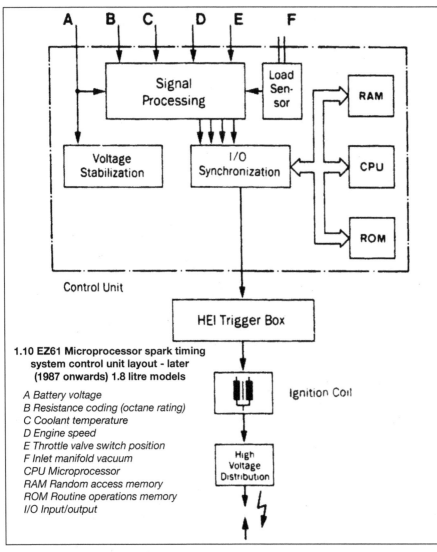

1.10 EZ61 Microprocessor spark timing system control unit layout - later (1987 onwards) 1.8 litre models

A Battery voltage
B Resistance coding (octane rating)
C Coolant temperature
D Engine speed
E Throttle valve switch position
F Inlet manifold vacuum
CPU Microprocessor
RAM Random access memory
ROM Routine operations memory
I/O Input/output

1 General information

1.3 litre models

On all 1.3 litre models a Delco breakerless electronic ignition system is used. This comprises of the HT ignition coil and the distributor, this being driven off the end of the camshaft.

The distributor contains an induction sensor (reluctor) mounted onto its shaft and an ignition module (pick-up) fixed to its body. The system operates as follows.

When the ignition is switched on but the engine is stationary the transistors in the module prevent current flowing through the ignition system primary (LT) circuit.

As the crankshaft rotates, the induction sensor moves through the magnetic field created by the module. When the teeth are in alignment with the module projections a small AC voltage is created. The module uses this voltage to switch the transistors in the unit and complete the ignition system primary (LT) circuit.

As the teeth move out of alignment with the module projections the AC voltage changes and the transistors are switched again to interrupt the primary (LT) circuit. This causes a high voltage to be induced in the coil secondary (HT) windings which then travels down the HT lead to the distributor and onto the relevant spark plug.

1.6 and early (pre 1987) 1.8 litre models

On these models a Bosch (Hall effect) ignition system is fitted. The system comprises of the HT ignition coil, the distributor and the ignition module **(see illustration)**.

The Hall effect system distributor incorporates a permanent magnet, a detector/amplifier, and four vanes. When a vane is masking the detector/amplifier no voltage is induced in the detector, and under these conditions the module passes current through the low tension windings of the coil.

Rotation of the distributor will uncover the detector and cause it to be influenced by the magnetic field of the permanent magnet. The Hall effect induces a small voltage in the detector plate which is then amplified and triggers the module to interrupt the low tension current in the coil.

The ignition module in the Hall effect system incorporates a circuit which switches off the low tension circuit if the time between consecutive signals exceeds 1.5 seconds. The coil and internal circuits are therefore protected if the ignition is left switched on inadvertently.

Later (1987 onwards) 1.8 litre models

On these models the ignition system is of the EZ61 Microprocessor spark timing system type. The ignition system consists solely of a control unit and the distributor **(see illustration)**.

The control unit receives signals from

various sensors and automatically adjusts the ignition timing to suit the constantly changing operating conditions of the engine. The distributor therefore merely functions as a high voltage distribution unit.

2.0 litre models

On 2.0 litre models the ignition system is integrated with the fuel injection system, both systems being under the control of the same control unit (See Chapter 4). The distributor therefore merely functions as a high voltage distribution unit.

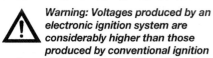

2 Ignition system - testing

⚠️ *Warning: Voltages produced by an electronic ignition system are considerably higher than those produced by conventional ignition systems. Extreme care must be taken when working on the system with the ignition switched on. Persons with surgically-implanted cardiac pacemaker devices should keep well clear of the ignition circuits, components and test equipment*

1.3, 1.6 and early (pre 1987) 1.8 litre models

Note: *Refer to the warning given in Section 1 of Part A of this Chapter before starting work. Always switch off the ignition before disconnecting or connecting any component and when using a multi-meter to check resistances.*

General

1 The components of electronic ignition systems are normally very reliable; most faults are far more likely to be due to loose or dirty connections or to "tracking" of HT voltage due to dirt, dampness or damaged insulation than to the failure of any of the system's components. **Always** check all wiring thoroughly before condemning an electrical component and work methodically to eliminate all other possibilities before deciding that a particular component is faulty.
2 The old practice of checking for a spark by holding the live end of an HT lead a short distance away from the engine is not recommended; not only is there a high risk of a powerful electric shock, but the HT coil or amplifier unit will be damaged. Similarly, **never** try to "diagnose" misfires by pulling off one HT lead at a time.

Engine will not start

3 If the engine either will not turn over at all, or only turns very slowly, check the battery and starter motor. Connect a voltmeter across the battery terminals (meter positive probe to battery positive terminal), disconnect the ignition coil HT lead from the distributor cap and earth it, then note the voltage reading obtained while turning over the engine on the starter for (no more than) ten seconds. If the

reading obtained is less than approximately 9.5 volts, first check the battery, starter motor and charging system as described in the relevant Sections of this Chapter.
4 If the engine turns over at normal speed but will not start, check the HT circuit by connecting a timing light (following the manufacturer's instructions) and turning the engine over on the starter motor; if the light flashes, voltage is reaching the spark plugs, so these should be checked first. If the light does not flash, check the HT leads themselves followed by the distributor cap, carbon brush and rotor arm.
5 If there is a spark, check the fuel system for faults referring to the relevant part of Chapter 4 for further information.
6 If there is still no spark, check the voltage at the ignition HT coil "+" terminal; it should be the same as the battery voltage (ie, at least 11.7 volts). If the voltage at the coil is more than 1 volt less than that at the battery, check the feed back through the fusebox and ignition switch to the battery and its earth until the fault is found.
7 If the feed to the HT coil is sound, check the coil's primary and secondary winding resistance as described later in this Section; renew the coil if faulty, but be careful to check carefully the condition of the LT connections themselves before doing so, to ensure that the fault is not due to dirty or poorly-fastened connectors.
8 If the HT coil is in good condition, the fault is probably within the amplifier unit or distributor stator assembly. Testing of these components should be entrusted to a Vauxhall dealer.

Engine misfires

9 An irregular misfire suggests either a loose connection or intermittent fault on the primary circuit, or an HT fault on the coil side of the rotor arm.
10 With the ignition switched off, check carefully through the system ensuring that all connections are clean and securely fastened. If the equipment is available, check the LT circuit as described above.
11 Check that the HT coil, the distributor cap and the HT leads are clean and dry. Check the leads themselves and the spark plugs (by substitution, if necessary), then check the distributor cap, carbon brush and rotor arm as described in Chapter 1.
12 Regular misfiring is almost certainly due to a fault in the distributor cap, HT leads or spark plugs. Use a timing light (paragraph 4 above) to check whether HT voltage is present at all leads.
13 If HT voltage is not present on any particular lead, the fault will be in that lead or in the distributor cap. If HT is present on all leads, the fault will be in the spark plugs; check and renew them if there is any doubt about their condition.
14 If no HT is present, check the HT coil; its secondary windings may be breaking down under load.

Later (1987 onwards) 1.8 litre models and all 2.0 litre models

15 If a fault appears in the ignition system first ensure that the fault is not due to a poor electrical connection or poor maintenance; ie, check that the air cleaner filter element is clean, the spark plugs are in good condition and correctly gapped, that the engine breather hoses are clear and undamaged, referring to Chapter 1 for further information. Also check that the accelerator cable is correctly adjusted as described in the relevant part of Chapter 4. If the engine is running very roughly, check the compression pressures (Chapter 2).
16 If these checks fail to reveal the cause of the problem the vehicle should be taken to a suitably equipped Vauxhall dealer for testing using special diagnostic equipment. The tester will locate the fault quickly and simply alleviating the need to test all the system components individually which is a time consuming operation that carries a high risk of damaging the control unit.
17 The only ignition system checks which can be carried out by the home mechanic are those described in Chapter 1, relating to the spark plugs, and the ignition coil test described in this Chapter. If necessary, the system wiring and wiring connectors can be checked as described in Chapter 12 ensuring that the control unit wiring connector(s) have first been disconnected.

3 Distributor - removal and refitting

Removal

1.3 litre models

1 Remove the spark plugs (Chapter 1).
2 Undo the distributor cap retaining screws, lift of the cap and place it to one side.
3 With the transmission in gear and the handbrake released, pull the car forwards, until, with a finger over the plug hole, compression can be felt in No 1 cylinder (the cylinder nearest the crankshaft pulley). Continue moving the car forwards until the notch on the crankshaft pulley is aligned with the timing pointer **(see illustration)**. (On automatic transmission models, turn the

3.3 Crankshaft pulley timing notch (arrowed) aligned with pointer

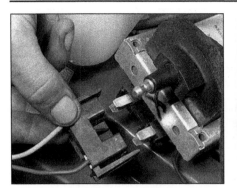

3.4 Disconnecting the distributor wiring connector at the ignition coil

3.5 Removing the distributor from the camshaft housing

3.6a Unplugging the distributor LT connector

engine by means of a spanner on the crankshaft bolt.) If the distributor cap is temporarily placed in position, the distributor rotor should be pointing towards the No 1 spark plug lead segment in the cap.

4 Disconnect the distributor wiring connector at the ignition coil **(see illustration)**, and detach the vacuum advance pipe from the distributor vacuum unit.

5 Undo the distributor clamp retaining nut (or bolt), lift off the clamp plate, and withdraw the distributor from the camshaft housing **(see illustration)**.

1.6 and early (pre 1987) 1.8 litre models

6 The procedure is similar to that just described in paragraphs 1 to 5, with the

following differences.

a) *The wiring connector must be unplugged from the distributor, not from the coil* **(see illustration)**.

b) *The distributor cap is secured by two spring clips, not by screws* **(see illustration)**.

c) *There is a mark on the edge of the distributor body to indicate the rotor position for No 1 cylinder firing, but the rotor and flash shield must be removed to expose it* **(see illustration)**. *The rotor can then be refitted to confirm the alignment.*

d) *The distributor is secured by two nuts, not by a clamp plate* **(see illustration)**.

e) *The distributor drive is by means of an offset peg and hole, not by a slot and dogs* **(see illustration)**.

Later (1987 onwards) 1.8 litre models and 2.0 litre models

7 Disconnect the battery leads.

8 Undo the retaining screws and remove the distributor cap from the distributor **(see illustration)**.

9 Extract the insulator. This is an interference fit in the housing, via an O-ring seal located in a groove on its outer edge, so ease it out of position taking great care not to damage the rotor arm **(see illustration)**.

10 Undo the two retaining screws and remove the rotor arm **(see illustrations)**.

11 If necessary, extract the rotor hub and carefully lever the oil seal out from the cylinder head **(see illustrations)**.

3.6b Removing the distributor cap

3.6c Remove flash shield to expose reference mark (arrowed)

3.6d Removing the distributor upper securing nut

3.6e Removing the distributor - note peg-and-hole drive

3.8 On later 1.8 litre and 2. litre models, undo the distributor cap retaining screws

3.9 Extract the insulator

3.10a Undo the two rotor screws . . .

3.10b . . . and remove the rotor

3.11a Extract the rotor hub . . .

Refitting

1.3 litre models

12 Before refitting the distributor, check that the engine has not been inadvertently turned whilst the distributor was removed; if it has, return it to the original position as described in paragraph 3.

13 Position the distributor so that the rotor contact is in line with the arrow or notch in the distributor body. In this position, the offset lug on the distributor drive coupling will be in the correct position to engage the similarly-offset slot in the end of the camshaft (see illustrations).

14 Check that the O-ring seal is in place on the distributor body, then insert the distributor into its camshaft housing location. With the rotor contact and arrow on the distributor body still in line, refit and secure the distributor clamp.

15 Refit the distributor cap, spark plugs and leads, wiring plug and vacuum pipe.

16 Refer to Section 5 and adjust the ignition timing.

1.6 and early (pre 1987) 1.8 litre models

17 Refer to paragraphs 12 to 16, bearing in mind the information given in paragraph 6.

Later (1987 onwards) 1.8 litre models and 2.0 litre models

18 Lubricate the lips of the new seal and press the seal squarely into position in the cylinder head, making sure its sealing lip is facing inwards. If necessary, tap the seal into position using a suitable tubular drift which bears only on its hard outer edge.

19 Carefully ease the rotor hub into position aligning its holes with the retaining bolt holes in the camshaft flange (see illustration).

20 Refit the rotor arm and securely tighten its retaining screws.

21 Fit a new O-ring to the groove in the insulator. Apply a smear of oil to aid installation and ease the insulator into position (see illustration).

22 Refit the distributor cap, making sure it is correctly located, and securely tighten its retaining screws.

3.11b . . . and prise out the oil seal

3.13a Distributor rotor contact, and arrow on distributor body in alignment . . .

3.13b . . . causing the drive coupling to be aligned like this . . .

3.13c . . . to engage the offset slot in the camshaft

3.19 Align the camshaft and rotor hub bolt holes

3.21 Renewing the insulator sealing ring

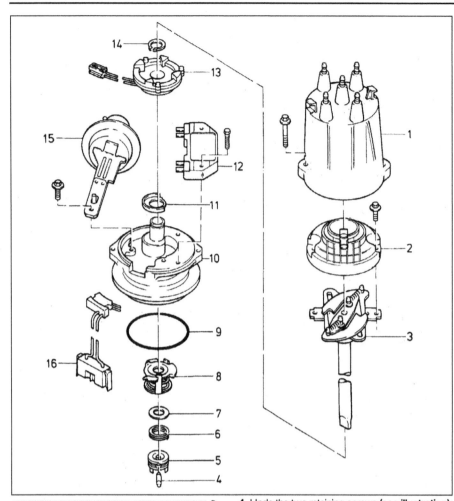

1 Distributor cap
2 Rotor
3 Shaft
4 Pin
5 Drive dog
6 Spring
7 Washer
8 Spring
9 O-ring
10 Body
11 Seal
12 Ignition module
13 Induction sensor
14 Circlip
15 Vacuum unit
16 Plug to coil

7 Check the distributor cap for corrosion of the segments, and for signs of tracking, indicated by a thin black line between the segments. Make sure that the carbon brush in the centre of the cap moves freely, and stands proud of its holder. Renew the cap if necessary.
8 If the metal portion of the rotor is badly burnt or loose, renew the rotor. If slightly burnt it may be cleaned with a fine file.
9 Suck on the end of the vacuum unit outlet, and check that the operating rod moves in as the suction is applied. Release the suction, and check that the rod returns to its original position. If this is not the case, renew the vacuum unit.
10 Inspect the distributor body and shaft assembly for excessive side movement of the shaft in its bushes. Check that the advance weights are free to move on their pivot posts, and that they return under the action of the springs. Check the security of all the components on the distributor shaft, and finally check for wear of the lug on the drive coupling.
11 Reassembly of the distributor is the reverse sequence to dismantling, but apply a few drops of engine oil to the advance weight pivot posts before refitting the rotor. If a new ignition module is being fitted, the new module will be supplied with a small quantity of silicone grease. This should be applied

4 Distributor - overhaul

1.3 litre models

1 Remove the distributor from the engine, as described in the previous Section.
2 Undo the two retaining screws and lift off the rotor **(see illustration)**.
3 Disconnect the two electrical plugs, one at each end, from the ignition module **(see illustration)**.

4 Undo the two retaining screws **(see illustration)**; withdraw the unit from the distributor.
5 Undo the two vacuum unit retaining screws **(see illustration)**, disengage the operating rod and remove the vacuum unit.
6 Due to its design and construction, this is the limit of dismantling possible on this distributor. It is possible to renew the rotor, vacuum unit, ignition module and distributor cap separately, but if inspection shows any of the components remaining on the distributor to be in need of attention, the complete distributor assembly must be renewed.

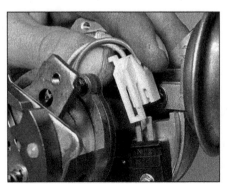

4.3 Disconnecting an electrical plug from the ignition module

4.4 Ignition module securing screws (arrowed)

4.5 Vacuum unit retaining screws (arrowed)

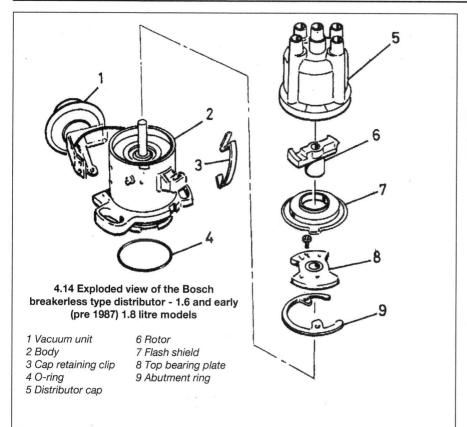

4.14 Exploded view of the Bosch breakerless type distributor - 1.6 and early (pre 1987) 1.8 litre models

1 Vacuum unit
2 Body
3 Cap retaining clip
4 O-ring
5 Distributor cap
6 Rotor
7 Flash shield
8 Top bearing plate
9 Abutment ring

4.16a Removing a vacuum unit retaining screw

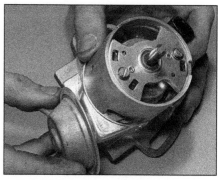

4.16b Removing the vacuum unit

between the module and its housing, to improve heat dissipation.

12 Refit the distributor as described in Section 3, after reassembly.

1.6 and early (pre 1987) 1.8 litre models

13 Remove the distributor as described in Section 3.

14 Pull off the rotor arm, and unclip the flash shield **(see illustration)**.

15 Although the top bearing plate can be removed after undoing its retaining screws, this is of academic interest, since no spare parts are available, neither are there any items requiring adjustment.

16 The vacuum unit can be renewed separately if required. Remove it by undoing the two retaining screws and unhooking the operating arm from the baseplate **(see illustrations)**. Note that the screws are not of equal length; the longer screw also secures one of the distributor cap clips.

17 Test the vacuum unit, as described in paragraph 9.

18 Inspect the distributor cap and rotor, as described in paragraphs 7 and 8.

19 Reassemble the distributor in the reverse order to that followed when dismantling. Make sure that the vacuum unit operating arm is correctly engaged with the peg on the baseplate; several attempts may be needed to reconnect it.

20 Refit the distributor as described in Section 3, after reassembly.

Later (1987 onwards) 1.8 litre models and 2.0 litre models

21 Refer to Section 3.

5 Ignition timing - adjustment

> ⚠️ Warning: Voltages produced by an electronic ignition system are considerably higher than those produced by conventional ignition systems. Extreme care must be taken when working on the system with the ignition switched on. Persons with surgically-implanted cardiac pacemaker devices should keep well clear of the ignition circuits, components and test equipment.

1.3, 1.6 and early (pre 1987) 1.8 litre models

Models using leaded (4-star) petrol

1 Static timing cannot be checked with the breakerless ignition system. However, if the distributor is correctly refitted (Section 3), the timing should be accurate enough to start the engine and permit it to run.

2 Dynamic timing, using a stroboscopic timing light, is carried out as described in Part B, Section 8, paragraphs 10, 11 and 12. Note, however, that the distributor is secured by two nuts instead of a clamp bolt.

3 Dwell angle checking and adjustment is not necessary with breakerless distributors.

Models using unleaded petrol

4 The engines used in Cavalier models are designed to run on high octane unleaded petrol, but the manufacturers recommend that the ignition timing is adjusted in accordance with the following guidelines.

Carburettor engines

5 If detonation ("pinking" or "knock") occurs, the timing should be retarded by 3° (see Part B, Section 8). If detonation occurs, it may be necessary to retard the ignition timing even further; some experimentation may be worthwhile to achieve satisfactory running.

Fuel injection engines

6 When using high octane unleaded petrol, the timing **must** be retarded by 3° as such fuel can cause inaudible high speed knock, which can lead to engine damage. The procedure is given in Part B, Section 8.

Later (1987 onwards) 1.8 litre models and 2.0 litre models

7 On these models the ignition timing can be checked using a stroboscopic light but no adjustment is possible. If the ignition timing is incorrect, there must be a fault in the system and the car should be taken to a Vauxhall dealer for testing.

6.2 Disconnecting a coil LT lead (1.8 litre model shown)

6.3 Ignition module wiring plug

6.4a Removing a coil securing bolt

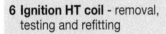
6 Ignition HT coil - removal, testing and refitting

Removal

1 Disconnect the battery leads.
2 Disconnect the LT wiring connectors from the coil, noting there correct fitted positions **(see illustration)**.
3 Disconnect the HT lead from the coil. where necessary, also disconnect the wiring connector from the ignition module **(see illustration)**.
4 Undo the retaining bolts and remove the coil from the car. If necessary, undo the clamp screw and remove the coil from its mounting bracket **(see illustrations)**.

Testing

5 Testing of the coil consists of using a multimeter set to its resistance function, to check the primary (LT '+' to '-' terminals) and secondary (LT '+' to HT lead terminal) windings for continuity, bearing in mind that on the four output, static type HT coil there are two sets of each windings. Compare the results obtained to those given in the Specifications at the start of this Chapter. Note the resistance of the coil windings will vary slightly according to the coil temperature, the results in the Specifications are approximate values for when the coil is at 20ºC.
6 Check that there is no continuity between the HT lead terminal and the coil body/mounting bracket.

7 If the coil is thought to be faulty, have your findings confirmed by a Vauxhall dealer before renewing the coil.

Refitting

8 Refitting is a reversal of the relevant removal procedure ensuring that the wiring connectors are correctly and securely reconnected.

7 Ignition module (control unit) - removal and refitting

1.3 litre models

1 The ignition module is located in the distributor. See Section 4 for details.

1.6 and early (pre 1987) 1.8 litre models

2 The ignition module is located on the coil mounting plate. To gain access, first remove the coil, as described in Section 6.
3 With the coil removed from its bracket, the module can be unbolted from the mounting plate **(see illustration)**.
4 If a new module is being fitted, it should be supplied with a small quantity of silicone grease, which must be applied to the mounting plate to improve heat dissipation **(see illustration)**. Similar heat sink compounds can also be obtained from shops selling radio and electronic components.
5 Refit the ignition module in the reverse order to removal. Make sure that the locating pins

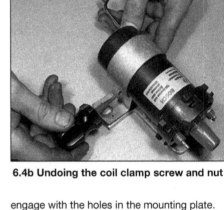

6.4b Undoing the coil clamp screw and nut

engage with the holes in the mounting plate.

Later 1.8 (1987 onwards) litre models

6 The ignition control unit is located in the engine compartment where it is mounted onto the suspension strut turret. To remove the unit, first disconnect the battery leads.
7 Release the spring retaining tangs and disconnect the wiring connector **(see illustration)**.
8 Undo the retaining screws and remove the unit from its mounting bracket.
9 Refitting is the reverse of removal

2.0 litre models

10 Refer to Chapter 4.

7.3 Unbolting the ignition module

7.4 Ignition module and mounting plate - note locating pins (arrowed)

7.7 Disconnecting the control unit wiring plug - later 1.8 litre model

Chapter 6
Clutch

Contents

Clutch - adjustment 2
Clutch - removal, inspection and refitting 5
Clutch cable - removal and refitting 3
Clutch pedal - removal and refitting 4
Clutch release bearing, lever, bushes and seal - removal and
    refitting 6
General information 1

Degrees of difficulty

Easy, suitable for novice with little experience	**Fairly easy,** suitable for beginner with some experience	**Fairly difficult,** suitable for competent DIY mechanic	**Difficult,** suitable for experienced DIY mechanic	**Very difficult,** suitable for expert DIY or professional

Specifications

Type	Single dry plate with diaphragm spring. Cable actuation	
Torque wrench settings	**Nm**	**lbf ft**
Clutch cover bolts	15	11
Release fork to lever bolt	35	26
Flywheel housing cover plate bolts	7	5
Flywheel housing-to-engine	75	55
End cover screw plug (F10, F10.4, F16.4)	50	37
End cover screw plug (F10.5, F16.5)	30	22
End cover retaining bolts	22	16

1 General information

All models covered by this manual are fitted with a single plate diaphragm spring clutch which is enclosed in a pressed steel cover bolted to the flywheel. The gearbox input shaft projects through the clutch and is located at its forward end in a needle roller spigot bearing within the centre of the crankshaft.

The clutch driven plate is located between the flywheel and the clutch pressure plate and it can slide on splines on the gearbox input shaft. When the clutch is engaged, the diaphragm spring forces the pressure plate to grip the driven plate against the flywheel and drive is transmitted from the crankshaft, through the driven plate, to the gearbox input shaft. On disengaging the clutch the pressure plate is lifted to release the driven plate with the result that the drive to the gearbox is disconnected.

The clutch is operated by a foot pedal suspended under the facia and a cable connected to the clutch release lever mounted on the clutch bellhousing. Depressing the pedal causes the release lever to move the thrust bearing against the release fingers of the diaphragm spring in the pressure plate

assembly. The spring is sandwiched between two rings which act as fulcrums. As the centre of the spring is moved in, the periphery moves out to lift the pressure plate and disengage the clutch. The reverse takes place when the pedal is released.

As wear takes place on the driven plate with usage, the foot pedal will rise progressively relative to its original position. Periodic adjustment is not required.

An unusual feature of the design of this particular clutch is that the driven plate, release bearing and seal can be renewed without having to remove either the engine or the transmission from the car.

2 Clutch - adjustment

1 The clutch is normally self-adjusting, but if the cable or driven plate are renewed, the following initial adjustment will be required.
2 Take a measurement from the edge of the steering wheel to the centre of the clutch pedal and then take another measurement with the pedal fully depressed. These measurements can be taken using a suitable strip of wood or metal as the important figure is the difference between the two measurements, ie the

movement (stroke) of the pedal itself. This should be 138 mm and if this is not the case, the nut on the threaded end of the cable where it fits into the clutch release lever must be adjusted to obtain the correct pedal movement. Before adjusting the nut, remove the spring clip, and refit it after the adjustment has been made. Recheck the pedal movement on completion **(see illustrations)**.
3 After some period in use, it will not be possible to adjust the cable in this fashion and it will be an indication that the driven plate is due for renewal. Note that when correctly adjusted, the clutch pedal will be slightly

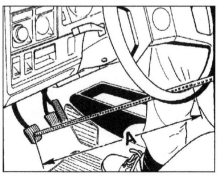

2.2a Clutch pedal released measurement (A)

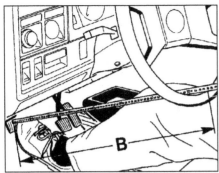

2.2b Clutch pedal depressed measurement (B)

higher than the brake pedal and it is incorrect for the two pedals to be in alignment. If they are aligned the clutch cable needs adjusting. Note also that there should be no play in the clutch pedal of these vehicles.

3 Clutch cable - removal and refitting

Removal

1 The common reason for having to renew the clutch cable is breakage, but it may also be necessary if the pedal action is stiff or jerky.
2 Before disturbing the installation, take a measurement of the length of the threaded end of the cable fitting protruding through the adjusting nut at the release lever end. This will enable you to preset the new cable and so simplify its installation.
3 Remove the spring clip from the cable, slacken the adjusting nut and disconnect the cable from the release lever. The cable assembly can now be extracted from the lug on the bellhousing case **(see illustration)**.
4 Working inside the car, unhook the return spring from the clutch foot pedal and disconnect the cable from the pedal lever **(see illustration)**.
5 The cable assembly can now be withdrawn into the engine compartment by pulling it through the bulkhead.
6 If a headlamp washer system is installed, then the fluid reservoir will have to be moved aside.

3.3 Removing the spring clip from the clutch cable

Refitting

7 Refitting the clutch cable is the reverse of the removal procedure. Position the cable adjusting nut initially so that the same amount of thread protrudes through the nut as noted during removal, then adjust the clutch as described in Section 2.

4 Clutch pedal - removal and refitting

Removal

1 Remove the cardboard trim panel from under the instrument panel.
2 Refer to the previous Section and disconnect the clutch cable from the release lever and the clutch pedal, but there is no need to remove the assembly from the lug on the bellhousing case or withdraw the assembly from the car. Release the pedal return spring.
3 Remove the wire locking clip from the pedal pivot retaining nut; remove the nut and washer.
4 Push the pivot out of the support bracket and remove the clutch pedal and the return spring.

Refitting

5 Refitting is the reverse of the removal procedure. Before inserting the pedal pivot, lightly smear the bearing surface with a molybdenum disulphide grease. Refit the cable as described in the previous Section and adjust if necessary.

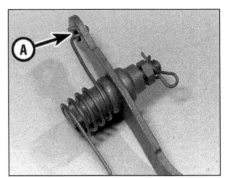

3.4 Clutch pedal assembled as when in place on the vehicle. Cable is retained by return spring (A) - pedal removed for clarity

5 Clutch - removal, inspection and refitting

Removal

1 A feature of these models is being able to renew the clutch pressure plate, the driven plate, the release bearing, the release pivot bushes and the clutch seal without having to remove either the engine or the transmission.
2 Although the maker's procedure requires the use of special tools, these are not essential and the work can be carried out using the tools normally available to the home mechanic.
3 Some of the operations are best carried out by working under the front of the vehicle, so apply the handbrake fully, jack up the front of the vehicle and support securely on axle stands (see "*Jacking and Vehicle Support*").. Bolt and remove the flywheel housing cover plate from the base of the clutch bellhousing.
4 On early models (up to approximately mid-1988), unscrew and remove the plug from the transmission casing end cover. On later models there is no plug in the end cover. On these models, unscrew the nut and disconnect the earth lead from the end cover. Position a suitable container beneath the end cover then undo the retaining bolts, noting each ones correct fitted location as it is removed, and remove the casing end cover and gasket from the transmission **(see illustrations)**.

5.4a Threaded plug in transmission end cover (arrowed) (4-speed transmission)

5.4b Unscrewing threaded plug (4-speed transmission)

5.4c On later models, remove the end cover to gain access to the input shaft end

5.5 Extracting the input shaft circlip

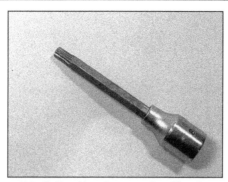

5.6a Splined key for removing 12-point socket-head screws

5.6b Removing the input shaft screw

5 Extract the circlip, now exposed, from the end of the input shaft using a pair of circlip pliers **(see illustration)**.

6 Underneath the circlip is a socket-headed (12-point) screw, which will require a 12-point splined key to extract it. Motor accessory tool shops usually stock this type of key. Remove the screw **(see illustrations)**.

7 The shaft can now be slid out of engagement with the splined hub of the clutch driven plate. To do this, the makers provide a special tool, but an effective substitute is to remove one of the four bolts which secure the gearchange mechanism cover to the top of the transmission case. Using this bolt as a pattern, obtain one similar, but of at least 40.0 mm in length. Screw the bolt into the end of the input shaft and use the bolt to pull the shaft out of its stop. Refit the bolt to the cover on the transmission case. On some 5-speed

transmissions, it is not unknown for the input shaft to be very tight, in which event it may prove difficult to withdraw it without using the special tool or a puller of some sort. In extreme cases a slide hammer will have to be attached to the end of the shaft to enable it to be withdrawn **(see illustrations)**.

8 Before the clutch can be removed the pressure plate must be compressed against the tension of the diaphragm spring, otherwise the clutch assembly will be too thick to pass through the space between the flywheel and the edge of the bellhousing when removing it.

9 The vehicle makers can supply three special clamps (KM526) for this job, but substitutes can be made up from strips of 3 mm thick steel strip. The clamps should be U-shaped with a distance of approximately 15 mm between the inner faces of each side of the clamp **(see illustration)**.

10 Bevel the edges of the clamps to make it easier to fit them. Have an assistant depress the clutch pedal fully and then fit each clamp securely over the edge of the clutch cover/plate assembly engaging them in the apertures spaced around the rim of the clutch cover. Turn the crankshaft by means of the pulley bolt to bring each clip location into view.

11 Once the clips have been fitted, release the clutch pedal.

12 Progressively loosen and remove each of the six bolts which hold the clutch cover to the flywheel **(see illustration)**.

13 Although positioning dowels are not used to locate the clutch cover to the flywheel, the coloured spot on the flywheel should be in alignment with the notch in the rim of the clutch cover.

14 Withdraw the clutch assembly downwards and out of the bellhousing. The pressure plate

5.7a Screwing bolt into input shaft

5.7b Withdrawing input shaft to stop

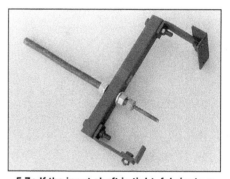

5.7c If the input shaft is tight, fabricate a tool similar to that shown . . .

5.7d . . . to disengage the shaft from the clutch

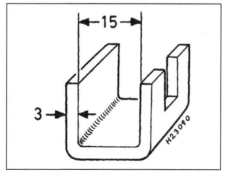

5.9 Clutch pressure plate retaining clamp dimensions (mm)

5.12 Unscrewing clutch cover bolts

5.14 Removing clutch with retaining clips fitted

can be compressed in a vice in order to be able to remove the clips **(see illustration)**.

Inspection

15 In the normal course of events, clutch dismantling and reassembly involves simply fitting a new clutch pressure plate, driven plate and release bearing. Under no circumstances should the diaphragm spring clutch unit be dismantled. If a fault develops in the pressure plate assembly, a new or exchange replacement unit must be fitted.

16 Do not attempt to reline a driven plate yourself, it is just not worth it, but obtain a new component. The necessity for renewing the plate will be apparent if the lining material has worn down to the rivets or the linings are oil stained. If the latter, rectify the faulty engine or transmission oil seal which must be the cause. The driven plate may also have broken torsion springs or worn hub splines.

17 If a new clutch is being fitted, it is false economy not to renew the release bearing at the same time (see Section 6). This will preclude having to replace it at a later date.

18 Check the machined faces of the flywheel and the pressure plate. If either is badly grooved it should be machined until smooth, or replaced with a new item. If the pressure plate is cracked or split it must be renewed.

Refitting

19 Some clutch assemblies are supplied already compressed with the retaining clips fitted. If this is not the case, the pressure plate should be compressed evenly in a vice; using protectors to prevent damage to the machined face of the plate. Alternatively, use a heavy bolt and nut with two metal strips having a hole drilled in them to do the job. Fit the clips.

20 Apply a smear of molybdenum disulphide grease to the splines of the driven plate hub and then offer the plate to the flywheel so that the greater projecting side of it is away from the flywheel. Hold the plate against the flywheel while the clutch pressure plate assembly (compressed) is offered into position.

21 Push the input shaft through the hub of the driven plate and engage its end in the pilot bearing in the end of the crankshaft. Note that it is not permissible to use hammer blows to assist in refitting the input shaft.

5.26 Applying sealant to end cover plug (4-speed transmission)

22 If the input shaft cannot be pushed home by hand, steady pressure should be exerted by means of a screw or hydraulic device. The special tool KM-564, is produced expressly for the purpose, but it should be possible to press the shaft into position using the improvised tool (or something similar) shown in **illustration 5.7c**. If the shaft is hammered home, transmission damage may result.

23 Bolt the clutch cover to the flywheel and tighten them to the specified torque.

24 Have your assistant depress the clutch pedal and then remove the temporary clips.

25 To the end of the input shaft, screw in the recessed screw and fit a new circlip.

26 On early models screw the plug into the transmission end cover, on four-speed transmissions apply a smear of sealant to the plug threads prior to installation. Tighten to the specified torque noting that the plug should not project more than 4.0 mm (0.16 in) from the face of the end cover when correctly fitted **(see illustration)**.

27 On later models, ensure that the end cover and transmission mating surfaces are clean and dry and fit a new gasket. Refit the cover and screw in the retaining bolts, making sure each one is fitted in its original location. Tighten the bolts evenly and progressively to the specified torque then reconnect the earth strap and securely tighten its retaining nut.

28 Check the clutch adjustment (Section 2).

29 Fit the cover plate to the flywheel housing.

30 Lower the front of the vehicle to the ground and check the transmission oil level as described in Chapter 1.

6.3a Withdrawing release lever shaft

Removal

1 Wear of the clutch release bearing is indicated by a squealing noise when the clutch pedal is depressed with the engine running.

2 To gain access to the release bearing, remove the clutch unit (Section 5).

3 After removing the clutch, undo the clamp bolt securing the release fork to the release lever pivot shaft. Disconnect the clutch cable from the release lever (Section 3), and then pull the release lever pivot shaft up and out of the housing and remove the release fork. Unscrew the three bolts securing the release bearing guide to the transmission and remove the guide. Prise the old (input shaft) seal out of the release bearing guide location. If required, the bushes supporting the release lever pivot can be drifted out of the case using a drift **(see illustrations)**.

Refitting

4 Refitting is the reverse of the removal procedure but note the following points:

a) After fitting a new input shaft seal to the release bearings guide fill the space between the lips of the seal with a good quality general purpose grease.

b) When fitting the new O-ring seal to the casing at the release bearing guide location do not use any grease or oil as this seal should be fitted dry.

c) Lightly smear the release bearing guide surface, on which the bearing slides with molybdenum disulphide grease and tighten the bolts securely.

d) If being renewed, drift the new release lever bushes into their housings, ensure that their locating tongues are engaged in the slots in the case, and coat the inner surfaces of the bushes with molybdenum disulphide grease.

e) Fit the release bearing and the release fork together and tighten the release fork clamp bolt to the specified torque.

f) Refit the clutch as described in Section 5.

g) Check the adjustment as described in Section 2.

6.3b Release lever shaft bushes

Chapter 7A
Manual transmission

Contents

Gearchange lever - removal and refitting .3
Gearchange lever reverse selector cable - removal and refitting 4
Gearchange linkage - removal, refitting and adjustment 5
General information 1
Oil seals - renewal 6
Reversing lamp switch - testing, removal and refitting 7
Speedometer drive - removal and refitting .8
Transmission - draining and refilling 2
Transmission - removal and refitting 9
Transmission oil level check .See Chapter 1
Transmission overhaul - general information 10

Degrees of difficulty

Easy, suitable for novice with little experience	Fairly easy, suitable for beginner with some experience	Fairly difficult, suitable for competent DIY mechanic	Difficult, suitable for experienced DIY mechanic	Very difficult, suitable for expert DIY or professional

Specifications

Type . . . . Four or five forward speeds (all with synchromesh) and reverse. Unit transversely mounted at front of car

Designation
1.3 up to 1982 . . . . F10 (4-speed)
1.3 from 1983 . . . . F10.4, F13.4 (4-speed) or F10.5, F13.5 (5-speed)
1.6, 1.8 and 2.0 . . . . F16, F16.4 (4-speed) or F16.5 (5-speed)

Torque wrench settings
	Nm	lbf ft
Differential cover plate bolts	30	22
Flywheel housing-to-engine bolts	75	55
Exhaust bracket to transmission casing	60	44
Mounting bracket bolts to transmission	30	22
Mounting bolts to bodyframe	40	29
Reverse lamp switch	20	15

1 General information

The transmission is contained in a cast-aluminium alloy casing bolted to the engine's left-hand end, and consists of the gearbox and final drive differential - often called a transaxle.

Drive is transmitted from the crankshaft via the clutch to the input shaft, which has a splined extension to accept the clutch friction plate, and rotates in sealed ball-bearings. From the input shaft, drive is transmitted to the output shaft, which rotates in a roller bearing at its right-hand end, and a sealed ball-bearing at its left-hand end. From the output shaft, the drive is transmitted to the differential crownwheel, which rotates with the differential case and planetary gears, thus driving the sun gears and driveshafts. The rotation of the planetary gears on their shaft allows the inner roadwheel to rotate at a slower speed than the outer roadwheel when the car is cornering.

The input and output shafts are arranged side by side, parallel to the crankshaft and driveshafts, so that their gear pinion teeth are in constant mesh. In the neutral position, the output shaft gear pinions rotate freely, so that drive cannot be transmitted to the crownwheel.

Gear selection is via a floor-mounted lever and selector rod mechanism. The selector rod causes the appropriate selector fork to move its respective synchro-sleeve along the shaft, to lock the gear pinion to the synchro-hub. Since the synchro-hubs are splined to the output shaft, this locks the pinion to the shaft, so that drive can be transmitted. To ensure that gear-changing can be made quickly and quietly, a synchro-mesh system is fitted to all forward gears, consisting of baulk rings and spring-loaded fingers, as well as the gear pinions and synchro-hubs. The synchro-mesh cones are formed on the mating faces of the baulk rings and gear pinions.

2 Transmission - draining and refilling

1 Since transmission oil draining and refilling is not specified by Vauxhall as a routine service operation, the transmission is regarded as a sealed unit and therefore has no drain plug. If, for any reason, it is wished to drain the oil, the differential cover plate must be removed as follows.
2 From underneath the vehicle, remove all traces of dirt from around the transmission differential cover plate.
3 Position a suitable container beneath the plate then slacken and remove the retaining bolts and allow the oil to drain into the container. Remove the cover plate and recover the gasket.
4 Once all the oil has drained, remove all traces of oil and dirt from the mating surfaces of the cover plate and transmission.

3.8 Later type gear lever-to-floor mounting

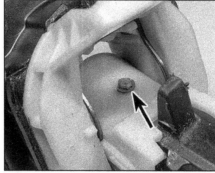

3.9a Remove the C-clip (arrowed) from the pin groove . . .

3.9b . . . withdraw the pin . . .

5 Fit a new gasket to the plate and refit the plate to the transmission. Tighten the plate retaining bolts evenly and progressively to the specified torque setting.
6 Fill the transmission with the specified type and quantity of oil via the breather/filler plug and check the oil level (Chapter 1).

3 Gearchange lever - removal and refitting

Removal

Early models

1 Set the gearchange lever in neutral then release the rubber boot at the base and slide it up the lever.
2 If a central console is fitted, it may be necessary to remove it for access, depending on type (see Chapter 11).
3 Extract the circlip from its groove in the housing.
4 Press the gearchange lever to the left-hand side and withdraw it.
5 If essential, the gearchange lever housing complete with insulator can be removed from the underside of the floor. Renew the complete assembly.
6 If the boot is to be renewed, the knob can be pulled off if it is first heated in hot water.

Later models

7 Proceed as described in paragraphs 1 and 2.

8 Undo the four selector unit-to-floor securing bolts and lift the lever assembly clear **(see illustration)**.
9 To remove the selector housing unit, prise free the C-clip, extract the pin and withdraw the housing unit from the lever bottom end **(see illustrations)**.
10 The selector lever ball rubber can be removed by prising it free from the groove in the ball **(see illustration)**.
11 The gear lever knob and rubber boot are removed in the manner described for earlier models (paragraph 6).
12 Removal and dismantling of the gearchange gate unit is possible as required, but take a note of the fitting orientation of any components removed to assist when reassembling.

Refitting

Early models

13 Refitting is a reversal of removal, but observe the following points:
 a) *Apply grease to the pivot ball and socket.*
 b) *Note that the tab on the underside of the boot is towards the front of the vehicle.*
 c) *When fitting the gear lever knob, align it with the stop on reverse gear sleeve.*

Later models

14 Refit in the reverse order of removal, observing the following points:
 a) *Lubricate the pivot ball and socket with grease.*

 b) *Ensure that the gear lever knob is correctly aligned and all gearchange control components are correctly orientated before refitting.*
 c) *When refitted, ensure that the alignment markings on the side of the selector housing and gate change unit align when the lever is in neutral (see illustration).*

4 Gearchange lever reverse selector cable - removal and refitting

Removal

1 The reverse blocker mechanism, which is released by lifting the collar on the gear lever when engaging reverse gear, is operated by a cable which runs inside the gear lever. If the cable breaks it may be renewed as follows, but check first that the necessary parts are available.
2 Remove the gear lever, as described in Section 3.
3 Pull the knob from the gear lever, first heating the knob in boiling water. Even after heating, it is likely that the knob will be destroyed during removal. Extract the spring from below the knob.
4 Remove the two grub screws from the top of the gear lever. The top screw has a recessed hexagonal head and is undone with an Allen key; the lower screw has a slotted

3.9c . . . and separate the lever from the housing (later models)

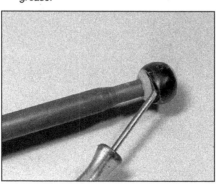

3.10 Rubber insulator removal from the selector lever ball (later models)

3.14 Alignment marks for neutral on lever and housing - arrowed (later models)

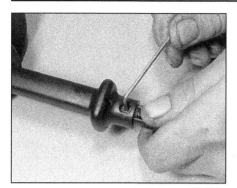

4.4 Removing a grub screw from the gear lever (early models)

4.5 Drive out the roll pins

5.4 Protective boot at base of gear lever

head and is undone with a small screwdriver **(see illustration)**.

5 Drive out the roll pins which secure the plastic coupling and shift finger to the gear lever. It is likely that the coupling will be destroyed during removal. Remove the cable and its end fitting **(see illustration)**.

Refitting

6 Refit in the reverse order to removal, using new roll pins and (where necessary) a new plastic coupling and gear lever knob. No adjustment procedure is described, so the position in which the cable is clamped by the grub screws will have to be determined by trial and error.

5 Gearchange linkage - removal, refitting and adjustment

Removal

1 Working at the transmission, slacken the pinch-bolt at the gearchange rod coupling.
2 Remove the screws which hold the gearchange rod protective housing and detach the rubber cover at the end of the housing.
3 Separate the base of the gearchange lever from the eye in the gearchange rod and then withdraw the linkage assembly from the vehicle.
4 Withdraw the bellows and boot from the protective housing **(see illustration)**.

5 The assembly may be further dismantled to renew worn components by driving out the retaining pin from the intermediate lever and control rod.
6 Tap the rod out of the lever.
7 The universal joint may be dismantled by grinding off the rivet heads.
8 Use a rod to remove the bushes from the protective housing.

Refitting

9 Commence reassembly by filling the protective housing sleeve bush grooves with grease and inserting the bushes into the housing.
10 Special pins with circlips are available to replace the original rivets when reassembling the universal joints.
11 Connect the intermediate lever to the control rod using a new pin, but make sure that it is aligned with the clamp as shown **(see illustration)**.
12 Fit the bellows and boot to the protective housing and apply silicone grease liberally inside the boot.
13 Slide the gearchange rod into the housing and fit to the floorpan.
14 Adjust the linkage as described below.

Adjustment

15 Set the gearchange lever in neutral.
16 If fitted, remove the centre console (see Chapter 11).
17 Slacken the pinch-bolt on the gearchange rod coupling **(see illustration)**.

18 Prise out the small blanking plug from the transmission cover.
19 Looking towards the front of the vehicle, grip the gearchange rod and twist it in an anti-clockwise direction until a 4.5 mm diameter twist drill can be inserted into the hole left by removal of the plug. Insert the drill until it fully enters the hole in the selector lever as shown **(see illustration)**.
20 The help of an assistant will now be required to withdraw the gearchange lever boot upwards and to move the lever across the neutral gate until it is aligned with the 1st/2nd (centre) point of the gate, up against the reverse stop.
21 Without moving the set position of the gearchange lever, tighten the rod coupling pinch-bolt.
22 Withdraw the twist drill and refit the plug. To prevent oil leakage when the vehicle is operating, it is vital that this plug seals perfectly, if not, renew it.
23 Refit the gear lever boot and the centre console.

6 Oil seals - renewal

Driveshaft oil seal

1 Position a suitable container beneath the transmission to catch any oil which may leak from the transmission during the following operation.

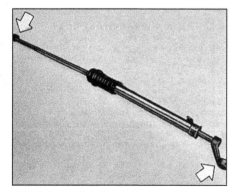

5.11 Intermediate lever to clamp alignment - arrowed

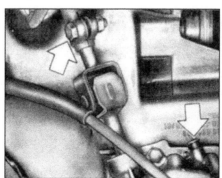

5.17 Transmission adjuster hole and clamp pinch-bolt - arrowed

5.19 Setting gearchange rod (shown with casing removed for clarity)

2 Working as described in Chapter 8, free the inner end of the driveshaft from the transmission and position it clear of the seal, noting that there is no need to unscrew the driveshaft retaining nut; the driveshaft can be left secured to the hub. Support the driveshaft to avoid placing any strain on the driveshaft joints or gaiters.

3 Carefully prise the oil seal out of the transmission using a large flat-bladed screwdriver.

4 Remove all traces of dirt from the area around the oil seal aperture then apply a smear of grease to the outer lip of the new oil seal. Fit the new seal into its aperture and drive it squarely into position using a suitable tubular drift (such as a socket) which bears only on the hard outer edge of the seal, until it abuts its locating shoulder.

5 Refit the driveshaft as described in Chapter 8.

6 Check and, if necessary top-up, the transmission oil level as described in Chapter 1.

Input shaft oil seal

7 Refer to Chapter 6, Section 6.

7 Reversing lamp switch - testing, removal and refitting

Testing

1 The reversing lamp circuit is controlled by a plunger-type switch that is screwed into the top of the transmission casing. If a fault develops in the circuit first ensure that the circuit fuse has not blown.

2 To test the switch, disconnect the wiring connector and use a multimeter (set to the resistance function) or a battery and bulb test circuit to check that there is continuity between the switch terminals only when reverse gear is selected. If this is not the case and there are no obvious breaks or other damage to the wires, the switch is faulty and must be renewed.

Removal

3 To improve access to the switch, remove the battery as described in Chapter 5.

4 Disconnect the wiring connector(s) from the switch then unscrew it from the transmission casing and remove it along with its sealing washer **(see illustration)**.

Refitting

5 Fit a new sealing washer to the switch then screw it back into position in the top of the transmission housing and tighten it to the specified torque setting. Reconnect the wiring connector(s) then refit the battery and test the operation of the circuit.

8 Speedometer drive - removal and refitting

Removal

1 Disconnect the speedometer cable from the transmission by unscrewing its knurled retaining ring.

2 Undo the retaining bolt and recover the speedometer drive retaining plate from the transmission housing.

3 Withdraw the speedometer drive assembly from the transmission.

4 Slide the drive gear out from its housing and remove the O-ring and seal from the housing.

Refitting

5 Press a new seal into the housing and fit a new O-ring to the housing groove. Apply a smear of oil to the seal and O-ring and slide the drive gear into position.

6 Refit the assembly to the transmission, making sure the drive gear engages correctly.

7 Refit the retaining plate, making sure it is correctly engaged with the drive gear, and securely tighten its retaining bolt.

8 Reconnect the speedometer cable.

9 Transmission - removal and refitting

Removal

1 Disconnect the clutch operating cable from the release lever.

2 Disconnect the leads from the reverse lamp switch.

3 Disconnect the gearchange rod by removing the bolt from the coupling clamp.

4 Disconnect the speedometer drive cable from the transmission casing by unscrewing the knurled ring or unbolting the retainer plate according to type.

5 Raise the front of the vehicle and support it securely on axle stands (see *"Jacking and Vehicle Support"*)..

6 Remove the left-hand front roadwheel.

7 Disconnect the earth strap which runs between the transmission and the bodyframe **(see illustration)**.

8 Remove the long exhaust pipe bracket from the transmission (if applicable).

9 Disconnect the anti-roll bar from the left-hand suspension lower control arm.

10 Unbolt the suspension control arm support, as described in Chapter 10. With the suspension arm and support suspended by the stub axle carrier balljoint, swivel the assembly to one side out of the way.

11 Release the driveshaft from the transmission using a suitable tool as described in Chapter 8. Anticipate some loss of oil as the driveshafts are released. Withdraw the left-hand driveshaft from the transmission by pulling it towards you.

12 Slide the input shaft out of engagement with the clutch plate as described in Chapter 6.

13 Take the weight of the engine on a hoist or jack. Place a jack, preferably of trolley type, under the transmission.

14 Disconnect the left rear mounting bracket from both the transmission case and the flexible mount **(see illustration)**.

15 Disconnect the left-hand front mounting bracket from the transmission case and the flexible mount.

16 Clear controls, cables and electrical leads away from the transmission casing.

17 Remove the transmission bellhousing-to-engine connecting bolts.

18 Unbolt and remove the cover plate from the lower part of the flywheel housing. This is the cover that faces towards the timing belt end of the engine.

19 Lower the transmission. The right-hand driveshaft will drop out, be ready to support it. Remove the transmission from under the vehicle.

7.4 Reversing lamp switch

9.7 Transmission earth strap

9.14 Transmission left-rear mounting bracket

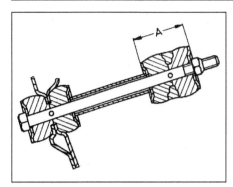

9.27 Anti-roll bar end fitting diagram
A = 38. mm (1.5 in)

20 Clean away external dirt. If overhaul is to be carried out, place the unit securely on a bench or other firm working surface.

Refitting

21 Manoeuvre the transmission under the vehicle and raise it on a jack to connect with the engine. If the clutch has been dismantled, ensure that the driven plate is centralised behind the clutch cover. As the transmission is raised, engage the right-hand driveshaft with it.
22 Insert the connecting bolts at the flywheel housing flange and tighten to the specified torque. Refit the flywheel cover plate.
23 Refit the front engine mountings followed by the rear ones.
24 Reconnect the driveshafts to the transmission case and secure their locking rings by applying a heavy drift to the driveshaft joint weld bead and then giving the drift a sharp blow with a hammer (refer to Chapter 8).
25 Refit the suspension control arm and support as described in Chapter 10.
26 Ensure that the control arm support bolts are cleaned of old thread sealant. Apply new sealant before tightening to the specified torque (Chapter 10).
27 Reconnect the anti-roll bar to the control arm. Do not overtighten the connecting bolt or nut, but only enough to maintain the dimension (A) as shown **(see illustration)**.
28 Push the input shaft into engagement with the clutch driven plate splined hub and fit all disturbed components as described in Chapter 6.
29 Reconnect the earth strap.
30 Refit the roadwheel.
31 Reconnect the reverse lamp switch leads, the clutch and speedometer cables.
32 Reconnect and adjust the gearchange control rod (Section 5).
33 Lower the vehicle to the floor.
34 Fill the transmission with the correct grade and quantity of oil.

10 Transmission overhaul - general information

Overhauling a manual transmission is a difficult and involved job for the DIY home mechanic. In addition to dismantling and reassembling many small parts, clearances must be precisely measured and, if necessary, changed by selecting shims and spacers. Internal transmission components are also often difficult to obtain and in many instances, extremely expensive. Because of this, if the transmission develops a fault or becomes noisy, the best course of action is to have the unit overhauled by a specialist repairer or to obtain an exchange reconditioned unit.

Nevertheless, it is not impossible for the more experienced mechanic to overhaul the transmission if the special tools are available and the job is done in a deliberate step-by-step manner so that nothing is overlooked.

The tools necessary for an overhaul include internal and external circlip pliers, bearing pullers, a slide hammer, a set of pin punches, a dial test indicator and possibly a hydraulic press. In addition, a large, sturdy workbench and a vice will be required.

During dismantling of the transmission, make careful notes of how each component is fitted to make reassembly easier and accurate.

Before dismantling the transmission, it will help if you have some idea what area is malfunctioning. Certain problems can be closely related to specific areas in the transmission which can make component examination and replacement easier. Refer to the Fault diagnosis Section at the end of this manual for more information.

Notes

Chapter 7B
Automatic transmission

Contents

Automatic transmission - removal and refitting 5
Automatic transmission fluid level check . . . . .See Chapter 1
Automatic transmission fluid renewal . . . . .See Chapter 1
Automatic transmission overhaul - general information 6
General information 1
Kickdown cable - removal, refitting and adjustment 2
Speed selector control cable - removal, refitting and adjustment . . .3
Starter inhibitor switch - adjustment 4

Degrees of difficulty

Easy, suitable for novice with little experience	Fairly easy, suitable for beginner with some experience	Fairly difficult, suitable for competent DIY mechanic	Difficult, suitable for experienced DIY mechanic	Very difficult, suitable for expert DIY or professional

Specifications

Type	General Motors Hydromatic Torque converter (fluid coupling) with chain drive to gear trains. Three forward and one reverse gear
Designation	125 THM

Torque wrench settings	Nm	lbf ft
Fluid pan bolts	16	12
Fluid cooling hose connections to transmission	38	28
Torque converter housing-to-engine bolts	75	55
Torque converter-to-driveplate bolts:		
1.3 litre models	65	48
All other models	60	44
Fluid cooling hose to cooler	22	16
Mounting bracket bolts to transmission	22	16
Mounting bolts to bodyframe	40	30

1 General information

The automatic transmission is of General Motors design and manufacture and is optionally available on most models. The unit provides three forward speeds and reverse with a "kickdown" facility. As with manual transmission, the differential and final drive are built into the transmission casing.

The main components are a torque converter (fluid coupling), which transmits power to the gear trains through a chain drive, and a hydraulic circuit which regulates the selection of gears, clutches and brakes according to speed and engine load. Due to the close tolerances to which the unit operates, cleanliness is absolutely essential whenever fluid is being added or any component removed. Entry of grit or dirt into the transmission will cause a malfunction of the valves and possible damage to the internal components.

The automatic transmission is a complex piece of equipment and the home mechanic should limit himself to undertaking the operations described in the following Sections. More extensive operations should be left to your dealer or automatic transmission specialist.

2 Kickdown cable - removal, refitting and adjustment

Removal

1 Remove the air cleaner from the carburettor (where necessary).
2 Disconnect the kickdown cable from the adjuster mechanism (A) by first relieving the spring pressure and then pulling out the securing pin - hook a piece of wire through the hole in the pin to pull it out if necessary **(see illustration)**. Prise the cupped end fitting (B) from the ball-stud on the lever.
3 Working at the transmission end of the cable, remove the locking bolt from the sleeve and pull the sleeve upwards. Disconnect the inner cable from the transmission.
4 Release the cable adjusting mechanism from its support bracket by depressing the lugs.

Refitting

5 Refit the cable by first connecting at the transmission, keeping the cable tight, and refitting the sleeve. The cable must be routed between the brake pipes at the master cylinder. The cable will not operate smoothly if routed under the brake pipes.

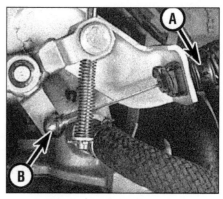

2.2 Kickdown cable connection at carburettor

A Cable adjuster   *B Ball cap end fitting*

6 Push the cable adjusting mechanism into its support bracket, ensuring that the lugs locate correctly.
7 Reconnect the cable to the carburettor and adjusted it as follows.

Adjustment

8 First depress the accelerator pedal until it just contacts the kickdown switch. Check that in this position the throttle valve plate is fully open. If not adjust the throttle cable at the carburettor. Now release the accelerator pedal, and check that there is no free play in the cable at this idle position. If the cable is slack, adjustment can be made using the adjuster on the pedal mechanism.
9 Slowly depress the accelerator until the kickdown switch has been actuated. The kickdown cable adjustment mechanism will automatically set itself - operation of the ratchet should confirm this. Adjustment will now remain automatically in this position.
10 Release the accelerator pedal, and refit the air cleaner to the carburettor.

3 Speed selector control cable - removal, refitting and adjustment

Removal

1 From the centre console extract the four retaining screws, lift the selector lever cover, turn it and remove it; disconnecting the lamp electrical lead as it is withdrawn.
2 Extract the two console securing screws, set the selector lever in "P" and remove the console.
3 Working at the transmission, release the selector cable by pulling-off the retaining clip (A) and then unscrewing the cable from the support (B) **(see illustration)**.
4 Working inside the vehicle, disconnect the cable from the selector hand control lever.
5 Release the cable from the clamp (A), loosen and remove sleeve (B) **(see illustration)**.
6 Withdraw the cable assembly by pulling it into the engine compartment.

Refitting

7 Fitting a new cable is a reversal of the removal operations, but observe the following points: Check that the cable grommet at the bulkhead makes a good seal. Set the cable in its sleeve so that it is not under tension. When connecting the cable make sure that the hand control lever is in "P".

Adjustment

8 With the help of an assistant check that with the hand control lever in each position, the lever on the transmission can be felt to be positively positioned in its correct detent and not under any tension. Where this is not the case, adjust the cable at (A) adjacent to the hand control lever **(see illustration 3.5)**.
9 Refit the centre console and selector lever cover.

3.3 Selector cable retaining clip (A) and support (B)

4 Starter inhibitor switch - adjustment

1 The starter inhibitor switch should prevent the starter motor operating in any selector position other than "N" or "P". If this is not the case, adjust as follows.
2 Remove the selector lever cover, which is secured by four screws, and select "P".
3 Loosen the two screws which secure the starter inhibitor switch. Turn the switch against the direction of travel of the lever until the engine can be started.
4 Tighten the screws and check that the engine can only be started in positions "P" and "N". If the correct adjustment is difficult to achieve, place a washer of thickness 1 to 2 mm (0.04 to 0.08 in) under the switch rear mounting bracket, then try again.
5 Refit the selector lever cover when adjustment is correct.

5 Automatic transmission - removal and refitting

Removal

1 Removal of the automatic transmission together with the engine is described in Chapter 2. To remove the transmission independently, proceed in the following way.
2 Disconnect and remove the battery.
3 Disconnect the earth strap from the transmission.
4 Remove the kickdown cable (Section 2).
5 Disconnect the selector cable from the lever on the transmission.
6 Extract the retaining clip and pull the lever from the transmission.
7 Unscrew the selector cable support bracket, there is no need to disconnect the cable from the bracket.
8 Unscrew and remove the bolts which connect the torque converter housing to the engine.
9 Remove the remaining bolt and lift away the starter motor and tie it up with a piece of wire. There is no need to disconnect the electrical leads.

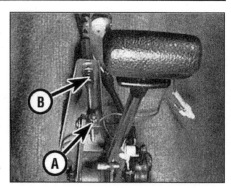

3.5 Selector cable attachment at hand control lever

A Clamp   *B Sleeve*

10 Disconnect the speedometer cable from the transmission.
11 Remove the fluid dipstick.
12 Raise the front of the car sufficiently high so that the transmission will pass out under the front end when removing it.
13 Remove the front left-hand roadwheel.
14 Attach a suitable hoist to the engine or support it on a jack.
15 Disconnect the left rear transmission to bodymember mounting.
16 Disconnect the anti-roll bar from the left-hand suspension lower arm.
17 Disconnect the left-hand lower suspension control arm support from the bodyframe as described in Chapter 10.
18 Disconnect the left-hand driveshaft from the transmission as described in Chapter 8.
19 Release the right-hand driveshaft from the transmission as described in Chapter 8.
20 Disconnect the oil cooler lines at the transmission end and plug the hoses.
21 Unbolt and remove the torque converter cover plate.
22 Unscrew the driveplate-to-torque converter connecting bolts. Jam the starter ring gear while releasing each bolt. The driveplate will have to be rotated to bring each bolt head to an accessible position. Do this by turning the crankshaft pulley or torsional damper bolt. New bolts must be fitted on reassembly.
23 Unbolt and remove the left-hand front mounting.
24 Unbolt the exhaust bracket from the transmission and swing the bracket upwards.
25 Pull out the dipstick guide/filler tube. Be prepared for some loss of fluid.
26 Support the transmission on a jack, preferably of trolley type.
27 Working under the vehicle, disconnect the left-hand rear mounting bracket from the bodyframe member, also the two bolts from the engine mounting bracket.
28 Pull the transmission from the engine to clear the positioning dowels and then lower the transmission jack. Withdraw the transmission from under the front of the vehicle.

Refitting

29 Refitting is a reversal of removal, noting the following points.

a) *Before offering the transmission to the engine, check that the torque converter is fully meshed with the oil pump. To do this, measure (A) as shown in the diagram. This should be between 9.00 and 10.00 mm. If it is not, turn the converter at the same time applying hand pressure* **(see illustration)**.

b) *Apply a smear of molybdenum disulphide grease to the torque converter pilot spigot.*

c) *When bolting the torque converter to the driveplate, align the white spot on the plate with the coloured spot on the torque converter.*

d) *When connecting the kickdown cable, first attach it to the transmission. Adjust as described in Section 2.*

e) *Fill the transmission with oil (Chapter 1).*

f) *Check all nuts and bolts have been tightened to the specified torque and that thread locking compound has been applied to the threads (clean) of the suspension control arm support bolts.*

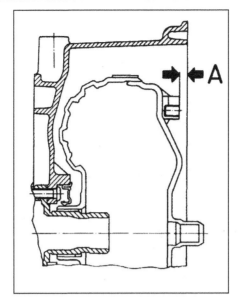

5.29 Torque converter installation diagram
A = 9. to 10. mm

6 Automatic transmission overhaul
- general information

1 In the event of a fault occurring on the transmission, it is first necessary to determine whether it is of an electrical, mechanical or hydraulic nature and to do this special test equipment is required. It is therefore essential to have the work carried out by a Vauxhall dealer if a transmission fault is suspected.

2 Do not remove the transmission from the car for possible repair before professional fault diagnosis has been carried out, since most tests require the transmission to be in the vehicle.

Notes

Chapter 8
Driveshafts

Contents

Driveshaft - removal and refitting 2
Driveshaft gaiter - renewal 3
Driveshaft gaiter check . . . . .See Chapter 1
Driveshaft joint - renewal 4
Driveshaft overhaul - general information .5
General information 1

Degrees of difficulty

Easy, suitable for novice with little experience	Fairly easy, suitable for beginner with some experience	Fairly difficult, suitable for competent DIY mechanic	Difficult, suitable for experienced DIY mechanic	Very difficult, suitable for expert DIY or professional

Specifications

Torque wrench settings	Nm	lbf ft
Driveshaft to hub carrier:		
Stage 1	100	74
Slacken then Stage 2	20	15
Stage 3*	Tighten through a further 90°	
Suspension lower arm bolts:		
Smaller bolts	110	81
Large centre bolts	130	96
Roadwheel bolts	90	66

Turn nut back if necessary to align split pin hole. Do not tighten to align

1 General information

Drive is transmitted from the differential to the front wheels by means of two solid steel driveshafts of unequal length. The right-hand driveshaft is longer than the left-hand due to the position of the transmission.

Both driveshafts are splined at their outer ends to accept the wheel hubs and are threaded so that each hub can be fastened by a large nut. The inner end of each driveshaft is splined to accept the differential sun gear.

Constant velocity (CV) joints are fitted to each end of the driveshafts to ensure that the smooth and efficient transmission of drive at all the angles possible as the roadwheels move up and down with the suspension, and as they turn from side to side under steering. Both inner and outer constant velocity joints are of the ball-and-cage type.

2 Driveshaft - removal and refitting

Removal

1 Raise the front of the vehicle and support it securely.

2 Remove the front roadwheel.

3 Extract the split pin from the castellated nut or nut lock at the end of the driveshaft. Unscrew the nut. This nut is very tight and will require the use of a long knuckle bar to release it. To prevent the driveshaft turning, have an assistant apply the brake pedal or bolt a bar to two of the wheel bolt holes as shown **(see illustration)**. There is no need to remove the brake caliper.

4 Disconnect the anti-roll bar from the suspension lower control arm.

5 Disconnect the suspension lower control arm support from the bodyframe side-member

(Chapter 10) and, with it suspended by its balljoint, swivel the control arm aside.

6 A tool will now be required for insertion between the transmission casing and the inner driveshaft joint. In the absence of the official tool a flat steel bar with a good chamfer on

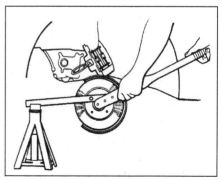

2.3 Releasing a driveshaft nut

2.6a Suitable driveshaft releasing tool

2.6b Releasing a driveshaft from the differential

2.7 Driveshaft released from hub carrier

one end will serve as a substitute. Drive the tool into the gap between the joint and casing to release the shaft snap-ring from the differential. Be prepared for some loss of oil and plug the hole (even with a piece of rag) to prevent loss of oil and entry of dirt **(see illustrations)**.

7 It should now be possible to push the driveshaft out of the hub using finger pressure. If it is not, use a hub puller **(see illustration)**.

8 When removing the left-hand driveshaft, it may be found difficult to engage a suitable tool to release it from the transmission. In this case, apply a long steel rod to the edge of the joint and drive it out.

9 On models produced after October 1982, shafts are fitted to 1.6, 1.8 and 2.0 models with automatic transmission which incorporate a modified inboard joint **(see illustration)**. This type of joint does not incorporate a stop to restrict the sliding travel within the joint. *Great care must therefore be taken when removing or handling this type of driveshaft not to pull on the shaft, or the joint members will become separated and the complete shaft ruined.*

10 On 1.6, 1.8 and 2.0 models with manual transmission, the longer right-hand driveshaft has a two-part weight fitted to act as a torsional vibration damper. If this is removed for any reason, it is important that it is refitted so that the distance between the inner end of the outer joint gaiter and the outer face of the weight is 260 mm (10.24 in).

11 Do not move the vehicle on its wheels with one or both driveshafts removed from their hubs. If this precaution is not observed, the front wheel bearings may be damaged.

12 The driveshaft-to-hub nut should be renewed every time it is disturbed.

Refitting

13 Before refitting a driveshaft, make sure that the contact surfaces of the shaft joint and hub bearing are absolutely clean. Apply some grease to the shaft splines and insert into the hub carrier. Screw on the shaft nut finger tight. Fit a new snap-ring to the inboard end of the driveshaft **(see illustrations)**.

14 Insert the inboard end of the driveshaft into the transmission as far as it will go **(see illustration)**.

15 Now apply a screwdriver to the weld bead of the inboard joint, **not** the metal cover, and drive the driveshaft into the differential until the retaining snap-ring engages positively. Pull on the driveshaft to check the engagement **(see illustration)**.

16 Reconnect the suspension arm and the anti-roll bar as described in Chapter 10 and tighten all nuts and bolts to the specified torque.

17 Tighten the new driveshaft/hub nut to the specified torque in stages (see Specifications).

18 Fit the nut lock (where installed) and insert a new split pin. Bend over the ends of the pin.

19 Fit the roadwheel and lower the vehicle to the ground.

20 Top-up the transmission oil (Chapter 1).

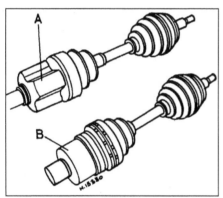

2.9 Driveshaft inboard joint comparison on automatic transmission models

A From 1983   B Earlier models

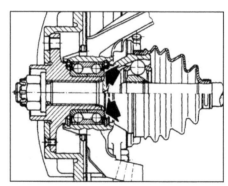

2.13a Sectional view of front hub
Clean the surfaces indicated

2.13b Driveshaft inboard joint snap-ring (arrowed)

2.14 Inserting driveshaft into transmission

2.15 Securing driveshaft joint to transmission

3.1 Driveshaft inboard joint showing gaiter retaining clips (arrowed)

3 Driveshaft gaiter - renewal

1 With the driveshaft removed from the vehicle as described in the preceding Section, remove the retaining clips and slide the gaiter from the joint **(see illustration)**.
2 Expand the retaining circlip and remove the joint from the splines of the driveshaft.
3 Slide the defective gaiter from the driveshaft.
4 Clean away the old grease from the joint and repack liberally with the specified grease. If excessively worn or damaged, a driveshaft joint must be renewed as a unit (Section 4).

5 Slide the new gaiter onto the shaft so that the smaller diameter opening is located in the groove on the driveshaft.
6 Refit the joint so that the retaining circlip engages in its groove, then slide the gaiter over the joint and squeeze them to expel as much air as possible.
7 Fit new gaiter retaining clips. There are many suitable types available, but those used as original equipment will require the use of special pliers to tighten them.

4 Driveshaft joint - renewal

1 A worn driveshaft joint cannot be overhauled, only renewed as a complete assembly. Remove the driveshaft (Section 2).
2 Release the securing band and slide the gaiter off the worn joint.
3 Expand the circlip which secures the joint to the driveshaft **(see illustration)**.
4 Using a plastic-faced hammer, tap the joint from the driveshaft **(see illustration)**.
5 Tap on the new joint until the securing circlip engages in its groove.
6 Repack the joint with the specified grease.
7 Refit the gaiter as described in the preceding Section.
8 Fit the driveshaft to the vehicle.

5 Driveshaft overhaul - general information

1 If any of the checks described in Chapter 1 reveal wear in any driveshaft joint, first remove the roadwheel trim or centre cap (as appropriate).
2 If the split pin is in position, the driveshaft nut should be correctly tightened. If in doubt remove the split pin then slacken the nut and tighten it through all the stages listed in the Specifications at the start of this Chapter. Once tightened, secure the nut in position with a new split pin then refit the centre cap or trim. Repeat this check on the remaining driveshaft nut.
3 Road test the vehicle and listen for a metallic clicking from the front as the vehicle is driven slowly in a circle on full lock. If a clicking noise is heard this indicates wear in the outer constant velocity joint. This means that the joint must be renewed; reconditioning is not possible.
4 If vibration, consistent with road speed, is felt through the car when accelerating, there is a possibility of wear in the inner constant velocity joints.
5 To check the joints for wear, remove the driveshafts, then dismantle them as described in Sections 3 and 4; if any wear or free play is found, the affected joint must be renewed.

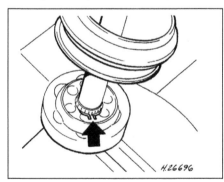

4.3 Driveshaft joint retaining circlip - arrowed

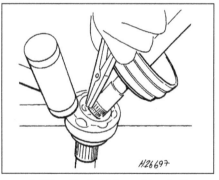

4.4 Tapping joint from driveshaft

Notes

Chapter 9
Braking system

Contents

Brake light switch - removal and refitting .20
Brake pedal - removal and refitting 19
Brake pedal remote control assembly (pre-1985 models) - removal
  and refitting 14
Brake pedal remote control rod (pre-1985 models) - removal and
  refitting 15
Front brake caliper - removal, overhaul and refitting 8
Front brake disc - inspection removal and refitting 6
Front brake pad wear check . . . . .See Chapter 1
Front brake pads - renewal 4
General description 1
Handbrake - adjustment . . . . .See Chapter 1
Handbrake cables - renewal 16
Handbrake lever - removal, overhaul and refitting 17
Handbrake warning light switch - removal and refitting 18
Hydraulic fluid level check . . . . .See "Weekly checks"
Hydraulic fluid renewal . . . . .See Chapter 1
Hydraulic pipes and hoses - renewal 3
Hydraulic system - bleeding 2
Master cylinder - removal, overhaul and refitting 10
Pressure regulating valves - testing, removal and refitting 11
Rear brake drum - removal, inspection and refitting 7
Rear brake shoe wear check . . . . .See Chapter 1
Rear brake shoes - renewal 5
Rear brake wheel cylinder - removal, overhaul and refitting 9
Vacuum servo unit (booster) - testing, removal and refitting 13
Vacuum servo unit hose - renewal 12

Degrees of difficulty

Easy, suitable for novice with little experience	Fairly easy, suitable for beginner with some experience	Fairly difficult, suitable for competent DIY mechanic	Difficult, suitable for experienced DIY mechanic	Very difficult, suitable for expert DIY or professional

Specifications

Front brakes

Type	Disc, with single piston sliding caliper
Disc diameter:	
2.0 litre models with 20 SEH engine	256 mm
All other models	236 mm
Disc thickness:	
New:	
1.3 and 1.6 litre models	12.7 mm
1.8 litre models	20.0 mm
2.0 litre models:	
20NE engine	20.0 mm
20SEH engine	24.0 mm
Minimum thickness (after refinishing*):	
1.3 and 1.6 litre models	10.7 mm
1.8 litre models	18.0 mm
2.0 litre models:	
20NE engine	18.0 mm
20SEH engine	22.0 mm
Maximum disc run-out	0.1 mm
Brake pad thickness (including backing plate):	
New	15.5 to 15.9 mm
Minimum	7.0 mm

*When this dimension is reached, only one more set of brake pads are permissible, then renew the discs

Rear brakes

Type:	
Pre-1984 models	Single leading shoe drum
1984 onwards models	Self-adjusting single leading shoe drum
Drum diameter:	
New:	
Saloon and Hatchback	200 mm
Estate	230 mm
Maximum diameter:	
Saloon and Hatchback	201 mm
Estate	231 mm
Maximum drum out-of-round	0.1 mm
Minimum friction material-to-rivet head depth	0.5 mm

Torque wrench settings

	Nm	lbf ft
Master cylinder stop bolt	6	4
Vacuum servo unit to support bracket	18	13
Vacuum servo to bulkhead	18	13
Pressure regulator to master cylinder:		
GMF type	40	30
ATE type	12	9
Caliper mounting bolts	95	70
Roadwheel bolts	90	66
Bleed screw	9	7
Caliper banjo union hollow bolt	25	18
Brake pedal support bracket to bulkhead	20	15
Pedal cross-shaft nut	18	13
Rear wheel cylinder to backplate	9	7
Master cylinder mounting nuts	18	13
Vacuum servo union nut to manifold	15	11
Hydraulic pipeline union nuts	11	8
Handbrake cable locknut	20	15
Handbrake lever to floor	20	15

1 General description

The braking system is of the servo-assisted, dual circuit hydraulic type. The arrangement of the hydraulic system is such that each circuit operates one front and one rear brake from a tandem master cylinder. Under normal circumstances both circuits operate in unison. However, in the event of hydraulic failure in one circuit, full braking force will still be available at two wheels.

All models were equipped with front disc brakes and rear drum brakes.

The front disc brakes are actuated by single piston sliding type calipers which ensure that equal pressure is applied to each disc pad.

The rear drum brakes incorporate leading and trailing shoes which are actuated by twin piston wheel cylinders. On early (pre-1984) models, the rear brakes require regular adjustment to operate correctly. On later (1984 onwards) models, a self-adjust mechanism is incorporated to automatically compensate for brake shoe wear. As the brake shoe linings wear, the footbrake operation automatically operates the adjuster mechanism which effectively lengthens the shoe strut and repositions the brake shoes to remove the lining to drum clearance.

Pressure regulating valves are screwed into the master cylinder ports to control the pressure applied to the rear brakes. These valves are non-adjustable.

The handbrake provides an independent mechanical means of rear brake application.

Note: *When servicing any part of the system, work carefully and methodically; also observe scrupulous cleanliness when overhauling any part of the hydraulic system. Always renew components (in axle sets, where applicable) if in doubt about their condition, and use only genuine replacement parts, or at least those of known good quality. Note the warnings given in 'Safety first' and at relevant points in this Chapter concerning the dangers of asbestos dust and hydraulic fluid.*

2 Hydraulic system - bleeding

⚠️ *Warning: Hydraulic fluid is poisonous; wash off immediately and thoroughly in the case of skin contact and seek immediate medical advice if any fluid is swallowed or gets into the eyes. Certain types of hydraulic fluid are inflammable and may ignite when allowed into contact with hot components; when servicing any hydraulic system it is safest to assume that the fluid is inflammable and to take precautions against the risk of fire as though it is petrol that is being handled. Hydraulic fluid is also an effective paint stripper and will attack plastics; if any is spilt, it should be washed off immediately using copious quantities of fresh water. Finally, it is hygroscopic (it absorbs moisture from the air) - old fluid may be contaminated and unfit for further use. When topping-up or renewing the fluid, always use the recommended type and ensure that it comes from a freshly opened sealed container.*

General

1 The correct operation of any hydraulic system is only possible after removing all air from the components and circuit; this is achieved by bleeding the system.

2 During the bleeding procedure, add only clean, unused hydraulic fluid of the recommended type; never re-use fluid that has already been bled from the system. Ensure that sufficient fluid is available before starting work.

3 If there is any possibility of incorrect fluid being already in the system, the brake components and circuit must be flushed completely with uncontaminated, correct fluid and new seals should be fitted to the various components.

4 If hydraulic fluid has been lost from the system, or air has entered, because of a leak ensure that the fault is cured before proceeding further.

5 Park the vehicle on level ground, switch off the engine and select first or reverse gear, then chock the wheels and release the handbrake.

6 Check that all pipes and hoses are secure, unions tight and bleed screws closed. Clean any dirt from around the bleed screws.

7 Unscrew the master cylinder reservoir cap and top the master cylinder reservoir up to the 'MAX' level line; refit the cap loosely and remember to maintain the fluid level at least above the 'MIN' level line throughout the procedure or there is a risk of further air entering the system.

8 There are a number of one-man, do-it-yourself brake bleeding kits currently available from motor accessory shops. It is recommended that one of these kits is used whenever possible as they greatly simplify the bleeding operation and also reduce the risk of expelled air and fluid being drawn back into the system. If such a kit is not available the basic (two-man) method must be used which is described in detail below.

9 If a kit is to be used, prepare the vehicle as described previously and follow the kit manufacturer's instructions as the procedure may vary slightly according to the type being used; generally they are as outlined below in the relevant sub-section.

10 Whichever method is used, the same sequence must be followed (paragraphs 11 and 12) to ensure that the removal of all air from the system.

Bleeding sequence

11 If the system has been only partially disconnected and suitable precautions were taken to minimise fluid loss, it should be necessary only to bleed that part of the system (ie. the primary or secondary circuit).

12 If the complete system is to be bled, then it should be done working in the following sequence.

a) Left-hand rear brake.
b) Right-hand front brake.
c) Right-hand rear brake.
d) Left-hand front brake.

Bleeding - basic (two-man) method

13 Collect a clean glass jar, a suitable length of plastic or rubber tubing which is a tight fit over the bleed screw and a ring spanner to fit the screw. The help of an assistant will also be required.

14 Remove the dust cap from the first screw in the sequence. Fit the spanner and tube to the screw, place the other end of the tube in the jar and pour in sufficient fluid to cover the end of the tube.

15 Ensure that the master cylinder reservoir fluid level is maintained at least above the `MIN' level line throughout the procedure.

16 Have the assistant fully depress the brake pedal several times to build up pressure, then maintain it on the final stroke.

17 While pedal pressure is maintained, unscrew the bleed screw (approximately one turn) and allow the compressed fluid and air to flow into the jar. The assistant should maintain pedal pressure, following it down to the floor if necessary and should not release it until instructed to do so. When the flow stops, tighten the bleed screw again, release the pedal slowly and recheck the reservoir fluid level.

18 Repeat the steps given in paragraphs 16 and 17 until the fluid emerging from the bleed screw is free from air bubbles. If the master cylinder has been drained and refilled and air is being bled from the first screw in the sequence, allow approximately five seconds between cycles for the master cylinder passages to refill.

19 When no more air bubbles appear, tighten the bleed screw securely, remove the tube and spanner and refit the dust cap. Do not overtighten the bleed screw.

20 Repeat the procedure on the remaining screws in the sequence until all air is removed from the system and the brake pedal feels firm again.

Bleeding - using a one-way valve kit

21 As their name implies, these kits consist of a length of tubing with a one-way valve fitted to prevent expelled air and fluid being drawn back into the system; some kits include a translucent container which can be positioned so that the air bubbles can be more easily seen flowing from the end of the tube.

22 The kit is connected to the bleed screw, which is then opened. The user returns to the driver's seat and depresses the brake pedal with a smooth, steady stroke and slowly releases it; this is repeated until the expelled fluid is clear of air bubbles.

23 Note that these kits simplify work so much that it is easy to forget the master cylinder reservoir fluid level; ensure that this is maintained at least above the `MIN' level line at all times.

Bleeding - using a pressure bleeding kit

24 These kits are usually operated by the reservoir of pressurised air contained in the spare tyre, although note that it will probably be necessary to reduce the pressure to a lower limit than normal; refer to the instructions supplied with the kit.

25 By connecting a pressurised, fluid-filled container to the master cylinder reservoir, bleeding can be carried out simply by opening each screw in turn (in the specified sequence) and allowing the fluid to flow out until no more air bubbles can be seen in the expelled fluid.

26 This method has the advantage that the large reservoir of fluid provides an additional safeguard against air being drawn into the system during bleeding.

27 Pressure bleeding is particularly effective when bleeding `difficult' systems or when bleeding the complete system at the time of routine fluid renewal.

All methods

28 When bleeding is complete and firm pedal feel is restored, wash off any spilt fluid, tighten the bleed screws securely and refit their dust caps.

29 Check the hydraulic fluid level and top-up if necessary as described in "Weekly checks".

30 Discard any hydraulic fluid that has been bled from the system; it will not be fit for re-use.

31 Check the feel of the brake pedal. If it feels at all spongy, air must still be present in the system and further bleeding is required. Failure to bleed satisfactorily after a reasonable repetition of the bleeding procedure may be due to worn master cylinder seals.

3 Hydraulic pipes and hoses - renewal

Note: *Before starting work, refer to the note at the beginning of Section 2 concerning the dangers of hydraulic fluid.*

1 If any pipe or hose is to be renewed, minimise fluid loss by removing the master cylinder reservoir cap and then tightening it down onto a piece of polythene to obtain an airtight seal. Alternatively flexible hoses can be sealed, if required, using a proprietary brake hose clamp, while metal brake pipe unions can be plugged (if care is taken not to allow dirt into the system) or capped immediately they are disconnected. Place a wad of rag under any union that is to be disconnected to catch any spilt fluid.

2 If a flexible hose is to be disconnected, unscrew the brake pipe union nut before removing the spring clip which secures the hose to its mounting bracket.

3 To unscrew the union nuts it is preferable to obtain a brake pipe spanner of the correct size; these are available from most large motor accessory shops. Failing this a close-fitting open-ended spanner will be required, though if the nuts are tight or corroded their flats may be rounded-off if the spanner slips. In such a case a self-locking wrench is often the only way to unscrew a stubborn union, but it follows that the pipe and the damaged nuts must be renewed on reassembly. Always clean a union and surrounding area before disconnecting it. If disconnecting a component with more than one union make a careful note of the connections before disturbing any of them.

4 If a brake pipe is to be renewed it can be obtained, cut to length and with the union nuts and end flares in place, from Vauxhall/Opel dealers. All that is then necessary is to bend it to shape, following the line of the original, before fitting it to the car. Alternatively, most motor accessory shops can make up brake pipes from kits, but this requires very careful measurement of the original to ensure that the replacement is of the correct length. The safest answer is usually to take the original to the shop as a pattern.

5 On refitting, do not overtighten the union nuts. It is not necessary to exercise brute force to obtain a sound joint.

6 Ensure that the pipes and hoses are correctly routed with no kinks and that they are secured in the clips or brackets provided. After fitting, remove the polythene from the reservoir and bleed the hydraulic system as described in Section 2. Wash off any spilt fluid and check carefully for fluid leaks.

4 Front brake pads - renewal

Warning: Renew both sets of front brake pads at the same time - never renew the pads on only one wheel as uneven braking may result. Note that the dust created by wear of the pads may contain asbestos, which is a health hazard. Never blow it out with compressed air and don't inhale any of it. An approved filtering mask should be worn when working on the brakes. DO NOT use petroleum-based solvents to clean brake parts. Use brake cleaner or methylated spirit only.

1 Raise the front of the vehicle. If the roadwheels have been balanced on the vehicle (new vehicles are balanced this way in production) then mark the relative position of the roadwheel to the hub so that it can be aligned correctly when refitting.

2 Inspect the thickness of the friction material on each pad. If any one is at or below the

4.4 Removing a disc pad spring

4.5 Outboard disc pad partially withdrawn

4.6 Withdrawing the inboard disc pad

specified minimum, renew the pads as an axle set (four pads) in the following way.

3 Drive out the pad retaining pins by applying a punch to their inboard ends.

4 Remove the springs **(see illustration)**.

5 Using a pair of pliers, withdraw the outboard pad **(see illustration)**.

6 Remove the inboard pad. If it is very tight, move the pad sideways slightly to depress the caliper piston **(see illustration)**.

7 In order to accommodate the new thicker pads, the caliper piston must be depressed fully into its cylinder using a flat bar of metal such as a tyre lever. The action of depressing the piston will cause the fluid in the reservoir to rise, so anticipate this by syphoning some off using an old (clean) hydrometer or similar.

8 Brush out the jaws of the caliper, *taking care not to inhale the dust*.

9 Insert the pads, making sure that the lining side is against the disc. When fitting disc pads supplied by the vehicle manufacturer, it may be found that two pads out of the four have white marks on their backing plates. Where this is the case, the pads with the marks should be fitted to the piston sides of the calipers. On later ATE type brake units, a shim may be fitted between the inner brake pad and the caliper piston. Where applicable, ensure that the shim is inserted with the inner pad **(see illustration)**.

10 Locate the spreader springs and drive in the retaining pins **(see illustrations)**.

11 Repeat the operations on the opposite brake.

12 Refit the roadwheels and lower the vehicle.

13 Apply the footbrake hard several times to position the pads against the discs.

14 Top-up the fluid reservoir to the correct level.

15 New brake pads need to be carefully bedded in and, where possible, heavy braking should be avoided during the first 120 miles (200 km).

5 Rear brake shoes - renewal

⚠️ *Warning: Brake shoes must be renewed on both rear wheels at the same time - never renew the shoes on only one wheel as uneven braking may result. Also, the dust created by wear of the shoes may contain asbestos, which is a health hazard. Never blow it out with compressed air and don't inhale any of it. An approved filtering mask should be worn when working on the brakes. DO NOT use petroleum based solvents to clean brake parts. Use brake cleaner or methylated spirit only.*

1 Remove the brake drum as described in Section 7.

2 Working carefully and taking the necessary precautions, remove all traces of brake dust from the brake drum, backplate and shoes.

3 Measure the depth from the friction material to each of the rivets. If this is equal or less than the specified minimum, all four shoes must be renewed as a set. Also, the shoes should be renewed if any are fouled with oil or grease; there is no satisfactory way of degreasing friction material once contaminated.

4 If any of the brake shoes are worn unevenly or fouled with oil or grease, trace and rectify the cause before reassembly. If the shoes are to be renewed proceed as described below. If all is well refit the drums as described in Section 7.

Early (pre-1984) models with adjustable rear brakes

5 Note the location and orientation of all components before dismantling, as an aid to reassembly.

6 Disconnect the upper shoe return spring using a pair of pliers.

7 Remove the shoe steady clips. These are of spring wire type, the ends of which should be compressed to release the clip from the brake backplate **(see illustration)**.

8 Pull the shoes apart until they can be released from the bottom anchorage.

9 Detach the shoe lower return spring and remove the strut from between the shoes **(see illustration)**.

10 Disconnect the end of the handbrake cable from the lever on the brake shoe and withdraw the shoes.

11 Although linings are available separately (without shoes), renewal of the shoes

4.9 Inner disc pad and shim - ATE type brake unit

4.10a Inserting disc pad pin

4.10b Disc pads reassembled

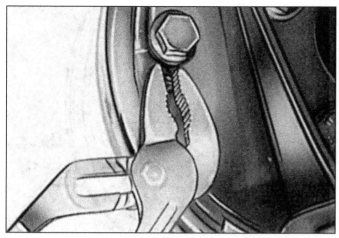

5.7 Compressing shoe steady spring - early models

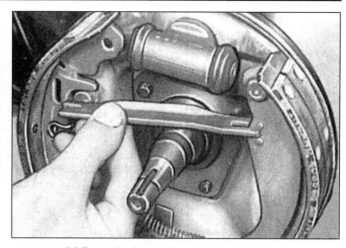

5.9 Removing brake shoe strut - early models

complete with linings is to be preferred, unless the necessary skills and equipment are available to fit new linings to the old shoes.

12 Examine the return springs. If they are distorted, or if they have seen extensive service, renewal is advisable. Weak springs may cause the brakes to bind.

13 If a new handbrake operating lever was not supplied with the new shoes (where applicable), transfer the lever from the old shoes. The lever may be secured with a pin and circlip, or by a rivet, which will have to be drilled out. It may also be necessary to transfer the adjusting lever pivot pin and clip from the original front shoe to the new shoe.

14 Peel back the rubber protective caps and check the wheel cylinder for fluid leaks or other damage and that both cylinder pistons are free to move easily.

15 Prior to installation clean the backplate and apply a thin smear of high-temperature brake grease or anti-seize compound to all those surfaces of the backplate which bear on the shoes, particularly the wheel cylinder pistons and lower pivot point. Do not allow the lubricant to foul the friction material.

16 Lay the shoes out on the bench, making sure that they are correctly located with regard to handbrake lever and shoe lining leading and trailing ends **(see illustration)**.

17 Fit the lower return spring.

18 Pull the shoes apart and engage their lower ends in the anchorage, then attach the handbrake cable.

19 Fit the strut and the shoe return upper spring.

20 Fit new shoe steady spring clips.

21 Refit the brake drum as described in Section 7 and adjust the rear brake shoes.

22 Check and, if necessary, adjust the

handbrake as described in Chapter 1.

23 On completion check the hydraulic fluid level as described in "Weekly checks".

Later (1984 onwards) models with self-adjusting rear brakes

24 Note the location and orientation of all components before dismantling, as an aid to reassembly **(see illustrations)**.

25 Remove the steady pins and clips or

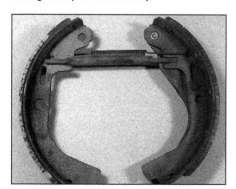

5.16 Rear brake shoes ready for fitting - early models

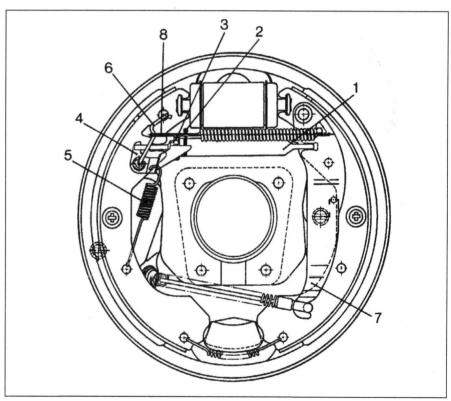

5.24a Self-adjusting rear brake components - later Saloon and Hatchback

1 Strut
2 Thermoclip
3 Adjuster pinion
4 Adjuster lever
5 Adjuster lever return spring
6 Return spring bracket
7 Handbrake lever
8 Upper return spring

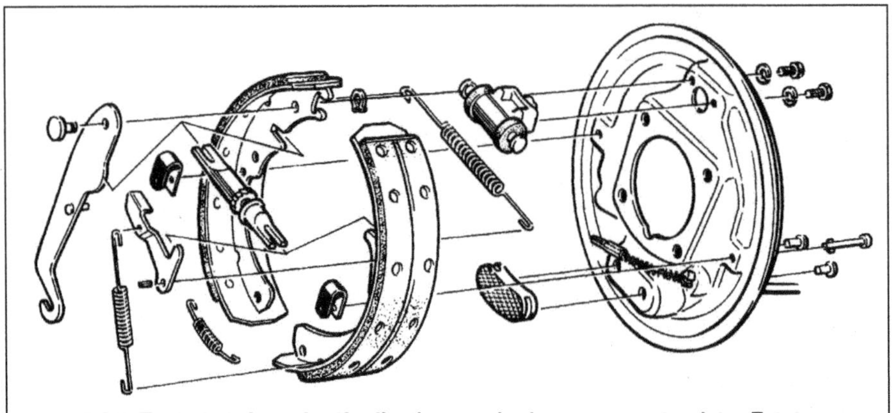

5.24b Exploded view of self-adjusting rear brake components - later Estate

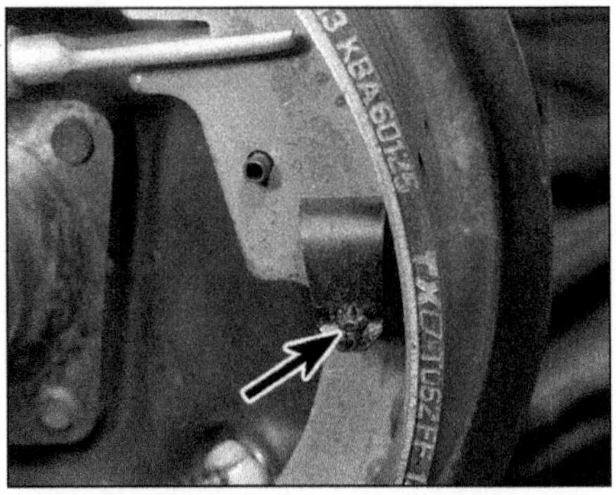

5.25a Brake shoe steady clip (Estate). Twist retainer (arrowed) 90° . . .

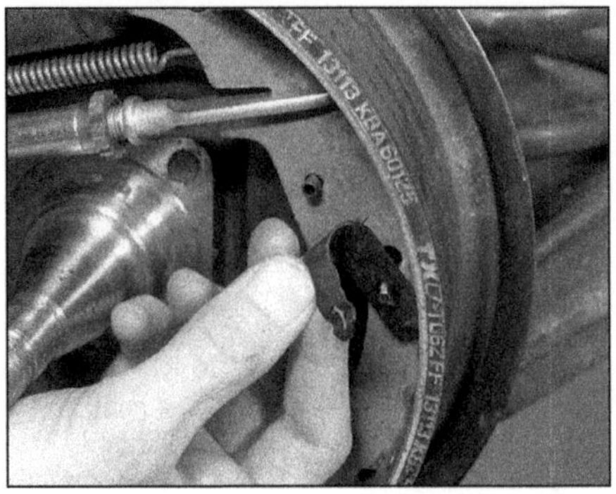

5.25b . . . and remove the clip

springs and washers. Renew them if they are damaged **(see illustrations)**.

26 Disconnect the handbrake cable from the operating lever **(see illustration)**. If there is insufficient slack in the cable, disconnect it at the equaliser.

27 The return springs may be unhooked now and the shoes removed separately, or the assembly of shoes, strut and springs may be removed together. The second course is particularly easy if the rear hub is removed, as has been done for photographic purposes here. Be careful not to damage the wheel cylinder rubber boots. Do not depress the brake pedal while the shoes are off. As a precaution, wrap a strong elastic band around the wheel cylinder pistons to retain them.

28 Dismantle the shoes, strut and springs. Note how the springs are fitted, and which way round the strut goes. Be careful not to interchange left-hand and right-hand adjuster components: on all except Estate models, the threaded rod is marked "L" or "R", and the other "handed" components are colour-coded black for the left-hand side and silver for the right **(see illustration)**.

29 Dismantle and clean the adjusting strut. Apply a smear of silicone-based lubricant to the adjuster threads.

30 Carry out the operations described above in paragraphs 11 to 16,

31 Assemble the new shoes, springs and adjuster components. Transfer the shoe return springs to their correct holes in the new shoes and locate the self-adjuster components. The threaded strut should be clean and lightly greased and fully retracted by turning the star wheel before fitting it between the shoes. Note that the shorter leg of the strut fork should be towards you. On Saloon and Hatchback variants, the cup spring securing the adjuster lever pivot pin on the shoe web should be renewed. Refer to the appropriate accompanying photographs for the reassembly details **(see illustrations)**.

32 Prior to reassembling the brake shoe assemblies to their fitted positions, apply a smear of copper-based anti-seize compound, or other suitable product, to the shoe rubbing areas on the brake backplate.

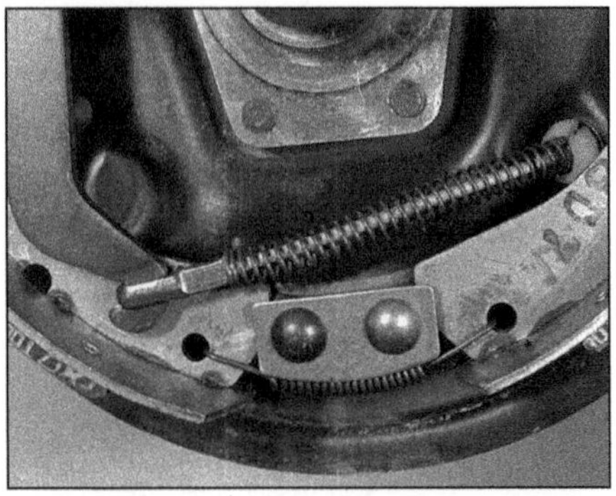

5.26 Disconnect the handbrake cable

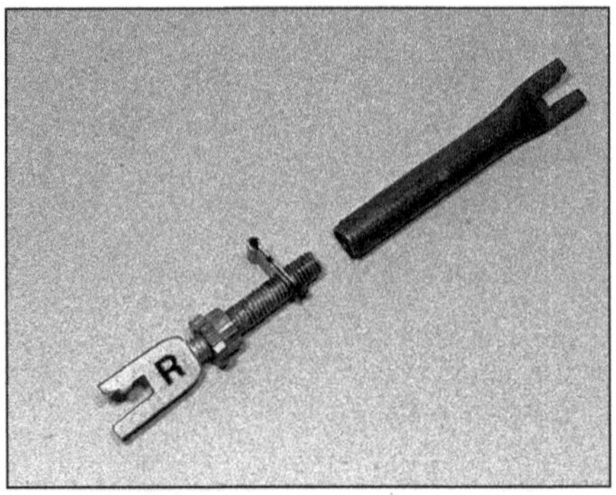

5.28 Self-adjusting strut components - right-hand side

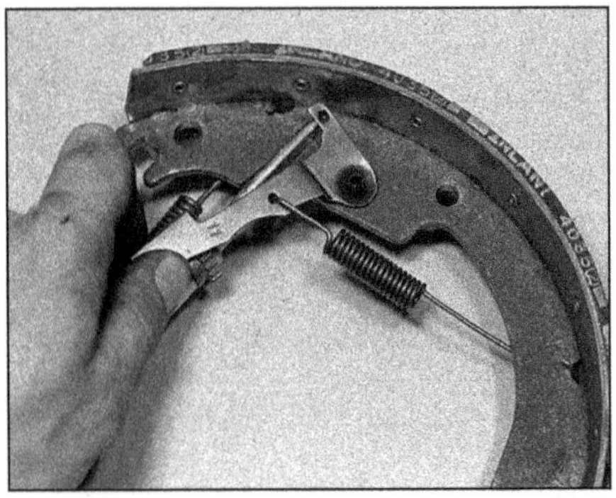

5.31a Fitting the adjuster lever (Estate)

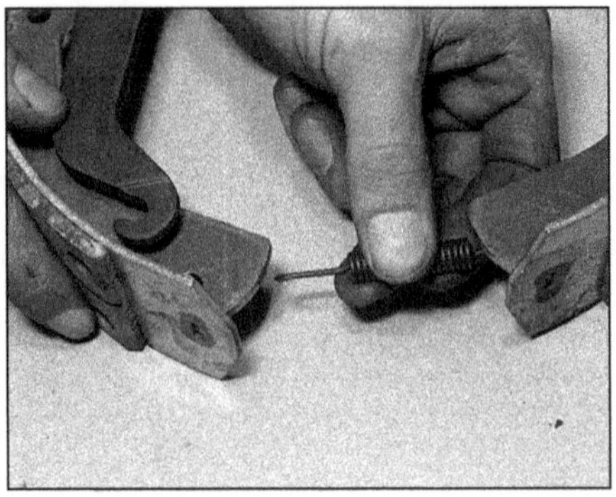

5.31b Fitting the lower return spring (Estate)

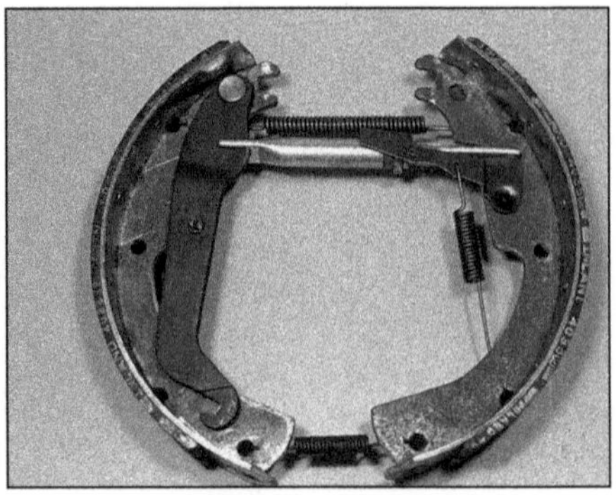

5.31c Rear brake components ready for refitting (Estate)

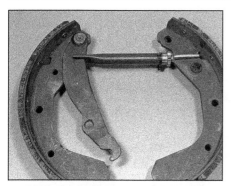

5.31d Self-adjusting strut correctly fitted (Saloon/Hatchback)

5.31e Fitting the upper return spring (Saloon/Hatchback)

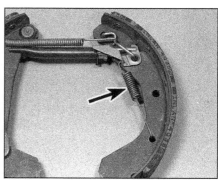

5.31f Adjuster lever spring fitted (Saloon/Hatchback)

33 Offer the shoes to the brake backplate. Be careful not to damage the wheel cylinder boots or to displace the pistons. When the shoes are in position, insert and secure the steady pins. Reconnect the handbrake cable, and refit and adjust the hub if it was removed **(see illustrations)**.

34 If fitting the shoes and springs together is found too difficult, it is possible to fit the shoes and secure them with the steady pins, then to introduce the adjuster strut and fit the springs and adjuster lever.

35 Back off the adjuster pinion to reduce the length of the strut until the brake drum will pass over the new linings. Make sure that the handbrake lever is correctly positioned (pin on the edge of the shoe web, not riding on top of it). Refit the brake drum (Section 7).

5.33a Fitting rear brake components (Estate)

5.33b Rear brake components installed - (Saloon/Hatchback)

36 Repeat the operations on the other rear brake, then adjust the brakes by operating the footbrake (Saloon/Hatchback) or the handbrake (Estate) at least ten times. A clicking noise will be heard at the drums as the automatic adjusters operate; when the clicking stops, adjustment is complete.

37 Check and, if necessary, adjust the handbrake as described in Chapter 1.

38 On completion check the hydraulic fluid level as described in *"Weekly checks"*.

6 Front brake disc - inspection, removal and refitting

Note: Before starting work, refer to the note at the beginning of Section 4 concerning the dangers of asbestos dust.

Inspection

Note: If either disc requires renewal, both should be renewed at the same time to ensure even and consistent braking.

1 Firmly apply the handbrake, jack up the front of the car and support it on axle stands (see *"Jacking and Vehicle Support"*). Remove the appropriate front roadwheel, marking its correct fitted position on the hub.

2 Slowly rotate the brake disc so that the full area of both sides can be checked; remove the brake pads if better access is required to the inner surface. Light scoring is normal in the area swept by the brake pads, but if heavy scoring is found the disc must be renewed.

3 It is normal to find a lip of rust and brake dust around the disc's perimeter; this can be scraped off if required. If, however, a lip has formed due to excessive wear of the brake pad swept area then the disc's thickness must be measured using a micrometer. Take measurements at several places around the disc at the inside and outside of the pad swept area; if the disc has worn at any point to the specified minimum thickness or less, the disc must be renewed.

4 If the disc is thought to be warped it can be checked for run-out either using a dial gauge mounted on any convenient fixed point, while the disc is slowly rotated, or by using feeler blades to measure (at several points all around the disc) the clearance between the disc and a

fixed point such as the caliper mounting bracket. To ensure that the disc is squarely seated on the hub, fit two wheel bolts complete with spacers approximately 10 mm thick and tighten them securely. If the measurements obtained are at the specified maximum or beyond, the disc is excessively warped and must be renewed; however it is worth checking first that the hub bearing is in good condition (Chapters 1 and/or 10).

5 Check the disc for cracks, especially around the wheel bolt holes, and any other wear or damage and renew if necessary.

Removal

6 Remove the brake pads as described in Section 4.

7 Extract the small retaining screw and then tilt the disc and withdraw it from the hub **(see illustration)**.

Refitting

8 Refitting is the reverse of the removal procedure, noting the following points.

   a) *Ensure that the mating surfaces of the disc and hub are clean and flat.*
   b) *If a new disc has been fitted, use a suitable solvent to wipe any preservative coating from the disc before refitting the caliper.*
   c) *On vehicles which are equipped with light alloy roadwheels, a facing sleeve is mounted on the collar of the brake disc.*
   d) *Refit the brake pads as described in Section 4.*

6.7 Removing the brake disc retaining screw

e) *Refit the roadwheel, aligning the marks made on removal, then lower the vehicle to the ground and tighten the roadwheel bolts to the specified torque. On completion, repeatedly depress the brake pedal until normal (non-assisted) pedal pressure returns.*

7 Rear brake drum - removal, inspection and refitting

Note: *Before starting work, refer to the note at the beginning of Section 5 concerning the dangers of asbestos dust.*

Removal

1 Chock the front wheels then jack up the rear of the vehicle and support it on axle stands (see *"Jacking and Vehicle Support"*). Remove the appropriate rear wheel, marking its correct fitted position on the drum, and proceed as described under the relevant sub-heading.

Early (pre-1984) models with adjustable rear brakes

2 Extract the drum securing screw then release the handbrake and remove the drum. If the drum is tight on the hub, tap it off with a plastic hammer **(see illustration)**. If the drum is grooved due to wear, the cam adjusters may have to be backed off right off before the drum can be pulled off and the shoes cleared from the grooves.

Later (1984 onwards) models with self-adjusting rear brakes

3 Remove the brake drum securing screw then release the handbrake and pull off the drum. If it is tight, collapse the brake shoes by removing the plug in the brake backplate and pushing the handbrake operating lever outwards with a screwdriver **(see illustration)**.

Inspection

Note: *If either drum requires renewal, both should be renewed at the same time to ensure even and consistent braking.*

4 Working carefully, remove all traces of brake dust from the drum, but *avoid inhaling the dust as it is injurious to health.*

5 Scrub clean the outside of the drum and check it for obvious signs of wear or damage

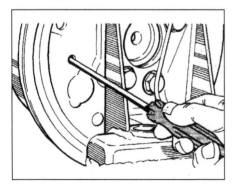

7.3 Release the handbrake lever by pushing a screwdriver through the hole

7.2 Brake drum retaining screw

such as cracks around the roadwheel bolt holes; renew the drum if necessary.

6 Examine carefully the inside of the drum. Light scoring of the friction surface is normal, but if heavy scoring is found the drum must be renewed. It is usual to find a lip on the drum's inboard edge which consists of a mixture of rust and brake dust; this should be scraped away to leave a smooth surface which can be polished with fine (120 to 150 grade) emery paper. If, however, the lip is due to the friction surface being recessed by excessive wear, then the drum must be renewed.

7 If the drum is thought to be excessively worn, or oval, its internal diameter must be measured at several points using an internal micrometer. Take measurements in pairs, the second at right angles to the first, and compare the two to check for signs of ovality. Provided that it does not enlarge the drum to beyond the specified maximum diameter, it may be possible to have the drum refinished by skimming or grinding; if this is not possible, the drums on both sides must be renewed. Note that if the drum is to be skimmed, both drums must be refinished to maintain a consistent internal diameter on both sides.

Refitting

Early (pre-1984) models with adjustable rear brakes

8 If a new brake drum is to be installed, use a suitable solvent to remove any preservative coating that may have been applied to its interior.

9 Ensure that the drum and hub flange mating surfaces are clean and dry and remove all traces of corrosion. Locate the drum on the hub noting that it may be necessary to rotate the adjuster cams to allow the drum to pass over the brake shoes.

10 Refit the drum retaining screw and tighten it securely.

11 Ensure that the handbrake is fully released then apply the footbrake hard a couple of times to centralise the shoes.

12 Turn one hexagon adjuster on the brake backplate while turning the drum in the normal forward direction until the wheel locks. Then back it off until the wheel rotates freely without binding **(see illustration)**.

HAYNES HiNT *In order to combat corrosion occurring in the adjusters, apply some lubricant to the hexagon head periodically, and apply a little grease to prevent water penetrating the backplate.*

13 Repeat the adjustment on the second adjuster.

14 With the brake shoes correctly adjusted check, and if necessary, adjust the handbrake as described in Chapter 1.

15 Refit the roadwheel, aligning the marks made on removal, then lower the vehicle to the ground and tighten the wheel bolts to the specified torque setting.

Later (1984 onwards) models with self-adjusting rear brakes

16 If a new brake drum is to be installed, use a suitable solvent to remove any preservative coating that may have been applied to its interior.

17 Ensure that the drum and hub flange mating surfaces are clean and dry and remove all traces of corrosion.

18 Make sure that the handbrake lever stop peg is correctly repositioned against the edge of the brake shoe web then locate the drum on the hub. Note that it may be necessary to shorten the adjuster strut length by rotating the strut wheel to allow the drum to pass over the brake shoes.

19 Refit the drum retaining screw and tighten it securely.

20 Adjust the lining to drum clearance by repeatedly applying the footbrake (Saloon/Hatchback) or handbrake (Estate models) at least ten times. Whilst applying the brake have an assistant listen to the rear drums to check that the adjuster strut is functioning correctly; if this is so a clicking sound will be emitted by the strut as the pedal is depressed.

21 With the lining to drum clearance set check, and if necessary, adjust the handbrake as described in Chapter 1.

22 Refit the roadwheel, aligning the marks made on removal, then lower the vehicle to the ground and tighten the wheel bolts to the specified torque setting.

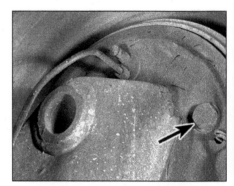

7.12 Rear brake hexagon adjuster (arrowed) - early models

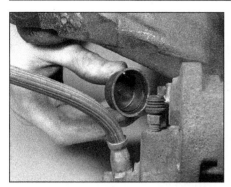

8.6a On GMF type caliper, remove the bolt caps . . .

8.6b . . . then unscrew the mounting bolts . . .

8.6c . . . and remove the caliper from the vehicle

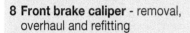

8 Front brake caliper - removal, overhaul and refitting

Note: *Before starting work, refer to the note at the beginning of Section 2 concerning the dangers of hydraulic fluid and to the warning at the beginning of Section 4 concerning the dangers of asbestos dust.*

Removal

1 Apply the handbrake, then jack up the front of the vehicle and support it on axle stands (see *"Jacking and Vehicle Support"*). Remove the appropriate roadwheel, marking its correct fitted position on the wheel hub.

2 Minimise fluid loss either by removing the master cylinder reservoir cap and then tightening it down onto a piece of polythene to obtain an airtight seal, or by using a brake hose clamp, a G-clamp or a similar tool to clamp the flexible hose.

3 Clean the area around the caliper brake hose union. Slacken and remove the union bolt and recover the sealing washer from either side of the hose union; discard the washers new ones must be used on refitting. Plug the hose end and caliper hole to minimise fluid loss and prevent the ingress of dirt into the hydraulic system.

4 Remove the brake pads (Section 4).

5 On models with ATE type calipers, slacken and remove the two caliper mounting bolts and remove the caliper assembly from the vehicle.

6 On models with GMF type calipers, prise off the mounting bolt caps to gain access to the bolts. Slacken and remove the bolts and remove the caliper from the vehicle **(see illustrations)**.

Overhaul

ATE type caliper

7 With the caliper on the bench, wipe away all traces of dust and dirt, but *avoid inhaling the dust as it is injurious to health.*

8 Separate the caliper body from its bracket by sliding them apart. On the early type caliper recover the guide springs.

9 Using a screwdriver, prise off the retaining ring from the dust excluder then remove the excluder from the caliper.

10 Withdraw the partially ejected piston from the caliper body and remove the dust excluder. The piston can be withdrawn by hand, or if necessary pushed out by applying compressed air to the brake hose union hole. Only low pressure should be required such as is generated by a foot pump.

11 Once the piston has been removed, pick out the seal from its groove in the cylinder, using a plastic or wooden instrument.

12 Thoroughly clean all components using only methylated spirit, isopropyl alcohol or clean hydraulic fluid as a cleaning medium. Never use mineral-based solvents such as petrol or paraffin which will attack the hydraulic system's rubber components. Dry the components immediately using

compressed air or a clean, lint-free cloth. Use compressed air to blow clear the fluid passages.

13 Check all components and renew any that are worn or damaged. Check particularly the cylinder bore and piston; these should be renewed (note that this means the renewal of the complete body assembly) if they are scratched, worn or corroded in any way.

14 If the assembly is fit for further use, obtain the necessary components from your Vauxhall dealer. Renew the caliper seals as a matter of course; these should never be re-used.

15 On the later type caliper inspect the mounting bracket location pegs and caliper guide rubbers for signs of wear or damage. Both should be undamaged and a reasonably tight, sliding fit in each other. The location guide rubbers can be removed for renewal if required. Extract the nylon compression sleeve from within each rubber, then carefully compress the sleeve shoulder and push it through to remove it on the inboard side. Refit the location rubber and insert the compression sleeve. Take care not to damage the rubber and sleeve during fitting and ensure that the shoulder of the rubber guide bush is fully engaged **(see illustrations)**.

16 On reassembly, ensure that all components are absolutely clean and dry.

17 Soak the piston and the new seal in clean hydraulic fluid. Smear clean fluid on the cylinder bore surface.

18 Fit the new seal using only the fingers to manipulate it into the cylinder bore groove.

8.15a Extract the nylon compression sleeve . . .

8.15b . . . and withdraw the rubber bush from the caliper (later type)

8.15c Location bush refitted to the caliper (later type)

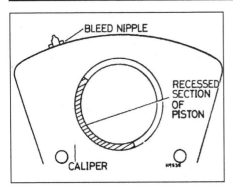

8.19 Caliper piston recess setting diagram

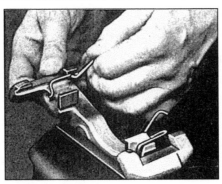

8.22 Fitting caliper bracket guide springs

19 Fit the new dust seal to the piston and refit it to the cylinder bore using a twisting motion, and ensure that the piston enters squarely into the bore. Push the piston into the caliper bore making sure that the piston step is positioned as shown (**see illustration**).

20 When the piston has been partially depressed, engage the dust excluder with the rim of the cylinder and fit the retaining clip.

21 Depress the piston fully into its cylinder bore.

22 On the early type caliper, secure the caliper bracket in a vice and install the guide springs (**see illustration**). Slide the caliper body into the bracket splines until the body and bracket are flush.

23 On the later type caliper, engage the location pegs with the guides and slide the bracket onto the caliper.

GMF type caliper

24 With the caliper on the bench, wipe away all traces of dust and dirt, but *avoid inhaling the dust as it is injurious to health.*

25 Prise the sliding sleeve inner dust caps from the caliper housing.

26 Push the caliper sliding sleeves inwards so that the dust caps can be disengaged from the sleeve grooves and removed.

27 Prise off the piston dust excluder.

28 Remove the piston dust excluder from the caliper.

29 Carry out the operations described earlier in paragraphs 10 to 12.

30 Press the sliding sleeves out from the caliper body, noting which way around they are fitted, and recover their sealing rings. Inspect the sleeves and caliper body for signs of wear or damage. Both should be undamaged and a reasonably tight, sliding fit in each other.

31 Check all components and renew any that are worn or damaged. Check particularly the cylinder bore and piston; these should be renewed (note that this means the renewal of the complete body assembly) if they are scratched, worn or corroded in any way.

32 If the assembly is fit for further use, obtain the necessary components from your Vauxhall/Opel dealer. Renew the caliper seals as a matter of course; these should never be re-used.

33 On reassembly, ensure that all components are absolutely clean and dry.

34 Soak the piston and the new seal in clean hydraulic fluid. Smear clean fluid on the cylinder bore surface.

35 Fit the new seal using only the fingers to manipulate it into the cylinder bore groove.

36 Fit the new dust seal to the piston and refit it to the cylinder bore using a twisting motion, and ensure that the piston enters squarely into the bore.

37 When the piston has been partially depressed, engage the dust excluder with the rim of the cylinder then depress the piston fully into its cylinder bore.

38 Fit the new sealing rings to the sliding sleeve recesses and apply the grease supplied in the repair kit to the sleeves. Install the sleeves making sure they are fitted the correct way around.

39 Fit the inner dust caps, making sure they are correctly engaged with the sliding sleeves. Slide the sleeves into position and press the dust caps into position on the caliper body using a suitable tubular drift.

Refitting

40 Prior to refitting, remove all traces of locking compound from the caliper mounting bolt threads and the hub carrier holes. Apply a drop of fresh locking compound to the bolt threads.

41 Refit the caliper and insert the mounting bolts, tightening them to the specified torque setting.

42 Position a new sealing washer on each side of the hose union and connect the brake hose to the caliper. Ensure that the hose is correctly positioned against the caliper body lug then install the union bolt and tighten it to the specified torque setting.

43 Refit the brake pads as described in Section 4.

44 Remove the brake hose clamp or polythene, where fitted, and bleed the hydraulic system as described in Section 2. Note that providing the precautions described were taken to minimise brake fluid loss, it should only be necessary to bleed the relevant front brake.

45 Refit the roadwheel, aligning the marks

made on removal, then lower the vehicle to the ground and tighten the roadwheel bolts to the specified torque.

9 Rear brake wheel cylinder - removal, overhaul and refitting

Note: *Before starting work, refer to the note at the beginning of Section 2 concerning the dangers of hydraulic fluid and to the warning at the beginning of Section 5 concerning the dangers of asbestos dust.*

Removal

1 Remove the brake drum as described in Section 7.

2 Using pliers, carefully unhook the upper brake shoe return spring and remove it from both brake shoes. Pull the upper ends of the shoes away from the wheel cylinder to disengage them from the pistons.

3 Minimise fluid loss by either removing the master cylinder reservoir cap and then tightening it down onto a piece of polythene to obtain an airtight seal, or by using a brake hose clamp, a G-clamp or a similar tool to clamp the flexible hose at the nearest convenient point to the wheel cylinder.

4 Wipe away all traces of dirt around the brake pipe union at the rear of the wheel cylinder and unscrew the union nut. Carefully ease the pipe out of the wheel cylinder and plug or tape over its end to prevent dirt entry. Wipe off any spilt fluid immediately.

5 Unscrew the two wheel cylinder retaining bolts from the rear of the backplate and remove the cylinder taking great care not to allow surplus hydraulic fluid to contaminate the brake shoe linings.

Overhaul

6 Brush the dirt and dust from the wheel cylinder, taking care not to inhale it, and pull off the rubber dust excluders from the cylinder body (**see illustration**).

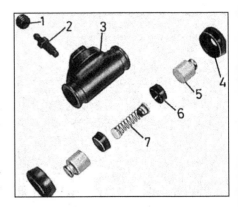

9.6 Exploded view of a rear wheel cylinder

1 Dust cap   5 Piston
2 Bleed screw   6 Seal
3 Cylinder   7 Spring
4 Dust excluder

7 The pistons will normally be ejected by pressure of the coil spring but if they are not, tap the end of the cylinder on a piece of hardwood or apply low air pressure from a tyre foot pump at the pipeline connection.

8 Inspect the surfaces of the piston and the cylinder bore for rust, scoring or metal-to-metal rubbed areas. If these are evident, renew the wheel cylinder complete.

9 If these components are in good order, discard the seals and dust excluders and obtain a repair kit which will contain all the renewable items.

10 Fit the piston seals (using the fingers only to manipulate them into position) so that the spring is between them. Dip the pistons in clean hydraulic fluid and insert them into the cylinder.

11 Fit the dust excluders.

Refitting

12 Ensure that the backplate and wheel cylinder mating surfaces are clean then spread the brake shoes and manoeuvre the wheel cylinder into position.

13 Engage the brake pipe and screw in the union nut two or three turns to ensure that the thread has started.

14 Insert the two wheel cylinder retaining bolts and tighten them to the specified torque setting. Now tighten the brake pipe union nut to the specified torque.

15 Remove the clamp from the flexible brake hose or the polythene from the master cylinder reservoir (as applicable).

16 Ensure that the brake shoes are correctly located in the cylinder pistons then carefully refit the brake shoe upper return spring, using a screwdriver to stretch the spring into position.

17 Refit the brake drum as described in Section 7.

18 Bleed the brake hydraulic system as described in Section 2. Providing suitable precautions were taken to minimise loss of fluid, it should only be necessary to bleed the relevant rear brake.

10 Master cylinder - removal, overhaul and refitting

Note: *Before starting work, refer to the warning at the beginning of Section 2 concerning the dangers of hydraulic fluid.*

Removal

1 Remove the master cylinder reservoir cap and syphon the hydraulic fluid from the reservoir. **Note:** *Do not syphon the fluid by mouth, as it is poisonous; use a syringe or an old poultry baster.* Alternatively, open any convenient bleed screw in the system and gently pump the brake pedal to expel the fluid through a plastic tube connected to the screw (see Section 2).

2 Release the cable retainer from around the master cylinder body (where applicable).

10.5 Unbolting the master cylinder from the servo unit (later models)

3 Wipe clean the area around the brake pipe unions on the side of the master cylinder and place absorbent rags beneath the pipe unions to catch any surplus fluid. Make a note of the correct fitted positions of the unions then unscrew the union nuts and carefully withdraw the pipes. Plug or tape over the pipe ends and master cylinder orifices to minimise the loss of brake fluid and to prevent the entry of dirt into the system. Wash off any spilt fluid immediately with cold water.

4 Two pressure regulating valves are screwed into the master cylinder and these should now be unscrewed.

5 Unbolt the master cylinder from the brake vacuum servo unit (booster) **(see illustration)**.

6 If the reason for removal was to renew the master cylinder, then retain the fluid reservoir for fitting to the new cylinder. To remove the reservoir from ATE type master cylinders, simply pull it from the rubber seals. On GMF type master cylinders, the fixing clips will first have to be pushed back with a screwdriver.

Overhaul

Note: *When overhauling the master cylinder unit, two types of repair kit are available. One is the "loose" seal type kit and the other more recently obtainable kit is one where the secondary piston comes ready assembled in a special tube which is used for fitting the piston. Proceed as applicable according to type as follows.*

ATE type cylinder

7 Remove all traces of dirt from the exterior of the master cylinder **(see illustration)**.

8 Prise the fluid reservoir from the cylinder body.

9 Extract the circlip from the end of the cylinder housing. To do this, the primary piston should be slightly depressed with a rod to relieve the tension on the circlip.

10 Withdraw the primary piston, noting which way the seals are fitted.

11 Insert a rod and depress the secondary piston so that the stop screw can be removed from the cylinder body.

12 Withdraw the secondary piston by tapping the end of the cylinder on a block of hardwood. Note which way the seals are fitted.

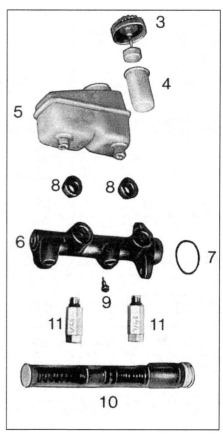

10.7 Exploded view of ATE master cylinder
3 Reservoir cap
4 Float guide sleeve
5 Reservoir
6 Cylinder body
7 O-ring
8 Plug
9 Stop screw
10 Packaged repair kit
11 Pressure regulating valve

13 Examine the surfaces of the pistons and the cylinder bore for rust, scoring or metal-to-metal rubbed areas. If evident, renew the master cylinder complete.

14 If the components are in good order, clean them in hydraulic fluid or methylated spirit - nothing else.

15 Obtain a repair kit which will contain all the necessary replaceable items.

Loose seal kit overhaul procedure

16 Install the new seals to the pistons, manipulating them into position with the fingers only. It is essential that the new seals are fitted the same way round as the old ones; they are tapered and will only function correctly if fitted the right way round.

17 Reassembly is a reversal of dismantling. Take great care not to trap or cut the lips of the piston seal as the pistons are entered into the cylinder bores. Dip each component in clean hydraulic fluid before assembling. Always fit a new circlip from the repair kit.

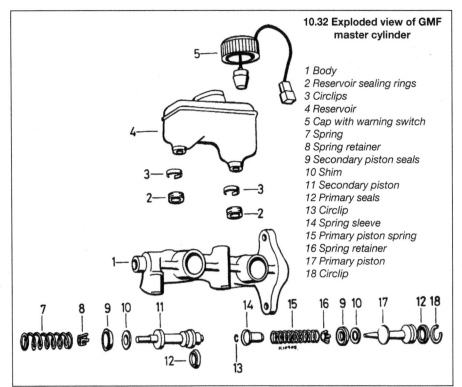

10.32 Exploded view of GMF master cylinder

1 Body
2 Reservoir sealing rings
3 Circlips
4 Reservoir
5 Cap with warning switch
7 Spring
8 Spring retainer
9 Secondary piston seals
10 Shim
11 Secondary piston
12 Primary seals
13 Circlip
14 Spring sleeve
15 Primary piston spring
16 Spring retainer
17 Primary piston
18 Circlip

18 Fit new rubber sealing rings and press the fluid reservoir into position on the cylinder body.

19 Pour some clean fluid into the reservoir and prime the master cylinder before installation by depressing the primary piston several times with a rod. A great deal of fluid will of course be ejected from the open ports of the cylinder.

Preassembled kit overhaul procedure

20 Lubricate the cylinder with brake fluid or brake rubber grease.

21 Clamp the cylinder in a soft-jawed vice with the bore more or less horizontal. Screw in the stop screw a little way, but not so far that it protrudes into the bore.

22 Remove the large plug from the assembly tube. Remove all the components from the short part of the tube and push the short part into the long part until they are flush.

23 Insert the assembly tube into the cylinder bore as far as the collar on the short sleeve. Use a blunt rod to push the secondary piston into the bore until it contacts the end of the cylinder. Nip up the stop screw, withdraw the rod and sleeve and tighten the stop screw fully.

24 Reposition the master cylinder in the vice with the bore opening facing upwards.

25 Smear the primary piston skirt and seal grooves with the special grease provided in the repair kit. Fit the stop washer to the piston.

26 Adjust the assembly tube so that the end of the long part is flush with the inner shoulder of the short part.

27 Fit the front seal to the primary piston with the open end of the seal facing the front of the master cylinder. Place the assembly tube over

the cylinder to compress the seal, insert the piston and tube part way into the bore and withdraw the tube.

28 Place the intermediate ring on the primary piston, then fit the other seal using the assembly tube in a similar manner.

29 Place the end washer on the primary piston, then depress the piston slightly and fit the circlip. Make sure that the circlip is properly seated and that the piston is free to move.

30 Fit new sealing rings and press the fluid reservoir into position.

31 Prime the cylinder by pouring clean brake fluid into the reservoir and working the pistons with a rod until fluid is ejected from all orifices.

GMF type cylinder

32 With the unit removed from the vehicle, clean away external dirt then release the retaining clips and remove the reservoir **(see illustration)**.

33 Insert a rod into the end of the cylinder and depress the piston until it can be held depressed by inserting a smooth pin or rod 3.0 mm in diameter through the primary outlet.

34 Extract the circlip from the end of the cylinder using circlip pliers or screwdrivers. Discard the circlip.

35 Remove the primary piston after first having pulled out the temporary retaining pin. Note which way the seals are fitted.

36 Remove the secondary piston by tapping the end of the cylinder on a piece of hardwood. Note which way the seals are fitted.

37 Dismantle the primary piston. This can be done by compressing the spring with a cap from an aerosol or similar in which a hole has

been drilled. As the circlip appears, prise it off with two screwdrivers and discard it.

38 Examine the surfaces of the pistons and the cylinder bore for scoring or metal-to-metal rubbed areas. If evident, renew the master cylinder complete.

39 If the components are in good order, clean them in hydraulic fluid or methylated spirit - nothing else.

40 Obtain a repair kit which will contain all the necessary replaceable items.

Loose seal kit overhaul procedures

41 Install the seals to the pistons, manipulating them into position with the fingers only. It is essential that the new seals are fitted the same way round as the old ones; they are tapered and will only function correctly if fitted the right way round.

42 Reassemble the primary piston using a new circlip. The circlip can be fully installed into its groove in the piston by tapping it down with a piece of tubing.

43 Dip the pistons in clean hydraulic fluid and fit the secondary piston, followed by the primary piston, into the cylinder.

44 Depress and hold the primary piston as described for dismantling while a new circlip is fitted.

45 Fit new rubber sealing rings and press the fluid reservoir into position on the cylinder body.

46 Pour some clean fluid into the reservoir and prime the master cylinder before installation by depressing the primary piston several times with a rod. A great deal of the fluid will of course be ejected from the open ports of the cylinder.

Preassembled kit overhaul procedure

47 Lubricate the cylinder bore with brake fluid or brake rubber grease. Clamp the cylinder with the bore horizontal.

48 Remove the plug from the assembly tube and insert the short part of the tube into the cylinder bore as far as the shoulder on the tube. Use a blunt rod to push the piston out of the tube and into the bore; retain the pistons in the bore with the smooth rod or needle used when dismantling. Withdraw the rod and the tube.

49 Fit a new circlip to the end of the cylinder. Depress the primary piston and withdraw the retaining rod or needle. Make sure that the circlip is properly seated and that the pistons are free to move.

50 Fit new sealing rings and press the reservoir into position.

51 Prime the cylinder, as described in paragraph 31.

Refitting

52 Refitting is a reversal of removal, use new reservoir rubber seals and tighten all bolts to the specified torque. On completion bleed the complete hydraulic system as described in Section 2.

11 Pressure regulating valves - testing, removal and refitting

Testing

1 Testing of the brake pressure valves can only be carried out by a Vauxhall dealer using specialist equipment. If the valves are found to be faulty they must be renewed; no adjustment is possible.

Removal

Note: *Renew both valves as a matched pair to ensure that the braking is not adversely effected.*
2 Carry out the operation described in paragraphs 1 to 4 of Section 10. On some later models, only one of the valves is screwed into the master cylinder port, the other one is mounted on the engine compartment bulkhead.

Refitting

3 Refitting is the reverse of removal, tightening the valves and brake pipe union nuts to their specified torque settings. On completion bleed the complete hydraulic system as described in Chapter 1.

12 Vacuum servo unit hose - renewal

1 Release the union nut on the inlet manifold and disconnect the vacuum hose **(see illustration)**.
2 Release the hose from the connector at the servo unit by unscrewing the clip. If the hose is of shrink-fit type, do not apply excessive force but rather ease the elbow from the rubber grommet in the servo shell.
3 Carefully cut a new length of servo hose to length allowing for the inclusion of the non-return valve.
4 Remove the non-return valve by cutting the hose lengthwise from the valve, but take care not to damage the valve. Cut the hose from the inlet manifold and servo unit connectors.
5 Reassemble making sure that the arrows on the non-return valve point towards the inlet manifold. Secure the hose to the manifold pipe with a clip.

12.1 Servo hose connection at manifold

13 Vacuum servo unit (booster) - testing, removal and refitting

Testing

1 With the engine switched off, depress the foot brake pedal several times then hold it down. Start the engine and the pedal should be felt to move downward a little. If it does not, check the vacuum hose and connections for leaks.
2 If a leak cannot be found then an internal fault in the servo unit must be suspected. The servo unit should not be dismantled, but if faulty, renew it.

Removal

Early (pre-1985) models

3 Where necessary, remove the air cleaner from the carburettor complete with ducting and hoses.
4 Disconnect the vacuum hose from the inlet manifold by unscrewing the union nut.
5 Disconnect the vacuum hose from the servo unit.
6 Disconnect the lead for the low level warning lamp switch on the master cylinder fluid reservoir.
7 Unbolt the master cylinder from the servo unit.
8 Carefully pull the master cylinder from the servo unit as far as the flexibility of the hydraulic pipelines will allow.
9 Working inside the vehicle, remove the cover located under the facia panel to provide access to the remote control support mounting nuts and bolt located on the inner face of the bulkhead.
10 Unscrew and remove the nuts and the bolt.
11 Disconnect the brake pedal return spring.
12 Extract the circlip from the brake pedal arm clevis pin, press out the pin to separate the pedal arm from under the servo unit pushrod.
13 Still working under the facia panel, unscrew the nuts which secure the brake pedal support bracket.
14 Working within the engine compartment, withdraw the servo unit and the brake remote

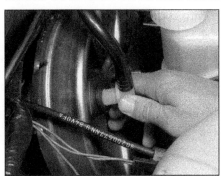

13.25 Disconnecting the servo vacuum hose

control assembly from the bulkhead.
15 Hold the remote control rod support in a vice.
16 Prise off the spring leg of the bellcrank lever. Then extract the circlip and take off the spring.
17 Tap out the lock pin which retains the bellcrank pivot.
18 Remove the bellcrank pivot.
19 Extract the circlip from the remote control rod eye pivot.
20 Remove the pivot to separate the remote control unit from the bellcrank lever at the servo unit.
21 Unscrew the mounting nuts and disconnect the servo unit from the remote control rod support.
22 Support the servo unit and unscrew the nut from the bellcrank lever mounting.
23 Remove the bellcrank lever by unscrewing it from the servo unit pushrod.

Later (1985 onwards) models

24 From 1985 model year, the servo and master cylinder are mounted on the right-hand side of the bulkhead. To remove the servo, proceed as follows.
25 Remove the air cleaner for ease of access if necessary, and disconnect the vacuum hose from the servo **(see illustration)**.
26 Remove the two nuts which secure the master cylinder to the servo. Disconnect the wires from the fluid level warning switch and carefully pull the master cylinder forwards until it clears the servo studs. Take care not to strain the hydraulic pipes; if necessary, release them from their clips on the bulkhead.
27 Inside the car, remove the cover from above the pedals. The cover is secured by clips and a strap.
28 Disconnect the return spring and the servo pushrod clevis from the brake pedal.
29 Still working inside the car, remove the four nuts which secure the servo bracket to the bulkhead.
30 Remove the servo and bracket from the engine bay by pulling the servo forwards and lifting it out. Do not displace the master cylinder further than necessary.
31 If the servo is to be renewed, unbolt it from its bracket.

Refitting

Early (pre-1985) models

32 Refitting is a reversal of removal, but apply grease to the bellcrank lever pivots and carry out the following adjustments. All nuts and bolts must be tightened to the specified torque wrench settings.
33 Pull the remote control rod fully towards the brake servo unit. Measure the lengths (A) of exposed thread on the rod as shown **(see illustration)**.
34 If adjustment is required, release the remote control rod locknut and rotate the rod. Once correctly adjusted, fit the dust excluder to the front of the pivot housing.

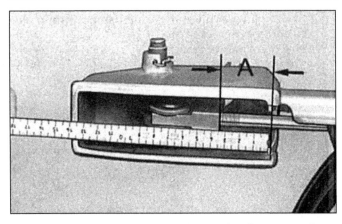

13.33 Remote control rod thread measuring diagram - early models
A = 28.5 to 29.5 mm

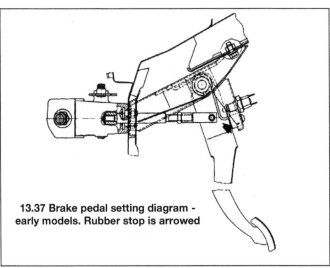

13.37 Brake pedal setting diagram - early models. Rubber stop is arrowed

13.39 Servo clevis and locknut (arrowed). Note seal putty on bracket flange

35 Having installed the assembly to the bulkhead, go inside the vehicle and release the pedal pushrod locknut.
36 Connect the clevis fork of the pushrod to the brake pedal arm.
37 Rotate the pushrod until the pedal arm just rests on the rubber stop **(see illustration)**. Tighten the pushrod locknut and then fit the pedal return spring.
38 Fit the master cylinder to the servo unit and reconnect the vacuum hose and the low fluid level warning lamp.

Later (1985 onwards) models

39 Refit in the reverse order to removal. If a new servo has been fitted, adjust the servo pushrod at the clevis to give 1.0 mm free play at the pedal. Tighten the locknut when adjustment is correct **(see illustration)**.

14 Brake pedal remote control assembly (pre-1985 models) - removal and refitting

Removal

1 The vehicle was originally designed for left-hand drive steering, therefore on pre-1985 right-hand drive versions, the brake pedal is connected to the vacuum servo unit by a remote control rod and bellcrank arrangement. This assembly enables force from the driver's foot to be transmitted to the left-hand side of the engine compartment where the vacuum servo unit and master cylinder are situated.
2 With the servo unit and remote control assembly withdrawn, as described in the preceding Section, extract the spring clip which secures the bellcrank lever pivot in the housing at the brake pedal end of the remote control rod **(see illustration)**.
3 Remove the pivot pin.
4 Pull the remote control rod with the bellcrank lever from the housing.
5 The bellcrank lever can be separated from the remote control rod after extracting the circlip.
6 The bellcrank lever is renewable complete with pedal pushrod.

Refitting

7 Refitting is a reversal of removal, apply grease to the pivots and adjust the remote control rod as described in Section 13, paragraphs 33 and 34.

15 Brake pedal remote control rod (pre-1985 models) - removal and refitting

Removal

1 Removal of the brake vacuum servo unit and the remote control assembly for pre-1985 models is described in earlier Sections. The following operations will enable the remote control rod to be removed independently from the vehicle should it be necessary to renew either the rod or bellcrank levers in the event of wear occurring in pivot bolts or bushes.
2 Remove the air cleaner for ease of access if necessary.
3 Working at the servo end of the remote control rod, prise off the spring leg and release the return spring.
4 Extract the spring clip and pull out the pivot

14.2 Bellcrank lever pivot spring clip - arrowed (early models)

to release the remote control rod and bellcrank lever. Use pliers to remove the pivot.
5 Working at the brake pedal end of the remote control rod, pull off the rubber cover from the bellcrank lever housing.
6 Rotate the remote control rod to unscrew it from the trunnion on the bellcrank lever.

Refitting

7 Screw the new rod into the trunnion, making sure that the dust excluding bellows are fitted to the rod.
8 Connect the remote control rod to the bellcrank lever at the servo unit.
9 Fit the pivot and spring clip. Reconnect the spring.
10 Check and adjust the remote control rod setting as described in Section 13, paragraphs 33 and 34.
11 Refit the components removed at the commencement of operations.

16 Handbrake cables - renewal

1 Pull the handbrake control lever to the second notch of its ratchet.
2 Raise the rear of the vehicle and remove the roadwheels and the brake drums.

16.4 Short handbrake cable and grommets (arrowed) - later models

16.11 Handbrake lever control rod/cable extension piece

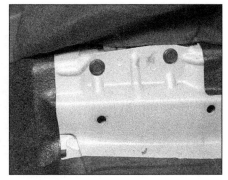

17.7 Handbrake lever mounting bolts

Shorter cable

3 Measure the length of exposed thread at the cable end fitting for ease of refitting and then unscrew the adjuster nut from the cable at the equaliser.
4 Detach the cable from its guide on the rear axle. On later models (1985 onwards) the handbrake cable guide tube was deleted and the cable routed through two grommets, held in position by a bracket welded to the rear axle. In this instance, detach the cable from the grommets **(see illustration)**.
5 Press out the cable sleeve from the brake backplate.
6 Unhook the handbrake cable from the shoe and pull the cable through the backplate.

Longer cable

7 Unscrew the nut from the threaded end fitting on the cable equaliser.
8 Detach the cable from the guide on the underbody. Bend the guide retaining tabs as necessary.
9 Detach the cable from the equaliser and the guide or grommets (as applicable - see paragraph 4) on the rear axle.
10 Disconnect the cable from the brake shoe.
11 Press out the cable sleeve from the backplate and withdraw the cable after disconnecting it from the extension piece on the handbrake lever pull rod **(see illustration)**.

Both cables

12 Refitting of both cables is a reversal of removal. Check and adjust the cables as described in Chapter 1 having first set the shorter cable end fitting to the measurement determined before removing.

17 Handbrake lever - removal, overhaul and refitting

Removal

1 Disconnect the shorter handbrake cable from the equaliser on the rear axle beam, after noting the length of exposed thread at the cable end fitting.
2 Disconnect the longer cable from the extension piece.

3 Disconnect the extension piece from the handbrake control lever pull rod.
4 Remove the grommet from the pullrod.
5 Remove the front passenger seat.
6 Where necessary, release and knock out the seat sliding rails and move them towards the rear.
7 Where applicable prise free and remove the plastic cover from the handbrake lever. Access to the handbrake-to-floor mounting bolts is through slits in the carpet. If no slits are provided, either carefully cut some or release and fold back the carpet. Unbolt the handbrake lever and withdraw it with pullrod until the handbrake ON switch lead can be disconnected **(see illustration)**.

Overhaul

8 A worn ratchet segment can be renewed by driving the sleeve from the control lever.
9 Drive the new sleeve supplied with the segment into the lever to permit a little play between segment and lever.
10 A new pawl can be fitted if the original pivot pin is drilled out.
11 Rivet the new pin so that the pawl is still free to move.

Refitting

12 Refitting is a reversal of the removal procedure. On completion adjust the handbrake as described in Chapter 1.

18 Handbrake warning light switch - removal and refitting

Removal

1 The handbrake ON warning light microswitch is bolted to the handbrake lever **(see illustration)**.
2 Access to the switch may be gained after removing the handbrake lever, (Section 17).
3 Undo the bolt and remove the microswitch.

Refitting

4 Refit in the reverse order.

19 Brake pedal - removal and refitting

Removal

1 Working under the facia panel, disconnect the pedal return spring.
2 Remove the clip and pull out the clevis pin to disconnect the pushrod clevis fork from the pedal arm.
3 Disconnect the electrical leads from the stop-lamp switch.
4 Pull the demister duct from the heater distributor housing.
5 Unbolt and remove the pedal support bracket.
6 Secure the support bracket in the jaws of a vice and extract the lockpin from the cross-shaft nut.
7 Unscrew and remove the nut and then pull the cross-shaft from the support bracket.
8 Withdraw the pedal and shaft spring.

Refitting

9 Refitting is a reversal of removal, but apply grease to the cross-shaft and tighten nuts and bolts to the specified torque.
10 Note that the cross-shaft nut is on the right-hand side when viewed from the driver's seat and the end of the shaft spring engages in the hole in the support bracket.

18.1 Handbrake warning light switch location and retaining bolt (arrowed)

20 Brake light switch - removal and refitting

Removal

1 The brake light switch is mounted on the pedal support bracket, in a "keyhole" type mounting (see illustration).

2 To remove the brake light switch, disconnect the electrical leads, turn the switch through 180° so that the keys line up with the slots and remove the switch.

Refitting

3 Refit in the reverse order, but pull the switch plunger out to its maximum extension before fitting the switch (see illustration).

4 The plunger will automatically adjust itself during use, but check that it becomes operational when the brake pedal travel exceeds 15 to 25 mm.

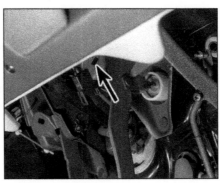

20.1 Brake light switch "keyhole" mounting (arrowed)

20.3 Brake light switch showing plunger fully extended (top) and retracted (bottom)

Chapter 10
Suspension and steering

Contents

Control arm balljoint - renewal 7
Control arm bushes - renewal 6
Control arm support - removal and refitting 8
Front anti-roll bar - removal and refitting .9
Front hub bearing - renewal 3
Front suspension control arm - removal and refitting 5
Front suspension strut - overhaul 4
Front suspension strut - removal and refitting 2
General information 1
Level control system component removal and refitting - general
    information 20
Level control system - description 18
Level control system (manual) - adjustment 19
Power steering pump - removal and refitting 30
Power steering system - bleeding 31
Rear anti-roll bar - removal and refitting 13
Rear axle - removal and refitting 16
Rear coil spring - removal and refitting .14
Rear hub bearings - adjustment 10
Rear hub bearings - renewal 11
Rear shock absorber - removal, testing and refitting 12
Rear suspension stub axle - removal and refitting 15
Steering column - overhaul 28
Steering column - removal and refitting 27
Steering column lock/ignition switch - removal and refitting 29
Steering damper - removal and refitting 25
Steering gear - overhaul 24
Steering gear - removal and refitting 22
Steering rack bellows - renewal 23
Steering wheel - removal and refitting 26
Tie-rod end - removal and refitting 21
Trailing arm flexible bushes - renewal 17
Wheel alignment and steering angles - general information 32
Wheel and tyre maintenance and tyre pressure
    checks . . . . .See "Weekly checks"

Degrees of difficulty

Easy, suitable for novice with little experience	**Fairly easy,** suitable for beginner with some experience	**Fairly difficult,** suitable for competent DIY mechanic	**Difficult,** suitable for experienced DIY mechanic	**Very difficult,** suitable for expert DIY or professional

Specifications

Front suspension
Type . . . .   Independent with MacPherson struts and coil springs. Anti-roll bar

Rear suspension
Type . . . .   Semi-independent torsion beam, with trailing arms, coilsprings and telescopic shock absorbers. Anti-roll bar on larger-engine models.

Steering
Type . . . .   Rack and pinion with power-assistance on certain models

Wheel alignment and steering angles
Front wheels:
  Camber (non adjustable):
    Laden*: . . . .   -1°15' to + 0°15'
    Maximum deviation side to side . . . .   1°
  Castor (non-adjustable):
    Laden*: . . . .   0 to +2°
    Maximum deviation side to side . . . .   1°
  Toe:
    Laden*:
      Up to 1985 . . . .   0.5 to 2.5 mm toe-out
      From 1985 onwards . . . .   1.0 mm toe-out to 1.0 mm toe-in
Rear wheels:
  Camber (non adjustable):
    Laden . . . .   0° to -1'
    Maximum deviation side-to-side . . . .   0°30'
  Toe-in:
    Laden . . . .   +0°20' to 1°00' (2.0 to 6.0 mm)
    Maximum deviation side-to-side . . . .   0°15'

*Laden indicates a vehicle containing two front seat occupants and a half-filled fuel tank

Roadwheels

Type	Pressed steel or aluminium alloy (depending on model)
Size	5J x 13, 5.5J x 13 or 5.5J x 14

Tyres

Size	155 SR 13, 165 SR 13, 165 HR 13, 185/70 SR 13, 185/70 HR 13, 185/70 TR 13 or 195/60 HR 14 (depending on model)

Torque wrench settings	Nm	lbf ft
Front suspension		
Control arm balljoint to stub axle carrier	70	52
Suspension strut top mounting nuts	20	15
Strut piston rod nut	55	41
Strut gland nut	200	148
Tie-rod balljoint to steering arm	60	44
Anti-roll bar U-clamps	20	15
Suspension control arm pivot bolts	110	81
Suspension control arm support (short type):		
Smaller bolts	110	81
Larger centre bolt	130	96
Suspension control arm support (longer type) bolts	110	81
Driveshaft to hub carrier castellated nut:		
Stage 1	100	74
Slacken then Stage 2	20	15
Stage 3	Tighten through further 90°	
Rear suspension		
Rear axle to underbody pivot bolts	100	74
Rear shock absorber mountings (Estate):		
Upper	20	15
Lower	55	41
Rear shock absorber lower mounting (Saloon/Hatchback):		
Up to VIN DV 144 510/D6 041 675	60	44
Later models	70	52
Level control pressure line unions	3	2
Anti-roll bar clamps	18	13
Stub axle flange to rear axle:		
Stage 1	60	44
Stage 2	Turn through further 30°	
Steering		
Adjustment screw locknut	60	44
Column spindle coupling clamp bolt	22	16
Pinion-to-coupling clamp bolt	22	16
Steering wheel nut	25	18
Steering gear unit mounting nuts	15	11
Pinion attachment bolt	40	30
Column-to-dash panel bolts	22	16
Damper bolts to steering gear housing	22	16
Tie-rod to steering gear	110	81
Tie-rod balljoint nut	60	44
Tie-rod clamp pinch-bolt	20	15
Power steering items:		
Flow and return pipes to steering gear (special retaining bolt)	37	27
High pressure hose union nut	42	31
Pump pressure lines union nut (to connectors)	28	21
Fluid reservoir bracket bolts	7	5
Support-to-cylinder block bolts	40	30
Oil pump bolts	15	11
Support tightening screw	40	30
Tightening piece to support bolts	15	11
Tightening piece bolt locknut	40	30
Roadwheels		
Roadwheel bolts	90	66

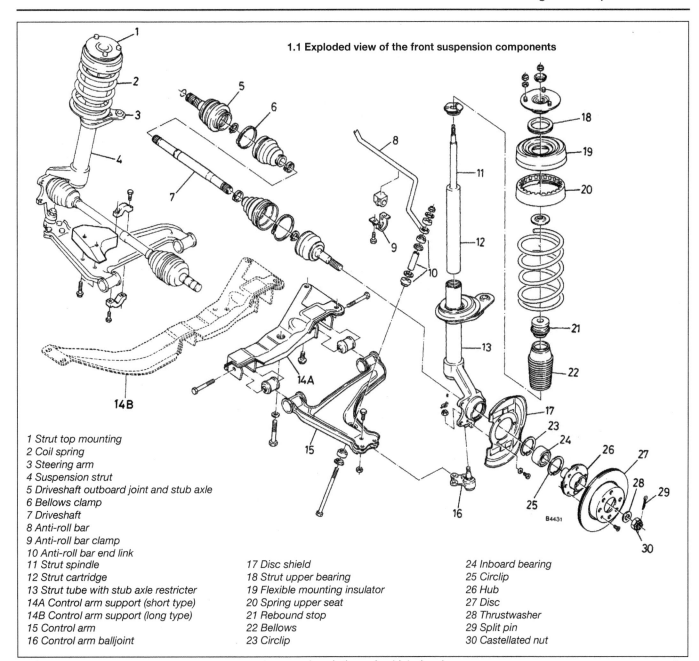

1.1 Exploded view of the front suspension components

1 Strut top mounting
2 Coil spring
3 Steering arm
4 Suspension strut
5 Driveshaft outboard joint and stub axle
6 Bellows clamp
7 Driveshaft
8 Anti-roll bar
9 Anti-roll bar clamp
10 Anti-roll bar end link
11 Strut spindle
12 Strut cartridge
13 Strut tube with stub axle restricter
14A Control arm support (short type)
14B Control arm support (long type)
15 Control arm
16 Control arm balljoint

17 Disc shield
18 Strut upper bearing
19 Flexible mounting insulator
20 Spring upper seat
21 Rebound stop
22 Bellows
23 Circlip

24 Inboard bearing
25 Circlip
26 Hub
27 Disc
28 Thrustwasher
29 Split pin
30 Castellated nut

1 General information

The front suspension consists of telescopic hydraulic struts, coil springs, anti-roll bar and a control arm **(see illustration)**.

The hub bearings are of double row ball type.

The rear suspension is of semi-independent type having a torsion beam and trailing arms with mini-block coil springs and telescopic shock absorbers **(see illustration)**.

The roadwheels may be of pressed steel or light alloy type dependent upon the particular model.

Some models are fitted with a level control system, a description of which is given elsewhere in this Chapter.

The steering gear is of rack-and-pinion type, movement being transmitted to the front wheels through tie-rods which are connected to the rack through a sliding sleeve.

The steering column consists of an outer column which incorporates a deformable section, and a shaft connected to a flexible coupling at its lower end.

As from 1983, power steering gear is fitted as standard to all 1.8 CD models and is available as an option on other models.

With this type of steering gear, a rotary slide valve design is employed which gives exceptionally precise steering with good "feel" and operational safety.

2 Front suspension strut - removal and refitting

Removal

1 Remove the centre trim plate from the roadwheel.

2 Extract the split pin from the castellated hub nut and release the nut.

3 Raise the vehicle, support securely and then remove the roadwheel. If the roadwheels have been balanced on the vehicle (new vehicles are balanced this way in production) then mark the relative position of the roadwheel to the hub so that it can be aligned correctly when refitting.

1.3 Exploded view of the rear suspension components

1 Shock absorber
2 Coil spring
3 Axle beam
4 Trailing link
5 Anti-roll bar
6 Stub axle
7 Oil seal
8 Inboard bearing
9 Hub
10 Outboard bearing
11 Thrustwasher
12 Split pin
13 Castellated nut
14 Dust cap

4 Prise off the mounting bolt caps (GMF caliper only) then slacken and remove the two caliper mounting bolts and slide the caliper off the brake disc. Support the caliper; do not allow it to hang on the hydraulic hose.

5 Unscrew the tie-rod end balljoint nut well up its threads and then, using a suitable balljoint extractor tool, disconnect the balljoint from the steering arm on the suspension strut.

6 Disconnect the control arm balljoint from the stub axle carrier in a similar way. It may be found that, owing to the limited clearance between the driveshaft joint and the balljoint nut, it is difficult to fit an extractor tool. In this case either push the driveshaft slightly out of the hub which will compress the joint and provide greater clearance for the tool or use forked wedges as an alternative.

7 Pull the stub axle carrier towards you until the driveshaft is detached from the carrier and then support the shaft on a block or jack.

Note: Do not move the vehicle on its wheels

with one or both driveshafts removed from their hubs, as damage to the front wheel hub bearings can occur.

8 Remove the suspension strut mounting nuts from the upper turret (see illustration).

9 Withdraw the suspension strut, complete with coil spring, from under the front wing.

Refitting

10 Refitting is a reversal of removal noting the following points.

a) Tighten all nuts and bolts to the specified torque settings (where given).

b) Prior to refitting the brake caliper, remove all traces of locking compound from the mounting bolt threads and hub carrier holes and apply a drop of fresh locking compound to the bolt threads. Refit the caliper and insert the mounting bolts, tightening them to the specified torque setting (see Chapter 9).

3 Front hub bearing - renewal

1 Remove the suspension strut as described in Section 2.

2 Extract the countersunk screw and remove the brake disc from the hub.

3 The hub should now be removed from the carrier using one of two methods. Either use a press or puller, or screw two roadwheel bolts into the hub flange and, using progressively thicker packing pieces, tighten the bolts to force off the hub (see illustrations).

4 Undo and remove the brake disc shield.

5 Extract the two bearing circlips (see illustrations).

6 Using a press or bearing puller remove the bearing from the stub axle carrier, applying pressure to the outer track.

7 Before installing the new bearing, insert the

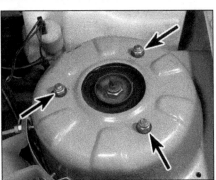

2.8 Front suspension strut top mounting nuts (arrowed)

3.3a Removing hub from carrier

3.3b Hub removed from carrier

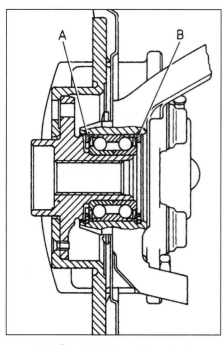

3.5a Sectional view of front hub
A and B Bearing circlips

circlip (A in illustration 3.5a) into the stub axle carrier. Make sure that it is positively located in its groove with its tabs pointing downward (when strut is in vehicle).
8 Press the new bearing into position until it

3.5b Extracting hub bearing circlip

contacts the circlip, applying pressure to the outer track **(see illustration)**.
9 Fit the remaining bearing circlip.
10 Fit the brake disc shield.
11 Press or draw (long bolt and washers) the hub, which is an interference fit, into the stub axle carrier. The bearing inner track must be supported during this operation.
12 Refit the suspension strut.

4 Front suspension strut - overhaul

1 The suspension struts are of renewable cartridge type which makes them very easy to recondition in the event of their losing their damping properties.

3.8 Hub bearing/seal

2 With the strut removed from the vehicle as described in Section 2, secure it by gripping the stub axle carrier in the jaws of a vice.
3 Fit a suitable spring compressor tool to the spring coils. These are available at most motor accessory shops. Tighten the compressor until all the tension is removed from the spring, then, as an additional safety measure, tighten a strap or chain around the compressor **(see illustration)**.
4 Unscrew and remove the strut spindle top nut and withdraw the top mounting **(see illustrations)**.
5 Lift off the spring upper seat. Note the detachable bearing. Remove the thrustwasher and the rebound stop **(see illustrations)**.
6 Carefully release the spring tension by unscrewing the compressor nuts evenly.

4.3 Strut coil spring with compressor and strap fitted

4.4a Strut top mounting plate

4.4b Strut spring upper seat

4.5a Strut mounting plate removal from spring upper seat

4.5b Strut upper bearing

4.5c Strut thrustwasher and rebound stop

4.7 Strut bellows

4.9a Method of unscrewing strut gland nut

4.9 b Removing strut gland nut

4.10 Removing strut cartridge

7 Take off the compressor and the coil spring **(see illustration)**.
8 Withdraw the strut bellows.
9 From the upper end of the strut, unscrew the gland nut. This is very tight and it will probably be found easier to grip the nut in a vice and to unscrew the strut from it using a long bar as shown **(see illustrations)**.
10 Withdraw the hydraulic damper cartridge and discard it **(see illustration)**.
11 Reassemble by inserting the new cartridge and tightening the gland nut to the specified torque.
12 Locate the bellows and stop plates.
13 Locate the coil spring so that the end of its lower coil locates correctly in the channel of the seat.
14 Fit the spring compressor and compress

the spring enough to be able to fit the top mounting.
15 Fit the top mounting with bearing. Ensure that the support bearing is correctly fitted and locate the stop washers as shown **(see illustration)**.
16 Hold the strut spindle from rotating while the mounting nut is tightened to the specified torque.
17 Carefully release the spring compressor and remove it.

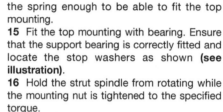

5 Front suspension control arm - removal and refitting

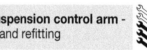

Removal

1 The control arm may be removed independently, leaving its support attached to the vehicle.
2 Raise the front of the vehicle and remove the roadwheel. If the roadwheels have been balanced on the vehicle (new vehicles are balanced this way in production) then mark the relative position of the roadwheel to the hub so that it can be aligned correctly when refitting.
3 Disconnect the anti-roll bar end link.
4 Using a suitable tool, disconnect the control arm balljoint from the stub axle carrier (see Section 2, paragraph 6) **(see illustrations)**.
5 Unbolt the control arm pivot bolts from the support. On some later models, the control arm support differs in that it is extended and

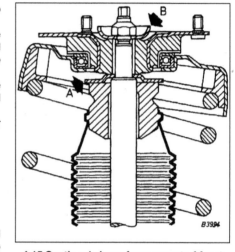

4.15 Sectional view of upper part of front suspension strut
A and B Support bearing stop washers

bolted to the front body crossmember; the removal of the control arm from this type of support remains the same **(see illustration)**.

Refitting

6 Refitting is a reversal of removal noting the following points.
a) *Always use new bolts which will be supplied pre-coated with thread locking compound. If they are not, apply a suitable locking compound to their threads prior to installation.*

5.4a Control arm balljoint

5.4b Control arm balljoint released

5.5 Long type control arm front mounting

5.6 Right-hand control arm damper weight

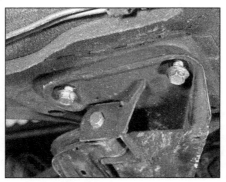

8.4 Unscrew the two smaller bolts

8.7a Control arm support removal tool

b) Remove all traces of locking compound from the bolt hole threads in the underbody, ideally by running a tap of the correct size and pitch down them. If a suitable tap is not available, cut two slots into the threads of one of the original bolts, and use the bolt to remove the locking compound from the threads.

c) Tighten the support bolts to the specified torque. When tightening the pivot bolts, support the control arm in the horizontal attitude and then tighten to the specified torque.

d) The right-hand control arm on some larger engine models is fitted with a damper weight. This is secured by socket-headed screws (see illustration).

6 Control arm bushes - renewal

1 The flexible bushes should preferably be removed and new ones fitted using a press. However, a bolt with suitable distance pieces and washers is equally effective as a means of drawing the bushes out or in.

2 The control arm should be removed as described in Section 6.

3 Apply soapy water as a lubricant to the new bushes before fitting them. Make sure that the flange at each end of the flexible bush projects equally from its control arm housing. Note that the bushes are not identical; the one incorporating the internal intermediate bush must be fitted to the front of the control arm.

7 Control arm balljoint - renewal

With the control arm removed from the vehicle as described in Section 5, drill out the balljoint rivets using a 12.0 mm drill. Remove the balljoint.

Fit the replacement balljoint using the nuts and bolts supplied and making sure that the nuts are located on the underside of the control arm.

8 Control arm support - removal and refitting

Removal

1 The purpose of removing the control arm support will normally be as preparation for removal of the engine, transmission or driveshaft, and the operations described here are directed towards this end. However, if the support is being removed for renewal or repair, then the control arm should first be detached from it by unscrewing the pivot bolts.

2 Raise the front of the vehicle and remove the roadwheel.

3 Disconnect the anti-roll bar from the control arm by unscrewing the nuts on the end link of the bar.

Shorter type support - 1.3 and 1.6 (except GLS) litre models

4 Unscrew the two smaller bolts which attach the support to the underbody (see illustration).

5 Unscrew the larger bolt from the centre underside of the support, but do not remove it.

6 The support is located on a positioning dowel and a puller will now be required to draw it off.

8.7b Withdrawing control arm support

7 A suitable tool can be made up by modifying a two-legged extractor as shown. The important part is the shape of the heads of the anchor bolts which must be inserted into the small rectangular cutouts in the underside of the support. These are then turned through 90° to give it firm anchorage to the tool (see illustrations).

8 If the extractor pressure bolt is now located against the head of the larger support bolt and screwed in, the action will force the support off its dowel and leave it hanging on its partially unscrewed centre bolt (see illustration).

9 Remove the centre bolt and lower the support (see illustration).

8.8 Short type control arm support positioning dowel

8.9 Removing control arm support larger fixing bolt

8.10a Centre and rear control arm support bolts (longer type support)

8.10b Front bolts on longer type control arm support

8.12 Torque tightening the control arm larger fixing bolt

Longer type support - 1.6 GLS, 1.8 and 2.0 litre models

10 On these models the control arm support is held in place by six bolts and the support is not located on a dowel as previously described for the shorter type support **(see illustrations)**.

11 Apart from this difference, and the fact that a special removal tool will not be required, the removal operations are similar to those previously described, but prior to removing the support, make an outline marking of the mounting positions at the front and rear to ensure exact realignment when refitting.

Refitting

12 Refitting is a reversal of removal noting the following points.

a) *Always use new bolts which will be supplied pre-coated with thread locking compound. If they are not, apply a suitable locking compound to their threads prior to installation.*

b) *Remove all traces of locking compound from the bolt hole threads in the underbody, ideally by running a tap of the correct size and pitch down them.* **Tip:** *If a suitable tap is not available, cut two slots into the threads of one of the original bolts, and use the bolt to remove the locking compound from the threads.*

c) *Tighten the support bolts to the specified torque* **(see illustration)**.

9.1 Front anti-roll bar end link

9 Front anti-roll bar - removal and refitting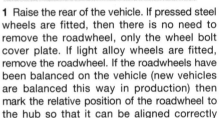

Removal

1 Raise the front of the vehicle and disconnect the anti-roll bar end links from the suspension control arms **(see illustration)**.

2 Release the control arm support from the bodyframe as described in the preceding Section. Do not remove it completely, but have it hanging on the centre bolt. This will provide sufficient clearance to withdraw the anti-roll bar sideways once the bar clamps have been released from the underbody.

Refitting

3 Refitting is a reversal of removal, but observe the procedure for the support bolts as described in the preceding Section. Tighten the anti-roll bar end link nut to give the specified rubber cushion compression shown **(see illustration)**.

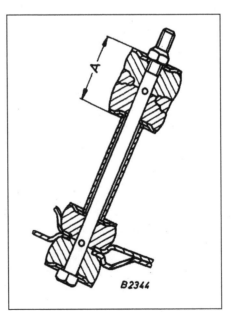

9.3 Front anti-roll bar end link
A = 38. mm (1.5 in)

10 Rear hub bearings - adjustment

1 Raise the rear of the vehicle. If pressed steel wheels are fitted, then there is no need to remove the roadwheel, only the wheel bolt cover plate. If light alloy wheels are fitted, remove the roadwheel. If the roadwheels have been balanced on the vehicle (new vehicles are balanced this way in production) then mark the relative position of the roadwheel to the hub so that it can be aligned correctly when refitting.

2 Prise off the small dust cap from the centre of the hub.

3 Extract the split pin from the castellated nut on the stub axle.

4 Tighten the nut to a torque of 25 Nm (18 lbf ft) while turning the roadwheel (or brake drum).

5 After tightening the nut to this initial torque, slacken the nut until the thrustwasher can *just* be moved. Determine this by trying to move the washer with a screwdriver blade. Do not lever against the hub, simply apply the blade directly to the washer.

6 If the split pin holes are not aligned with the nut castellations, tighten the nut until the first available alignment occurs and check whether the thrustwasher can still be moved. If it can, fit the split pin; if not, back off the nut to the next available position, then fit the split pin.

7 Check that the hub can rotate freely without binding then refit the dust cap.

11 Rear hub bearings - renewal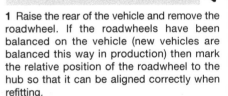

1 Raise the rear of the vehicle and remove the roadwheel. If the roadwheels have been balanced on the vehicle (new vehicles are balanced this way in production) then mark the relative position of the roadwheel to the hub so that it can be aligned correctly when refitting.

2 Remove the brake drums (Chapter 9).

3 Prise off the dust cap and extract the split pin from the castellated nut **(see illustration)**.

4 Remove the nut and the thrustwasher **(see illustration)**.

11.3 Rear hub nut and split pin

11.4 Removing the thrustwasher

11.9 Locate the new hub oil seal

5 Withdraw the hub from the stub axle.

6 Lever out the oil seal from the inboard end of the hub and then take out the inboard and outboard bearing inner races.

7 Press or drive out the bearing outer tracks from the hub.

8 Press or drive the new bearing outer tracks into the hub.

9 Fit the inboard bearing race and oil seal. Apply grease liberally to the bearing and the lips of the oil seal and half fill the space between the two bearing outer tracks with grease **(see illustration)**.

10 Fit the hub to the stub axle, insert the outboard bearing race, the thrustwasher and the nut.

11 Adjust as described in Section 10.

---

12 Rear shock absorber -
   removal, testing and refitting

Removal

1 Due to the design of the rear axle, it is essential that one shock absorber at a time be removed and refitted.

2 On models fitted with the level control system it is essential to depressurize the air in the system before removing the shock absorber(s). See Section 20, paragraph 3.

Hatchback/Saloon models

3 Open the luggage boot or tailgate and prise off the cap which covers the shock absorber top mounting.

4 Unscrew the nut(s) now exposed and take off the washer and rubber cushion **(see illustrations)**.

5 Drive the rear wheels up onto the ramps. If ramps are not available, raise and securely support the rear of the vehicle, but be prepared to compress the shock absorber slightly by jacking up under the axle arm **(see illustration)**.

6 Disconnect the level control system union from the shock absorber where applicable (after depressurizing the air in the system).

7 Disconnect the shock absorber lower mounting from the rear axle and then withdraw it from the vehicle.

8 To test the shock absorber unit, grip it vertically in the jaws of a vice so that it is held

by its lower mounting eye.

9 Fully extend and contract the shock absorber six or seven times. Any evidence of jerky movement or lack of resistance will indicate the need for renewal.

Estate models

10 The rear suspension on the Estate is similar to that on the other models. The main difference is in the shock absorber mountings: the shock absorbers are inclined at an angle to improve the load deck space.

11 Remove the mounting nuts and bolts from the top and bottom mountings, recover the spacer washers, and withdraw the shock absorber **(see illustrations)**.

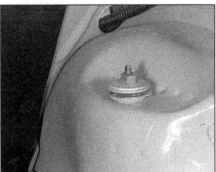
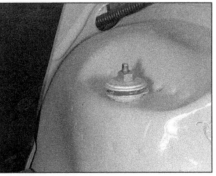

12.4a Rear shock absorber upper mounting

12.4b Rear shock absorber top mounting lower cushion

12.5 Rear shock absorber lower mounting (Saloon/Hatchback)

12.11a Rear shock absorber lower mounting (Estate)

12.11b Rear shock absorber upper mounting (Estate)

Refitting

12 Refitting is a reversal of removal noting the following points.

   a) Tighten all nuts and bolts to their specified torque settings (where given).

   b) On models with level control, ensure that the shock absorber is fitted with the pressure line facing the correct way round. Tighten the lower mounting bolt to the specified torque, and the upper mounting nut to give the exposed thread length shown (see illustrations). Reconnect the level control system hose to the shock absorber union, repressurize the system and check for any signs of air leaks (Section 19).

13 Rear anti-roll bar - removal and refitting

Removal

1 An anti-roll bar is fitted to the rear suspension system on some models. Although the mounting positions for the anti-roll bar differ on pre- and post 1985 models, due to the rear axle being modified in profile, the removal, servicing and refitting procedures are the same.

2 Raise and support the vehicle at the rear.

3 Disconnect the anti-roll bar mountings from the suspension trailing arm, and from the clamps on the rear axle. Remove the bar.

4 Renew the anti-roll bar and/or its mounting bushes if they are worn, perished or damaged.

Refitting

5 Refit in the reverse order of removal. Tighten the retaining bolts to the specified torque.

14 Rear coil spring - removal and refitting

Removal

1 On models fitted with the level control system first depressurize the system as described in Section 20.

2 Raise the rear of the vehicle and support under the rear jacking points under the sill and remove the roadwheels. If the roadwheels have been balanced on the vehicle (new vehicles are balanced this way in production) then mark the relative position of the roadwheel to the hub so that it can be aligned correctly when refitting.

3 Place a jack under the suspension trailing arm and raise it slightly.

4 Disconnect the shock absorber lower mounting and separate the shock absorber eye from the mounting bracket. Remove the jack. Disconnect and plug the brake flexible hoses if they are in danger of being strained by the movement of the rear axle (see Chapter 9 for details).

5 Disconnect the shock absorber on the other side of the vehicle in a similar way.

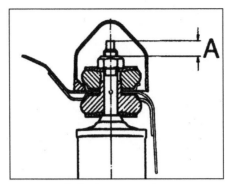

12.12a Rear shock absorber upper mounting - standard type
A = 9 mm (0.35 in)

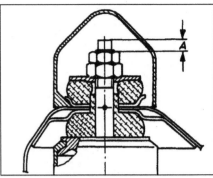

12.12b Rear shock absorber upper mounting - two retaining nut type
A = 6 mm (0.24 in)

6 Slightly lower the jack which is still supporting the trailing arm and then remove the coil spring from the opposite side of the vehicle first, followed by the remaining one. Take out the insulating rings from the spring seats.

Refitting

7 Refitting is a reversal of removal noting the following points.

   a) If there is any difficulty in holding the insulators in place while the coil spring is located, use impact type adhesive.

   b) Where necessary, reconnect the brake hoses and bleed the brake hydraulic system as described in Chapter 9.

   c) On models fitted with level control, repressurize the system (Section 19).

15 Rear suspension stub axle - removal and refitting

Removal

1 Remove the hub as described in Section 11.

2 Unscrew and remove the four bolts which hold the stub axle mounting flange to the axle flange. Remove the stub axle.

Refitting

3 Refitting is the reverse of removal noting the following.

   a) Always use new stub axle bolts which will be supplied pre-coated with thread locking compound. If they are not, apply a suitable locking compound to their threads prior to installation.

   b) Prior to refitting, remove all traces of locking compound from the bolt hole threads, ideally by running a tap of the correct size and pitch down them. If a suitable tap is not available, cut two slots into the threads of one of the original bolts, and use the bolt to remove the locking compound from the threads.

   c) Tighten the bolts through the stages given in the Specifications.

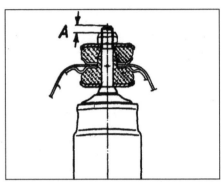

12.12c Rear shock absorber upper mounting - load levelling type
A = 6 mm (0.24 in)

16 Rear axle - removal and refitting

Removal

1 Raise the rear of the vehicle, support it securely under the jacking points and remove the roadwheels. If the roadwheels have been balanced on the vehicle (new vehicles are balanced this way in production) then mark the relative position of the roadwheel to the hub so that it can be aligned correctly when refitting.

2 Disconnect the rear flexible brake hydraulic hoses from the rigid pipeline connections (see Chapter 9) and cap the pipes and hoses to prevent loss of fluid.

3 Unscrew the self-locking nut on the shorter handbrake cable end fitting at the equaliser. Disconnect the cable from the equaliser.

4 Disconnect the longer handbrake cable from the extension piece on the lever pull rod.

5 Release the handbrake cable from the underbody guides by bending them open.

6 Remove the coil springs (Section 14).

7 Locate a jack, preferably of hydraulic type, under the centre of the rear axle.

8 Unscrew and remove the pivot bolts which connect the trailing arms to the underbody.

9 Lower the jack and withdraw the axle assembly from under the vehicle.

10 The axle may be dismantled as necessary by removing the brake components (Chapter 9), and the stub axle and hubs (Sections 11 and 15 of this Chapter).

Refitting

11 Reassembly and refitting are reversals of removal and dismantling, but observe the following requirements
  a) *Tighten all nuts and bolts to the specified torque but leave tightening the rear axle pivot bolts until the vehicle is free standing and laden with the equivalent of a driver and a front seat passenger.*
  b) *Bleed the brake hydraulic system with reference to Chapter 9.*
  c) *Adjust the handbrake (Chapter 9).*

17 Trailing arm flexible bushes - renewal

1 Support the body under the jacking points and remove the roadwheels. If the roadwheels have been balanced on the vehicle (new vehicles are balanced this way in production) then mark the relative position of the roadwheel to the hub so that it can be aligned correctly when refitting.
2 The rear axle must be supported, preferably on a trolley jack, and the brake hose clips removed from the underbody.
3 Unscrew and remove the pivot bolts which secure the trailing arms to the underbody **(see illustration)**.
4 Lower the jack very slowly and at the same time ease the brake hoses and the rigid lines, bending the latter if necessary to prevent straining them.
5 As soon as the flexible bushes in the trailing arms are clear of the underbody, support the rear axle on axle stands (see *"Jacking and Vehicle Support"*).
6 Using a sharp knife cut off the flange from the flexible bushes.
7 Tap round the bush housing to free the bush.
8 Use a bolt and distance pieces to draw the bush from the trailing arm. Removal will be facilitated if the housing is heated to between 60 and 70°C (140 and 158°F).

Warning; Do not use a flame to do this, owing to the proximity of the fuel tank, but heat with a soldering iron or rags soaked in boiling water.

9 Smear the new bush with grease and draw it into position, but make sure that the mouldings on the end of the bush are positioned as shown **(see illustration)**.
10 Always renew the bushes on both trailing links at the same time.
11 Refit the axle by reversing the removal operations. Tighten bolts to the specified torque, leaving tightening the rear axle pivot bolts until the vehicle is free standing and laden with the equivalent of a driver and a front seat passenger

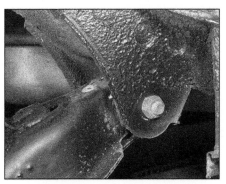

17.3 Rear trailing link pivot bolt

18 Level control system - description

1 This system is only available on certain models and its function is to compensate for the effect of heavy luggage or towing loads on the vehicle's rear suspension.
2 The system operates by varying the air pressure in the rear shock absorbers. On some models the pressure in the system is regulated automatically, whilst on others (and more commonly) the pressure can be manually adjusted.

Automatic system control

3 When the fully automatic system is fitted, an electrically-driven compressor is the source of compressed air and no driver action is necessary. Response to level change is

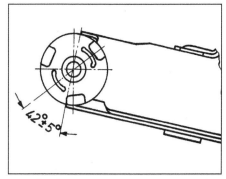

17.9 Trailing arm flexible bush positioning

inhibited for 20 seconds or so in order to prevent the system trying to compensate for bumps in the road.
4 The layout of the automatic level control system and the location of the various components is shown in the accompanying illustration **(see illustration)**.

Manual system control

5 With this more commonly fitted system, a compressed air line is connected to a union connection in the body of each shock absorber at the rear. The two hoses are interconnected to a single hose which is routed through the body side panels to an adjuster valve (similar to a tyre pressure valve) in the body at the rear. The location of this valve varies according to model, but will be in the luggage compartment or in the rain channel on the right rear corner (accessible with the boot lid open).

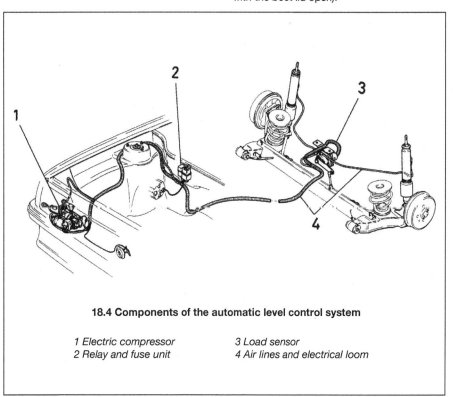

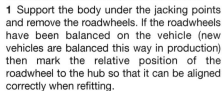

18.4 Components of the automatic level control system

1 Electric compressor
2 Relay and fuse unit
3 Load sensor
4 Air lines and electrical loom

19 Level control system (manual) - adjustment

1 Most vehicles will be equipped with the manually adjusted system. A compressed air line is used to increase the system pressure via a valve in the load area (see illustration). The procedure is as follows.

2 With the vehicle unladen, use a tyre pressure gauge on the level control valve to check that the system pressure is 0.8 bar (12 psi): adjust if necessary. Measure the distance from the centre of the rear bumper to the ground with the vehicle standing on a level surface (see illustration).

3 Load the vehicle and increase the pressure in the system to restore the previously measured height. Do not exceed a pressure of 5.0 bar (73 psi).

4 After unloading the vehicle, depressurize the system to correct the height, observing the minimum pressure of 0.8 bar (12 psi). Do not drive an unladen vehicle with the system fully inflated.

5 If it is necessary to check the rear wheel alignment, this should be done with the level control system inflated to 1.0 bar (15 psi).

20 Level control system component removal and refitting - general information

1 If a fault is suspected in the level control system it is essential that it is checked out by a Vauxhall dealer without delay. If a leak is suspected, inspect the system hoses and connections for condition and security.

2 If any part of the level control system is to be disconnected or removed, the system must first be depressurized.

3 Depressurize the level control system completely, either at the valve (manual system) or by slackening a pressure line union (automatic system).

4 If removing any of the electrical components of the automatic level control system, first disconnect the battery earth lead.

5 When refitting the system components, ensure that the line connections are tightened

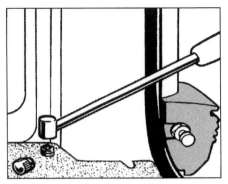

19.1 Level control system manual inflation valve on the Estate model

to the specified torque setting, also that the system hoses are correctly routed. Check for signs of air leaks when the system has been repressurized.

21 Tie-rod end - removal and refitting

Removal

1 Raise the front of the car and remove the roadwheel. If the wheels have been balanced on the vehicle (new vehicles are balanced this way in production) then mark the relative position of the roadwheel to the hub so that it can be aligned correctly when refitting.

2 Slacken the tie-rod end balljoint nut, release the ball-pin using a balljoint separator tool, and remove the nut (see illustration). Extract the balljoint from the steering arm.

3 Slacken the clamp bolt which secures the tie-rod end to the outer tie-rod. Mark the position of the tie-rod end on the outer tie-rod with paint or tape, then unscrew the tie-rod end.

4 Note that the tie-rod ends are handed. The right-hand end is marked with an "R"; the left-hand end has no marking.

Refitting

5 Screw the new tie-rod end onto the tie-rod to approximately the same position as was occupied by the old one. Secure it with the clamp bolt.

19.2 Measuring the rear ride height

6 Connect the tie-rod end to the steering arm, and secure it with a new self-locking nut, tightened to the specified torque.

7 Refit the roadwheel, and lower the car to the ground.

8 Check and adjust the front wheel alignment (toe setting), as described in Section 32.

22 Steering gear - removal and refitting

Removal

Manual steering

1 Remove the air cleaner.

2 If a headlamp washer system is fitted, release the fluid reservoir and move it to one side.

3 Disconnect the battery earth lead.

4 Working at the centre of the steering rack housing, remove both tie-rod bolts and remove the bolt locks and the spacer plate (see illustration).

5 On models fitted with a steering damper, detach the damper brackets from the steering gear housing and remove the damper.

6 Pull off the cardboard panel from under the facia panel to give access to the steering column shaft flexible coupling.

7 Set the steering wheel and front roadwheels in the straight-ahead position.

8 Unscrew the two pinch-bolts on the flexible coupling at the base of the steering column shaft (see illustration).

21.3 Typical balljoint extractor

22.4 Tie-rod connection to steering rack

22.8 Flexible coupling upper pinch-bolt (arrowed)

22.10 Steering rack showing mounting clamp (arrowed)

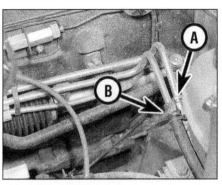

22.12 Power steering pressure pipe union (A) and return hose clip (B)

23 Steering rack bellows - renewal

9 Slide the flexible coupling upwards off the pinion.

10 Unbolt the steering gear mounting clamps and withdraw the rack-and-pinion housing through the front right-hand wheel arch **(see illustration)**.

Power steering

11 The operations are similar to those just described for the manual steering gear, except that the flow (pressure) and return pipes must be disconnected prior to removal.

12 Undo the pressure pipe union and slacken the return hose clip, then separate the pipe and hose unions **(see illustration)**.

13 Allow the fluid to drain from the open pipe and hose unions, then cover the unions with small plastic bags or tape to prevent dirt ingress.

Refitting

Manual steering

14 Refitting is a reversal of removal, but before connecting the flexible coupling to the pinion, the steering must be centred in the following way.

15 Jack up the front of the car and turn the pinion on the steering gear until the distance between the centre of the spacer plate and the rib on the mounting is as shown **(see illustration)**.

16 Set the steering wheel in its straight-ahead position.

17 Where a steering damper is fitted, bolt it to

the steering gear housing and tighten the bolts to the specified torque wrench setting.

18 Push the flexible coupling down and connect it with the pinion, then tighten the coupling bolt to its specified torque setting.

19 The upper clamp should now be lying so that the pinch-bolt is parallel with the steering housing. If it is not, this will indicate that the pinion is out of phase with the rack, and the components will have to be adjusted. Refer to your Vauxhall/Opel dealer for further information.

20 Check that the concave end of the mounting bracket is pointing downward when the steering gear is installed.

21 If the pinion sealing cap has been disturbed, make sure that its notch is engaged with the rib on the steering gear housing.

Power steering

22 When refitting the steering gear, centralise it by counting the number of turns from lock to lock while turning the pinion shaft. Then set the steering by turning the pinion shaft from the full lock position through half the number of turns counted.

23 Fit the flexible coupling to the pinion shaft (steering still centralised) so that the upper pinch-bolt lies horizontally and on top of the pinion shaft.

24 Reconnect the pipe and hose unions, then fill and bleed the system as described in Section 31.

1 To renew faulty bellows, the steering gear must first be removed from the vehicle as described in the preceding Section.

2 Remove the mounting bracket and its rubber insulator from the housing. If working on power steering, undo the banjo unions and remove the fluid pipes.

3 Remove the bellows clamp wires and pull the bellows from the housing. If both bellows are to be renewed, the complete bellows/sleeve assembly may be slid from the housing.

4 Refitting is a reversal of removal, but observe the following essential requirements.

  a) *The concave end of the mounting bracket bolt hole flange must be pointing down when the steering gear is installed.*

  b) *If the pinion sealing cap has been removed, make sure that its notch is engaged with the rib on the steering gear housing.*

  c) *On power steering gear, refit the banjo unions using new sealing washers.*

24 Steering gear - overhaul

1 Examine the steering gear assembly for signs of wear or damage and check that the rack moves freely throughout the full length of its travel with no signs of roughness or excessive free play between the steering gear pinion and rack. It is possible to overhaul the steering gear assembly components but this task should be entrusted to a Vauxhall/Opel dealer. The only components which can be renewed easily by the home mechanic are the steering gear bellows and the tie-rod ends which are covered elsewhere in this Chapter.

2 On models equipped with power-assisted steering inspect all the steering gear fluid unions for signs of leakage and check that all union nuts are securely tightened.

3 Inspect the rubber mountings and pinion gear cover renew them if the rubbers shown signs of wear or deterioration.

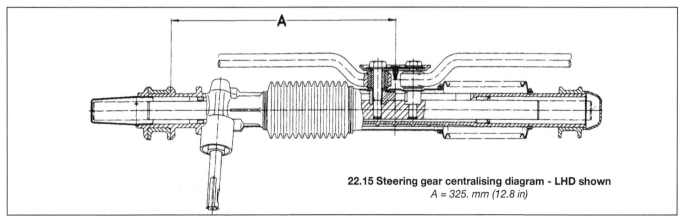

22.15 Steering gear centralising diagram - LHD shown
A = 325. mm (12.8 in)

25 Steering damper - removal and refitting

Removal

1 Certain models are equipped with a steering damper which is fitted between the rack and the rack housing.
2 First unbolt the damper from the rack bracket at the centre of the steering assembly and then unclamp it from the rack housing **(see illustration)**. Remove the damper.

Refitting

3 Refitting is a reversal of removal, but tighten the spindle nut only sufficiently to maintain the length (A) of exposed threads as shown in **illustration 25.3a**. The clamp should be set as shown in **illustration 25.3b**, before tightening all bolts to the specified torque.

26 Steering wheel - removal and refitting

Removal

1 Disconnect the battery negative lead.
2 Prise out the horn button from the centre of the steering wheel and detach the wiring connections **(see illustration)**.
3 Set the steering wheel in the straight-ahead position and unscrew the retaining nut.
4 Using a small two-legged puller with outward-facing legs inserted through the two holes in the wheel hub, withdraw the steering wheel from the shaft. Do not attempt to thump the wheel off or the safety type steering column may be damaged **(see illustration)**.
5 When necessary, the horn contact ring may be renewed by unclipping it from the wheel hub. When fitting the new ring, make sure that the direction indicator switch cancelling segment is to the left-hand side.

Refitting

6 Refit by reversing the removal operations. Check that the steering wheel is correctly aligned before tightening its retaining nut to the specified torque.

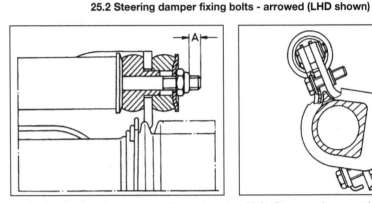

25.2 Steering damper fixing bolts - arrowed (LHD shown)

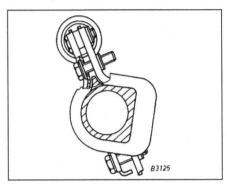

25.3a Steering damper mounting nut setting - LHD shown
A = 6. mm (0.24 in)

25.3b Damper clamp setting in relation to rack housing - LHD shown

27 Steering column - removal and refitting

Removal

1 Disconnect the battery earth lead. Extract the four screws and remove both halves of the steering column shroud.
2 Unclip the direction indicator and wiper switches by depressing the upper and lower locking tabs and sliding the switches from their grooves.
3 Pull out the wiring harness for the steering and ignition locks.
4 Set the steering wheel and the front roadwheels in the straight-ahead position.
5 Unscrew and remove the upper pinch-bolt

from the steering flexible coupling.
6 Unscrew and remove the bolt that secures the base of the column to the bulkhead.
7 The bolts must now be extracted from the column upper mounting bracket. The left-hand bolt is of shear-head type and must be centre-punched, drilled out (using an 1/8 inch bit) and a bolt extractor used to remove it. A self-locking nut is used on the right-hand side.
8 Withdraw the column assembly into the vehicle interior and then remove it from the vehicle. Handle the column carefully, avoid knocks or impact of any kind. Remove the steering wheel (Section 26).

Refitting

9 If a new column assembly is being installed, a plastic washer is located on the base of the shaft as an aid to centering the shaft in the column tube.
10 Centre the steering gear as described in Section 22, paragraphs 15 to 19.
11 Engage the plastic washer for centring the shaft in the column tube.
12 Offer the column into position and connect the coupling as described in Section 22, paragraphs 16 to 18.
13 Loosely connect the upper mounting using a new shear bolt **(see illustration)**.
14 Loosely screw in the column lower fixing bolt and the coupling pinch-bolt.
15 Tighten the lower fixing bolt to its specified torque. Tighten the shear-head bolt until its head breaks off.

26.2 Horn button removed

26.4 Removing steering wheel

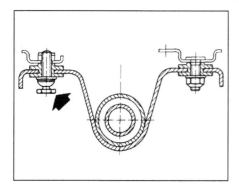

27.13 Steering column upper bracket mounting bolts. Shear-head bolt arrowed

16 Pull up on the steering shaft until contact is made with the shaft bearing stop. Tighten the coupling pinch-bolt.
17 Remove the temporary plastic centering washer.
18 Refit the wiring harness and column switches, also the column upper shrouds **(see illustration)**.
19 Refit the steering wheel and reconnect the battery.

28 Steering column - overhaul

The steering column incorporates a telescopic safety feature. In the event of a front end crash, the shaft housing collapses and prevents the steering wheel injuring the driver. Before refitting the steering column examine the column and mountings for signs of damage and deformation and check the steering shaft for signs of free play in the column bushes. If there are signs of damage or play, the column must be renewed. Overhaul of the column is possible but this is a fiddly task and should be entrusted to a Vauxhall/Opel dealer. Consult your Vauxhall/Opel dealer for further information.

29 Steering column lock/ignition switch - removal and refitting

1 To renew either the ignition switch or the steering lock cylinder, first remove the lower half of the steering column shroud by undoing and removing the securing screws. Disconnect the battery negative terminal and proceed as described under the relevant sub-heading.

Ignition switch wiring block

2 Disconnect the wiring block from the ignition switch.
3 Slacken the two small retaining screws and withdraw the wiring block from the end of the lock housing.
4 Refitting is the reverse of removal, ensuring that the switch centre is correctly engaged with the lock cylinder rod flats.

27.18 Steering column shroud screw

Steering lock cylinder

5 Disconnect the battery earth lead and, after removing the lower half of the steering column shroud, insert the ignition key and turn it to the "II" position.
6 Using a piece of wire or a drill shank (3 mm diameter), depress the lock spring retaining the cylinder and carefully withdraw the cylinder from its housing. It is important that the ignition switch is not removed or disturbed while the lock cylinder is not fitted.
7 Before fitting a new lock cylinder insert the ignition key and turn it to the "II" position. Insert the assembly into the steering lock housing and press it down until the retaining spring engages before removing the key.
8 Reconnect the battery earth lead and test the operation of the ignition switch before fitting the lower half shroud.

30 Power steering pump - removal and refitting

Removal

1 Remove the auxiliary drivebelt as described in Chapter 1.
2 Slacken the retaining clip and disconnect the fluid return hose from the pump then slacken the union nut and disconnect the

supply pipe from the pump along with its O-ring. Be prepared for some fluid spillage as the pipe and hose are disconnected and plug the hose/pipe end and pump unions to minimise fluid loss and prevent the entry of dirt into the system.
3 Slacken and remove the front and rear mountinging bolts securing the power steering pump to its mounting bracket and remove the pump from the engine compartment **(see illustration)**.
4 Remove the cap and empty the reservoir contents into a suitable container.
5 Overhaul of the pump is possible but this task should be entrusted to a Vauxhall dealer.

Refitting

6 Manoeuvre the pump into position and refit its mounting bolts, tightening them to the specified torque setting.
7 Fit a new O-ring to the supply pipe union then reconnect the pipe to the pump and tighten the union nut to the specified torque setting. Refit the return hose to the pump and securely tighten its retaining clip.
8 Refit the auxiliary drivebelt as described in Chapter 1.
9 On completion bleed the hydraulic system as described in Section 31.

31 Power steering system - bleeding

1 Fill the pump fluid reservoir to the full level with specified fluid.
2 Start the engine and allow it to idle.
3 Turn the steering slowly from one lock to the other. This will prove easier if the front roadwheels are first raised off the ground. Do not hold the steering on the full lock position in either direction for periods exceeding 10 seconds.
4 Repeat several times until the fluid level in the reservoir does not fall any further and then finally top-up to the mark and switch off the engine.

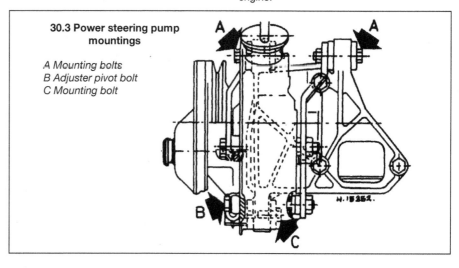

30.3 Power steering pump mountings

A Mounting bolts
B Adjuster pivot bolt
C Mounting bolt

32 Wheel alignment and steering angles - general information

1 Accurate front wheel alignment is essential to good steering and for even tyre wear. Before considering the steering angles, check that the tyres are correctly inflated, that the front wheels are not buckled, the hub bearings are not worn and that the steering linkage is in good order, without slackness or wear at the joints.

2 Wheel alignment consists of four factors:

Camber, is the angle at which the roadwheels are set from the vertical when viewed from the front or rear of the vehicle. Positive camber is the angle (in degrees) that the wheels are tilted outwards at the top from the vertical.

Castor, is the angle between the steering axis and a vertical line when viewed from each side of the vehicle. Positive castor is indicated when the steering axis is inclined towards the rear of the vehicle at its upper end.

Steering axis inclination, is the angle, when viewed from the front or rear of the vehicle, between the vertical and an imaginary line drawn between the upper and lower front suspension strut mountings.

Toe, is the amount by which the distance between the front inside edges of the roadwheel rims differs from that between the rear inside edges. If the distance between the front edges is less than that at the rear, the wheels are said to toe-in. If the distance between the front inside edges is greater than that at the rear, the wheels toe-out.

3 Due to the need for precision gauges to measure the small angles of the steering and suspension settings, it is preferable that checking of camber and castor is left to a service station having the necessary equipment. Camber and castor are set during production of the vehicle, and any deviation from the specified angle will be due to accident damage or gross wear in the suspension mountings.

4 To check the front wheel alignment, first make sure that the lengths of both tie-rods are equal when the steering is in the straight-ahead position. The tie-rods can be adjusted for length if necessary by releasing all the clamp pinch-bolts and turning the rods.

5 Obtain a tracking gauge. These are available in various forms from accessory stores, or one can be fabricated from a length of steel tubing suitably cranked to clear the sump and bellhousing and having a setscrew and locknut at one end.

6 With the gauge, measure the distance between the two wheel inner rims (at hub height) at the rear of the wheel. Push the vehicle forward to rotate the wheel through 180° (half a turn) and measure the distance between the wheel inner rims, again at hub height, at the front of the wheel. This last measurement should differ from the first by the appropriate toe-in/toe-out according to the Specifications. The vehicle must be on level ground.

7 Where the toe-in/toe-out is found to be incorrect, release the tie-rod clamp pinch-bolts and turn the tie-rods equally. Only turn them a quarter of a turn at a time before re-checking the alignment. Do not grip the threaded part of the tie-rod/balljoint during adjustment, but use an open-ended spanner on the flats provided. It is important not to allow the tie-rods to become unequal in length during adjustment otherwise the alignment of the steering wheel will become incorrect and tyre scrubbing will occur on turns. The maximum difference in lengths between the rods must not exceed 5 mm.

8 On completion, tighten the tie-rod clamps without disturbing their setting. Check that the balljoint is at the centre of its arc of travel and the openings in the clamps are aligned with the slots in the tie-rod balljoint socket, also that the clamp pinch-bolts have their nuts at the top.

Chapter 11
Bodywork and fittings

Contents

Bonnet - removal and refitting 6
Bonnet release cable - renewal 7
Centre console - removal and refitting 37
Door- removal and refitting 21
Door glass - removal and refitting 14
Door trim panel - removal and refitting 12
Exterior rear view mirror glass - removal and refitting 39
Exterior rear view mirror (manual) - removal and refitting 40
Exterior rear view mirror motor - removal and refitting 42
Exterior rear view mirror (electric) - removal and refitting 41
Facia panel - removal and refitting 35
Front bumper- removal and refitting 9
Front door exterior handle - removal and refitting 17
Front door lock - removal and refitting 16
Front door lock cylinder - removal and refitting 18
Front seat - removal and refitting 33
Front wing - removal and refitting 11
General description 1
Glove compartment - removal and refitting 36
Head restraints - removal and refitting 38
Load area trim panels (Estate) - removal and refitting 28
Luggage boot lid - removal and refitting 29
Luggage boot lid lock and cylinder - removal and refitting 30
Maintenance - bodywork and underframe 2

Maintenance - upholstery and carpets 3
Major body damage - repair 5
Minor body damage - repair 4
Opening side window - removal and refitting 32
Radiator grille - removal and refitting 8
Rear air deflector (Estate) - removal and refitting 44
Rear bumper - removal and refitting 10
Rear door exterior handle - removal and refitting 20
Rear door fixed quarter-light - removal and refitting 15
Rear door lock - removal and refitting 19
Rear seat - removal and refitting 34
Rear vent grille (Estate) - removal and refitting 45
Seat belts - care and maintenance 41
Sunroof - general information 43
Tailgate (Estate) - removal and refitting 25
Tailgate (Hatchback) - removal and refitting 22
Tailgate lock barrel (Estate) - removal and refitting 27
Tailgate lock (Estate) - removal and refitting 26
Tailgate lock (Hatchback) - removal and refitting 23
Tailgate struts (Hatchback and Estate) - removal and refitting ... 24
Window regulator - removal and refitting 13
Windscreen, tailgate and fixed rear quarter window - general
    information 31
Seat belts - care and maintenance 46

Degrees of difficulty

Easy, suitable for novice with little experience	Fairly easy, suitable for beginner with some experience	Fairly difficult, suitable for competent DIY mechanic	Difficult, suitable for experienced DIY mechanic	Very difficult, suitable for expert DIY or professional

Specifications

Torque wrench settings	Nm	lbf ft
Bumper mounting bolts	12	9
Tailgate strut ball-stud	20	15
Tailgate hinge bolts	20	15
Front seat U-clip bolts	20	15
Bonnet hinge bolts	20	15
Seat belt bolts	35	26

1 General description

The body and underframe are of all-welded steel construction. Models in the range include two and four-door Saloons, a five-door Hatchback, a five-door Estate and a two-door Convertible.

The only detachable "fixed" panels are the bolt-on front wings.

2 Maintenance - bodywork and underframe

1 The general condition of a vehicle's bodywork is the one thing that significantly affects its value. Maintenance is easy but needs to be regular. Neglect, particularly after minor damage, can lead quickly to further deterioration and costly repair bills. It is important also to keep watch on those parts of the vehicle not immediately visible, for instance the underside, inside all the wheel arches and the lower part of the engine compartment.

2 The basic maintenance routine for the bodywork is washing with a lot of water, from a hose. This will remove all the loose solids which may have stuck to the vehicle. It is important to flush these off in such a way as to prevent grit from scratching the finish. The wheel arches and underframe need washing in

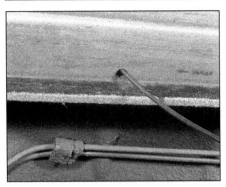

2.4a Clearing sill drain hole

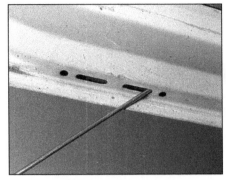

2.4b Clearing door drain hole

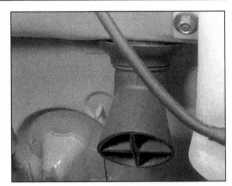

2.4c Bonnet scuttle drain tube

the same way to remove any accumulated mud which will retain moisture and tend to encourage rust. Strangely enough, the best time to clean the underframe and wheel arches is in wet weather when the mud is thoroughly wet and soft. In very wet weather the underframe is usually cleaned of large accumulations automatically and this is a good time for inspection.

3 Periodically, except on vehicles with a wax-based underbody protective coating, it is a good idea to have the whole of the underframe of the vehicle steam cleaned, engine compartment included, so that a thorough inspection can be carried out to see what minor repairs and renovations are necessary. Steam cleaning is available at many garages and is necessary for removal of the accumulation of oily grime which sometimes is allowed to become thick in certain areas. If steam cleaning facilities are not available, there are one or two excellent grease solvents available which can be brush applied. The dirt can then be simply hosed off. Note that these methods should not be used on vehicles with wax-based underbody protective coating or the coating will be removed. Such vehicles should be inspected annually, preferably just prior to winter, when the underbody should be washed down and any damage to the wax coating repaired. Ideally, a completely fresh coat should be applied. It would also be worth considering the use of such wax-based protection for injection into door panels, sills, box sections, etc, as an additional safeguard against rust damage where such protection is not provided by the vehicle manufacturer.

4 After washing paintwork, wipe off with a chamois leather to give an unspotted clear finish. A coat of clear protective wax polish will give added protection against chemical pollutants in the air. If the paintwork sheen has dulled or oxidised, use a cleaner/polisher combination to restore the brilliance of this shine. This requires a little effort, but such dulling is usually caused because regular washing has been neglected. Care needs to be taken with metallic paintwork, as special non abrasive cleaner/polisher is required to avoid damage to the finish. Always check that the door and ventilator opening drain holes

and pipes are completely clear so that water can be drained out **(see illustrations)**. Bright work should be treated in the same way as paint work. Windscreens and windows can be kept clear of the smeary film which often appears, by the use of a proprietary glass cleaner. Never use any form of wax or other body or chromium polish on glass.

Convertible

5 Convertible models should not be taken through a car wash, as the hood seams and the plastic rear window can be damaged. Clean the rear window with a soft damp cloth or a chamois leather. Do not use a scraper to remove frost and ice from the rear window, use a normal de-ice spray or warm water.
6 To clean the hood, brush it in the direction of the pile, do not use soap and water, or any other cleaning agent.

3 Maintenance - upholstery and carpets

Mats and carpets should be brushed or vacuum cleaned regularly to keep them free of grit. If they are badly stained remove them from the vehicle for scrubbing or sponging and make quite sure they are dry before refitting. Seats and interior trim panels can generally be kept clean by wiping with a damp cloth. If they do become stained (which can be more apparent on light coloured upholstery) use a little liquid detergent and a soft nail brush to scour the grime out of the grain of the material. Do not forget to keep the headlining clean in the same way as the upholstery. When using liquid cleaners inside the vehicle do not over-wet the surfaces being cleaned. Excessive damp could get into the seams and padded interior causing stains, offensive odours or even rot. If the inside of the vehicle gets wet accidentally it is worthwhile taking some trouble to dry it out properly, particularly where carpets are involved. Do not leave oil or electric heaters inside the vehicle for this purpose.

4 Minor body damage - repair

Repairs of minor scratches in bodywork

1 If the scratch is very superficial, and does not penetrate to the metal of the bodywork, repair is very simple. Lightly rub the area of the scratch with a paintwork renovator, or a very fine cutting paste, to remove loose paint from the scratch and to clear the surrounding bodywork of wax polish. Rinse the area with clean water.
2 Apply touch-up paint, or a paint film, to the scratch using a fine paint brush; continue to apply fine layers of paint until the surface of the paint in the scratch is level with the surrounding paintwork. Allow the new paint at least two weeks to harden, then blend it into the surrounding paintwork by rubbing the scratch area with a paintwork renovator or a very fine cutting paste. Finally apply wax polish.
3 Where the scratch has penetrated right through to the metal of the bodywork, causing the metal to rust, a different repair technique is required. Remove any loose rust from the bottom of the scratch with a penknife, then apply rust inhibiting paint, to prevent the formation of rust in the future. Using a rubber or nylon applicator fill the scratch with bodystopper paste. If required, this paste can be mixed with cellulose thinners, to provide a very thin paste which is ideal for filling narrow scratches. Before the stopper-paste in the scratch hardens, wrap a piece of smooth cotton rag around the top of a finger. Dip the finger in cellulose thinners and quickly sweep it across the surface of the stopper-paste in the scratch; this will ensure that the surface of the stopper-paste is slightly hollowed. The scratch can now be painted over as described earlier in this Section.

Repairs of dents in bodywork

4 When deep denting of the vehicle's bodywork has taken place, the first task is to pull the dent out, until the affected bodywork almost attains its original shape. There is little

point in trying to restore the original shape completely, as the metal in the damaged area will have stretched on impact and cannot be reshaped fully to its original contour. It is better to bring the level of the dent up to a point which is about 3 mm below the level of the surrounding bodywork. In cases where the dent is very shallow anyway, it is not worth trying to pull it out at all. If the underside of the dent is accessible, it can be hammered out gently from behind, using a mallet with a wooden or plastic head. Whilst doing this, hold a block of wood firmly against the outside of the panel to absorb the impact from the hammer blows and thus prevent a large area of the bodywork from being 'belled-out'.

5 Should the dent be in a section of the bodywork which has a double skin or some other factor making it inaccessible from behind, a different technique is called for. Drill several small holes through the metal inside the area - particularly in the deeper section. Then screw long self-tapping screws into the holes just sufficiently for them to gain a good purchase in the metal. Now the dent can be pulled out by pulling on the protruding heads of the screws with a pair of pliers.

6 The next stage of the repair is the removal of the paint from the damaged area, and from an inch or so of the surrounding 'sound' bodywork. This is accomplished most easily by using a wire brush or abrasive pad on a power drill, although it can be done just as effectively by hand using sheets of abrasive paper. To complete the preparation for filling, score the surface of the bare metal with a screwdriver or the tang of a file, or alternatively, drill small holes in the affected area. This will provide a really good 'key' for the filler paste.

7 To complete the repair see the Section on filling and respraying.

Repairs of rust holes or gashes in bodywork

8 Remove all paint from the affected area and from an inch or so of the surrounding 'sound' bodywork, using an abrasive pad or a wire brush on a power drill. If these are not available a few sheets of abrasive paper will do the job most effectively. With the paint removed you will be able to judge the severity of the corrosion and therefore decide whether to renew the whole panel (if this is possible) or to repair the affected area. New body panels are not as expensive as most people think and it is often quicker and more satisfactory to fit a new panel than to attempt to repair large areas of corrosion.

9 Remove all fittings from the affected area except those which will act as a guide to the original shape of the damaged bodywork (eg. headlights etc). Then, using tin snips or a hacksaw blade, remove all loose metal and any other metal badly affected by corrosion. Hammer the edges of the hole inwards in order to create a slight depression for the filler paste.

10 Wire brush the affected area to remove the powdery rust from the surface of the remaining metal. Paint the affected area with rust inhibiting paint; if the back of the rusted area is accessible treat this also.

11 Before filling can take place it will be necessary to block the hole in some way. This can be achieved by the use of aluminium or plastic mesh, or aluminium tape.

12 Aluminium or plastic mesh or glass fibre matting, is probably the best material to use for a large hole. Cut a piece to the approximate size and shape of the hole to be filled, then position it in the hole so that its edges are below the level of the surrounding bodywork. It can be retained in position by several blobs of filler paste around its periphery.

13 Aluminium tape should be used for small or very narrow holes. Pull a piece off the roll and trim it to the approximate size and shape required, then pull off the backing paper (if used) and stick the tape over the hole; it can be overlapped if the thickness of one piece is insufficient. Burnish down the edges of the tape with the handle of a screwdriver or similar, to ensure that the tape is securely attached to the metal underneath.

Bodywork repairs - filling and respraying

14 Before using this Section, see the Sections on dent, deep scratch, rust holes and gash repairs.

15 Many types of bodyfiller are available, but generally speaking those proprietary kits which contain a tin of filler paste and a tube of resin hardener are best for this type of repair. A wide, flexible plastic or nylon applicator will be found invaluable for imparting a smooth and well contoured finish to the surface of the filler.

16 Mix up a little filler on a clean piece of card or board - measure the hardener carefully (follow the maker's instructions on the pack) otherwise the filler will set too rapidly or too slowly. Using the applicator apply the filler paste to the prepared area; draw the applicator across the surface of the filler to achieve the correct contour and to level the surface. As soon as a contour that approximates to the correct one is achieved, stop working the paste - if you carry on too long the paste will become sticky and begin to 'pick-up' on the applicator. Continue to add thin layers of filler paste at twenty minute intervals until the level of the filler is just proud of the surrounding bodywork.

17 Once the filler has hardened, excess can be removed using a metal plane or file. From then on, progressively finer grades of abrasive paper should be used, starting with a 40 grade production paper and finishing with a 400 grade wet-and-dry paper. Always wrap the abrasive paper around a flat rubber, cork, or wooden block - otherwise the surface of the filler will not be completely flat. During the smoothing of the filler surface the wet-and-dry paper should be periodically rinsed in water. This will ensure that a very smooth finish is imparted to the filler at the final stage.

18 At this stage the 'dent' should be surrounded by a ring of bare metal, which in turn should be encircled by the finely 'feathered' edge of the good paintwork. Rinse the repair area with clean water, until all of the dust produced by the rubbing-down operation has gone.

19 Spray the whole area with a light coat of primer - this will show up any imperfections in the surface of the filler. Repair these imperfections with fresh filler paste or bodystopper, and once more smooth the surface with abrasive paper. If bodystopper is used, it can be mixed with cellulose thinners to form a really thin paste which is ideal for filling small holes. Repeat this spray and repair procedure until you are satisfied that the surface of the filler, and the feathered edge of the paintwork are perfect. Clean the repair area with clean water and allow to dry fully.

20 The repair area is now ready for final spraying. Paint spraying must be carried out in a warm, dry, windless and dust free atmosphere. This condition can be created artificially if you have access to a large indoor working area, but if you are forced to work in the open, you will have to pick your day very carefully. If you are working indoors, dousing the floor in the work area with water will help to settle the dust which would otherwise be in the atmosphere. If the repair area is confined to one body panel, mask off the surrounding panels; this will help to minimise the effects of a slight mis-match in paint colours. Bodywork fittings (eg. trim strips, door handles etc) will also need to be masked off. Use genuine masking tape and several thicknesses of newspaper for the masking operations.

21 Before commencing to spray, agitate the aerosol can thoroughly, then spray a test area (an old tin, or similar) until the technique is mastered. Cover the repair area with a thick coat of primer; the thickness should be built up using several thin layers of paint rather than one thick one. Using 400 grade wet-and-dry paper, rub down the surface of the primer until it is really smooth. While doing this, the work area should be thoroughly doused with water, and the wet-and-dry paper periodically rinsed in water. Allow to dry before spraying on more paint.

22 Spray on the top coat, again building up the thickness by using several thin layers of paint. Start spraying in the centre of the repair area and then, using a circular motion, work outwards until the whole repair area and about 2 inches of the surrounding original paintwork is covered. Remove all masking material 10 to 15 minutes after spraying on the final coat of paint.

23 Allow the new paint at least two weeks to harden, then, using a paintwork renovator or a very fine cutting paste, blend the edges of the paint into the existing paintwork. Finally, apply wax polish.

Plastic components

24 With the use of more and more plastic body components by the vehicle manufacturers (eg. bumpers, spoilers, and in some cases major body panels), rectification of more serious damage to such items has become a matter of either entrusting repair work to a specialist in this field, or renewing complete components. Repair of such damage by the DIY owner is not really feasible owing to the cost of the equipment and materials required for effecting such repairs. The basic technique involves making a groove along the line of the crack in the plastic using a rotary burr in a power drill. The damaged part is then welded back together by using a hot air gun to heat up and fuse a plastic filler rod into the groove. Any excess plastic is then removed and the area rubbed down to a smooth finish. It is important that a filler rod of the correct plastic is used, as body components can be made of a variety of different types (eg. polycarbonate, ABS, polypropylene).

25 Damage of a less serious nature (abrasions, minor cracks etc) can be repaired by the DIY owner using a two-part epoxy filler repair material. Once mixed in equal proportions, this is used in similar fashion to the bodywork filler used on metal panels. The filler is usually cured in twenty to thirty minutes, ready for sanding and painting.

26 If the owner is renewing a complete component himself, or if he has repaired it with epoxy filler, he will be left with the problem of finding a suitable paint for finishing which is compatible with the type of plastic used. At one time the use of a universal paint was not possible owing to the complex range of plastics encountered in body component applications. Standard paints, generally speaking, will not bond to plastic or rubber satisfactorily. However, it is now possible to obtain a plastic body parts finishing kit which consists of a pre-primer treatment, a primer and coloured top coat. Full instructions are normally supplied with a kit, but basically the method of use is to first apply the pre-primer to the component concerned and allow it to dry for up to 30 minutes. Then the primer is applied and left to dry for about an hour before finally applying the special coloured top coat. The result is a correctly coloured component where the paint will flex with the plastic or rubber, a property that standard paint does not normally posses.

5 Major body damage - repair

Where serious damage has occurred, or large areas need renewal due to neglect, it means that complete new panels will need welding in, and this is best left to professionals. If the damage is due to impact, it will also be necessary to check completely the alignment of the bodyshell, and this can

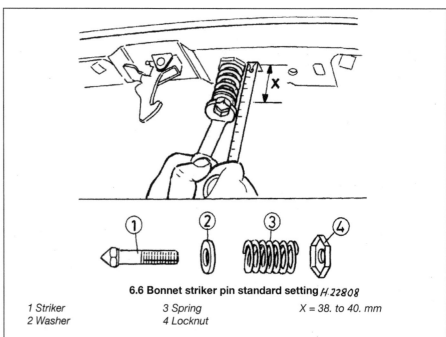

6.6 Bonnet striker pin standard setting *H.22808*

1 Striker   3 Spring   X = 38. to 40. mm
2 Washer   4 Locknut

only be carried out accurately by a Vauxhall/Opel dealer using special jigs. If the body is left misaligned, it is primarily dangerous as the car will not handle properly, and secondly, uneven stresses will be imposed on the steering, suspension and possibly transmission, causing abnormal wear, or complete failure, particularly to such items as the tyres.

6 Bonnet - removal and refitting

Removal

1 Open the bonnet and support it in the fully open position.
2 Mark the position of the hinges on the underside of the bonnet.
3 With the help of an assistant, support the weight of the bonnet and unbolt and remove it from the vehicle.
4 It is unlikely that the bonnet hinges will ever have to be removed but if they are, the wiper arm and linkage will first have to be withdrawn (Chapter 12) and the rivets drilled out of the hinged holder brackets.

Refitting

5 Refitting is a reversal of removal, but check the bonnet alignment (even gap between edge of bonnet and wing) before finally tightening the hinge bolts.
6 When closing the bonnet, it should close smoothly and positively with moderate hand pressure. If it does not, align the dovetail and plate and adjust the projection of the dovetail by releasing its locknut and turning it by using a screwdriver in its end slot. The standard setting is as shown **(see illustration)**.

7 Bonnet release cable - renewal

1 Remove the cable clip from the top of the front cross rail.
2 Using a screwdriver, prise the cable end fitting out of the release slide.
3 Working inside the vehicle, pull the bonnet release handle and holder assembly sharply rearwards to disengage the holder lug from the body locating slot **(see illustration)**.
4 Pull the cable assembly through its grommet in the engine compartment rear bulkhead into the engine compartment.
5 Fit the new cable by reversing the removal operations, then adjust the cable to remove any slackness by altering the cable setting at the clip on the top rail.
6 The cable should release the bonnet with a gentle pull on the control handle. If it is still stiff, check the setting of the catch dovetail as described in the preceding Section.
7 Apply some grease to the bonnet release slide and to the lock dovetail.

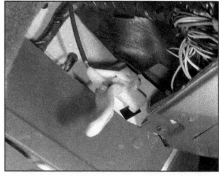

7.3 Removing the bonnet release handle and holder assembly

8.1 Radiator grille lower spigot

8.2 Radiator grille top clip

Estate

Centre section

9 Refit in the reverse order to removal. Apply non-hardening sealing compound around the bolt holes before fitting the bumper.

Side section

10 Refit in the reverse order to removal. Make sure that the interlocking pin engages correctly with the centre section.

11 Front wing - removal and refitting

Removal

1 Remove the front roadwheel.
2 Remove the protective liner from under the wing after having unclipped it and extracted the screws which hold it in place.
3 Remove the front bumper as described in Section 9.
4 Open the bonnet and unscrew and remove the seven bolts from the top edge of the wing.
5 Working under the wing, remove the four bolts which hold the wing to the lower front body panel.
6 Working inside the vehicle, remove the side trim panel at the footwell to expose the two bolts at the lower part of the windscreen A-pillar.
7 Remove the screw from the base of the pillar at the sill flange.
8 Cut around the seams of the wing with a sharp knife to release the mastic and then lift the wing away.

Refitting

9 Clean away all old mastic sealer from the body mating flange and apply a thick bead of new sealer.
10 Offer the new wing into position and screw in the bolts finger tight.
11 Now align the wing with the adjacent body panels and then tighten all bolts and screws.
12 Apply protective coating to the underside of the wing and refinish the outer surface to match the body colour.
13 When the protective coating is dry, refit the bumper, the protective liner and the footwell trim panel.

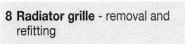

8 Radiator grille - removal and refitting

Removal

1 The grille is held in place at its upper edge by clips and the bottom is secured by pegs engaging in sockets **(see illustration)**.
2 Lever out the grille clips and lift the grille up and away from the front of the vehicle **(see illustration)**.

Refitting

3 Refit in the reverse order to removal.

9 Front bumper - removal and refitting

Removal

1 The bumpers are constructed of impact-resistant plastic material bolted directly to the front bodyframe and wings.
2 Reach under the front wings and unscrew the securing bolts.
3 Withdraw the bumper.
4 If necessary, remove the number plate.

Refitting

5 Refitting is a reversal of removal making sure the end slides engage with their brackets.

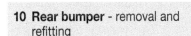

10 Rear bumper - removal and refitting

Removal

Saloon and Hatchback

1 Remove the rear number plate lamp from the bumper as described in Chapter 12 and then disconnect the lead from it.
2 Unbolt the bumper from the support brackets located inside the lower rear body panel.
3 Withdraw the bumper, disengaging the end slides from the brackets.

Estate

Centre section

4 Remove the tailgate interior trim panel.
5 Remove the bolts which secure the bumper to the tailgate and remove the bumper **(see illustration)**.

Side section

6 Open the tailgate and remove the two bolts which secure the side section to its rear bracket **(see illustration)**.
7 Slide the bumper section off rearwards. If the sliding bracket is stuck, unbolt it: access to the bolt is by removing the washer reservoir (right-hand side) or the rear quarter interior trim panel (left-hand side) **(see illustration)**.

Refitting

Saloon and Hatchback

8 Refitting is a reversal of removal.

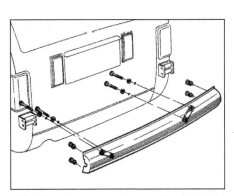

10.5 Rear bumper centre section (Estate)

10.6 Estate rear bumper side section retaining bolts (arrowed)

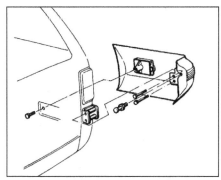

10.7 Rear bumper side section (Estate)

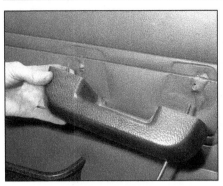

12.2a Removing door armrest (early models)

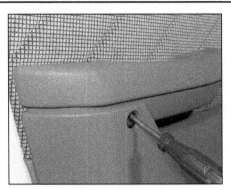

12.2b Removing door armrest/door oddment tray panel screw (later models)

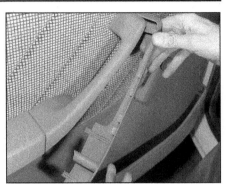

12.2c Removing door pull trim (later models)

12 Door trim panel - removal and refitting

Removal

1 Remove the securing clip from the window regulator handle. To do this, force back the trim bezel, located between the handle and the door trim, and pull out the clip using a length of wire with a hooked end. Alternatively, introduce a strip of rag between the handle and the door trim, and work it back and forth to pick up the ends of the clip. Remove the handle, trim bezel and clip.
2 Extract the two screws and remove the armrest. On later models fitted with a combined armrest/oddment tray, prise free the

plastic plug for access to the rear retaining screw, then prise free and withdraw the lower section of the door pull to gain access to the three forward retaining screws **(see illustrations)**. Remove the door pull trim.
3 Unscrew and remove the lock plunger knob **(see illustration)**.
4 Insert the fingers or a broad blade between the trim panel and the door and pull the panel from the door. Use a jerking action to do this in order to free the plastic securing clips from the holes in the door panel. The clips are rather brittle and it is a wise precaution to purchase some spare ones as replacements for any broken during the work.
5 As the trim panel is withdrawn, the door lock remote control handle escutcheon plate bezel will be freed **(see illustration)**.

Refitting

6 Refitting is a reversal of removal. Note that the regulator handle spring clip is fitted to the handle before the handle is fitted. The handle complete with clip is then simply driven onto the splined shaft of the regulator by striking it with the palm of the hand **(see illustration)**.

13 Window regulator - removal and refitting

Removal

1 Remove the trim panel (Section 12).
2 Carefully peel away the plastic sheet.
3 Temporarily refit the regulator handle and set the glass as if half open. Chock the lower edge of the glass channel with a wooden prop.
4 Remove the regulator mounting screws and withdraw the regulator mechanism sideways through the aperture in the door panel as the regulator arm disengages from the guide channel **(see illustrations)**. On some later models, the regulator is secured by rivets instead of screws, in which case carefully drill out the rivets to release the mechanism.

Refitting

5 Refitting is a reverse of removal; apply some molybdenum disulphide grease to the mechanism before fitting. If applicable, use new blind rivets to secure the regulator unit.
6 Refer to Chapter 12 for details of power operated windows.

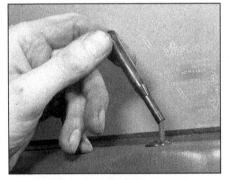

12.3 Removing door lock plunger

12.5 Door remote control handle escutcheon

12.6 Window regulator handle ready for fitting

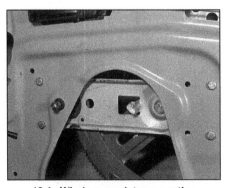

13.4a Window regulator mounting

13.4b Regulator arm engaged in channel

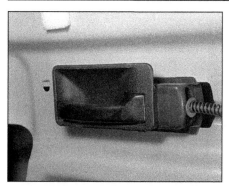

16.8 Remote control handle assembly

14 Door glass - removal and refitting

Removal
1 Remove the window regulator (Section 13).
2 Working at the glass slot in the door, prise off the clips and remove the weather strips.
3 Withdraw the glass divider channel upwards from rear doors having first released its securing screws.
4 Withdraw the glass upwards tilting it slightly to remove it.

Refitting
5 Refit by reversing the removal operations, but adjust the glass slide channels as necessary to ensure smooth positive movement of the glass.
6 Refer to Chapter 12 for details of power operated windows.

15 Rear door fixed quarter-light - removal and refitting

Removal
1 Remove the main door glass (Section 14).
2 Pull the quarter-light complete with rubber seal out of the door frame.

Refitting
3 Refitting is a reversal of removal.

16 Front door lock - removal and refitting

Removal
1 Remove the door trim panel (Section 12).
2 Peel back the plastic waterproof sheet.
3 Wind up the window fully.
4 Release the glass guide channel screws.
5 Pull out the rubber weather strip and then withdraw the guide channels out through the apertures in the door inner panel.
6 Disconnect the control rods from the lock by prising off the clips.

7 Working at the edge of the door, remove the lock securing screws and withdraw the lock.
8 The remote control handle can be removed from its retaining slot if it is pushed towards the front of the vehicle (see illustration).

Refitting
9 Refitting is a reversal of removal.

17 Front door exterior handle - removal and refitting

Removal
1 Remove the door trim panel (Section 12).
2 Peel away the plastic waterproof sheet as necessary to gain access, and then disconnect the control rod from the door lock.
3 Remove the handle screws and take the handle from the door panel.

Refitting
4 Refitting is a reversal of removal, but adjust the control rod by means of its threaded coupling so approximately 8 mm of the threaded rod end is exposed.

18 Front door lock cylinder - removal and refitting

Removal
1 Remove the door trim panel (Section 12).
2 Peel away the waterproof sheet to give access to the lock cylinder.
3 Disconnect the control rod from the lock arm (see illustration).
4 Prise out the forked spring clip and remove the lock cylinder assembly.
5 To dismantle, insert the ignition key in the lock and then force a screwdriver between the housing and the arm to force off the retaining circlip.
6 Separate the lock components, noting their fitted correct fitted locations prior to removal (see illustration).

Refitting
7 Refitting is a reversal of removal, making sure the spring is correctly engaged with the housing, and the arm is correctly engaged with the spring. Use a new circlip.

19 Rear door lock - removal and refitting

Removal
1 Wind up the window fully.
2 Remove the trim panel as described in Section 12.
3 Peel back the plastic waterproof sheet to give access to the lock.
4 Disconnect the control rods from the lock and the remote control handle by moving it in the direction of the front of the vehicle.

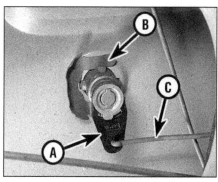

18.3 Door lock cylinder viewed from inside door showing arm (A), spring clip (B) and control rod (C)

5 Working at the edge of the door, extract the securing screws and remove the door lock by swinging it around the door glass guide channel and out through the aperture in the door panel.

Refitting
6 Refit in the reverse order of removal.

20 Rear door exterior handle - removal and refitting

Removal
1 Remove the door trim panel as described in Section 12.
2 Peel away the plastic waterproof sheet as necessary to give access to the door lock exterior handle.
3 Disconnect the control rod from the lock.
4 Unscrew the two handle fixing screws and withdraw the handle.

Refitting
5 Refitting is a reversal of removal, but adjust the control rod by means of its threaded coupling so that approximately 8 mm of the threaded rod end is exposed.

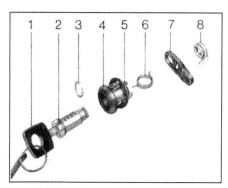

18.6 Exploded view of lock cylinder

1 Key	5 Seal
2 Cylinder	6 Spring
3 Circlip	7 Arm
4 Housing	8 End piece

21 Door - removal and refitting

Removal

1 The door hinges are welded onto the door frame and the body pillar so that there is no provision for adjustment or alignment.
2 To remove a door, open it fully and support it under its lower ends on blocks covered with pads of rag.
3 Disconnect the door check and drive out the hinge pins. Remove the door **(see illustration)**.
4 If the door can be moved up and down on its hinge due to wear in the pivot pins or holes, it may be possible to drill out the holes and fit slightly oversize pins.

Refitting

5 Refitting is the reverse of removal. Door closure may be adjusted by moving the socket-headed striker **(see illustration)**.

22 Tailgate (Hatchback) - removal and refitting

Removal

1 Disconnect the electrical leads from the heated rear window.
2 Disconnect the hose for the tailgate washer jets.
3 Remove the supports for the luggage compartment cover.
4 Open the tailgate fully and have an assistant support it.
5 Disconnect the support strut from its mounting on the tailgate by extracting the retaining ring from the ball end fitting.
6 Prise off the hinge pin retaining rings and then drive out the pins towards the centre line of the vehicle.
7 Lift the tailgate from the vehicle.

Refitting

8 Refitting is a reversal of removal, but before fully tightening the hinge bolts adjust the tailgate to give an equal gap at each side and positive closure when shut.

23 Tailgate lock (Hatchback) - removal and refitting

Removal

1 Open the tailgate and unclip the tailgate trim panel to remove it.
2 Extract the four screws which hold the lock.
3 Prise out the forked spring clips which secure the lock cylinder housing.
4 Pull the lock cylinder outwards, complete with control linkage.
5 Remove the lock through the opening in the tailgate inner panel.

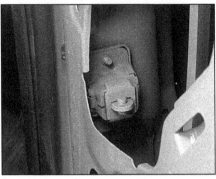

21.3 Door check strap attachment inside door edge

Refitting

6 Refitting is a reversal of removal.
7 To dismantle the lock cylinder, refer to Section 30.

24 Tailgate struts (Hatchback and Estate) - removal and refitting

Removal

1 The strut end fittings are of ball type with a retaining ring.
2 To remove, open the tailgate fully and have an assistant support it.
3 Remove the rings and disconnect the struts. The struts are gas pressurised and should not be punctured or cut open, or subjected to heat.

Refitting

4 Refitting is a reversal of removal.

25 Tailgate (Estate) - removal and refitting

Removal

1 Open the tailgate and remove the ten screws which secure the bottom and sides of the trim panel.

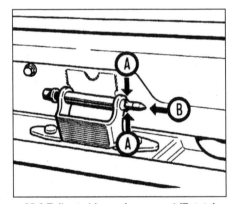

25.6 Tailgate hinge pin removal (Estate)

A Depress retainer   *B Drive out pin*

21.5 Door lock striker

2 Carefully free the trim panel, disengaging the fasteners from its top edge.
3 Disconnect the loudspeaker wiring (when fitted), and remove the trim panel.
4 Disconnect the wiring connectors from the tailgate electrical components, and the screen washer pipe from its nozzle. Remove the wiring harness and the pipe from the tailgate.
5 Have an assistant support the tailgate. Disconnect the support struts from the tailgate by prising free their balljoints.
6 Still with the tailgate supported, depress the hinge pin retainers and drive out the pins **(see illustration)**. Remove the tailgate.

Refitting

7 Refit in the reverse order to removal.

26 Tailgate lock (Estate) - removal and refitting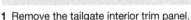

1 Remove the tailgate interior trim panel.
2 Release the spring clip and withdraw the connecting rod from the lock **(see illustration)**.
3 Remove the screws which secure the lock to the tailgate. Remove the lock.

Refitting

4 Refit in the reverse order to removal. Check for correct operation of the lock before refitting the trim panel.

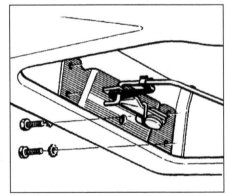

26.2 Tailgate lock details

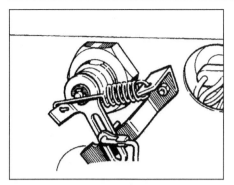

27.2 Tailgate lock barrel details - early models

27.6 On later models remove the trim moulding over the lock barrel . . .

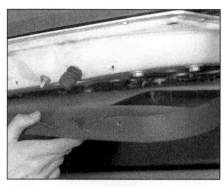

27.7 . . . then remove the tailgate interior trim panel

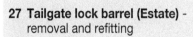

27 Tailgate lock barrel (Estate) - removal and refitting

Removal

Early models

1 Remove the tailgate interior trim panel.
2 Release the retaining clip and withdraw the connecting rod from the barrel yoke (see illustration).
3 Disconnect the return spring from the yoke.
4 Remove the circlip which secures the yoke to the lock barrel. Remove the yoke.
5 Remove the nut which secures the lock barrel to the tailgate. Remove the tailgate handle, which is secured by four screws, and extract the lock barrel.

Later models

6 Open the tailgate and undo the screws securing the outer body trim moulding over the lock barrel (see illustration).
7 Remove the tailgate inner trim panel (see illustration).
8 Using pliers, unhook the return spring from the lock barrel lever (see illustration).
9 Extract the circlip and washer then remove the lock barrel lever from the end of the barrel.
10 Undo the retaining nut, and withdraw the lock barrel from the tailgate.
11 If necessary, undo the retaining nut, remove the washer, and withdraw the handle from the control lever and tailgate (see illustration).

Refitting

12 Refit in the reverse order to removal. Check for correct operation of the lock before refitting the trim panel.

28 Load area trim panels (Estate) - removal and refitting

Removal

Load area carpet

1 The carpet in the rear section of the load area is secured by Velcro strips. Separate the

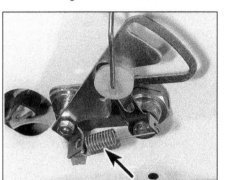

27.8 Release the return spring (arrowed) from the lock barrel lever

strips to remove the carpet; press them home on refitting.
2 The covering on the seat backs, which becomes the load area floor when the seat backs are lowered, is secured by plastic pegs. With care these pegs may be prised out undamaged, and re-used on refitting.

Side and roof trim panels

3 Refer to illustration 28.3 to identify the panels.
4 In each case the various panels are secured by screws and/or plastic clips. Take care not to

27.11 Removing the lock handle - later models

break the plastic clips when prising them free.
5 If removing the tailgate body trim panel, it will be necessary first to remove the rear carpet, the upper and rear quarter upper trim panels and the tailgate strut (see Section 24) from the side concerned.
6 When removing the rear quarter interior trim panel, also remove the rear seat belt upper mounting (if fitted).

Refitting

7 Refitting is a reversal of removal. Renew any broken retaining clips.

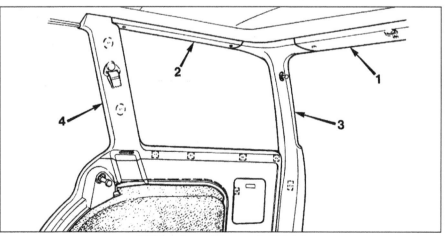

28.3 Load area trim panels (Estate)

1 Tailgate opening inner upper   2 Rear quarter upper   3 Tailgate body pillar   4 Rear quarter interior

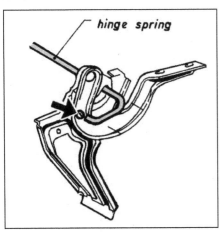

29.4 Luggage boot lid hinge and counterbalance spring
Release spring from hole (arrowed)

29 Luggage boot lid - removal and refitting

Removal

1 Open the lid and mark the position of the hinges on the underside of the lid.
2 With the help of an assistant, unbolt the hinges from the lid and lift the lid away.
3 The hinges themselves should not normally be disturbed, but if they must be removed then the counterbalance springs will have to be released and removed.
4 Unhook them using a lever of sufficient length to be able to counteract the tension of the spring rods **(see illustration)**.
5 If the hinges are unbolted from the body, fit new sealing washers in order to prevent water seepage into the luggage compartment.

Refitting

6 Refitting is the reverse of removal

30 Luggage boot lid lock and cylinder - removal and refitting

Removal

1 Open the boot lid and unscrew the lock fitting screws. Withdraw the lock **(see illustration)**.
2 To remove the lock cylinder, prise the retaining clip out using a screwdriver. Withdraw the cylinder assembly.
3 To dismantle, insert the key into the cylinder and then extract the circlip using a thin screwdriver.
4 Note the fitted position of the lock components.

Refitting

5 Reassembly and refitting are reversals of removal and dismantling, but when fitting the lock to the boot lid apply pressure to the lock

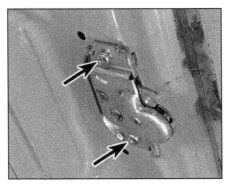

30.1 Luggage boot lid lock retaining screws (arrowed)

cylinder from the key hole end until the forked retaining clip can be felt to engage fully. Adjust the height of the striker if necessary to ensure smooth positive closure **(see illustration)**.

31 Windscreen, tailgate and fixed rear quarter window - general information

These areas of glass are secured by the tight fit of the weatherstrip in the body aperture and are bonded in position with a special adhesive. The removal and refitting of these areas of fixed glass is a difficult, messy and time-consuming task which is beyond the scope of the home mechanic. It is difficult, unless one has plenty of practice, to obtain a secure, waterproof fit. Furthermore, the task carries a high risk of breakage; this applies especially to the laminated glass windscreen. In view of this, owners are strongly advised to have this sort of work carried out by one of the many specialist windscreen fitters.

32 Opening side window - removal and refitting

Removal

1 This type of window is fitted to two-door Saloon models.
2 Unscrew the window catch.
3 Disconnect the window at the hinges.

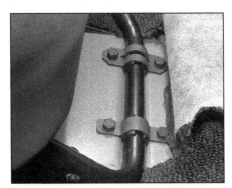

33.1 Front seat mounting bolts

30.5 Luggage boot lid lock striker

4 The toggle type lock can be removed if the pivot pin peening is drilled out and the pin then driven out.
5 Unscrew the anchor plate from the glass.

Refitting

6 Refitting is the reverse of removal and dismantling, but peen the edges of the pivot pin holes to prevent the pin dropping out whilst in service.

33 Front seat - removal and refitting

Removal

Early models

1 Unbolt and remove the U-shaped clips which secure the tubular crossmembers of the seats to the floor **(see illustration)**.
2 Release the seat adjuster and move the seats rearwards off their slide rails **(see illustration)**.

Later models

3 Withdraw the front trim grommet and the rear plastic trim covers which conceal the four bolts securing the seat rails to the floor.
4 Undo the two front bolts and two rear bolts and withdraw the seat assembly from the car. Where necessary, disconnect any electrical wiring connectors from the seat as they become accessible.

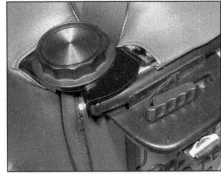

33.2 Front seat slide and rake adjuster

Refitting

Early models

5 Refit by reversing the removal operations, but make sure that the plastic slippers are not displaced as the seats are engaged on the runners.

Later models

6 Refitting is the reverse of removal.

34 Rear seat - removal and refitting

Removal

Saloon models

1 Pull the two loops at the base of the seat cushion to release the retainers **(see illustration)**.
2 Remove the cushion.
3 Prise up the metal tabs at the base of the seat back, then lift the seat back upwards off the securing hooks **(see illustration)**.

Hatchback models

4 Before removing the rear seat on these models, remove the luggage compartment cover and then depress the seat back locking plungers.
5 Fold down the seat back and unbolt the seat from the floor.

Refitting

6 Refitting is a reversal of removal.

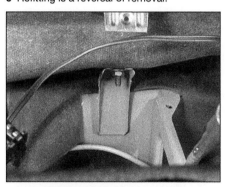
35.7 Facia mounting bracket

35.8a Facia lower mounting screw (over steering column)

34.1 Rear seat cushion catch (Saloon)

35 Facia panel - removal and refitting

Removal

1 Disconnect the battery.
2 Remove the instrument panel (Chapter 12).
3 Take off the lower cover panels from under the facia panel.
4 Remove the switches, switch panels, radio, clock and other electrical accessories as described in Chapter 12.
5 Disconnect the heater control panel as described in Chapter 3.
6 Remove the glove compartment (Section 36 of this Chapter).
7 Reach through the apertures left by removal of the instrument panel and the glove compartment and unscrew the nuts from the facia retaining brackets **(see illustration)**.
8 Remove the facia panel lower mounting screws **(see illustrations)**.
9 Remove the shrouds from the upper part of the steering column.
10 Disconnect the air ducts from the windscreen demister outlet slots.
11 Prise out the fresh air grilles and the door window demister grilles from the facia panel **(see illustration)**.
12 Pull the facia panel towards you and remove it sideways from the vehicle interior.

Refitting

13 Refitting is a reversal of removal.

35.8b Facia lower mounting screw (underside on right, near fusebox)

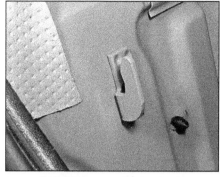
34.3 Rear seat retaining hook

36 Glove compartment - removal and refitting

Removal

1 Open the door of the glove compartment and unscrew and remove the fixing screws from around the edge of the liner.
2 On some models a glove compartment lamp is fitted which is actuated by a "door open" type plunger switch. Where the lamp is fitted, withdraw the liner carefully until the electrical leads can be disconnected.

Refitting

3 Refitting is a reversal of removal.

37 Centre console - removal and refitting

Removal

Short console

1 Release the gear lever gaiter from the console base, and move it up the gear lever **(see illustration)**.
2 Carefully prise up the front edge of the trim around the gear lever using a screwdriver, then release the two locating tabs at the rear. Remove the trim up and over the gear lever.
3 Withdraw the oddments box, then release the console cover from the top console.

35.11 Removing fresh air vents and switch panel

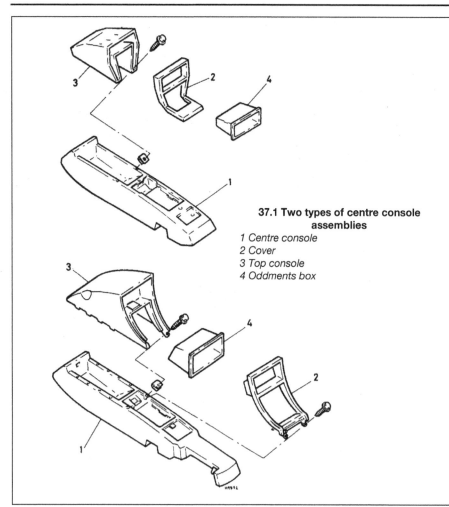

37.1 Two types of centre console assemblies

1 Centre console
2 Cover
3 Top console
4 Oddments box

37.9a Undo the two console cover lower screws . . .

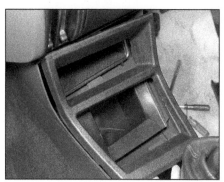

37.9b . . . then lift the cover and disengage the tags at the top

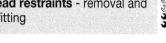

38 Head restraints - removal and refitting

Removal

Standard seats

1 Using a piece of hooked wire pull out the spring clips from the head restraint mounting stems **(see illustration)**.
2 Pull the head restraint up and out of the seat back.

Sports seats

3 Press the head restraint downwards as far as it will go.

4 Undo the screws, now visible, securing the top console to the centre console base, and remove the top console.
5 Remove the small plastic covers (where fitted) then undo the screws securing the centre console base to the floor.
6 Disengage the front of the centre console base from the locating peg on the floor, and remove the unit from the car.

Long console

7 Release the gear lever gaiter from the console base, and move it up the gear lever.
8 Carefully prise up the front edge of the trim around the gear lever using a screwdriver, then release the two locating tabs at the rear. Remove the trim up and over the gear lever.
9 Undo the two console lower screws, then lift the cover and disengage the locating tags at the top **(see illustrations)**. Remove the cover.
10 Undo the two lower screws securing the top console, disengage the top console from the console base, and remove the top console **(see illustration)**.
11 Carefully prise out the small plastic cover, and undo the console base retaining screw forward of the handbrake lever **(see illustration)**. Undo the second retaining screw at the rear of the handbrake lever.

12 Pull up the handbrake lever as far as possible, and pull the console base rearward to disengage the locating peg at the front. Manoeuvre the console base over the handbrake and gear lever and remove it from the car. Note that if insufficient clearance exists, it may be necessary to back off the handbrake adjustment slightly to allow the lever to be pulled up far enough.

Refitting

13 Refitting is a reversal of removal.

37.10 Undo the two top console securing screws

37.11 Prise out the plastic cover to reveal the console base retaining screw

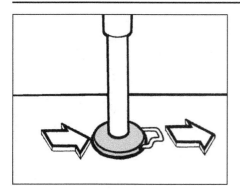

38.1 Head restraint clip removal in direction of arrows

4 Have an assistant press the seat backrest at the points shown to release the springs **(see illustration)**. With the assistant applying pressure, pull sharply upwards on the head restraint to remove it.

Refitting

Standard seats

5 Before fitting a head restraint, fit the clip so that its shaped section is towards the rear of the vehicle.

Sports seats

6 Refit by inserting the head restraint rods into the backrest. It should be possible to feel the retaining springs engaging with the notches in the rods.

39.1a Remove mirror glass by levering with wooden wedge

40.1 Remove exterior mirror handle cover . . .

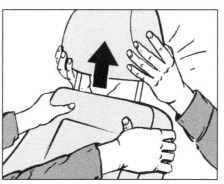

38.4 Head restraint removal from Sports seat

39 Exterior rear view mirror glass - removal and refitting

Removal

Insert a wooden or Plastic wedge at the outside edge of the mirror glass and carefully lever the glass free. Disconnect the adjuster links and heater wires, as applicable, and remove the glass **(see illustrations)**.

Refitting

Refit in the reverse order to removal. Be careful when pressing the glass home: the sudden movement as the ball enters its socket may cause the glass to break.

39.1b With glass freed from balljoint, disconnect linkage

40.2 . . . then remove the cover plate . . .

40 Exterior rear view mirror (manual) - removal and refitting

Removal

1 Working inside the vehicle, prise off the mirror remote control handle cover **(see illustration)**.
2 Prise off the triangular shaped plate **(see illustration)**.
3 Extract the three mirror mounting screws which are now exposed and have an assistant support the mirror head on the outside of the vehicle **(see illustration)**.

Refitting

4 Refitting is a reversal of removal.

41 Exterior rear view mirror (electric) - removal and refitting

Removal

1 Remove the door trim panel, as described in Section 12, and unplug the mirror wiring harness connector.
2 Prise off the mounting cover and remove the three mounting screws, supporting the mirror as the screws are removed. Remove the mirror from the vehicle.

Refitting

3 Refit in the reverse order to removal.

42 Exterior rear view mirror motor - removal and refitting

Removal

1 Remove the mirror glass, as just described.
2 Remove the door trim panel, as described in Section 12, and unplug the mirror wiring harness connector.
3 Fold the mirror forwards and unscrew and remove the motor.

Refitting

4 Refit in the reverse order to removal.

40.3 . . . and extract the mounting screws

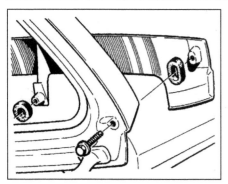

44.2 Air deflector seal washers (Estate)

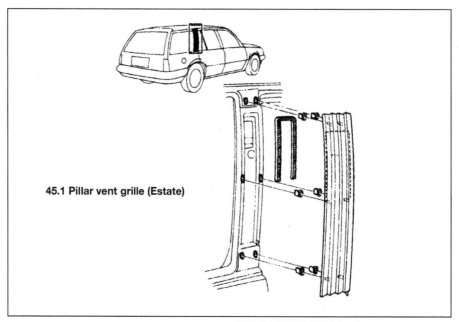

45.1 Pillar vent grille (Estate)

43 Sunroof - general information

A tilt/slide manual sunroof was offered as an optional extra on most models and was fitted as standard equipment on some models.

Due to the complexity of the sunroof mechanism considerable expertise is needed to repair, replace or adjust the sunroof components successfully. Removal of the roof first requires the headlining to be removed which is a complex and tedious operation and not a task to be undertaken lightly. Therefore any problems with the sunroof should be referred to a Vauxhall/Opel dealer.

44 Rear air deflector (Estate) - removal and refitting

Removal

1 Open the tailgate and remove the four screws which secure the air deflector to the tailgate.
2 Remove the air deflector, noting the position of the sealing washers **(see illustration)**.

Refitting

3 Refit in the reverse order to removal.

45 Rear vent grille (Estate) - removal and refitting

Removal

1 The pillar vent grille is a snap fit into the body pillar. Remove it by prising it free, being careful not to damage the paintwork or the attaching lugs **(see illustration)**.
2 When fitting new grommets, use non-hardening sealing compound in the grommet holes.

Refitting

3 Refit the grille by snapping it home.

46 Seat belts - care and maintenance

1 Periodically inspect the seat belts for fraying or other damage. If evident, renew the belt.
2 Cleaning of the belt fabric should be done with a damp cloth and a little detergent only.
3 Never alter the original belt anchorage and, if the belts are ever removed, always take careful note of the sequence of mounting components. If the washers or collars are incorrectly positioned, the belt will not swivel as it has been designed to do.
4 On two-door models, the belt retractor is hidden behind the rear quarter trim panel. For access to the retractor, remove the trim panel.
5 This is carried out by first removing the seat cushion and then pulling the trim panel clips out of their holes by jerking the panel away with the fingers.

Wiring diagrams

Colour code

BL	Blue
BR	Brown
GE	Yellow
GN	Green
GR	Grey
HBL	Light blue
LI	Lilac
RT	Red
SW	Black
VI	Violet
WS	White

Abbreviations

ABS	Anti-lock braking
BR	Trip computer
EMP	Receiver (radio)
EST	Electronic spark timing (ignition advance)
EV61	Electronic carburettor
EZ61	Microprocessor spark timing system
EZF	EST
EZV	Electronic carburettor
HEI	High energy ignition system
MZV	Microprocessor-controlled ignition system
SAS	Overrun cut-off
SSS	Stop-start system
TBI	Throttle body injection
TFL	Day running lights
TSZ	HEI

Wiring identification

eg GE WS 1.5

GE	Basic colour
WS	Identification colour
1.5	Section (mm^2)

Explanatory note

The following wiring diagrams are laid out using a grid reference system, with the bottom line being the earth track. Using grid reference 55 at the bottom of Diagram 1 as an example, follow the line upwards past switch S50 to lamp H20, through connector X2 and finally to a number in a box (20). Referring back to grid reference 20 at the bottom of the diagram, it will be seen that a number 55 in a box aligns with this reference near the top of the diagram. The line from this boxed number is a continuation of grid reference 55 and shows the live feed to lamp H20 through the 20 amp fuse F6.

Key to diagram 1 (Models from introduction to 1984)

No	Description	Grid reference	No	Description	Grid reference
E1	RH parking light	47	F22	Fuse (mixture preheater)	360
E2	RH tail light	48	F24	Fuse (level control)	379
E3	Number plate light	49	F25	Voltage stabiliser	19
E4	LH parking light	44	G1	Battery	1
E5	LH tail light	45	G2	Alternator	14
E6	Engine compartment light	52	H1	Radio	95
E7	RH high beam	60	H2	Horn	109
E8	LH high beam	59	H3	Turn signal warning light	76
E9	RH low beam	63	H4	Oil pressure warning light	27
E10	LH low beam	62	H5	Handbrake/brake fluid warning light	26
E11	Instrument lights	51	H6	Hazard warning system warning light	72
E12	Selector lever light	100	H7	No-charge warning light	15
E13	Boot light	81	H8	Main beam warning light	61
E14	Courtesy light	92	H9	RH stop-light	67
E15	Glovebox light	105	H10	LH stop-light	65
E16	Cigarette lighter light	102	H11	RH front turn signal light	76
E17	RH reversing light	108	H12	RH rear turn signal light	78
E18	LH reversing light	107	H13	LH front turn signal light	73
E19	Heated rear window	40	H14	LH rear turn signal light	75
E20	LH foglight	158	H16	Preheater warning light	173
E21	RH foglight	159	H17	Trailer turn signal warning light	199
E22	LH spot light	151	H18	Dual horns	110
E23	RH spot light	153	H19	Headlights on warning buzzer	280, 283
E24	Rear foglight	163	H20	Choke on warning light	55
E25	LH heated front seat	181 to 184	H23	Radio with electric aerial	269
E30	RH heated front seat	186 to 189	H25	Mirror heater warning light	330
E31	Symbol insert light	166	K1	Heated rear window relay	39
E32	Clock light	98	K2	Flasher unit	69
E33	Ashtray light	103	K4	Spotlight relay	149
E34	Heater control light	167	K5	Foglight relay	156
E38	Computer light	309	K8	Windscreen wiper intermittent relay	120 to 123
E39	RH rear foglight	162	K9	Headlamp washer relay	129
F1 to F18	Fuses in fusebox		K10	Trailer flasher unit	200, 201
F19	Fuse (window motors)	274, 385	K15	Fuel injection timing control	213 to 225
F20	Fuse (central locking)	367	K19	Level control relay	378, 379

Key to diagram 1 (Models from introduction to 1984) (continued)

No	Description	Grid reference
K20	Ignition module	8 to 10
K21	Level control sensor	375 to 378
K25	Preheater relay	174 to 178
K28	Running light relay	240, 241
K29	Electric aerial relay	259 to 267
K30	Rear wiper relay	142 to 144
K31	Fuel pump relay	206 to 208
K35	Heated exterior mirror delay relay	335 to 338
K36	Computer relay	312 to 314
K37	Central locking relay	366 to 370
K39	Time delay relay	247 to 249
K45	Mixture preheater relay	360, 361
K46	Ignition timing control	345 to 350
K52	Ignition module	342, 343
L2	Ignition coil (Hall sensor)	9
L3	Ignition coil (inductive sensor)	343, 344
L4	Ignition coil (inductive sensor, EZ 61)	411, 412
M1	Starter motor	7
M2	Windscreen wiper motor	119
M3	Heater fan motor	89
M4	Radiator fan motor	17
M5	Washer pump	117
M6	LH headlight wiper motor	130
M7	RH headlight wiper motor	135
M8	Rear window wiper motor	140
M9	Rear window washer pump	145
M12	Starter motor (Diesel)	168 to 171
M14	LH front door window motor	273, 275, 394, 396
M15	RH front door window motor	276, 278, 388, 390
M16	LH rear door window motor	392, 394
M17	RH rear door window motor	396, 398
M18	Front door locking motor	369, 372
M19	LH rear door locking motor	369, 372
M20	RH rear door locking motor	369, 372
M21	Fuel pump	211
M22	Level control compressor	379
M26	Electric aerial motor	259 to 267
M28	LH exterior mirror adjustment	318 to 320
M30	LH exterior mirror adjustment and heating	325 to 328
M31	RH exterior mirror adjustment and heating	332 to 335
P1	Fuel gauge	22
P2	Temperature gauge	20
P3	Clock	96
P4	Fuel sensor	22, 310
P5	Temperature sensor	20
P7	Tachometer	113
P8	Oil pressure gauge	115
P9	Voltmeter	114
P10	Oil pressure sensor	115
P11	Airflow meter	235
P12	Temperature probe (coolant)	235
P13	Outside air temperature sensor	312
P14	Distance sensor	303, 304, 356, 357
P15	Fuel flowmeter	305, 306
R2	Carburettor preheater	199
R3	Cigarette lighter	101
R5	Glow plugs	175, 176
R7	Mixture preheater	360
R12	Automatic choke	202
S1	Starter motor switch	6, 7
S2.1	Light switch	52, 53
S2.2	Courtesy light switch	90
S3	Heater fan switch	86 to 89
S4	Heated rear window switch	39
S5.2	Headlight dip switch	57

No	Description	Grid reference
S5.3	Turn signal switch	78
S5.5	Horn switch	109
S7	Reversing light switch	107
S8	Stop-light switch	65
S9.2	Windscreen wiper switch (intermittent)	117 to 121
S9.3	Rear window wiper switch (intermittent)	143, 144
S10	Automatic transmission switch	7
S11	Brake fluid level switch	24
S13	Handbrake warning light switch	26
S14	Oil pressure switch	27
S15	Boot light switch	81
S16	RH courtesy light switch	93
S17	LH courtesy light switch	92
S18	Glove box light switch	105
S21	Foglight switch	156
S22	Rear foglight switch	163,164
S23	Boot lid release switch	204
S29	Radiator fan switch	17
S30	LH heated seat switch	180,181
S31	LH rear door courtesy light switch	91
S32	RH rear door courtesy light switch	93
S37	LH front door window motor switch	272 to 275, 374 to 377
S38	RH front door window motor switch, or rear window isolating switch	276 to 279, 383
S39	LH rear door window motor switch	392 to 394
S40	RH rear door window motor switch	366, 367
S41	Central locking door switch	366, 367
S44	Throttle valve switch	235
S46	Heated seat switch	184 to 186
S47	Doors open/headlamps on warning switch	283
S50	Choke on warning switch	55
S52	Hazard light switch	69 to 75
S60	Clutch pedal switch	264
S66	Vacuum switch	348
S67	LH exterior mirror adjustment switch	317 to 320
S68	Exterior mirror switch	323 to 332
S73	Temperature switch	361
S74	Engine temperature switch	351
S75	Oil temperature switch	351
S77	Distance switch	353 to 356
S78	RH front door window motor switch	388 to 391
S79	LH rear door remote window motor switch	392 to 395
S80	RH rear door remote window motor switch	396 to 399
U1	Day running lights transformer	241 to 245
U3	Computer	304 to 313
U3.1	Clock switch	311
U3.2	Function selector switch	311
U3.3	Reset/stopwatch/adjustment switch	311
X1	Trailer socket	190 to 197
X2	Auxiliary connector	55, 95, 100, 181, 185, 204, 266, 274, 280, 322, 367, 385
Y3	Boot lid release solenoid	204
Y4	Headlight washer solenoid valve	134
Y5	Diesel solenoid valve	179
Y6	Auxiliary air slide valve	235
Y7	Fuel injectors	235
Y9	Level control solenoid	377
Y10	Distributor	12
Y11	Hall sensor	9, 10, 345,346
Y15	Inductive sensor	410, 411
Y17	Idle cut-off solenoid valve	203
Y18	Dashpot solenoid valve	246,249
Y22	Distributor	348
Y23	Distributor	415

Not all items are fitted to all models

Refer to page WD•1 for colour codes

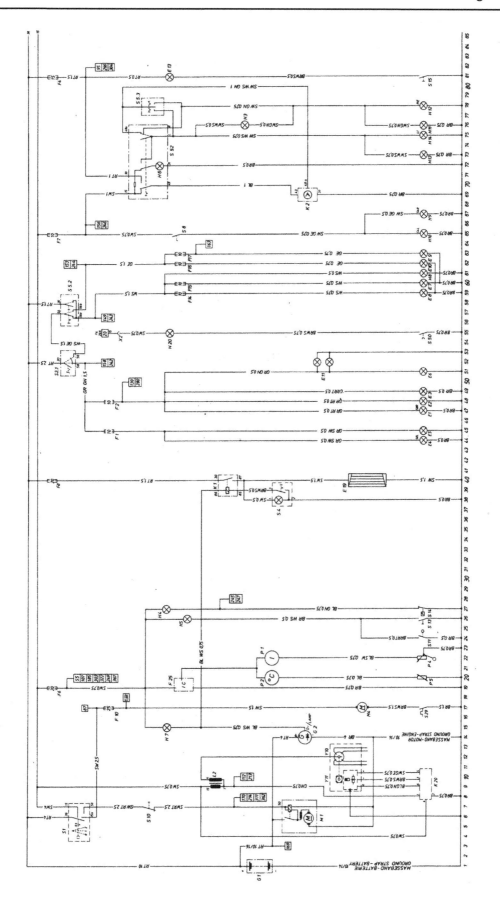

Diagram 1: Typical diagram for all models 1981 to 1984

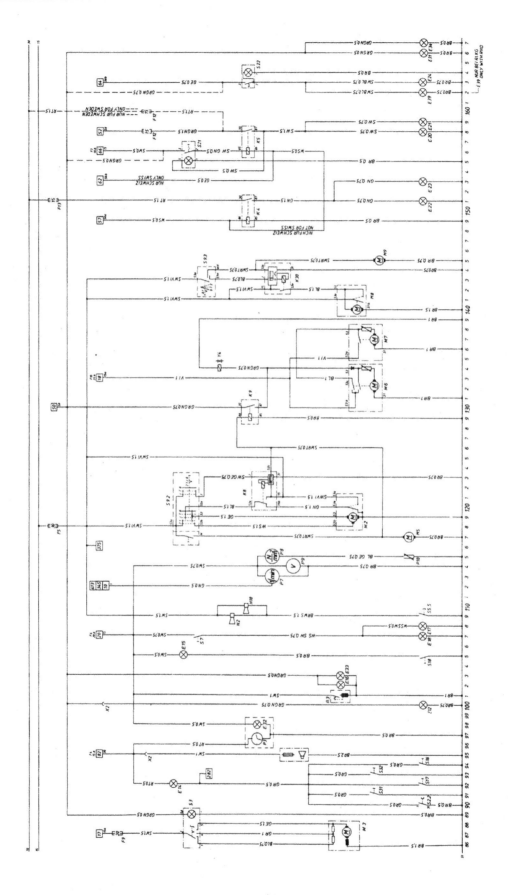

Diagram 1: Typical diagram for all models 1981 to 1984 (continued)

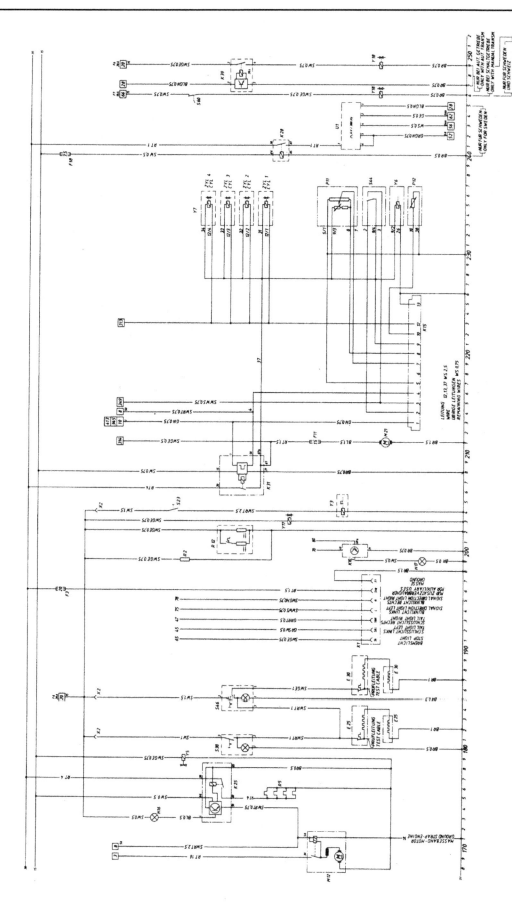

Diagram 1: Typical diagram for all models 1981 to 1984 (continued)

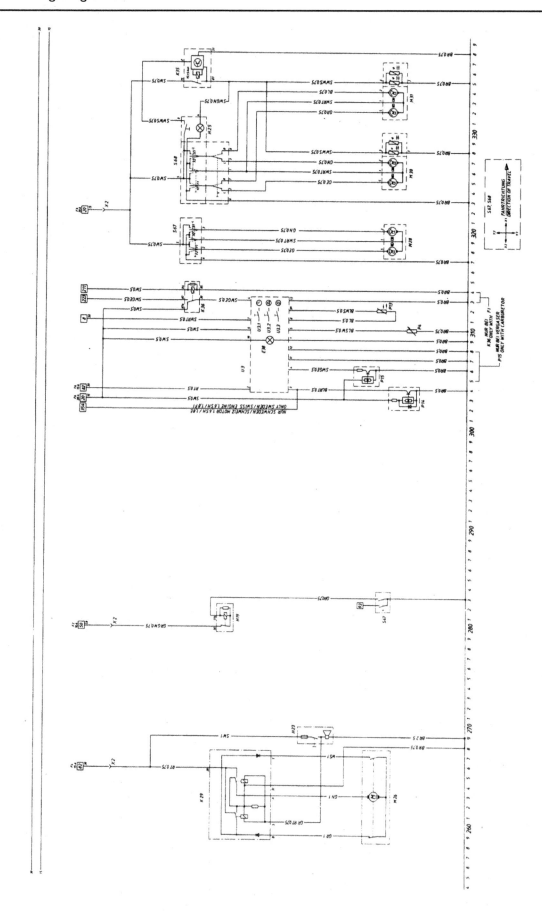

**Diagram 1: Typical diagram for all models
1981 to 1984 (continued)**

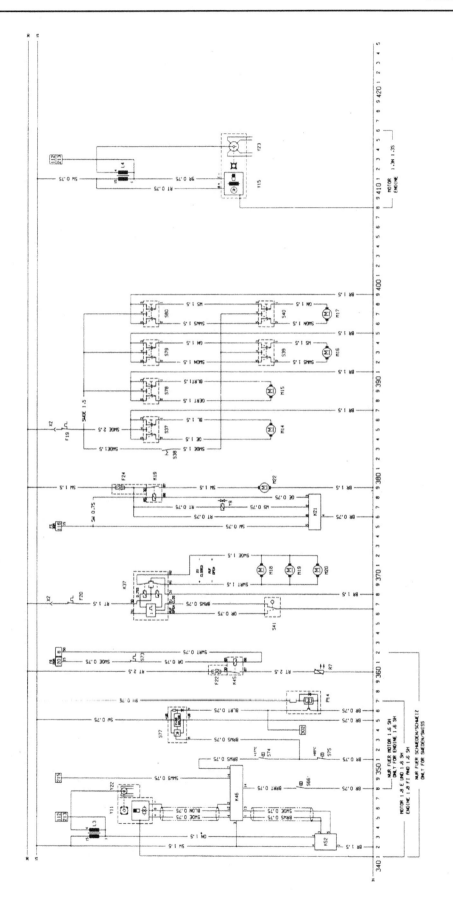

Diagram 1: Typical diagram for all models 1981 to 1984 (continued)

Key to diagram 2 (Models from 1985 to 1986)

No	Description	Grid reference	No	Description	Grid reference
E1	LH parking light	236	H12	LH rear turn signal light	285
E2	LH tail light	237	H13	RH front turn signal light	288
E3	Number plate light	243	H14	LH rear turn signal light	289
E4	RH parking light	241	H16	Preheater warning light	170
E5	RH tail light	242	H17	Trailer turn signal warning light	280
E6	Engine compartment light	245	H18	Dual horns	345
E7	LH high beam	251	H19	Headlights on warning buzzer	291, 292
E8	RH high beam	252	H20	Choke on warning light	224
E9	LH low beam	254	H23	Radio with electric aerial	310, 311
E10	RH low beam	255	H25	Mirror heater warning light	383, 393
E11	Instrument lights	246	H33	LH repeater turn signal light	283
E12	Selector lever light	248	H34	RH repeater turn signal light	287
E13	Boot light	293	K1	Headed rear window relay	209, 210
E14	Courtesy light	294	K2	Flasher unit	281
E15	Glovebox light	225	K4	Spotlight relay	270, 271
E16	Cigarette lighter light	230	K5	Foglight relay	263, 264
E17	LH reversing light	226	K8	Windscreen wiper intermittent relay	317 to 320
E18	RH reversing light	227	K9	Headlamp washer relay	324, 325
E19	Heated rear window	210	K10	Trailer flasher unit	280, 281
E20	LH foglight	262	K15	Fuel injection timing control	181 to 191, 475 to 487
E21	RH foglight	263	K19	Level control relay	350, 351
E22	LH spot light	269	K20	Ignition module	112 to 116
E23	RH spot light	270	K21	Level control sensor	347 to 350
E24	Rear foglight (LH on some models)	259	K25	Preheater relay	170 to 173
E25	LH heated front seat	370	K29	Electric aerial relay	306 to 310
E30	RH heated front seat	374	K30	Rear wiper relay	339 to 341
E31	Symbol insert light	245	K31	Fuel pump relay	177 to 179, 471 to 473
E32	Clock light	301	K35	Heated exterior mirror delay relay	397, 399
E33	Ashtray light	231	K36	Computer relay	413 to 415
E34	Heater control light	245	K37	Central locking relay	361 to 365
E38	Computer light	408	K39	Time delay relay	160, 162
E39	RH rear foglight	258	K42	Stop/start control unit	419 to 427
E41	Courtesy light (with delay)	297, 298	K43	Stop/start relay	427, 428
F1 to F18	Fuses in fusebox		K45	Mixture preheater relay	136, 137
F19	Fuse (window motors)	435	K46	Ignition timing control	144, 149, 460 to 467
F20	Fuse (central locking)	362	K52	Ignition module	141, 142, 457, 458
F22	Fuse (mixture preheater)	136	K58	Fuel pump relay (TBI)	
F24	Fuse (level control)	351	K59	Day running light relay	354 to 359
F25	Voltage stabiliser	213	L2	Ignition coil (Hall sensor)	113, 114, 142, 143, 458
G1	Battery	101	L3	Ignition coil (inductive sensor)	122, 123, 423
G2	Alternator	109, 110	M1	Starter motor	106, 107
H1	Radio	304	M2	Windscreen wiper motor	315 to 318
H2	Horn	344	M3	Heater fan motor	203 to 205
H3	Turn signal warning light	286	M4	Radiator fan motor	202
H4	Oil pressure warning light	222	M5	Washer pump	314
H5	Handbrake/brake fluid warning light	221	M6	LH headlight wiper motor	327 to 330
H6	Hazard warning system warning light	283	M7	RH headlight wiper motor	332 to 334
H7	No-charge warning light	110	M8	Rear window wiper motor	337 to 339
H8	Main beam warning light	253	M9	Rear window washer pump	342
H9	LH stop-light	227	M12	Starter motor (Diesel)	168, 169
H10	RH stop-light	278	M14	LH front door window motor	438, 440
H11	LH front turn signal light	284	M15	RH front door window motor	442, 444

Key to diagram 2 (Models from 1985 to 1986) (continued)

No	Description	Grid reference	No	Description	Grid reference
M16	LH rear door window motor	446, 448	S22	Rear foglight switch	259, 260
M17	RH rear door window motor	450, 452	S23	Boot lid release switch	232
M19	LH rear door locking motor	364, 367	S29	Radiator fan switch	202
M20	RH rear door locking motor	364, 367	S30	LH heated seat switch	369, 370
M21	Fuel pump	177, 471	S31	LH rear door courtesy light switch	297
M22	Level control compressor	351	S32	RH rear door courtesy light switch	298
M26	Electric aerial motor	306 to 308	S37	LH front door window motor switch	438 to 441
M30	LH exterior mirror adjustment and heating	378 to 381, 387 to 390	S38	Rear window isolating switch	437
			S39	LH rear door window motor switch	446, 448
M31	RH exterior mirror adjustment and heating	394 to 397	S40	RH rear door window motor switch	450, 452
M32	Front door locking motor	364, 367	S41	Central locking door switch	361, 362
M33	Idle control unit		S44	Throttle valve switch	197, 494
M37	Boot lid/tailgate locking motor	364, 367	S46	Heated seat switch	373, 374
P1	Fuel gauge	214	S47	Doors open/headlamps on warning switch	291, 292
P2	Temperature gauge	215	S50	Choke on warning switch	224
P3	Clock	302	S52	Hazard light switch	281 to 285
P4	Fuel sensor	214	S60	Clutch pedal switch	158
P5	Temperature sensor	215	S64	Horn switch	344
P7	Tachometer	217	S66	Vacuum switch	147
P11	Airflow meter	197, 494	S68	Exterior mirror switch	
P12	Temperature probe (coolant)	197, 494	S68.1	Exterior mirror adjustment switch	377 to 380, 385 to 389
P13	Outside air temperature sensor	412, 413	S68.2	Exterior mirror heater switch	383, 392
P14	Distance sensor	155, 156, 404, 405	S68.3	Exterior mirror left/right switch	386 to 390
P15	Fuel flowmeter	406, 407	S73	Temperature switch	137
P32	Heated Lambda sensor	494	S74	Engine temperature switch	150
R2	Carburettor preheater	129	S75	Oil temperature switch	150
R3	Cigarette lighter	229	S77	Distance switch	152 to 155
R5	Glow plugs	172, 173	S78	RH front door window motor switch	442 to 445
R7	Mixture preheater	136	S79	LH rear door remote window motor switch	446 to 449
R11	Instrument lights dimmer	245	S80	RH rear door remote window motor switch	450 to 453
R12	Automatic choke	131, 132	S85	Stop/start clutch pedal switch	419
S1	Starter motor switch	106 to 108	S86	Stop/start switch	418, 419
S2.1	Light switch	241 to 243, 429 to 430	U3	Computer	405 to 414
S2.2	Courtesy light switch	294	U3.1	Clock switch	412
S3	Heater fan switch	203 to 206	U3.2	Function selector switch	412
S4	Heated rear window switch	208, 209	U3.3	Reset/stopwatch/adjustment switch	412
S5.2	Headlight dip switch	253, 254, 431	X1	Trailer socket	238, 240, 274, 275, 276, 286, 290
S5.3	Turn signal switch	287, 288	X2	Auxiliary connector	224, 232, 248, 304, 362, 370, 375, 435
S7	Reversing light switch	227	Y3	Boot lid release solenoid	232
S8	Stop-light switch	278	Y4	Headlight washer solenoid valve	325
S9.2	Windscreen wiper switch (intermittent)	314 to 318	Y5	Diesel solenoid valve	174
S9.3	Rear window wiper switch (intermittent)	340, 341	Y6	Auxiliary air slide valve	197, 494
S10.1	Automatic transmission switch	107	Y7	Fuel injectors	197, 494
S11	Brake fluid level switch	220	Y9	Level control solenoid	349
S13	Handbrake warning light switch	221	Y10	Distributor	118
S14	Oil pressure switch	222	Y11	Hall sensor	114 to 116, 460 to 462
S15	Boot light switch	293	Y15	Inductive sensor	121 to 122, 429
S16	RH courtesy light switch	295	Y17	Idle cut-off solenoid valve	130
S17	LH courtesy light switch	296	Y18	Dashpot solenoid valve	158, 162
S18	Glovebox light switch	225	Y22	Distributor	148, 464
S21	Foglight switch	265 to 267	Y23	Distributor	125, 432

Not all items are fitted to all models

Refer to page WD•1 for colour codes

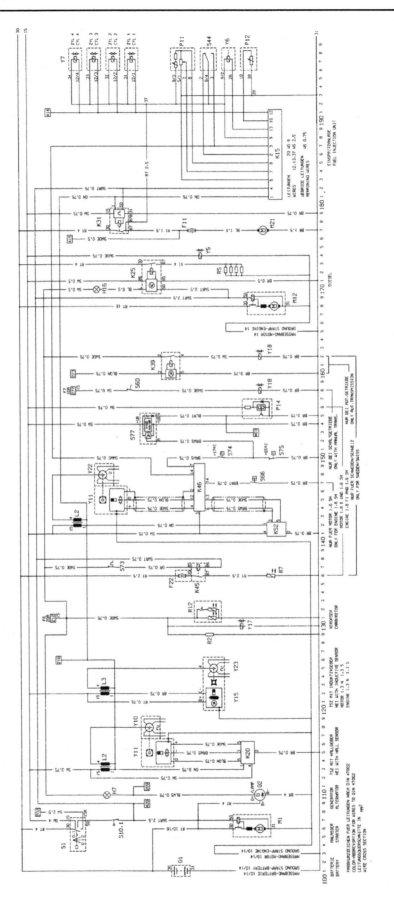

**Diagram 2: Typical diagram for all models
1985 to 1986**

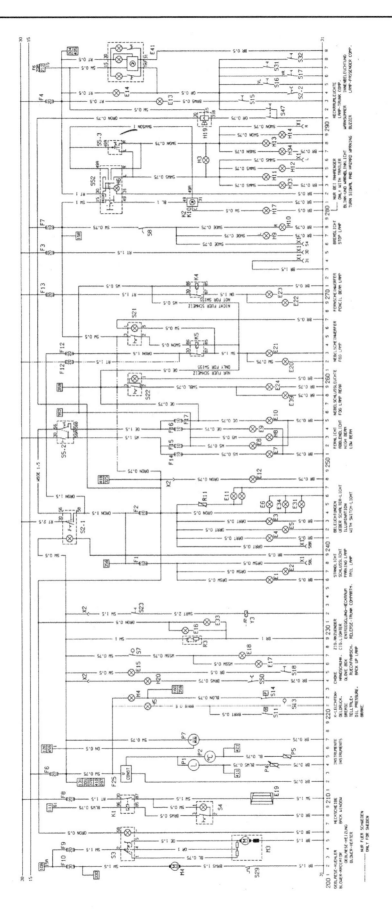

**Diagram 2: Typical diagram for all models
1985 to 1986 (continued)**

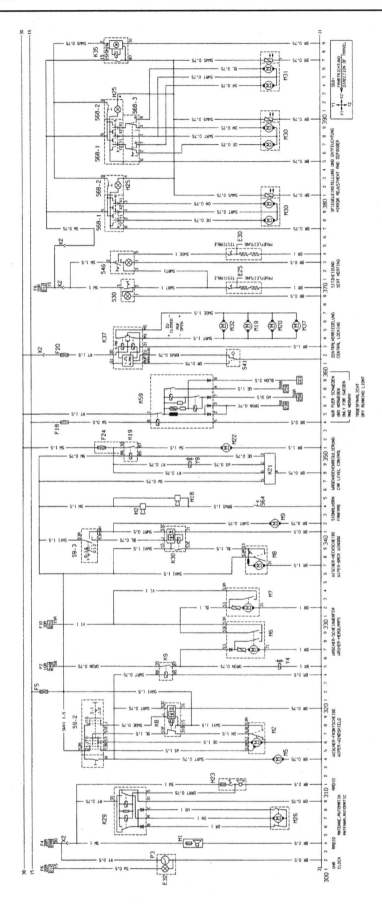

Diagram 2: Typical diagram for all models 1985 to 1986 (continued)

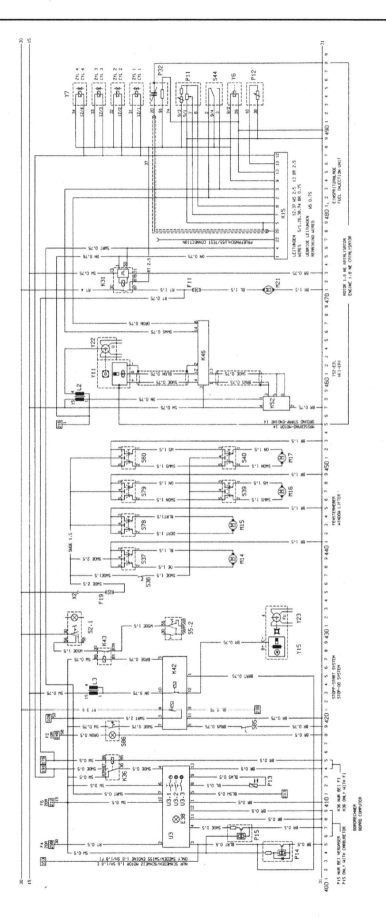

Diagram 2: Typical diagram for all models 1985 to 1986 (continued)

Key to diagram 3 (Models from 1987-on)

No	Description	Grid reference	No	Description	Grid reference
E1	LH parking light	329	H25	Mirror heater warning light	483, 493
E2	LH tail light	330	H26	ABS warning light	589
E3	Number plate light	336	H30	Engine warning light	148, 176
E4	RH parking light	334	H33	LH repeater turn signal light	391
E5	RH tail light	335	H34	RH repeater turn signal light	395
E6	Engine compartment light	337	H44	EZV warning light	255
E7	LH high beam	359	K1	Heated rear window relay	306, 307
E8	RH high beam	360	K2	Flasher unit	389
E9	LH low beam	362	K4	Spotlight relay	378, 379
E10	RH low beam	363	K5	Foglight relay	371, 372
E11	Instrument lights	338	K8	Windscreen wiper intermittent relay	432 to 435
E12	Selector lever light	341	K9	Headlamp washer relay	439, 440
E13	Boot light	405	K10	Trailer flasher unit	388, 389
E14	Courtesy light	406	K15	Fuel injection timing control	284 to 291
E15	Glovebox light	319	K19	Level control relay	465, 466
E16	Cigarette lighter light	324	K20	Ignition module	216 to 218
E17	LH reversing light	320	K21	Level control sensor	462 to 465
E18	RH reversing light	321	K25	Preheater relay	209 to 212
E19	Heated rear window	307	K29	Electric aerial relay	419 to 423
E20	LH foglight	370	K30	Rear wiper relay	454 to 456
E21	RH foglight	371	K35	Heated exterior mirror delay relay	497, 499
E22	LH spot light	377	K36	Computer relay	513 to 515
E23	RH spot light	378	K37	Central locking relay	558 to 562
E24	LH rear foglight	367	K45	Mixture preheater relay	263, 264
E25	LH heated front seat	470	K47	Over-voltage protection, relay	570, 571
E26	Light switch light	334	K50	ABS timing control	574, 588
E30	RH heated front seat	474	K53	Timing control (EV 61)	273 to 282
E31	Symbol insert light	337	K54	Carburettor control unit (EZV)	240 to 260
E32	Clock light	414	K55	Carburettor relay (EZV)	238, 239
E33	Ashtray light	325	K57	Control unit (TBI)	143 to 161
E34	Heater control light	337	K58	Fuel pump relay (TBI)	163, 164
E38	Computer light	508	K59	Day running light relay	344 to 350
E39	RH rear foglight	366	K61	Control unit (Motronic)	171 to 195
E41	Courtesy light (with delay)	409, 410	K62	Control unit (dim-dip lights)	353 to 357
F1 to F18 Fuses in fusebox			K68	Fuel injection relay	196 to 199, 295 to 299
F19	Fuse (window motors)	536	K73	Ignition module (EZ 61)	270, 271
F20	Fuse (central locking)	559	K74	Control unit (MZV)	225 to 234
F24	Fuse (level control)	466	L2	Ignition coil (Hall sensor)	215, 216
F25	Voltage stabiliser	310	L3	Ignition coil (inductive sensor)	126, 127, 137, 138, 172,
F31	Fuse (EZV carburettor)	238			173, 227, 228, 258, 259
F32	Fuse (mixture preheater)	264	L4	Ignition coil (inductive sensor, EZ 61)	271, 272
G1	Battery	101	M1	Starter motor	106, 107, 300, 302
G2	Alternator	110, 111, 205	M2	Windscreen wiper motor	430 to 433
G3	Battery (Diesel)	201	M4	Radiator fan motor	114
H1	Radio	417	M5	Washer pump	429
H2	Horn	459	M6	LH headlight wiper motor	442 to 445
H3	Turn signal warning light	394	M7	RH headlight wiper motor	447 to 449
H4	Oil pressure warning light	317	M8	Rear window wiper motor	452 to 454
H5	Handbrake/brake fluid warning light	316	M9	Rear window washer pump	457
H6	Hazard warning system warning light	390	M12	Starter motor (Diesel)	207, 208
H7	No-charge warning light	111	M14	LH front door window motor	539, 541
H8	Main beam warning light	361	M15	RH front door window motor	543, 545
H9	LH stop-light	385	M16	LH rear door window motor	547, 549
H10	RH stop-light	386	M17	RH rear door window motor	551, 553
H11	LH front turn signal light	392	M19	LH rear door locking motor	561, 564
H12	LH rear turn signal light	393	M20	RH rear door locking motor	561, 564
H13	RH front turn signal light	396	M21	Fuel pump	197, 164, 295
H14	RH rear turn signal light	397	M22	Level control compressor	466
H16	Preheater warning light	209	M26	Electric aerial motor	419 to 421
H17	Trailer turn signal warning light	388	M30	LH exterior mirror adjustment and heating	478 to 481, 487 to 490
H18	Dual horns	460	M31	RH exterior mirror adjustment and heating	494 to 497
H19	Headlights on warning buzzer	403, 404	M32	Front door locking motor	561, 564
H20	Choke on warning light	122	M33	Idle control unit	183, 184, 149 to 152
H23	Radio with electric aerial	423, 424	M37	Boot lit/tailgate locking motor	561, 564

Key to diagram 3 (Models from 1987-on) (continued)

No	Description	Grid reference
P1	Fuel gauge	311
P2	Temperature gauge	312
P3	Clock	415
P4	Fuel sensor	311
P5	Temperature sensor	312
P7	Tachometer	314
P11	Airflow meter	185 to 189
P12	Temperature probe (coolant)	178, 289
P13	Outside air temperature sensor	512, 513
P14	Distance sensor	142, 143, 170, 171, 504, 505
P15	Fuel flowmeter	506, 507
P17	LH front wheel sensor (ABS)	574, 575
P18	RH front wheel sensor (ABS)	576, 577
P19	LH rear wheel sensor (ABS)	578, 579
P20	RH rear wheel sensor (ABS)	580, 581
P23	Inlet manifold vacuum sensor	155 to 157, 225 to 227
P24	Coolant temperature sensor (EV 61)	277, 278, 231, 232
P29	Inlet manifold temperature sensor	247
P30	Coolant temperature sensor	153, 248
P31	Main throttle potentiometer	248, 250
P32	Heated Lambda sensor	193, 194
P33	Lambda sensor	157
P34	Throttle valve position sensor	158 to 160
P35	Crankshaft inductive sensor	189 to 191, 274 to 276, 257 to 259
R2	Carburettor preheater	116, 262
R3	Cigarette lighter	323
R5	Glow plugs	211, 212
R7	Mixture preheater	264
R11	Instrument lights dimmer	338
R12	Automatic choke	118
R15	Resistor	161, 162
S1	Starter motor switch	106, 107, 205, 206
S2	Light switch	
S2.1	Main light switch	334 to 337
S2.2	Courtesy light switch	406
S3	Heater fan switch	300 to 303
S4	Heated rear window switch	305, 306
S5.2	Headlight dip switch	361, 362
S5.3	Turn signal switch	395, 396
S7	Reversing light switch	321
S8	Stop-light switch	386
S9.2	Windscreen wiper switch (intermittent)	429 to 433
S9.3	Rear window wiper switch (intermittent)	455, 456
S10.1	Automatic transmission switch	107
S10.2	Reversing light switch	322
S10.3	Park/neutral switch	159
S11	Brake fluid level switch	315
S13	Handbrake warning light switch	316
S14	Oil pressure switch	317
S15	Boot lid switch	405
S16	RH courtesy light switch	407
S17	LH courtesy light switch	408
S18	Glovebox light switch	319
S21	Foglight switch	373 to 375
S22	Rear foglight switch	367, 368
S23	Boot lid release switch	326
S30	LH heated seat switch	469, 470
S31	LH rear door courtesy light switch	409
S32	RH rear door courtesy light switch	410
S37	LH front door window motor switch	539 to 542
S38	Rear window isolating switch	538

No	Description	Grid reference
S39	LH rear door window motor switch	547 to 549
S40	RH rear door window motor switch	551 to 553
S41	Central locking door switch	558, 559
S44	Throttle valve switch	173, 174, 285, 286
S46	Heated seat switch	472 to 474
S47	Doors open/headlamps on warning switch	403, 404
S50	Choke on warning switch	122
S52	Hazard light switch	389 to 393
S61	Power steering pressure switch	121
S67	Horn switch	459
S68.1	Exterior mirror adjustment switch	477 to 480, 485 to 489
S68.2	Exterior mirror heater switch	483, 492
S68.3	Exterior mirror left/right switch	486 to 490
S78	RH front door window motor switch	543 to 546
S79	LH rear door remote window motor switch	547 to 550
S80	RH rear door remote window motor switch	551 to 554
S91	Oil pressure switch (TBI)	166, 167
U3	Computer	505 to 514
U3.1	Clock switch	512
U3.2	Function selector switch	512
U3.3	Reset/stopwatch/adjustment switch	512
U4	ABS system	572 to 586
U4.1	ABS relay	573 to 576
U4.2	ABS solenoid valve relay	583 to 586
U4.3	ABS pump	572
U4.4	ABS diode	585
U4.5	LH front ABS solenoid valve	578
U4.6	RH front ABS solenoid valve	580
U4.7	LH rear ABS solenoid valve	579
U4.8	RH rear ABS solenoid valve	581
X1	Trailer socket	331, 333, 382 to 384, 394 to 398
X2	Auxiliary connector	122, 341, 326, 417, 470, 475, 536, 559
X10	Ignition timing adjustment connector	233, 234
X11	5-pin connector (TBI)	145, 148, 164, 167
X13	Test connector	175, 176, 178, 147, 153, 154, 255
X15	Connector - octane number	229, 230, 243, 244, 280, 281, 154, 155, 184 to 186
X15F	4-pin connector	270, 271, 291, 295
X16	Connector - wiring harness	255, 258, 261, 262
X17	8-pin connector (Motronic)	171, 172, 176, 181
Y1	Air conditioning compressor	
Y2	Revolution acceleration solenoid valve	
Y3	Boot lid release solenoid	326
Y4	Headlight washer solenoid valve	440
Y5	Diesel solenoid valve	213
Y6	Auxiliary air slide valve	293
Y7	Fuel injectors	186 to 193, 279 to 286
Y9	Level control solenoid	464
Y10	Distributor	220
Y11	Hall sensor	216 to 218
Y14	Inductive sensor (EV 61)	133 to 137, 225 to 227
Y15	Inductive sensor	125, 126
Y17	Idle cut-off solenoid valve	117
Y23	Distributor	129
Y24	Distributor	140, 230
Y25	Revolution acceleration solenoid valve	121
Y26	Throttle valve positioner	238 to 244
Y27	Pre-throttle valve	252, 253
Y32	Injection valve (TBI)	144
Y33	Distributor	174, 260, 274
Y34	Tank ventilation valve	195, 196

Not all items are fitted to all models
Refer to page WD•1 for colour codes

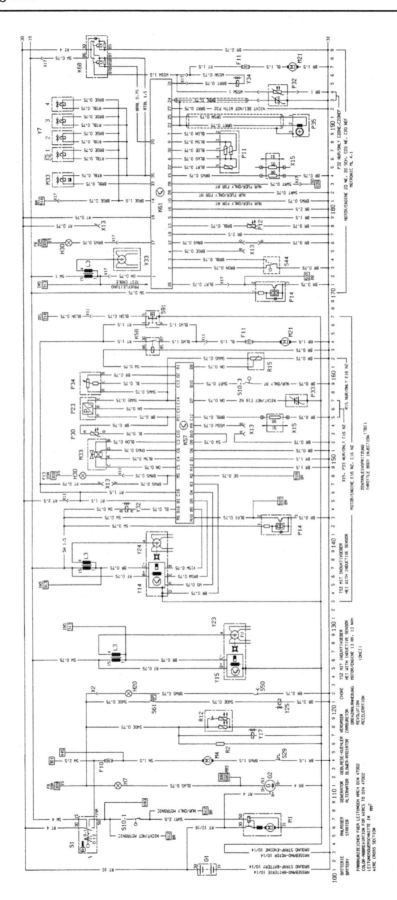

Diagram 3: Typical diagram for all models from 1987-on

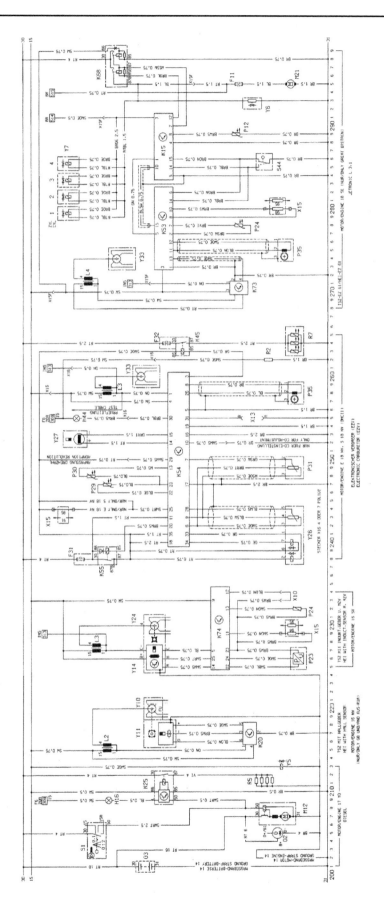

Diagram 3: Typical diagram for all models from 1987-on (continued)

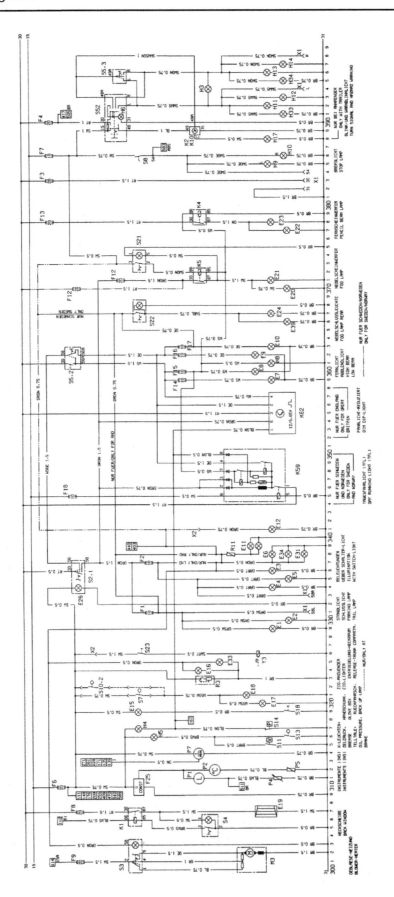

Diagram 3: Typical diagram for all models from 1987-on (continued)

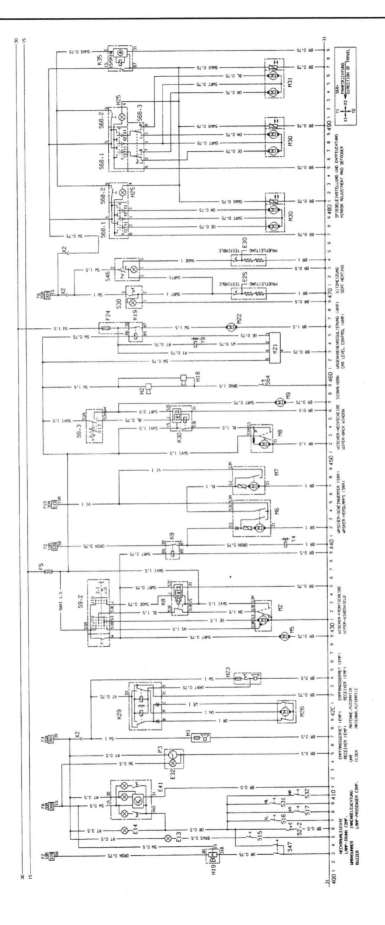

Diagram 3: Typical diagram for all models from 1987-on (continued)

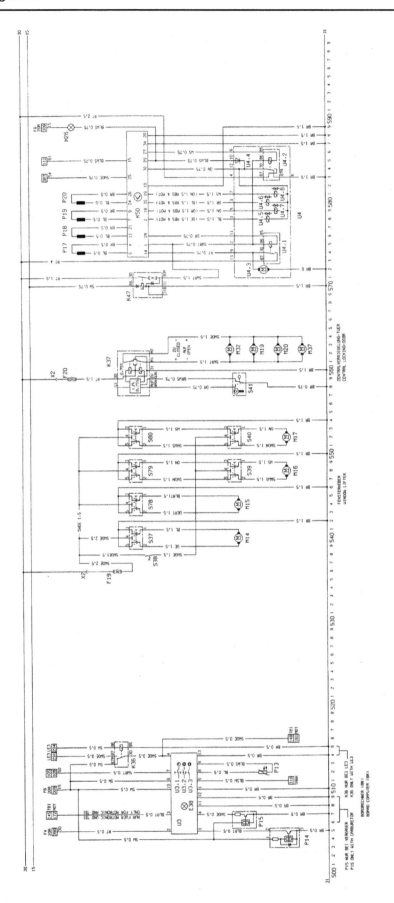

Diagram 3: Typical diagram for all models from 1987-on (continued)

Chapter 12
Body electrical system

Contents

Battery - removal and refitting ....See Chapter 5A
Battery check and maintenance ....See "Weekly checks"
Bulbs - renewal 11
Central locking system - general information and component removal
   and refitting 21
Cigarette lighter - removal and refitting 7
Clock - removal and refitting 6
Electrical fault finding - general information 2
Exterior lamps - removal and refitting 12
Fuses and relays - general information 3
General information 1
Headlamp beam adjustment - general information 13
Headlamp dim-dip system (UK models) - general information 14
Headlamp wash/wipe system - general information 20
Horn(s) - removal and refitting 5

Instrument panel - removal and refitting 8
Instrument panel components - removal and refitting 9
Loudspeakers - removal and refitting 24
Power operated windows - general information 26
Radio aerial - removal and refitting 25
Radio/cassette player - removal and refitting 23
Speedometer cable - removal and refitting 10
Switches - removal and refitting 4
Tailgate washer system - general information 19
Tailgate wiper motor- removal and refitting 17
Trip computer - general information and component renewal 22
Windscreen washer system - general information 18
Windscreen wiper motor and linkage - removal and refitting 16
Wiper blades and arms - removal and refitting 15

Degrees of difficulty

Easy, suitable for novice with little experience		**Fairly easy,** suitable for beginner with some experience		**Fairly difficult,** suitable for competent DIY mechanic		**Difficult,** suitable for experienced DIY mechanic		**Very difficult,** suitable for expert DIY or professional	

Specifications

System type .... 12V negative earth

Fuses - early models

Fuse	Rating (amps)		Circuit(s) protected
1	7.5		LH parking and tail, number plate, instrument illumination and engine compartment lamps
2	7.5		RH parking and tail lamps
3	7.5		Rear foglamps
4	15		Interior, luggage compartment and hazard warning lamps. Clock and radio
5	30		Windscreen wipers and washers and horn
6	20		Reversing lamps, cigarette lighter, automatic choke and instruments
7	10		Direction indicator and stop lamps
8	20		Heated rear screen
9	20		Heater blower motor
10	25		Radiator cooling fan
11	-		Not used
12	-		Not used
13	-		Not used
14	-		Not used
15	-		Not used
16	-		Not used
17	-		Not used

Note: *Not all items fitted to all models*

Fuses - later models

Fuse	Rating (amps)	Circuit(s) protected
1	7.5	LH parking and tail lamps
2	7.5	RH parking and tail lamps
3	-	Not used
4	15	Interior lamps, hazard warning lamps, clock and radio
5	30	Windscreen and tailgate wipers and washers and horn
6	20	Reversing lamps, cigarette lighter, automatic choke andinstruments
7	10	Direction indicator and stop lamps
8	20	Heated rear window
9	20	Heater blower motor
10	25	Radiator cooling fan
11	15	Fuel injection system
12	15	Front foglights
13	15	Auxiliary driving lights
14	10	LH main beam
15	10	RH main beam
16	10	LH dipped beam
17	10	RH dipped beam
18	-	Not used
19	30	Electric windows
20	30	Central locking

Note: *Not all items fitted to all models*

Bulbs

Lamp	Wattage
Headlamp	60/55
Front parking lamp	4
Direction indicator lamp	21
Stop/tail lamp	21/5
Rear number plate lamp	10
Reversing lamp	21
Engine compartment lamp	10
Luggage compartment lamp	10
Glovebox	5
Instrument warning (except ignition/charge warning) lamps	1.2
Ignition/charge warning lamp	3
Cigar lighter illumination	1.2
Switch illumination	1.2
Rear foglamps	21
Ashtray lamp	1.2
Clock illumination	1.2
Selector lever index (automatic transmission)	1.2
Choke ON switch	1.2
Direction indicator side repeater lamp	5
Auxiliary driving lamps	55
Vehicle interior lamp	10

1 General information

⚠ **Warning: Before carrying out any work on the electrical system, read through the precautions given in Safety First! at the start of this manual and Chapter 5**

The electrical system is of the 12 volt negative earth type. Power for the lights and all electrical accessories is supplied by a lead/acid type battery which is charged by the alternator.

This Chapter covers repair and service procedures for the various electrical components not associated with engine. Information on the battery, alternator and starter motor can be found in Chapter 5.

It should be noted that prior to working on any component in the electrical system, the battery negative terminal should first be disconnected to prevent the possibility of electrical short circuits and/or fires.

2 Electrical fault finding - general information

Note: *Refer to the precautions given in 'Safety first!' and in Section 1 of this Chapter before starting work. The following tests relate to testing of the main electrical circuits, and* should not be used to test delicate electronic circuits (such as anti-lock braking systems), particularly where an electronic control module is used.

General

1 A typical electrical circuit consists of an electrical component, any switches, relays, motors, fuses, fusible links or circuit breakers related to that component, and the wiring and connectors which link the component to both the battery and the chassis. To help to pinpoint a problem in an electrical circuit, wiring diagrams are included at the end of this Chapter.

2 Before attempting to diagnose an electrical fault, first study the appropriate wiring diagram

to obtain a complete understanding of the components included in the particular circuit concerned. The possible sources of a fault can be narrowed down by noting if other components related to the circuit are operating properly. If several components or circuits fail at one time, the problem is likely to be related to a shared fuse or earth connection.

3 Electrical problems usually stem from simple causes, such as loose or corroded connections, a faulty earth connection, a blown fuse, a melted fusible link, or a faulty relay (refer to Section 3 for details of testing relays). Visually inspect the condition of all fuses, wires and connections in a problem circuit before testing the components. Use the wiring diagrams to determine which terminal connections will need to be checked in order to pinpoint the trouble spot.

4 The basic tools required for electrical fault-finding include a circuit tester or voltmeter (a 12-volt bulb with a set of test leads can also be used for certain tests); a self-powered test light (sometimes known as a continuity tester); an ohmmeter (to measure resistance); a battery and set of test leads; and a jumper wire, preferably with a circuit breaker or fuse incorporated, which can be used to bypass suspect wires or electrical components. Before attempting to locate a problem with test instruments, use the wiring diagram to determine where to make the connections.

5 To find the source of an intermittent wiring fault (usually due to a poor or dirty connection, or damaged wiring insulation), a 'wiggle' test can be performed on the wiring. This involves wiggling the wiring by hand to see if the fault occurs as the wiring is moved. It should be possible to narrow down the source of the fault to a particular section of wiring. This method of testing can be used in conjunction with any of the tests described in the following sub-Sections.

6 Apart from problems due to poor connections, two basic types of fault can occur in an electrical circuit - open circuit, or short circuit.

7 Open circuit faults are caused by a break somewhere in the circuit, which prevents current from flowing. An open circuit fault will prevent a component from working, but will not cause the relevant circuit fuse to blow.

8 Short circuit faults are caused by a 'short' somewhere in the circuit, which allows the current flowing in the circuit to 'escape' along an alternative route, usually to earth. Short circuit faults are normally caused by a breakdown in wiring insulation, which allows a feed wire to touch either another wire, or an earthed component such as the bodyshell. A short circuit fault will normally cause the relevant circuit fuse to blow.

Finding an open circuit

9 To check for an open circuit, connect one lead of a circuit tester or voltmeter to either the negative battery terminal or a known good earth.

10 Connect the other lead to a connector in the circuit being tested, preferably nearest to the battery or fuse.

11 Switch on the circuit, bearing in mind that some circuits are live only when the ignition switch is moved to a particular position.

12 If voltage is present (indicated either by the tester bulb lighting or a voltmeter reading, as applicable), this means that the section of the circuit between the relevant connector and the battery is problem-free.

13 Continue to check the remainder of the circuit in the same fashion.

14 When a point is reached at which no voltage is present, the problem must lie between that point and the previous test point with voltage. Most problems can be traced to a broken, corroded or loose connection.

Finding a short circuit

15 To check for a short circuit, first disconnect the load(s) from the circuit (loads are the components which draw current from a circuit, such as bulbs, motors, heating elements, etc).

16 Remove the relevant fuse from the circuit, and connect a circuit tester or voltmeter to the fuse connections.

17 Switch on the circuit, bearing in mind that some circuits are live only when the ignition switch is moved to a particular position.

18 If voltage is present (indicated either by the tester bulb lighting or a voltmeter reading, as applicable), this means that there is a short circuit.

19 If no voltage is present, but the fuse still blows with the load(s) connected, this indicates an internal fault in the load(s).

Finding an earth fault

20 The battery negative terminal is connected to 'earth' - the metal of the engine/transmission and the car body - and most systems are wired so that they only receive a positive feed, the current returning via the metal of the car body. This means that the component mounting and the body form part of that circuit. Loose or corroded mountings can therefore cause a range of electrical faults, ranging from total failure of a circuit, to a puzzling partial fault. In particular, lights may shine dimly (especially when another circuit sharing the same earth point is in operation), motors (eg. wiper motors or the radiator cooling fan motor) may run slowly, and the operation of one circuit may have an apparently unrelated effect on another. Note that on many vehicles, earth straps are used between certain components, such as the engine/transmission and the body, usually where there is no metal-to-metal contact between components due to flexible rubber mountings, etc.

21 To check whether a component is properly earthed, disconnect the battery and connect one lead of an ohmmeter to a known good earth point. Connect the other lead to the wire or earth connection being tested. The resistance reading should be zero; if not, check the connection as follows.

22 If an earth connection is thought to be faulty, dismantle the connection and clean back to bare metal both the bodyshell and the wire terminal or the component earth connection mating surface. Be careful to remove all traces of dirt and corrosion, then use a knife to trim away any paint, so that a clean metal-to-metal joint is made. On reassembly, tighten the joint fasteners securely; if a wire terminal is being refitted, use serrated washers between the terminal and the bodyshell to ensure a clean and secure connection. When the connection is remade, prevent the onset of corrosion in the future by applying a coat of petroleum jelly or silicone-based grease or by spraying on (at regular intervals) a proprietary ignition sealer or a water dispersant lubricant.

3 Fuses and relays - general information

Fuses

1 The fuses are located behind a panel on the drivers side of the facia, behind a removable cover.

2 To gain access to fusebox, unclip the access panel from the driver's side of the facia (see illustrations).

3 The fuse number is marked on the fusebox next to each fuse, a list of the circuits each fuse protects is given in the Specifications at the start of this Chapter.

3.2a Detaching fuse box cover

3.2b Fuses and relays

4 To remove a fuse, first switch off the circuit concerned (or the ignition), then pull the fuse out of its terminals. The wire within the fuse is clearly visible; if the fuse is blown it will be broken or melted.

5 Always renew a fuse with one of an identical rating; never use a fuse with a different rating from the original or substitute anything else. Never renew a fuse more than once without tracing the source of the trouble. The fuse rating is stamped on top of the fuse; note that the fuses are also colour-coded for easy recognition.

6 If a new fuse blows immediately, find the cause before renewing it again; a short to earth as a result of faulty insulation is most likely. Where a fuse protects more than one circuit, try to isolate the defect by switching on each circuit in turn (if possible) until the fuse blows again. Always carry a supply of spare fuses of each relevant rating on the vehicle, a spare of each rating should be clipped into the base of the fusebox.

Relays

7 The majority of relays are located in the fusebox behind the driver's side lower facia panel and can be reached once the fusebox cover has been removed. Some relays (such as the lights on warning buzzer relay) are fitted to the base of the fusebox and can be reached once the lower panel has been removed from underneath the drivers side of the facia **(see illustration)**.

8 The rear wiper motor relay is located in the luggage compartment, behind the trim panel on the left-hand side. Release the panel fasteners at the rear and side as necessary, pull back the panel and remove the wiring plug and relay retaining screw. Additional relays can also be found in the engine compartment **(see illustration)**.

9 If a circuit or system controlled by a relay develops a fault and the relay is suspect, operate the system; if the relay is functioning it should be possible to hear it click as it is energized. If this is the case the fault lies with the components or wiring of the system. If the relay is not being energized then either the relay is not receiving a main supply or a switching voltage or the relay itself is faulty. Testing is by the substitution of a known good

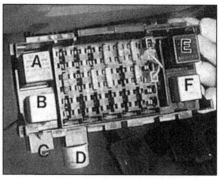

3.7 Relays on fusebox

A *Direction indicator*   D *Lights-on buzzer*
B *Heated rear screen*   E *Wiper delay*
C *Headlamp*   F *Rear foglamp*

unit but be careful; while some relays are identical in appearance and in operation, others look similar but perform different functions.

10 To renew a relay first ensure that the ignition switch is off. The relay can then simply be pulled out from the socket and the new relay pressed in.

4 Switches - removal and refitting

Removal

1 Before removing a switch, disconnect the battery negative lead.

Heater blower switch

2 The blower switch is retained by spring tabs which should be depressed with a knife blade inserted behind the switch bezel as the switch is pulled out of the panel.

3 If there is any difficulty in releasing the switch, an alternative method may be used by withdrawing the switch panel after extracting the panel securing screws **(see illustration)**.

4 Disconnect the switch wiring plug.

Heated rear window switch

5 Access to the switch is obtained after first extracting the switch panel screws and pulling the panel from the facia **(see illustration)**.

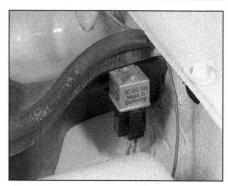

3.8 Relay in engine compartment of 1.8 SRi model

Lighting switch

6 The spring-loaded tabs which retain the switch should be depressed by inserting a blade behind the switch bezel, and the switch then pulled out of the facia panel until its wiring plug can be disconnected.

7 Alternatively, the switch panel can be withdrawn after extracting the securing screws **(see illustration)**. Removal of the switch panel also gives access to the instrument lighting dimmer switch, fitted to some models.

Hazard warning lamp switch

8 Access to the switch is as described for the heated rear window switch.

Steering column switches

9 Extract the securing screws and remove the lower shroud from the upper part of the steering column.

10 Remove the upper shroud. It should be possible to prise the shroud over the steering lock bezel, but if there is any difficulty, the lock can be removed if its retaining plunger is depressed with a thin rod. The ignition key must be in position 1.

11 Depress the switch retaining tabs and withdraw the switch far enough to be able to disconnect the wiring plug. Remove the switch **(see illustrations)**.

Courtesy lamp switch

12 This is located in the door pillar and is of plunger type.

4.3 Switch panel securing screw removal

4.5 Heater blower/heated rear window/hazard warning switches and mounting panel

4.7 Lighting switch panel screw

4.11a Depressing steering column switch retaining tabs

4.11b Removing a steering column switch

4.13 Courtesy lamp switch

13 To remove the switch, extract the fixing screw and withdraw it from the pillar **(see illustration)**.

14 If the switch is to be removed, tape the wires to the pillar to prevent them slipping into the interior of the pillar.

15 Apply petroleum jelly to the moving parts of the switch before refitting in order to prevent corrosion.

Rear foglamp switch

16 Access to this switch and its adjacent switches is best obtained by extracting the fixing screws and pulling the complete switch panel from the facia **(see illustration)**. Access to the two fixing screws can be achieved by removing the left-hand plastic blanking plate.

17 The wiring plugs and the switches can then be released by prising aside the tabs of their retaining clips.

Luggage area light switch (Estate)

18 Remove the tailgate interior trim panel as described in Chapter 11, Section 25.

19 Depress the switch plunger and disconnect the wire from the back of the switch. Press the switch body out of the tailgate **(see illustrations)**.

Power operated window switches

20 When fitted these are located on the top face of the centre console.

21 To remove, prise free the switch concerned, then lift it clear and detach the

wiring connections from it **(see illustrations)**.

Exterior mirror adjustment switch

22 Access to the switch is as described for the power operated window switches.

Horn switch

23 Prise the horn button out from the centre of the steering wheel and disconnect its wiring connectors **(see illustration)**.

Refitting

24 Refitting is the reversal of removal; check for correct switch operation before refitting. Switches which are retained by spring tabs only need to be pushed home.

4.16 Rear foglamp switch panel

4.19a Removing the luggage area light switch (Estate)

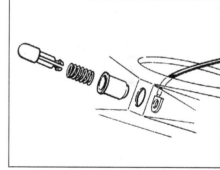

4.19b Luggage area light switch - Estate

4.21a Removing the powered exterior mirror adjuster switch

4.21b Exterior mirror adjustment switch lead connectors

4.23 Horn button removal

5.1a Single horn location

5.1b Second horn location - twin horns

6.1 Clock withdrawal

5 Horn(s) - removal and refitting

Removal

1 Where a single horn is fitted, it is located just ahead of the radiator. If twin horns are fitted, the second horn is attached to a bracket on the left-hand side underneath near the radiator (see illustrations). Where necessary, to improve access remove the radiator grille as described in Chapter 11 (Section 8).
2 Disconnect the wiring connectors then undo the retaining nut/bolt (as applicable) and remove the horn.

7.3 Cigar lighter mounting plate/ashtray housing screw

Refitting

3 Refitting is the reverse of removal.

6 Clock - removal and refitting

Removal

1 Disconnect the battery then carefully, taking great care not to mark the facia, prise the clock out of position (see illustration).
2 Disconnect the wiring connectors and remove the clock.

Refitting

3 Refitting is a reversal of removal.

7 Cigarette lighter - removal and refitting

Removal

1 Disconnect the battery.
2 Remove the lighter element from its socket.
3 Extract the retaining screw and remove the ashtray housing until the electrical leads can be pulled off the cigar lighter socket terminals (see illustration).
4 Remove the lighter socket from the ashtray housing.

Refitting

5 Refitting is a reversal of removal, but make sure that the earth lead (A) is located under the lug (B) of the lighter socket (see illustration).

8 Instrument panel - removal and refitting

Removal

1 Disconnect the battery.
2 Remove the cover panel from under the facia panel.
3 Reach up behind the instrument panel and disconnect the speedometer cable by prising down the plastic retainer (see also Section 10).
4 Extract the two screws from under the instrument panel hood (see illustration).
5 Withdraw and remove the hood.
6 Extract the instrument panel fixing screws (see illustration).
7 Swivel the top of the panel towards you until the multi-plugs at the rear can be disconnected.
8 Continue to swivel the instrument panel until the lugs at its base are free and the panel can be withdrawn.

Refitting

9 Refitting is a reversal of removal.

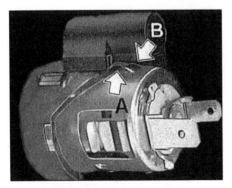

7.5 Cigar lighter connections

A Earth lead   *B Lug*

8.4 Instrument panel hood screw

8.6 Instrument panel fixing screw

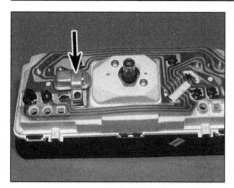

9.4 Instrument voltage stabilizer (arrowed)

10.2 Releasing speedometer drive cable

10.3 Speedometer drive cable at transmission

9 Instrument panel components - removal and refitting

Removal

1 Once the instrument panel has been withdrawn, the individual instruments can be detached.

2 To do this, unclip and remove the bezel and transparent sheet from the front of the dials.

3 Unscrew the securing nuts and withdraw the instruments from the printed circuit board. Take care not to damage the circuit board.

4 Should the coolant temperature gauge and the fuel gauge malfunction at the same time, then this will probably be due to a faulty instrument voltage stabiliser. This can be renewed after extracting the fixing screw **(see illustration)**.

Refitting

5 Refitting is a reversal of removal.

10 Speedometer cable - removal and refitting

Removal

1 Remove the cover panel from under the facia.

2 Reach up and disconnect the cable from the speedometer head by prising the retainer

aside **(see illustration)**. This method may prove difficult, in which case proceed from paragraph 5.

3 Disconnect the opposite end of the cable from the transmission by unbolting the retaining plate or unscrewing the knurled retaining ring according to model **(see illustration)**.

4 Feed the cable through the grommet into the engine compartment and remove it.

5 If difficulty is experienced in reaching up under the instrument panel to disconnect the cable, proceed as follows.

6 Disconnect the battery earth lead.

7 Disconnect the speedometer cable at the transmission end by unscrewing the knurled nut or removing the retaining plate, as applicable.

8 Remove the instrument panel hood (two screws).

9 Remove the screw(s) which secure the instrument panel and free the panel securing lugs.

10 Draw the instrument panel forwards while an assistant feeds the speedometer cable through the bulkhead. Release the cable from the speedometer by pressing the retaining clip.

11 Withdraw the cable into the engine compartment.

Refitting

12 Fit the new cable by reversing the removal procedure, making sure the cable is correctly routed.

11 Bulbs - renewal

General

1 Whenever a bulb is renewed, note the following points.

 a) *Disconnect the battery negative lead before starting work.*

 b) *Remember that if the light has just been in use the bulb may be extremely hot.*

 c) *Always check the bulb contacts and holder, ensuring that there is clean metal-to-metal contact between the bulb and its live(s) and earth. Clean off any corrosion or dirt before fitting a new bulb.*

 d) *Wherever bayonet-type bulbs are fitted (see Specifications) ensure that the live contact(s) bear firmly against the bulb contact.*

 e) *Always ensure that the new bulb is of the correct rating and that it is completely clean before fitting it; this applies particularly to headlight/foglight bulbs.*

Headlamp and front parking lamp

2 At the rear of the headlamp, prise the clip aside and pull off this protective cap **(see illustration)**.

3 Pull off the now exposed wiring plug **(see illustration)**.

4 Depress the bulb retainer and turn it through 1/8 of a turn **(see illustration)**.

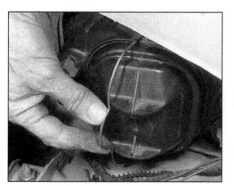

11.2 Headlamp rear cover clip

11.3 Headlamp rear cover removed

11.4 Removing bulb retainer

11.5 Bulbs and retainer removed from the headlamp

11.9 Front flasher bulb and holder removal

11.18a Rear lamp cluster covering trim

5 Withdraw the retainer complete with headlamp and parking lamp bulbs **(see illustration)**.
6 The headlamp bulbs are of halogen type and should not be touched with the fingers. If they are, clean their glass by wiping with a cloth moistened in methylated spirit.
7 Renew the bulb with one of similar type and refit the retainer by reversing the removal operations.

Front flasher lamp

8 Open the bonnet and reach down beside the headlamp.
9 Release the bayonet type bulbholder **(see illustration)**.
10 Renew the bulb with one of similar type and refit the bulbholder.

Front flasher side repeater lamp

11 Two different types of side repeater lamp fitted to the models are covered in this manual, both of which look similar.
12 On the first type, rotate the lamp unit to release it from the wing and withdraw the complete unit. Remove the bulbholder from the rear of the lens and remove the bulb. Fit the new bulb, securely refit the bulbholder to the lens and refit the lamp to the wing.
13 On the second type, rotate the lens anti-clockwise and remove it from the light unit. The bulb can then be removed. Fit the new bulb and securely refit the lens.

Front foglamp

14 Remove the single screw from the bottom of the lamp; remove the lens and reflector unit.

15 Release the spring clip, free the bulb from its holder and unplug the electrical connector.
16 Do not touch the glass of the new bulb with the fingers; if it is accidentally touched, clean it with methylated spirit.
17 Fit the new bulb, making sure that the lugs on the reflector engage with the slots in the holder. Secure with the spring clip and refit the lens and reflector.

Rear lamp cluster (Saloon and Hatchback)

18 Access to these bulbs is obtained by unclipping the cover or carpeting within the luggage compartment and then releasing the bulbholder retaining lugs and withdrawing the bulbholder **(see illustrations)**.
19 Renew the bulb with one of similar type.

Rear lamp cluster (Estate)

20 Remove the four securing screws and lift off the light unit. One of the screws is not immediately visible **(see illustration)**.
21 Release the bulbholder by depressing the lever on the side of the holder. Rotate the bulbholder and remove it **(see illustration)**.
22 Renew the bulb and refit the bulbholder, rotating the holder until it clicks into position.
23 Refit the light unit, securing with the screws.

Rear number plate lamp (Saloon and Hatchback)

24 Insert a thin screwdriver in the notch provided and prise the lamp from the bumper bar **(see illustrations)**.

11.18b Rear lamp bulbholder (retaining clips arrowed)

11.20 Rear light cluster (Estate) secured by four screws - screwdriver on hidden screw

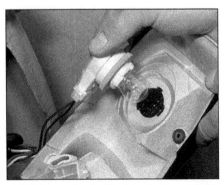

11.21 Removing bulbholder from rear light cluster (Estate)

11.24a Prise free the rear number plate lamp . . .

11.24b . . . from the bumper aperture

11.25 Rear number plate bulb

11.31 Removing a tailgate-mounted light bulb - Estate

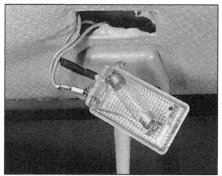

11.33a Interior lamp and bulb - standard type

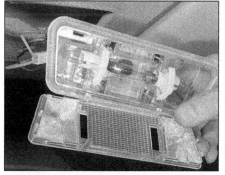

11.33b Combined interior lamp and reading lamp bulbs (unit removed for photo)

11.35 Luggage boot or area lamp

11.38 Instrument panel warning lamp bulb and holder

25 Renew the bulb with one of similar type **(see illustration)**.

Rear number plate lamp (Estate)

26 Remove the tailgate handle, which is secured by four screws.
27 Remove the two screws which secure the lens and pull it off.
28 Pull the old bulb out of its socket and press in a new bulb.
29 Refit by reversing the removal procedure.

Reversing lamps and rear foglamps (Estate)

30 Remove the tailgate interior trim panel (Chapter 11, Section 25).
31 Rotate and pull the bulbholder to remove it **(see illustration)**.
32 Renew the bulb, refit the holder and the trim panel.

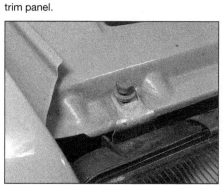

12.2 Headlamp retaining screw

Interior lamps

33 The lamp lens complete with festoon type bulbs can be removed from the headlining above the mirror by careful prising **(see illustrations)**.
34 Renew the bulb with one of similar type and refit the lamp. Note: On later models having a delay feature on the courtesy lamp, the bulb does not go out, the delay unit itself may be faulty.
35 Bulb renewal for the luggage area is carried out in a similar way **(see illustration)**.

Instrument panel lamps

36 These bulbs are accessible if the instrument panel is partially withdrawn as described in Section 8.
37 There is no need to disconnect the speedometer cable provided the cable is

12.3 Headlamp unit removal

eased through the bulkhead grommet as the panel is withdrawn.
38 Twist the bulbholders from their holes in the instrument panel and pull out the wedge type bulbs **(see illustration)**.

---

12 Exterior lamps - removal and refitting

Note: *Disconnect the battery negative lead before removing any lamp, and reconnect the lead after refitting*

Headlamp

Note: *On cars equipped with a headlamp wash/wipe system, it will first be necessary to remove the front bumper (Chapter 11) followed by the headlamp wiper blade on the side concerned (Section 20)*

1 To remove a headlamp unit; first disconnect the battery, then remove the radiator grille as described in Chapter 11.
2 Unscrew the two top headlamp mounting screws **(see illustration)**.
3 Pull the lamp unit forward to release the lower retaining lugs **(see illustration)**.
4 Press the spring clip aside on the rear cover of the lamp and take off the cover.
5 Pull out the wiring plug and withdraw the lamp unit.
6 Refitting is a reversal of removal. On completion adjust the headlight aim as described in Section 13.

Front flasher lamp

7 Remove the headlamp as described above. It is not necessary to remove the lamp completely, just enough to gain the required clearance to allow the flasher lamp to be removed.

8 Twist the flasher bulbholder anti-clockwise and release it from the rear of the lamp.

9 Release the two spring clips and remove the flasher lamp from the vehicle.

10 Refitting is the reverse of removal.

Rear light cluster

Saloon and Hatchback

11 Remove the rear quarter trim on the side concerned to gain access to the wiring harness.

12 Unclip and withdraw the lamp bulbholder.

13 Untwist and remove the foglamp bulbholder.

14 Undo the four retaining nuts and withdraw the light unit from the body.

15 Refit in reverse order of removal.

Estate

16 Remove the rear quarter trim panel on the side concerned to gain access to the wiring harness. Unplug the connector for the rear light unit.

17 Remove the four securing screws and lift off the unit. Extract the grommet and remove the light unit, wiring and grommet.

18 Refit in the reverse order to removal.

Reversing lights and rear foglights (Estate)

19 Remove the tailgate interior trim panel (Chapter 11, Section 25).

20 Undo the retaining, disconnect the wiring harness and extract the light unit from the tailgate.

21 Refit in the reverse order to removal.

13 Headlamp beam adjustment - general information

1 Accurate adjustment of the headlight beam is only possible using optical beam setting equipment and this work should therefore be carried out by a Vauxhall/Opel dealer or suitably equipped workshop.

2 For reference the headlights can be adjusted using the adjuster assemblies fitted to the top and bottom of each light unit. The top adjuster alters the horizontal position of the beam whilst the bottom adjuster alters the vertical aim of the beam **(see illustration)**.

Note: *Adjustment of the front foglights is correct when their outer edges are parallel with the front spoiler or front bumper. In this position each beam diverges from the longitudinal axis by 10°. Adjustment is made by turning the horizontal and/or vertical adjuster screws for each lamp as required. The adjuster screws are accessible through the front of the grille panel.*

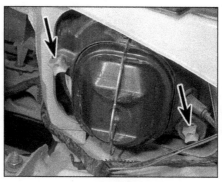

13.2 Headlamp beam adjustment screws (arrowed)

14 Headlamp dim-dip system (UK models) - general information

1 On UK models produced after October 1986, to comply with new lighting legislation, all UK models produced from the above date are fitted with a "dim-dip" system in the headlamp circuit. The function of the system is to ensure that the car cannot be driven on parking lights only.

2 The system is activated by a dim-dip control unit which, when activated, reduces the voltage supply to the headlamps. This system is designed as a safeguard only and normal lighting legislation requirements still apply and must be observed.

3 Access to the "dim-dip" control unit can be gained by removing the flexible padded trim panel located below the facia on the passenger's side. With the panel removed, the control unit will be seen bolted to the side of the body panel.

15 Wiper blades and arms - removal and refitting

Removal

1 Before removing a wiper arm make sure that it is in its parked position having been switched off by the wiper switch and not the ignition key.

2 To help re-alignment of the arms on the

15.4 Wiper arm nut

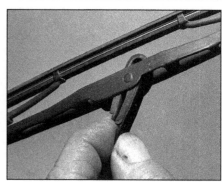

15.3 Removing a windscreen wiper blade

screen, stick a length of masking tape on the glass parallel to the blade before removing the arm.

3 Pull the wiper arm away from the glass, swivel the blade on the arm and then depress the catch on the U-shaped retainer and slide the blade from the wiper arm **(see illustration)**.

4 Flip up the plastic cover and unscrew the arm retaining nut **(see illustration)**.

5 Pull the arm from the driving spindle.

Refitting

6 Refitting is a reversal of removal, do not overtighten the nut.

16 Windscreen wiper motor and linkage - removal and refitting

Removal

1 Remove the wiper arms as described in the preceding Section.

2 Unscrew and remove the nuts from the drive spindles on the scuttle. Note the fitted sequence of seals and spacer.

3 Open the bonnet and remove the water deflector (where fitted).

4 Pull the wiring multi-plug from the wiper motor **(see illustration)**.

5 Disconnect the motor earth cable.

6 Unscrew the motor mounting screws and withdraw the complete motor/linkage assembly from the car.

16.4 Windscreen wiper motor

7 Disconnect the crank arm from the motor. When unscrewing the nut, counter the turning torque with an open-ended spanner applied to the crank otherwise the internal gearwheel teeth may be damaged.
8 Unbolt the motor from its mounting plate.

Refitting

9 Refitting is a reversal of removal, but again restrain the motor crank when tightening the crank arm nut.

17 Tailgate wiper motor - removal and refitting

Removal

1 Remove the rear wiper arm by undoing its securing nut and pulling it off. From beneath the arm remove the rubber boot, the second nut, the dust cap and the seal.
2 Remove the tailgate interior panel (Chapter 11, Section 25).
3 Disconnect the wiring connectors from the wiper motor.
4 Remove the two securing bolts and lift away the wiper motor **(see illustrations)**.

Refitting

5 Refit in the reverse order to removal. Position the wiper arm so that the blade is parallel with the base of the window in the parked position, (Estate models) or vertically (Hatchback models).

18 Windscreen washer system - general information

1 This consists of a fluid reservoir mounted adjacent to the strut turret within the engine compartment, an electrically-operated pump and a steering column washer/wiper switch **(see illustration)**.
2 A faulty pump can be renewed by "rocking" it out of its sealing grommet in the fluid reservoir. Use a new seal when refitting.
3 A rubber connecting sleeve is used to join the plastic pipe to the pump nozzle as attempting to force the stiff plastic pipe onto the nozzle could cause it to fracture.

17.4a Removing a rear wiper motor bolt (Estate). Other bolt is out of picture to right

4 The washer jets should be adjusted so that the stream of fluid strikes the screen just above the wiper blades in their parked position. Use a pin to adjust the jet nozzles.

19 Tailgate washer system - general information

Hatchback

1 The arrangement is similar to that described for the windscreen washer except that the fluid reservoir and pump are located within the "thickness" of the luggage compartment back panel.
2 Should the jet require adjustment, use a pin to do it and check that the water jet strikes the glass (vehicle stationary) near the centre.

Estate

3 The rear screen washer reservoir and pump are located behind the right-hand quarter trim panel **(see illustration)**.
4 To remove the pump or reservoir, remove the trim panel (Chapter 11, Section 25).
5 Disconnect the electrical and fluid unions from the pump. Lift the reservoir and pump off the retaining bracket.
6 The pump is a snap-fit in the base of the reservoir. Empty the reservoir before removal.
7 Access to the washer pipe is gained by removing the appropriate trim panels.
8 The washer jet is secured between the roof and the air deflector assembly by two screws.

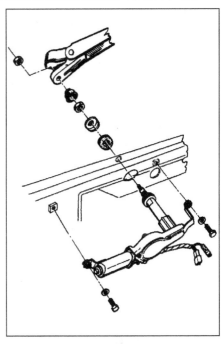
17.4b Rear wiper motor fitting details - Estate

9 Refitting of all washer components is in the reverse order to removal. Check for correct operation before refitting the trim panels.

20 Headlamp wash/wipe system - general information

1 This is available as a factory-fitted option.
2 Where this system is fitted then a combined windscreen and headlamp washer fluid reservoir is used, located under the bonnet.
3 The washer jet can be adjusted using a pin so that the fluid strikes the headlamp glass. If required the jet unit can be removed by carefully prising it free from the bumper **(see illustration)**, then disconnecting the hose.
4 Remove the wiper arm and blade in a similar manner to that described for the windscreen wiper arms and blades. Access to the wiper arm retaining nut and the wiper motor retaining nuts is much improved by first removing the front bumper.

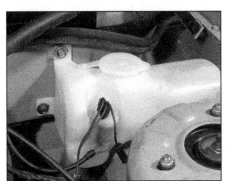
18.1 Washer fluid reservoir

19.3 Rear screen washer reservoir and pump - Estate

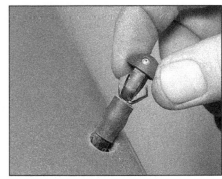
20.3 Headlamp washer jet removal

20.5 Headlamp wiper motor. Note that the motor for each side is handed (left and right) and are marked accordingly (L and R)

5 The wiper motor is located under the forward end of the wheel arch **(see illustration)**. To remove the motor, detach the wiper arm and blade, then undo the two retaining bolts and withdraw the motor unit from the wheel arch side. Disconnect the wiring in the line connection.

6 Refitting of all components is a reversal of the removal procedure. Check for satisfactory operation of the wiper, washer and headlamp unit on completion.

7 Check the headlamp beam for satisfactory alignment, (Section 13). Ensure that the wiper arm is fitted so that it is in contact with the retaining plate in the parked position.

8 Adjust the washer jet using a pin so it strikes the centre of the headlamp lens.

21 Central locking system - general information and component removal and refitting

1 The central locking system ensures, by means of switches, servo motors and associated wiring, that all passenger door locks follow the position of the driver's door lock **(see illustration)**. Locking or unlocking the driver's door, from the inside or outside, produces the same state in the other door locks.

2 A safety switch below the facia panel unlocks all the doors in the event of an accident involving impact.

3 If for any reason the central locking system is disabled, the doors can still be locked and unlocked by hand.

Driver's door switch - removal and refitting

4 Remove the door trim panel (Chapter 11). Free the waterproof sheet around the switch.

5 Unplug the electrical connectors from the switch - they are different sizes so they cannot be connected wrongly.

6 Remove the centre pin and the screw which secures the switch to the door **(see illustration)**. Remove the switch components from the door, unhooking the transfer lever from the linkage.

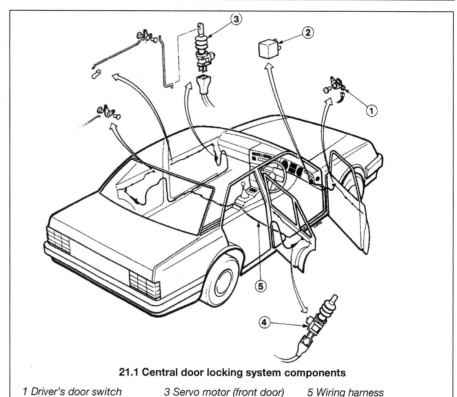

21.1 Central door locking system components

1 Driver's door switch
2 Safety switch
3 Servo motor (front door)
4 Servo motor (rear door)
5 Wiring harness

7 Refit in the reverse order to removal. Before tightening the contact plate screw, position the plate in the middle of the travel allowed by the slot **(see illustration)**. Check for correct operation before refitting the door trim.

Servo motor - removal and refitting

8 Remove the door trim panel (Chapter 11). Free the plastic sheet for access to the motor.

9 Remove the two bolts which secure the motor to the door. Disconnect the mechanical linkage and the electrical connector and remove the motor **(see illustrations)**.

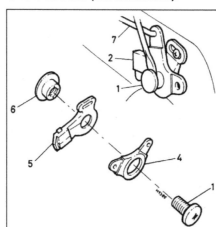

21.6 Removing the driver's door switch

1 Central pin
2 Electrical connectors
4 Transfer lever
5 Contact plate
6 Bush
7 Linkage

10 Refit in the reverse order to removal. Use new micro-encapsulated (self-locking) bolts. M6 x 8mm, available from a dealer. Check for correct function before refitting the door trim.

Tailgate lock mode - Hatchback from 1985

11 The tailgate lock barrel may be turned to one of three positions, which affects the operation of the central locking system on the tailgate lock, as shown **(see illustration)**.

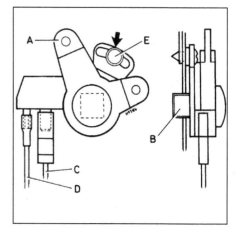

21.7 Fitting the driver's door switch: adjust slot to mid-position (arrowed)

A Transfer lever
B Bush
C Brown/white lead
D Grey lead
E Contact plate screw

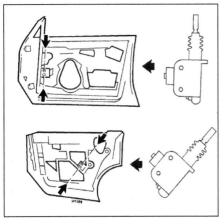

21.9a Location of door locking servo motors in front door (top) and rear door (bottom)

Fit motors in orientation indicated by arrows

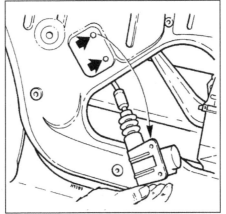

21.9b Removing a door locking servo motor - mounting bolts arrowed

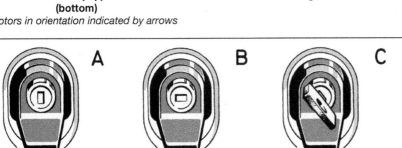

21.11 Tailgate lock mode - central locking

A Locked - tailgate cannot be opened irrespective of central door locking selection
B Unlocked - tailgate can only be opened if central locking is unlocked
C Over-ride position - tailgate can be opened even if central locking is to "locked". Button and key twist must be depressed to release tailgate lock. To remove key, turn back to either of positions A or B after tailgate has been opened

Safety switch and relay - removal and refitting

12 Disconnect the battery.
13 Release the trim fasteners securing the side trim panel in the footwell on the driver's side, using a wide-bladed screwdriver.
14 Remove the panel, disconnect the wiring connectors, and remove the safety switch or relay as applicable.
15 Refitting is a reversal of removal.

22 Trip computer - general information and component renewal

1 A trip computer is fitted to some later models. Fuel consumption and distance data are collected and evaluated with respect to time, thus enabling the computer to provide information on fuel consumption (both instantaneous and average), average speed and range on fuel remaining. Normal time clock and stopwatch functions are available, and an external temperature sensor is also provided.
2 Refer to the owner's handbook provided with the vehicle for operating instructions.
3 Although testing of the computer and its components is beyond the scope of the

average DIY mechanic, there is no reason why defective components should not be renewed, as described in the following paragraphs.

Component renewal

Computer relay

4 The trip computer relay is mounted on the lower face of the fusebox (see Section 3).
5 Remove the lower panelling to gain access and unplug the relay from its socket.
6 Plug in the new relay and refit the panelling.

Temperature sensor

7 The temperature sensor is located under the left-hand front wing. Disconnect the wiring plug and push the sensor out of its grommet.
8 Fit the new sensor into the grommet and connect the wiring plug.

Distance sender

9 The distance sender is screwed into the speedo drive take-off on the transmission; the cable screws into the back of the sender.
10 Unscrew the speedometer cable from the sender. Disconnect the wiring plug from the sender and unscrew the sender from the transmission.
11 Fit the new sender, making sure that it is of the same type as that removed. (Senders

carrying the reference 12 V 15 IMP work into the frequency divider mounted on the bulkhead, senders labelled 12 V8 IMP work directly into the computer). Connect the wiring plug and the speedo cable.

Computer

12 To remove the computer itself, first remove the facia switch panel.
13 Pull the computer out of the panel and disconnect the multi-plug.
14 Refit in the reverse order to removal, but note that a new computer will need to be calibrated on the vehicle by a GM dealer.

Computer display lighting

15 Remove the computer, as first described.
16 Extract the bulbholder from the top of the computer by twisting it with pliers. Renew the capless bulb.
17 Refit the bulbholder. Check that the new bulb works (computer plugged in, instrument lighting on) before refitting the switch panel.

23 Radio/cassette player - removal and refitting

Removal

Early models

1 Disconnect the battery.
2 Remove the ashtray and the central switch plate (6 screws) from the facia panel.
3 Reach around the radio and unscrew the mounting screws from the brackets.
4 Withdraw the radio sufficiently far to be able to disconnect the power, aerial, earth and loudspeaker leads from it.

Later models

5 On later models, the radio/cassette players fitted by Vauxhall/Opel have DIN standard fixings. Two special tools, obtainable from most car accessory shops, are required for removal. Alternatively tools can be fabricated from 3 mm diameter wire or welding rod.
6 Disconnect the battery negative lead.
7 Unscrew the four grub screws from the corners of the radio/cassette player, using a suitable Allen key **(see illustration)**.

23.7 On later models, unscrew the blanking screws . . .

8 Insert the tools into the holes exposed by removal of the grub screws, and push them until they snap into place. The radio/cassette player can then be slid out of the facia **(see illustration)**.

9 Disconnect the wiring connectors from the rear of the unit and remove the radio/cassette from the car **(see illustration)**. A diagram attached to the unit provides information on the wiring connections. In addition to this, each of the speaker plugs and sockets should be colour-coded to avoid confusion.

Refitting

10 Refitting is the reverse of removal.

24 Loudspeakers - removal and refitting

Removal

1 Speakers are positioned at each end of the facia panel, and, according to model, at each end of the parcel shelf or in the tailgate.

2 Access to the facia-mounted speakers can be gained after removal of the relevant side heater vent (Chapter 2). Although clearance is limited, it is just possible to disconnect the wiring, release the speaker retaining nuts, and withdraw the speaker through the vent aperture **(see illustration)**. If difficulty is experienced, greater working clearance can be gained if the glovebox or instrument panel (as applicable) are removed.

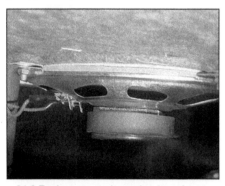

24.2 Facia-mounted speaker location as viewed through the heater vent aperture

23.8 . . . then insert the removal tools . . .

3 Where tailgate speakers are fitted, these can be removed after removal of the tailgate trim panel (see Chapter 11). The speaker can then be unscrewed, the wiring disconnected, and the speaker removed **(see illustrations)**.

Refitting

4 Refitting is the reverse of removal.

25 Radio aerial - removal and refitting

Removal

1 Remove the wheel arch liner on the right-hand side. It is secured by one screw and some clips.

2 Undo the slotted nut on the top of the aerial. If a proper spanner is not available, use a screwdriver in one of the slots, being careful to protect the car's paintwork. Remove the slotted nut and the top half mounting components **(see illustration)**.

3 Unbolt the aerial lower steady bracket (if fitted) and withdraw the aerial into the wing. Recover any loose mounting components.

4 Remove the radio/cassette as described in Section 23.

5 Release the aerial lead from its securing clips, removing trim as necessary for access. Feed the lead into the wing panel and recover the grommet.

23.9 . . . and slide out the radio/cassette unit and disconnect its wiring connectors

Refitting

6 Refit in the reverse order to removal. Use a new grommet where necessary and ensure that there is good metal-to-metal contact between the aerial and the underside of the wing.

26 Power operated windows - general information

1 This facility is a standard feature on some models.

2 Operation of the windows is controlled from switches mounted in the centre console.

3 In the event of a fault occurring, first check the circuit fuse and then the wiring connections for security.

4 Access to the door-mounted electric motors is obtained after removing the door trim panel as described in Chapter 11.

5 Disconnect the battery and then disconnect the wiring plugs from the motor.

6 Withdraw the motor mounting screws, or drill out the rivets, and release the window operating arm from the glass channel as described for manually-operated windows in Chapter 11. Withdraw the motor/arm assembly.

7 It is not recommended that the motor should be overhauled, but obtain a new sealed unit.

24.3a Remove the tailgate trim panel . . .

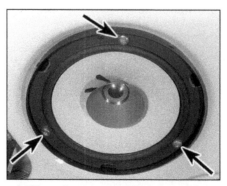

24.3b . . . for access to the rear speaker screws (arrowed) on Estate models

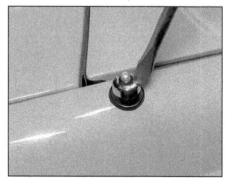

25.2 Undoing the aerial slotted nut with a screwdriver

Dimensions and Weights . . . . **REF•1**   Tools and Working Facilities . . . . **REF•5**
Conversion Factors . . . . **REF•2**   MOT Test Checks . . . .**REF•7**
Buying Spare Parts . . . .**REF•3**   Fault Diagnosis . . . . **REF•11**
Vehicle Identification Numbers . . . . **REF•3**   Glossary of Technical Terms . . . . **REF•18**
General Repair Procedures . . . . **REF•4**   Index . . . . **REF•23**

Dimensions and Weights

Note: *All figures are approximate, and may vary according to model. Refer to manufacturer's data for exact figures.*

Dimensions

Overall length:	
Saloon and Estate	4366 mm
Hatchback	4264 mm
Overall width	1668 mm
Overall height:	
Saloon	1395 mm
Hatchback	1385 mm
Estate	1368 mm
Wheelbase	2573 mm
Track - front:	
1.3 litre models	1400 mm
All other models	1406 mm
Track - rear	1406 mm

Weights

Kerb weight*:	
1.3 litre models	940 to 1020 kg
1.6 litre models	1011 to 1066 kg
1.8 litre models	1031 to 1100 kg
2.0 litre models	1103 to 1185 kg
Maximum roof rack load:	
Saloon and Hatchback	80 kg
Estate	50 kg
Maximum towing weight*:	
Braked trailer	650 to 1300 kg
Unbraked trailer	475 to 500 kg
Maximum trailer nose weight	50 kg

*The kerb weights and maximum permissible towing weights given are for general reference. The weights can differ according to model and year, therefore, if specific weight requirements are wanted for a particular model, consult your vehicle handbook or a Vauxhall dealer

Conversion factors

Length (distance)
Inches (in)	x 25.4	= Millimetres (mm)	x 0.0394	= Inches (in)
Feet (ft)	x 0.305	= Metres (m)	x 3.281	= Feet (ft)
Miles	x 1.609	= Kilometres (km)	x 0.621	= Miles

Volume (capacity)
Cubic inches (cu in; in³)	x 16.387	= Cubic centimetres (cc; cm³)	x 0.061	= Cubic inches (cu in; in³)
Imperial pints (Imp pt)	x 0.568	= Litres (l)	x 1.76	= Imperial pints (Imp pt)
Imperial quarts (Imp qt)	x 1.137	= Litres (l)	x 0.88	= Imperial quarts (Imp qt)
Imperial quarts (Imp qt)	x 1.201	= US quarts (US qt)	x 0.833	= Imperial quarts (Imp qt)
US quarts (US qt)	x 0.946	= Litres (l)	x 1.057	= US quarts (US qt)
Imperial gallons (Imp gal)	x 4.546	= Litres (l)	x 0.22	= Imperial gallons (Imp gal)
Imperial gallons (Imp gal)	x 1.201	= US gallons (US gal)	x 0.833	= Imperial gallons (Imp gal)
US gallons (US gal)	x 3.785	= Litres (l)	x 0.264	= US gallons (US gal)

Mass (weight)
Ounces (oz)	x 28.35	= Grams (g)	x 0.035	= Ounces (oz)
Pounds (lb)	x 0.454	= Kilograms (kg)	x 2.205	= Pounds (lb)

Force
Ounces-force (ozf; oz)	x 0.278	= Newtons (N)	x 3.6	= Ounces-force (ozf; oz)
Pounds-force (lbf; lb)	x 4.448	= Newtons (N)	x 0.225	= Pounds-force (lbf; lb)
Newtons (N)	x 0.1	= Kilograms-force (kgf; kg)	x 9.81	= Newtons (N)

Pressure
Pounds-force per square inch (psi; lbf/in²; lb/in²)	x 0.070	= Kilograms-force per square centimetre (kgf/cm²; kg/cm²)	x 14.223	= Pounds-force per square inch (psi; lbf/in²; lb/in²)
Pounds-force per square inch (psi; lbf/in²; lb/in²)	x 0.068	= Atmospheres (atm)	x 14.696	= Pounds-force per square inch (psi; lbf/in²; lb/in²)
Pounds-force per square inch (psi; lbf/in²; lb/in²)	x 0.069	= Bars	x 14.5	= Pounds-force per square inch (psi; lbf/in²; lb/in²)
Pounds-force per square inch (psi; lbf/in²; lb/in²)	x 6.895	= Kilopascals (kPa)	x 0.145	= Pounds-force per square inch (psi; lbf/in²; lb/in²)
Kilopascals (kPa)	x 0.01	= Kilograms-force per square centimetre (kgf/cm²; kg/cm²)	x 98.1	= Kilopascals (kPa)
Millibar (mbar)	x 100	= Pascals (Pa)	x 0.01	= Millibar (mbar)
Millibar (mbar)	x 0.0145	= Pounds-force per square inch (psi; lbf/in²; lb/in²)	x 68.947	= Millibar (mbar)
Millibar (mbar)	x 0.75	= Millimetres of mercury (mmHg)	x 1.333	= Millibar (mbar)
Millibar (mbar)	x 0.401	= Inches of water (inH₂O)	x 2.491	= Millibar (mbar)
Millimetres of mercury (mmHg)	x 0.535	= Inches of water (inH₂O)	x 1.868	= Millimetres of mercury (mmHg)
Inches of water (inH₂O)	x 0.036	= Pounds-force per square inch (psi; lbf/in²; lb/in²)	x 27.68	= Inches of water (inH₂O)

Torque (moment of force)
Pounds-force inches (lbf in; lb in)	x 1.152	= Kilograms-force centimetre (kgf cm; kg cm)	x 0.868	= Pounds-force inches (lbf in; lb in)
Pounds-force inches (lbf in; lb in)	x 0.113	= Newton metres (Nm)	x 8.85	= Pounds-force inches (lbf in; lb in)
Pounds-force inches (lbf in; lb in)	x 0.083	= Pounds-force feet (lbf ft; lb ft)	x 12	= Pounds-force inches (lbf in; lb in)
Pounds-force feet (lbf ft; lb ft)	x 0.138	= Kilograms-force metres (kgf m; kg m)	x 7.233	= Pounds-force feet (lbf ft; lb ft)
Pounds-force feet (lbf ft; lb ft)	x 1.356	= Newton metres (Nm)	x 0.738	= Pounds-force feet (lbf ft; lb ft)
Newton metres (Nm)	x 0.102	= Kilograms-force metres (kgf m; kg m)	x 9.804	= Newton metres (Nm)

Power
Horsepower (hp)	x 745.7	= Watts (W)	x 0.0013	= Horsepower (hp)

Velocity (speed)
Miles per hour (miles/hr; mph)	x 1.609	= Kilometres per hour (km/hr; kph)	x 0.621	= Miles per hour (miles/hr; mph)

Fuel consumption*
Miles per gallon (mpg)	x 0.354	= Kilometres per litre (km/l)	x 2.825	= Miles per gallon (mpg)

Temperature
Degrees Fahrenheit = (°C x 1.8) + 32   Degrees Celsius (Degrees Centigrade; °C) = (°F - 32) x 0.56

It is common practice to convert from miles per gallon (mpg) to litres/100 kilometres (l/100km), where mpg x l/100 km = 282

Spare parts are available from many sources; for example, Vauxhall garages, other garages and accessory shops, and motor factors. Our advice regarding spare part sources is as follows.

Officially-appointed garages

This is the best source for parts which are peculiar to your car, and are not generally available (eg complete cylinder heads, internal gearbox components, badges, interior trim etc). It is also the only place at which you should buy parts if the vehicle is still under warranty. To be sure of obtaining the correct parts, it will be necessary to give the storeman your car's vehicle identification number, and if possible, take the old parts along for positive identification. Many parts are available under a factory exchange scheme - any parts returned should always be clean. It obviously makes good sense to go straight to the specialists on your car for this type of part, as they are best equipped to supply you.

Other garages and accessory shops

These are often very good places to buy materials and components needed for the maintenance of your car (eg oil filters, spark plugs, bulbs, drivebelts, oils and greases, touch-up paint, filler paste, etc). They also sell general accessories, usually have convenient opening hours, charge lower prices, and can often be found not far from home.

Motor factors

Good factors will stock all the more important components which wear out comparatively quickly, and can sometimes supply individual components needed for the overhaul of a larger assembly (eg brake seals and hydraulic parts, bearing shells, pistons, valves, alternator brushes). They may also handle work such as cylinder block reboring, crankshaft regrinding and balancing, etc.

Tyre and exhaust specialists

These outlets may be independent, or members of a local or national chain. They frequently offer competitive prices when compared with a main dealer or local garage, but it will pay to obtain several quotes before making a decision. When researching prices, also ask what "extras" may be added - for instance, fitting a new valve and balancing the wheel are both commonly charged on top of the price of a new tyre.

Other sources

Beware of parts or materials obtained from market stalls, car boot sales or similar outlets. Such items are not invariably sub-standard, but there is little chance of compensation if they do prove unsatisfactory. In the case of safety-critical components such as brake pads, there is the risk not only of financial loss but also of an accident causing injury or death.

Second-hand components or assemblies obtained from a car breaker can be a good buy in some circumstances, but this sort of purchase is best made by the experienced DIY mechanic.

Vehicle identification numbers

Modifications are a continuing and unpublicised process in vehicle manufacture, quite apart from major model changes. Spare parts manuals and lists are compiled upon a numerical basis, the individual vehicle identification numbers being essential to correct identification of the component concerned.

When ordering spare parts, always give as much information as possible. Quote the car model, year of manufacture, body and engine numbers as appropriate.

The Vehicle Identification Number (VIN) plate is riveted to the top of the body front crossmember, and can be viewed once the bonnet is open. The plate carries the VIN and vehicle weight information, and paint and trim colour codes (see illustration).

The engine number is stamped onto a machined flat on the front face of the cylinder block (see illustration).

The chassis number is stamped into the body floor panel, between the driver's seat and the door sill (see illustration).

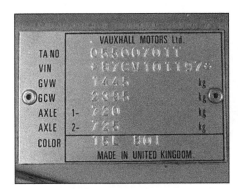
Vehicle identification plate

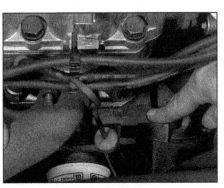
Engine number

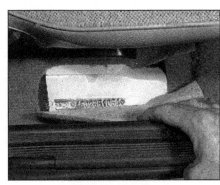
Chassis number

Whenever servicing, repair or overhaul work is carried out on the car or its components, it is necessary to observe the following procedures and instructions. This will assist in carrying out the operation efficiently and to a professional standard of workmanship.

Joint mating faces and gaskets

When separating components at their mating faces, never insert screwdrivers or similar implements into the joint between the faces in order to prise them apart. This can cause severe damage which results in oil leaks, coolant leaks, etc upon reassembly. Separation is usually achieved by tapping along the joint with a soft-faced hammer in order to break the seal. However, note that this method may not be suitable where dowels are used for component location.

Where a gasket is used between the mating faces of two components, ensure that it is renewed on reassembly, and fit it dry unless otherwise stated in the repair procedure. Make sure that the mating faces are clean and dry, with all traces of old gasket removed. When cleaning a joint face, use a tool which is not likely to score or damage the face, and remove any burrs or nicks with an oilstone or fine file.

Make sure that tapped holes are cleaned with a pipe cleaner, and keep them free of jointing compound, if this is being used, unless specifically instructed otherwise.

Ensure that all orifices, channels or pipes are clear, and blow through them, preferably using compressed air.

Oil seals

Oil seals can be removed by levering them out with a wide flat-bladed screwdriver or similar implement. Alternatively, a number of self-tapping screws may be screwed into the seal, and these used as a purchase for pliers or some similar device in order to pull the seal free.

Whenever an oil seal is removed from its working location, either individually or as part of an assembly, it should be renewed.

The very fine sealing lip of the seal is easily damaged, and will not seal if the surface it contacts is not completely clean and free from scratches, nicks or grooves. If the original sealing surface of the component cannot be restored, and the manufacturer has not made provision for slight relocation of the seal relative to the sealing surface, the component should be renewed.

Protect the lips of the seal from any surface which may damage them in the course of fitting. Use tape or a conical sleeve where possible. Lubricate the seal lips with oil before fitting and, on dual-lipped seals, fill the space between the lips with grease.

Unless otherwise stated, oil seals must be fitted with their sealing lips toward the lubricant to be sealed.

Use a tubular drift or block of wood of the appropriate size to install the seal and, if the seal housing is shouldered, drive the seal down to the shoulder. If the seal housing is unshouldered, the seal should be fitted with its face flush with the housing top face (unless otherwise instructed).

Screw threads and fastenings

Seized nuts, bolts and screws are quite a common occurrence where corrosion has set in, and the use of penetrating oil or releasing fluid will often overcome this problem if the offending item is soaked for a while before attempting to release it. The use of an impact driver may also provide a means of releasing such stubborn fastening devices, when used in conjunction with the appropriate screwdriver bit or socket. If none of these methods works, it may be necessary to resort to the careful application of heat, or the use of a hacksaw or nut splitter device.

Studs are usually removed by locking two nuts together on the threaded part, and then using a spanner on the lower nut to unscrew the stud. Studs or bolts which have broken off below the surface of the component in which they are mounted can sometimes be removed using a proprietary stud extractor. Always ensure that a blind tapped hole is completely free from oil, grease, water or other fluid before installing the bolt or stud. Failure to do this could cause the housing to crack due to the hydraulic action of the bolt or stud as it is screwed in.

When tightening a castellated nut to accept a split pin, tighten the nut to the specified torque, where applicable, and then tighten further to the next split pin hole. Never slacken the nut to align the split pin hole, unless stated in the repair procedure.

When checking or retightening a nut or bolt to a specified torque setting, slacken the nut or bolt by a quarter of a turn, and then retighten to the specified setting. However, this should not be attempted where angular tightening has been used.

For some screw fastenings, notably cylinder head bolts or nuts, torque wrench settings are no longer specified for the latter stages of tightening, "angle-tightening" being called up instead. Typically, a fairly low torque wrench setting will be applied to the bolts/nuts in the correct sequence, followed by one or more stages of tightening through specified angles.

Locknuts, locktabs and washers

Any fastening which will rotate against a component or housing in the course of tightening should always have a washer between it and the relevant component or housing.

Spring or split washers should always be renewed when they are used to lock a critical component such as a big-end bearing retaining bolt or nut. Locktabs which are folded over to retain a nut or bolt should always be renewed.

Self-locking nuts can be re-used in non-critical areas, providing resistance can be felt when the locking portion passes over the bolt or stud thread. However, it should be noted that self-locking stiffnuts tend to lose their effectiveness after long periods of use, and in such cases should be renewed as a matter of course.

Split pins must always be replaced with new ones of the correct size for the hole.

When thread-locking compound is found on the threads of a fastener which is to be re-used, it should be cleaned off with a wire brush and solvent, and fresh compound applied on reassembly.

Special tools

Some repair procedures in this manual entail the use of special tools such as a press, two or three-legged pullers, spring compressors, etc. Wherever possible, suitable readily-available alternatives to the manufacturer's special tools are described, and are shown in use. In some instances, where no alternative is possible, it has been necessary to resort to the use of a manufacturer's tool, and this has been done for reasons of safety as well as the efficient completion of the repair operation. Unless you are highly-skilled and have a thorough understanding of the procedures described, never attempt to bypass the use of any special tool when the procedure described specifies its use. Not only is there a very great risk of personal injury, but expensive damage could be caused to the components involved.

Environmental considerations

When disposing of used engine oil, brake fluid, antifreeze, etc, give due consideration to any detrimental environmental effects. Do not, for instance, pour any of the above liquids down drains into the general sewage system, or onto the ground to soak away. Many local council refuse tips provide a facility for waste oil disposal, as do some garages. If none of these facilities are available, consult your local Environmental Health Department for further advice.

With the universal tightening-up of legislation regarding the emission of environmentally-harmful substances from motor vehicles, most current vehicles have tamperproof devices fitted to the main adjustment points of the fuel system. These devices are primarily designed to prevent unqualified persons from adjusting the fuel/air mixture, with the chance of a consequent increase in toxic emissions. If such devices are encountered during servicing or overhaul, they should, wherever possible, be renewed or refitted in accordance with the vehicle manufacturer's requirements or current legislation.

OIL CARE

FOLLOW THE CODE

OIL BANK LINE
0800 66 33 66

Note: It is antisocial and illegal to dump oil down the drain. To find the location of your local oil recycling bank, call this number free.

Introduction

A selection of good tools is a fundamental requirement for anyone contemplating the maintenance and repair of a motor vehicle. For the owner who does not possess any, their purchase will prove a considerable expense, offsetting some of the savings made by doing-it-yourself. However, provided that the tools purchased meet the relevant national safety standards and are of good quality, they will last for many years and prove an extremely worthwhile investment.

To help the average owner to decide which tools are needed to carry out the various tasks detailed in this manual, we have compiled three lists of tools under the following headings: *Maintenance and minor repair*, *Repair and overhaul*, and *Special*. Newcomers to practical mechanics should start off with the *Maintenance and minor repair* tool kit, and confine themselves to the simpler jobs around the vehicle. Then, as confidence and experience grow, more difficult tasks can be undertaken, with extra tools being purchased as, and when, they are needed. In this way, a *Maintenance and minor repair* tool kit can be built up into a *Repair and overhaul* tool kit over a considerable period of time, without any major cash outlays. The experienced do-it-yourselfer will have a tool kit good enough for most repair and overhaul procedures, and will add tools from the *Special* category when it is felt that the expense is justified by the amount of use to which these tools will be put.

Maintenance and minor repair tool kit

The tools given in this list should be considered as a minimum requirement if routine maintenance, servicing and minor repair operations are to be undertaken. We recommend the purchase of combination spanners (ring one end, open-ended the other); although more expensive than open-ended ones, they do give the advantages of both types of spanner.

☐ *Combination spanners:*
  Metric - 8, 9, 10, 11, 12, 13, 14, 15, 17 & 19 mm
☐ *Adjustable spanner - 35 mm jaw (approx.)*
☐ *Spark plug spanner (with rubber insert)*
☐ *Spark plug gap adjustment tool*
☐ *Set of feeler blades*
☐ *Brake bleed nipple spanner*
☐ *Screwdrivers:*
  Flat blade - 100 mm long x 6 mm dia
  Cross blade - 100 mm long x 6 mm dia
☐ *Combination pliers*
☐ *Hacksaw (junior)*
☐ *Tyre pump*
☐ *Tyre pressure gauge*
☐ *Oil can*
☐ *Oil filter removal tool*
☐ *Fine emery cloth*
☐ *Wire brush (small)*
☐ *Funnel (medium size)*

Repair and overhaul tool kit

These tools are virtually essential for anyone undertaking any major repairs to a motor vehicle, and are additional to those given in the *Maintenance and minor repair* list. Included in this list is a comprehensive set of sockets. Although these are expensive, they will be found invaluable as they are so versatile - particularly if various drives are included in the set. We recommend the half-inch square-drive type, as this can be used with most proprietary torque wrenches. If you cannot afford a socket set, even bought piecemeal, then inexpensive tubular box spanners are a useful alternative.

The tools in this list will occasionally need to be supplemented by tools from the *Special* list.

☐ *Sockets (or box spanners) to cover range in previous list (including Torx sockets)*
☐ *Reversible ratchet drive (for use with sockets)*
☐ *Extension piece, 250 mm (for use with sockets)*
☐ *Universal joint (for use with sockets)*
☐ *Torque wrench (for use with sockets)*
☐ *Self-locking grips*
☐ *Ball pein hammer*
☐ *Soft-faced mallet (plastic/aluminium or rubber)*
☐ *Screwdrivers:*
  Flat blade - long & sturdy, short (chubby), and narrow (electricians) types
  Cross blade - Long & sturdy, and short (chubby) types
☐ *Pliers:*
  Long-nosed
  Side cutters (electricians)
  Circlip (internal and external)
☐ *Cold chisel - 25 mm*
☐ *Scriber*
☐ *Scraper*
☐ *Centre punch*
☐ *Pin punch*
☐ *Hacksaw*
☐ *Brake hose clamp*
☐ *Brake/clutch bleeding kit*
☐ *Selection of twist drills*
☐ *Steel rule/straight-edge*
☐ *Allen keys (inc. splined/Torx type)*
☐ *Selection of files*
☐ *Wire brush*
☐ *Axle-stands*
☐ *Jack (strong trolley or hydraulic type)*
☐ *Light with extension lead*

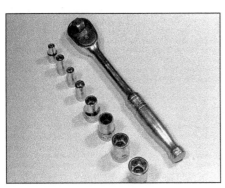

Sockets and reversible ratchet drive

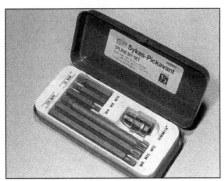

Spline bit set

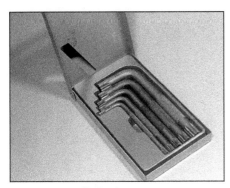

Spline key set

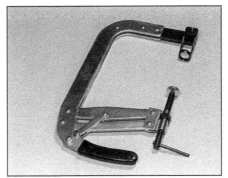

Valve spring compressor

Two- and three legged bearing puller

Special tools

The tools in this list are those which are not used regularly, are expensive to buy, or which need to be used in accordance with their manufacturers' instructions. Unless relatively difficult mechanical jobs are undertaken frequently, it will not be economic to buy many of these tools. Where this is the case, you could consider clubbing together with friends (or joining a motorists' club) to make a joint purchase, or borrowing the tools against a deposit from a local garage or tool hire specialist. It is worth noting that many of the larger DIY superstores now carry a large range of special tools for hire at modest rates.

The following list contains only those tools and instruments freely available to the public, and not those special tools produced by the vehicle manufacturer specifically for its dealer network. You will find occasional references to these manufacturers' special tools in the text of this manual. Generally, an alternative method of doing the job without the vehicle manufacturers' special tool is given. However, sometimes there is no alternative to using them. Where this is the case and the relevant tool cannot be bought or borrowed, you will have to entrust the work to a franchised garage.

☐ Valve spring compressor
☐ Valve grinding tool
☐ Piston ring compressor
☐ Piston ring removal/installation tool
☐ Cylinder bore hone
☐ Balljoint separator
☐ Coil spring compressors (where applicable)
☐ Two/three-legged hub and bearing puller
☐ Impact screwdriver
☐ Micrometer and/or vernier calipers
☐ Dial gauge
☐ Stroboscopic timing light
☐ Dwell angle meter/tachometer
☐ Universal electrical multi-meter
☐ Cylinder compression gauge
☐ Hand-operated vacuum pump and gauge
☐ Clutch plate alignment set
☐ Brake shoe steady spring cup removal tool
☐ Bush and bearing removal/installation set
☐ Stud extractors
☐ Tap and die set
☐ Lifting tackle
☐ Trolley jack

Buying tools

For practically all tools, a tool factor is the best source, since he will have a very comprehensive range compared with the average garage or accessory shop. Having said that, accessory shops often offer excellent quality tools at discount prices, so it pays to shop around.

Remember, you don't have to buy the most expensive items on the shelf, but it is always advisable to steer clear of the very cheap tools. There are plenty of good tools around at reasonable prices, but always aim to purchase items which meet the relevant national safety standards. If in doubt, ask the proprietor or manager of the shop for advice before making a purchase.

Care and maintenance of tools

Having purchased a reasonable tool kit, it is necessary to keep the tools in a clean and serviceable condition. After use, always wipe off any dirt, grease and metal particles using a clean, dry cloth, before putting the tools away. Never leave them lying around after they have been used. A simple tool rack on the garage or workshop wall for items such as screwdrivers and pliers is a good idea. Store all normal spanners and sockets in a metal box. Any measuring instruments, gauges, meters, etc, must be carefully stored where they cannot be damaged or become rusty.

Take a little care when tools are used. Hammer heads inevitably become marked, and screwdrivers lose the keen edge on their blades from time to time. A little timely attention with

emery cloth or a file will soon restore items like this to a good serviceable finish.

Working facilities

Not to be forgotten when discussing tools is the workshop itself. If anything more than routine maintenance is to be carried out, some form of suitable working area becomes essential.

It is appreciated that many an owner-mechanic is forced by circumstances to remove an engine or similar item without the benefit of a garage or workshop. Having done this, any repairs should always be done under the cover of a roof.

Wherever possible, any dismantling should be done on a clean, flat workbench or table at a suitable working height.

Any workbench needs a vice; one with a jaw opening of 100 mm is suitable for most jobs. As mentioned previously, some clean dry storage space is also required for tools, as well as for any lubricants, cleaning fluids, touch-up paints and so on, which become necessary.

Another item which may be required, and which has a much more general usage, is an electric drill with a chuck capacity of at least 8 mm. This, together with a good range of twist drills, is virtually essential for fitting accessories.

Last, but not least, always keep a supply of old newspapers and clean, lint-free rags available, and try to keep any working area as clean as possible.

Micrometer set

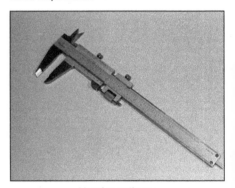

Vernier calipers

Stroboscopic timing light

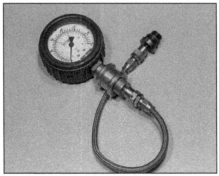

Cylinder compression gauge

Clutch plate alignment set

This is a guide to getting your vehicle through the MOT test. Obviously it will not be possible to examine the vehicle to the same standard as the professional MOT tester. However, working through the following checks will enable you to identify any problem areas before submitting the vehicle for the test.

Where a testable component is in borderline condition, the tester has discretion in deciding whether to pass or fail it. The basis of such discretion is whether the tester would be happy for a close relative or friend to use the vehicle with the component in that condition. If the vehicle presented is clean and evidently well cared for, the tester may be more inclined to pass a borderline component than if the vehicle is scruffy and apparently neglected.

It has only been possible to summarise the test requirements here, based on the regulations in force at the time of printing. Test standards are becoming increasingly stringent, although there are some exemptions for older vehicles. For full details obtain a copy of the Haynes publication Pass the MOT! (available from stockists of Haynes manuals).

An assistant will be needed to help carry out some of these checks.

The checks have been sub-divided into four categories, as follows:

1 Checks carried out **FROM THE DRIVER'S SEAT**

2 Checks carried out **WITH THE VEHICLE ON THE GROUND**

3 Checks carried out **WITH THE VEHICLE RAISED AND THE WHEELS FREE TO TURN**

4 Checks carried out on **YOUR VEHICLE'S EXHAUST EMISSION SYSTEM**

---

1 Checks carried out **FROM THE DRIVER'S SEAT**

Handbrake

☐ Test the operation of the handbrake. Excessive travel (too many clicks) indicates incorrect brake or cable adjustment.

☐ Check that the handbrake cannot be released by tapping the lever sideways. Check the security of the lever mountings.

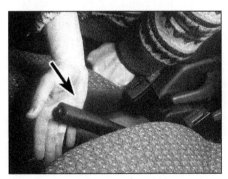

Footbrake

☐ Depress the brake pedal and check that it does not creep down to the floor, indicating a master cylinder fault. Release the pedal, wait a few seconds, then depress it again. If the pedal travels nearly to the floor before firm resistance is felt, brake adjustment or repair is necessary. If the pedal feels spongy, there is air in the hydraulic system which must be removed by bleeding.

☐ Check that the brake pedal is secure and in good condition. Check also for signs of fluid leaks on the pedal, floor or carpets, which would indicate failed seals in the brake master cylinder.

☐ Check the servo unit (when applicable) by operating the brake pedal several times, then keeping the pedal depressed and starting the engine. As the engine starts, the pedal will move down slightly. If not, the vacuum hose or the servo itself may be faulty.

Steering wheel and column

☐ Examine the steering wheel for fractures or looseness of the hub, spokes or rim.

☐ Move the steering wheel from side to side and then up and down. Check that the steering wheel is not loose on the column, indicating wear or a loose retaining nut. Continue moving the steering wheel as before, but also turn it slightly from left to right.

☐ Check that the steering wheel is not loose on the column, and that there is no abnormal

movement of the steering wheel, indicating wear in the column support bearings or couplings.

Windscreen and mirrors

☐ The windscreen must be free of cracks or other significant damage within the driver's field of view. (Small stone chips are acceptable.) Rear view mirrors must be secure, intact, and capable of being adjusted.

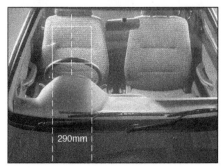

290mm

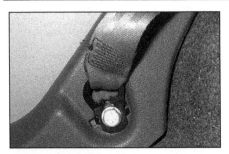

Seat belts and seats

Note: *The following checks are applicable to all seat belts, front and rear.*

☐ Examine the webbing of all the belts (including rear belts if fitted) for cuts, serious fraying or deterioration. Fasten and unfasten each belt to check the buckles. If applicable, check the retracting mechanism. Check the security of all seat belt mountings accessible from inside the vehicle.
☐ The front seats themselves must be securely attached and the backrests must lock in the upright position.

Doors

☐ Both front doors must be able to be opened and closed from outside and inside, and must latch securely when closed.

2 Checks carried out WITH THE VEHICLE ON THE GROUND

Vehicle identification

☐ Number plates must be in good condition, secure and legible, with letters and numbers correctly spaced – spacing at (A) should be twice that at (B).

☐ The VIN plate (A) and homologation plate (B) must be legible.

Electrical equipment

☐ Switch on the ignition and check the operation of the horn.
☐ Check the windscreen washers and wipers, examining the wiper blades; renew damaged or perished blades. Also check the operation of the stop-lights.

☐ Check the operation of the sidelights and number plate lights. The lenses and reflectors must be secure, clean and undamaged.
☐ Check the operation and alignment of the headlights. The headlight reflectors must not be tarnished and the lenses must be undamaged.
☐ Switch on the ignition and check the operation of the direction indicators (including the instrument panel tell-tale) and the hazard warning lights. Operation of the sidelights and stop-lights must not affect the indicators - if it does, the cause is usually a bad earth at the rear light cluster.
☐ Check the operation of the rear foglight(s), including the warning light on the instrument panel or in the switch.

Footbrake

☐ Examine the master cylinder, brake pipes and servo unit for leaks, loose mountings, corrosion or other damage.

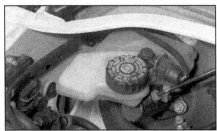

☐ The fluid reservoir must be secure and the fluid level must be between the upper (A) and lower (B) markings.

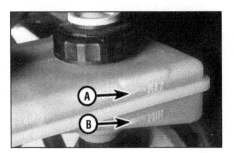

☐ Inspect both front brake flexible hoses for cracks or deterioration of the rubber. Turn the steering from lock to lock, and ensure that the hoses do not contact the wheel, tyre, or any part of the steering or suspension mechanism. With the brake pedal firmly depressed, check the hoses for bulges or leaks under pressure.

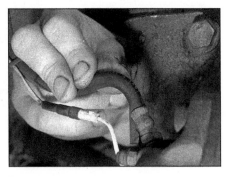

Steering and suspension

☐ Have your assistant turn the steering wheel from side to side slightly, up to the point where the steering gear just begins to transmit this movement to the roadwheels. Check for excessive free play between the steering wheel and the steering gear, indicating wear or insecurity of the steering column joints, the column-to-steering gear coupling, or the steering gear itself.
☐ Have your assistant turn the steering wheel more vigorously in each direction, so that the roadwheels just begin to turn. As this is done, examine all the steering joints, linkages, fittings and attachments. Renew any component that shows signs of wear or damage. On vehicles with power steering, check the security and condition of the steering pump, drivebelt and hoses.
☐ Check that the vehicle is standing level, and at approximately the correct ride height.

Shock absorbers

☐ Depress each corner of the vehicle in turn, then release it. The vehicle should rise and then settle in its normal position. If the vehicle continues to rise and fall, the shock absorber is defective. A shock absorber which has seized will also cause the vehicle to fail.

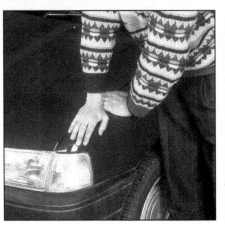

Exhaust system

☐ Start the engine. With your assistant holding a rag over the tailpipe, check the entire system for leaks. Repair or renew leaking sections.

3 Checks carried out WITH THE VEHICLE RAISED AND THE WHEELS FREE TO TURN

Jack up the front and rear of the vehicle, and securely support it on axle stands. Position the stands clear of the suspension assemblies. Ensure that the wheels are clear of the ground and that the steering can be turned from lock to lock.

Steering mechanism

☐ Have your assistant turn the steering from lock to lock. Check that the steering turns smoothly, and that no part of the steering mechanism, including a wheel or tyre, fouls any brake hose or pipe or any part of the body structure.

☐ Examine the steering rack rubber gaiters for damage or insecurity of the retaining clips. If power steering is fitted, check for signs of damage or leakage of the fluid hoses, pipes or connections. Also check for excessive stiffness or binding of the steering, a missing split pin or locking device, or severe corrosion of the body structure within 30 cm of any steering component attachment point.

Front and rear suspension and wheel bearings

☐ Starting at the front right-hand side, grasp the roadwheel at the 3 o'clock and 9 o'clock positions and shake it vigorously. Check for free play or insecurity at the wheel bearings, suspension balljoints, or suspension mountings, pivots and attachments.

☐ Now grasp the wheel at the 12 o'clock and 6 o'clock positions and repeat the previous inspection. Spin the wheel, and check for roughness or tightness of the front wheel bearing.

☐ If excess free play is suspected at a component pivot point, this can be confirmed by using a large screwdriver or similar tool and levering between the mounting and the component attachment. This will confirm whether the wear is in the pivot bush, its retaining bolt, or in the mounting itself (the bolt holes can often become elongated).

☐ Carry out all the above checks at the other front wheel, and then at both rear wheels.

Springs and shock absorbers

☐ Examine the suspension struts (when applicable) for serious fluid leakage, corrosion, or damage to the casing. Also check the security of the mounting points.

☐ If coil springs are fitted, check that the spring ends locate in their seats, and that the spring is not corroded, cracked or broken.

☐ If leaf springs are fitted, check that all leaves are intact, that the axle is securely attached to each spring, and that there is no deterioration of the spring eye mountings, bushes, and shackles.

☐ The same general checks apply to vehicles fitted with other suspension types, such as torsion bars, hydraulic displacer units, etc. Ensure that all mountings and attachments are secure, that there are no signs of excessive wear, corrosion or damage, and (on hydraulic types) that there are no fluid leaks or damaged pipes.

☐ Inspect the shock absorbers for signs of serious fluid leakage. Check for wear of the mounting bushes or attachments, or damage to the body of the unit.

Driveshafts (fwd vehicles only)

☐ Rotate each front wheel in turn and inspect the constant velocity joint gaiters for splits or damage. Also check that each driveshaft is straight and undamaged.

Braking system

☐ If possible without dismantling, check brake pad wear and disc condition. Ensure that the friction lining material has not worn excessively, (A) and that the discs are not fractured, pitted, scored or badly worn (B).

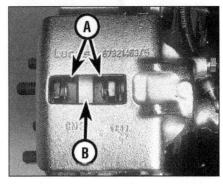

☐ Examine all the rigid brake pipes underneath the vehicle, and the flexible hose(s) at the rear. Look for corrosion, chafing or insecurity of the pipes, and for signs of bulging under pressure, chafing, splits or deterioration of the flexible hoses.

☐ Look for signs of fluid leaks at the brake calipers or on the brake backplates. Repair or renew leaking components.

☐ Slowly spin each wheel, while your assistant depresses and releases the footbrake. Ensure that each brake is operating and does not bind when the pedal is released.

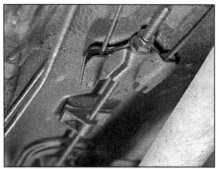

☐ Examine the handbrake mechanism, checking for frayed or broken cables, excessive corrosion, or wear or insecurity of the linkage. Check that the mechanism works on each relevant wheel, and releases fully, without binding.

☐ It is not possible to test brake efficiency without special equipment, but a road test can be carried out later to check that the vehicle pulls up in a straight line.

Fuel and exhaust systems

☐ Inspect the fuel tank (including the filler cap), fuel pipes, hoses and unions. All components must be secure and free from leaks.

☐ Examine the exhaust system over its entire length, checking for any damaged, broken or missing mountings, security of the retaining clamps and rust or corrosion.

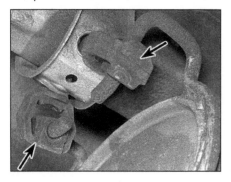

Wheels and tyres

☐ Examine the sidewalls and tread area of each tyre in turn. Check for cuts, tears, lumps, bulges, separation of the tread, and exposure of the ply or cord due to wear or damage. Check that the tyre bead is correctly seated on the wheel rim, that the valve is sound and

properly seated, and that the wheel is not distorted or damaged.

☐ Check that the tyres are of the correct size for the vehicle, that they are of the same size and type on each axle, and that the pressures are correct.

☐ Check the tyre tread depth. The legal minimum at the time of writing is 1.6 mm over at least three-quarters of the tread width. Abnormal tread wear may indicate incorrect front wheel alignment.

Body corrosion

☐ Check the condition of the entire vehicle structure for signs of corrosion in load-bearing areas. (These include chassis box sections, side sills, cross-members, pillars, and all suspension, steering, braking system and seat belt mountings and anchorages.) Any corrosion which has seriously reduced the thickness of a load-bearing area is likely to cause the vehicle to fail. In this case professional repairs are likely to be needed.

☐ Damage or corrosion which causes sharp or otherwise dangerous edges to be exposed will also cause the vehicle to fail.

4 Checks carried out on YOUR VEHICLE'S EXHAUST EMISSION SYSTEM

Petrol models

☐ Have the engine at normal operating temperature, and make sure that it is in good tune (ignition system in good order, air filter element clean, etc).

☐ Before any measurements are carried out, raise the engine speed to around 2500 rpm, and hold it at this speed for 20 seconds. Allow the engine speed to return to idle, and watch

for smoke emissions from the exhaust tailpipe. If the idle speed is obviously much too high, or if dense blue or clearly-visible black smoke comes from the tailpipe for more than 5 seconds, the vehicle will fail. As a rule of thumb, blue smoke signifies oil being burnt (engine wear) while black smoke signifies unburnt fuel (dirty air cleaner element, or other carburettor or fuel system fault).

☐ An exhaust gas analyser capable of measuring carbon monoxide (CO) and hydrocarbons (HC) is now needed. If such an instrument cannot be hired or borrowed, a local garage may agree to perform the check for a small fee.

CO emissions (mixture)

☐ At the time or writing, the maximum CO level at idle is 3.5% for vehicles first used after August 1986 and 4.5% for older vehicles. From January 1996 a much tighter limit (around 0.5%) applies to catalyst-equipped vehicles first used from August 1992. If the CO level cannot be reduced far enough to pass the test (and the fuel and ignition systems are otherwise in good condition) then the carburettor is badly worn, or there is some problem in the fuel injection system or catalytic converter (as applicable).

HC emissions

☐ With the CO emissions within limits, HC emissions must be no more than 1200 ppm (parts per million). If the vehicle fails this test at idle, it can be re-tested at around 2000 rpm; if the HC level is then 1200 ppm or less, this counts as a pass.

☐ Excessive HC emissions can be caused by oil being burnt, but they are more likely to be due to unburnt fuel.

Diesel models

☐ The only emission test applicable to Diesel engines is the measuring of exhaust smoke density. The test involves accelerating the engine several times to its maximum unloaded speed.

Note: *It is of the utmost importance that the engine timing belt is in good condition before the test is carried out.*

☐ Excessive smoke can be caused by a dirty air cleaner element. Otherwise, professional advice may be needed to find the cause.

Engine

- ☐ Engine fails to rotate when attempting to start
- ☐ Engine rotates, but will not start
- ☐ Engine difficult to start when cold
- ☐ Engine difficult to start when hot
- ☐ Starter motor noisy or excessively-rough in engagement
- ☐ Engine starts, but stops immediately
- ☐ Engine idles erratically
- ☐ Engine misfires at idle speed
- ☐ Engine misfires throughout the driving speed range
- ☐ Engine hesitates on acceleration
- ☐ Engine stalls
- ☐ Engine lacks power
- ☐ Engine backfires
- ☐ Oil pressure warning light illuminated with engine running
- ☐ Engine runs-on after switching off
- ☐ Engine noises

Cooling system

- ☐ Overheating
- ☐ Overcooling
- ☐ External coolant leakage
- ☐ Internal coolant leakage
- ☐ Corrosion

Fuel and exhaust systems

- ☐ Excessive fuel consumption
- ☐ Fuel leakage and/or fuel odour
- ☐ Excessive noise or fumes from exhaust system

Clutch

- ☐ Pedal travels to floor - no pressure or very little resistance
- ☐ Clutch fails to disengage (unable to select gears)
- ☐ Clutch slips (engine speed increases, with no increase in vehicle speed)
- ☐ Judder as clutch is engaged
- ☐ Noise when depressing or releasing clutch pedal

Manual gearbox

- ☐ Noisy in neutral with engine running
- ☐ Noisy in one particular gear
- ☐ Difficulty engaging gears
- ☐ Jumps out of gear
- ☐ Vibration
- ☐ Lubricant leaks

Automatic transmission

- ☐ Fluid leakage
- ☐ Transmission fluid brown, or has burned smell
- ☐ General gear selection problems
- ☐ Transmission will not downshift (kickdown) with accelerator fully depressed
- ☐ Engine will not start in any gear, or starts in gears other than Park or Neutral
- ☐ Transmission slips, shifts roughly, is noisy, or has no drive in forward or reverse gears

Driveshafts

- ☐ Clicking or knocking noise on turns (at slow speed on full-lock)
- ☐ Vibration when accelerating or decelerating

Braking system

- ☐ Vehicle pulls to one side under braking
- ☐ Noise (grinding or high-pitched squeal) when brakes applied
- ☐ Excessive brake pedal travel
- ☐ Brake pedal feels spongy when depressed
- ☐ Excessive brake pedal effort required to stop vehicle
- ☐ Judder felt through brake pedal or steering wheel when braking
- ☐ Brakes binding
- ☐ Rear wheels locking under normal braking

Suspension and steering systems

- ☐ Vehicle pulls to one side
- ☐ Wheel wobble and vibration
- ☐ Excessive pitching and/or rolling around corners, or during braking
- ☐ Wandering or general instability
- ☐ Excessively-stiff steering
- ☐ Excessive play in steering
- ☐ Lack of power assistance
- ☐ Tyre wear excessive

Electrical system

- ☐ Battery will not hold a charge for more than a few days
- ☐ Ignition/no-charge warning light remains illuminated with engine running
- ☐ Ignition/no-charge warning light fails to come on
- ☐ Lights inoperative
- ☐ Instrument readings inaccurate or erratic
- ☐ Horn inoperative, or unsatisfactory in operation
- ☐ Windscreen/tailgate wipers inoperative, or unsatisfactory in operation
- ☐ Windscreen/tailgate washers inoperative, or unsatisfactory in operation
- ☐ Electric windows inoperative, or unsatisfactory in operation
- ☐ Central locking system inoperative, or unsatisfactory in operation

Introduction

The vehicle owner who does his or her own maintenance according to the recommended service schedules should not have to use this section of the manual very often. Modern component reliability is such that, provided those items subject to wear or deterioration are inspected or renewed at the specified intervals, sudden failure is comparatively rare. Faults do not usually just happen as a result of sudden failure, but develop over a period of time. Major mechanical failures in particular are usually preceded by characteristic symptoms over hundreds or even thousands of miles. Those components which do occasionally fail without warning are often small and easily carried in the vehicle.

With any fault-finding, the first step is to decide where to begin investigations. Sometimes this is obvious, but on other occasions, a little detective work will be necessary. The owner who makes half a dozen haphazard adjustments or replacements may be successful in curing a fault (or its symptoms), but will be none the wiser if the fault recurs, and ultimately may have spent more time and money than was necessary. A calm and logical approach will be found to be more satisfactory in the long run. Always take into account any warning signs or abnormalities that may have been noticed in the period preceding the fault - power loss, high or low gauge readings, unusual smells, etc - and remember that failure of components such as fuses or spark plugs may only be pointers to some underlying fault.

The pages which follow provide an easy-reference guide to the more common problems which may occur during the operation of the vehicle. These problems and their possible causes are grouped under headings denoting various components or systems, such as Engine, Cooling system, etc. The Chapter and/or Section which deals with the problem is also shown in brackets. Whatever the fault, certain basic principles apply. These are as follows:

Verify the fault. This is simply a matter of being sure that you know what the symptoms are before starting work. This is particularly important if you are investigating a fault for someone else, who may not have described it very accurately.

Don't overlook the obvious. For example, if the vehicle won't start, is there petrol in the tank? (Don't take anyone else's word on this particular point, and don't trust the fuel gauge either!) If an electrical fault is indicated, look for loose or broken wires before digging out the test gear.

Cure the disease, not the symptom. Substituting a flat battery with a fully-charged one will get you off the hard shoulder, but if the underlying cause is not attended to, the new battery will go the same way. Similarly, changing oil-fouled spark plugs for a new set will get you moving again, but remember that the reason for the fouling (if it wasn't simply an incorrect grade of plug) will have to be established and corrected.

Don't take anything for granted. Particularly, don't forget that a "new" component may itself be defective (especially if it's been rattling around in the boot for months), and don't leave components out of a fault diagnosis sequence just because they are new or recently-fitted. When you do finally diagnose a difficult fault, you'll probably realise that all the evidence was there from the start.

Engine

Engine fails to rotate when attempting to start

- ☐ Battery terminal connections loose or corroded (Chapter 1).
- ☐ Battery discharged or faulty (Chapter 5A).
- ☐ Broken, loose or disconnected wiring in the starting circuit (Chapter 5A).
- ☐ Defective starter solenoid or switch (Chapter 5A).
- ☐ Defective starter motor (Chapter 5A).
- ☐ Starter pinion or flywheel ring gear teeth loose or broken (Chapters a and 5A).
- ☐ Engine earth strap broken or disconnected (Chapter 5A).
- ☐ Automatic transmission not in Park/Neutral position or starter inhibitor switch faulty (Chapter 7B).

Engine rotates, but will not start

- ☐ Fuel tank empty.
- ☐ Battery discharged (engine rotates slowly) (Chapter 5A).
- ☐ Battery terminal connections loose or corroded (Chapter 1).
- ☐ Ignition components damp or damaged (Chapters 1 and 5B or 5C).
- ☐ Broken, loose or disconnected wiring in the ignition circuit (Chapters 1 and 5B or 5C).
- ☐ Worn, faulty or incorrectly-gapped spark plugs (Chapter 1).
- ☐ Carburettor/fuel injection system fault (Chapter 4A or 4B).
- ☐ Major mechanical failure (eg camshaft drive) (Chapter 2).

Engine difficult to start when cold

- ☐ Battery discharged (Chapter 5A).
- ☐ Battery terminal connections loose or corroded (Chapter 1).
- ☐ Worn, faulty or incorrectly-gapped spark plugs (Chapter 1).
- ☐ Choke mechanism faulty - carburettor models (Chapter 4A).
- ☐ Faulty fuel cut-off solenoid - carburettor models (Chapter 4A).
- ☐ Fuel injection system fault - fuel-injected models (Chapter 4B).
- ☐ Other ignition system fault (Chapters 1 and 5B or 5C).
- ☐ Low cylinder compressions (Chapter 2).

Engine difficult to start when hot

- ☐ Air filter element dirty or clogged (Chapter 1).
- ☐ Choke mechanism faulty - carburettor models (Chapter 4A).
- ☐ Faulty fuel cut-off solenoid - carburettor models (Chapter 4A).
- ☐ Fuel injection system fault - fuel-injected models (Chapter 4B).
- ☐ Other ignition system fault (Chapters 1 and 5B or 5C).
- ☐ Low cylinder compressions (Chapter 2).

Starter motor noisy or excessively-rough in engagement

- ☐ Starter pinion or flywheel ring gear teeth loose or broken (Chapters 2 or 5A).
- ☐ Starter motor mounting bolts loose or missing (Chapter 5A).
- ☐ Starter motor internal components worn or damaged (Chapter 5A).

Engine starts, but stops immediately

- ☐ Loose or faulty electrical connections in the ignition circuit (Chapters 1 and 5B or 5C).
- ☐ Vacuum leak at the carburettor/throttle body or inlet manifold (Chapter 4A or 4B).
- ☐ Blocked carburettor jet(s) or internal passages - carburettor models (Chapter 4A).
- ☐ Blocked injector/fuel injection system fault - fuel-injected models (Chapter 4B).

Engine idles erratically

- ☐ Air filter element clogged (Chapter 1).
- ☐ Vacuum leak at the carburettor/throttle body or inlet manifold (Chapter 4A or 4B).
- ☐ Worn, faulty or incorrectly-gapped spark plugs (Chapter 1).
- ☐ Uneven or low cylinder compressions (Chapter 2).
- ☐ Camshaft lobes worn (Chapter 2A).
- ☐ Camshaft toothed belt incorrectly fitted (Chapter 2A).
- ☐ Blocked carburettor jet(s) or internal passages - carburettor models (Chapter 4A).
- ☐ Blocked injector/fuel injection system fault - fuel-injected models (Chapter 4B).

Engine misfires at idle speed

- ☐ Worn, faulty or incorrectly-gapped spark plugs (Chapter 1).
- ☐ Faulty spark plug HT leads (Chapter 1).
- ☐ Vacuum leak at the carburettor/throttle body, inlet manifold or associated hoses (Chapter 4A or 4B).
- ☐ Blocked carburettor jet(s) or internal passages - carburettor models (Chapter 4A).
- ☐ Blocked injector/fuel injection system fault - fuel-injected models (Chapter 4B).
- ☐ Distributor cap cracked or tracking internally (Chapter 1).
- ☐ Uneven or low cylinder compressions (Chapter 2).
- ☐ Disconnected, leaking, or perished crankcase ventilation hoses (Chapter 2).

Engine misfires throughout the driving speed range

- ☐ Fuel filter choked (Chapter 1).
- ☐ Fuel pump faulty, or delivery pressure low (Chapter 4A or 4B).
- ☐ Fuel tank vent blocked, or fuel pipes restricted (Chapter 4A or 4B).
- ☐ Vacuum leak at the carburettor/throttle body, inlet manifold or associated hoses (Chapter 4A or 4B).
- ☐ Worn, faulty or incorrectly-gapped spark plugs (Chapter 1).
- ☐ Faulty spark plug HT leads (Chapter 1).
- ☐ Distributor cap cracked or tracking internally (Chapter 1).
- ☐ Faulty ignition coil (Chapter 5B or 5C).
- ☐ Uneven or low cylinder compressions (Chapter 2).

☐ Blocked carburettor jet(s) or internal passages - carburettor models (Chapter 4A).
☐ Blocked injector/fuel injection system fault - fuel-injected models (Chapter 4B).

Engine hesitates on acceleration

☐ Worn, faulty or incorrectly-gapped spark plugs (Chapter 1).
☐ Vacuum leak at the carburettor/throttle body, inlet manifold or associated hoses (Chapter 4A or 4B).
☐ Blocked carburettor jet(s) or internal passages - carburettor models (Chapter 4A).
☐ Blocked injector/fuel injection system fault - fuel-injected models (Chapter 4B).

Engine stalls

☐ Vacuum leak at the carburettor/throttle body, inlet manifold or associated hoses (Chapter 4A or 4B).
☐ Fuel filter choked (Chapter 1).
☐ Fuel pump faulty, or delivery pressure low (Chapter 4A or 4B).
☐ Fuel tank vent blocked, or fuel pipes restricted (Chapter 4A or 4B).
☐ Blocked carburettor jet(s) or internal passages - carburettor models (Chapter 4A).
☐ Blocked injector/fuel injection system fault - fuel-injected models (Chapter 4B).

Engine lacks power

☐ Camshaft toothed belt incorrectly fitted (Chapter 2).
☐ Fuel filter choked (Chapter 1).
☐ Fuel pump faulty, or delivery pressure low (Chapter 4A or 4B).
☐ Uneven or low cylinder compressions (Chapter 2).
☐ Worn, faulty or incorrectly-gapped spark plugs (Chapter 1).
☐ Vacuum leak at the carburettor/throttle body, inlet manifold or associated hoses (Chapter 4A or 4B).
☐ Blocked carburettor jet(s) or internal passages - carburettor models (Chapter 4A).
☐ Blocked injector/fuel injection system fault - fuel-injected models (Chapter 4B or 4C).
☐ Brakes binding (Chapters 1 and 9).
☐ Clutch slipping - manual transmission models (Chapter 6).

Engine backfires

☐ Camshaft toothed timing belt incorrectly fitted (Chapter 2).
☐ Vacuum leak at the carburettor/throttle body, inlet manifold or associated hoses (Chapter 4A or 4B).
☐ Blocked carburettor jet(s) or internal passages - carburettor models (Chapter 4A).
☐ Blocked injector/fuel injection system fault - fuel-injected models (Chapter 4B).

Oil pressure warning light illuminated with engine running

☐ Low oil level, or incorrect oil grade (Chapter 1).
☐ Faulty oil pressure sensor (Chapter 5A).
☐ Worn engine bearings and/or oil pump (Chapter 2).
☐ High engine operating temperature (Chapter 3).
☐ Oil pressure relief valve defective (Chapter 2).
☐ Oil pick-up strainer clogged (Chapter 2).

Engine runs-on after switching off

☐ Excessive carbon build-up in engine (Chapter 2).
☐ High engine operating temperature (Chapter 3).
☐ Faulty fuel cut-off solenoid - carburettor models (Chapter 4A).
☐ Fuel injection system fault - fuel injection models (Chapter 4B).

Engine noises

Pre-ignition (pinking) or knocking during acceleration or under load

☐ Ignition timing incorrect/ignition fault (Chapters 1 and 5B or 5C).
☐ Incorrect grade of spark plug (Chapter 1).
☐ Incorrect grade of fuel (Chapter 1).
☐ Vacuum leak at the carburettor/throttle body, inlet manifold or associated hoses (Chapter 4A or 4B).
☐ Excessive carbon build-up in engine (Chapter 2).
☐ Blocked carburettor jet(s) or internal passages (Chapter 4A).
☐ Blocked injector/fuel injection fault (Chapter 4B).

Whistling or wheezing noises

☐ Leaking inlet manifold or carburettor/throttle body gasket (Chapter 4A or 4B).
☐ Leaking exhaust manifold gasket or pipe-to-manifold joint (Chapter 4A or 4B).
☐ Leaking vacuum hose (Chapters 4A, 4B and 9).
☐ Blowing cylinder head gasket (Chapter 2).

Tapping or rattling noises

☐ Worn valve gear or camshaft (Chapter 2).
☐ Ancillary component fault (water pump, alternator, etc) (Chapters 3, 5, etc).

Knocking or thumping noises

☐ Worn big-end bearings (regular heavy knocking, perhaps less under load) (Chapter 2).
☐ Worn main bearings (rumbling and knocking, perhaps worsening under load) (Chapter 2).
☐ Piston slap (most noticeable when cold) (Chapter 2).
☐ Ancillary component fault (water pump, alternator, etc) (Chapters 3, 5, etc).

Cooling system

Overheating

☐ Insufficient coolant in system (Chapter 1).
☐ Thermostat faulty (Chapter 3).
☐ Radiator core blocked, or grille restricted (Chapter 3).
☐ Electric cooling fan or thermoswitch faulty (Chapter 3).
☐ Pressure cap faulty (Chapter 3).
☐ Ignition timing incorrect (Chapters 1 and 5B or 5C).
☐ Inaccurate temperature gauge sender unit (Chapter 3).
☐ Airlock in cooling system (Chapter 1).

Overcooling

☐ Thermostat faulty (Chapter 3).
☐ Inaccurate temperature gauge sender unit (Chapter 3).

External coolant leakage

☐ Deteriorated or damaged hoses or hose clips (Chapter 1).
☐ Radiator core or heater matrix leaking (Chapter 3).
☐ Pressure cap faulty (Chapter 3).
☐ Water pump seal leaking (Chapter 3).
☐ Boiling due to overheating (Chapter 3).
☐ Core plug leaking (Chapter 2).

Internal coolant leakage

☐ Leaking cylinder head gasket (Chapter 2).
☐ Cracked cylinder head or cylinder bore (Chapter 2).

Corrosion

☐ Infrequent draining and flushing (Chapter 1).
☐ Incorrect coolant mixture or inappropriate coolant type (Chapter 1).

Fuel and exhaust systems

Excessive fuel consumption

- ☐ Air filter element dirty or clogged (Chapter 1).
- ☐ Choke mechanism faulty - carburettor models (Chapter 4A).
- ☐ Fuel injection system fault - fuel-injected models (Chapter 4B).
- ☐ Ignition timing incorrect/ignition fault (Chapters 1 and 5B or 5C).
- ☐ Tyres under-inflated (Chapter 1).

Fuel leakage and/or fuel odour

- ☐ Damaged/corroded fuel tank, pipes or connections (Chapter 4A or 4B).

- ☐ Carburettor float chamber flooding (float height incorrect) (Chapter 4A).

Excessive noise or fumes from exhaust system

- ☐ Leaking exhaust system or manifold joints (Chapters 1 and 4A or 4B).
- ☐ Leaking, corroded or damaged silencers or pipe (Chapters 1 and 4A or 4B).
- ☐ Broken mountings causing body or suspension contact (Chapter 1).

Clutch

Pedal travels to floor - no pressure or very little resistance

- ☐ Broken clutch cable (Chapter 6).
- ☐ Incorrect clutch cable adjustment (Chapter 6).
- ☐ Broken clutch release bearing or fork (Chapter 6).
- ☐ Broken diaphragm spring in clutch pressure plate (Chapter 6).

Clutch fails to disengage (unable to select gears)

- ☐ Incorrect clutch cable adjustment (Chapter 6).
- ☐ Clutch disc sticking on gearbox input shaft splines (Chapter 6).
- ☐ Clutch disc sticking to flywheel or pressure plate (Chapter 6).
- ☐ Faulty pressure plate assembly (Chapter 6).
- ☐ Clutch release mechanism worn or incorrectly assembled (Chapter 6).

Clutch slips (engine speed increases, with no increase in vehicle speed)

- ☐ Incorrect clutch cable adjustment (Chapter 6).

- ☐ Clutch disc linings excessively worn (Chapter 6).
- ☐ Clutch disc linings contaminated with oil or grease (Chapter 6).
- ☐ Faulty pressure plate or weak diaphragm spring (Chapter 6).

Judder as clutch is engaged

- ☐ Clutch disc linings contaminated with oil or grease (Chapter 6).
- ☐ Clutch disc linings excessively worn (Chapter 6).
- ☐ Clutch cable sticking or frayed (Chapter 6).
- ☐ Faulty or distorted pressure plate or diaphragm spring (Chapter 6).
- ☐ Worn or loose engine or gearbox mountings (Chapter 2).
- ☐ Clutch disc hub or gearbox input shaft splines worn (Chapter 6).

Noise when depressing or releasing clutch pedal

- ☐ Worn clutch release bearing (Chapter 6).
- ☐ Worn or dry clutch pedal bushes (Chapter 6).
- ☐ Faulty pressure plate assembly (Chapter 6).
- ☐ Pressure plate diaphragm spring broken (Chapter 6).
- ☐ Broken clutch disc cushioning springs (Chapter 6).

Manual gearbox

Noisy in neutral with engine running

- ☐ Input shaft bearings worn (noise apparent with clutch pedal released, but not when depressed) (Chapter 7A).*
- ☐ Clutch release bearing worn (noise apparent with clutch pedal depressed, possibly less when released) (Chapter 6).

Noisy in one particular gear

- ☐ Worn, damaged or chipped gear teeth (Chapter 7A).*

Difficulty engaging gears

- ☐ Clutch fault (Chapter 6).
- ☐ Worn or damaged gear linkage (Chapter 7A).
- ☐ Incorrectly-adjusted gear linkage (Chapter 7A).
- ☐ Worn synchroniser units (Chapter 7A).*

Jumps out of gear

- ☐ Worn or damaged gear linkage (Chapter 7A).

- ☐ Incorrectly-adjusted gear linkage (Chapter 7A).
- ☐ Worn synchroniser units (Chapter 7A).*
- ☐ Worn selector forks (Chapter 7A).*

Vibration

- ☐ Lack of oil (Chapter 1).
- ☐ Worn bearings (Chapter 7A).*

Lubricant leaks

- ☐ Leaking differential output oil seal (Chapter 7A).
- ☐ Leaking housing joint (Chapter 7A).*
- ☐ Leaking input shaft oil seal (Chapter 7A).*

Although the corrective action necessary to remedy the symptoms described is beyond the scope of the home mechanic, the above information should be helpful in isolating the cause of the condition, so that the owner can communicate clearly with a professional mechanic.

Automatic transmission

Note: *Due to the complexity of the automatic transmission, it is difficult for the home mechanic to properly diagnose and service this unit. For problems other than the following, the vehicle should be taken to a dealer service department or automatic transmission specialist.*

Fluid leakage

☐ Automatic transmission fluid is usually deep red in colour. Fluid leaks should not be confused with engine oil, which can easily be blown onto the transmission by air flow.

☐ To determine the source of a leak, first remove all built-up dirt and grime from the transmission housing and surrounding areas, using a degreasing agent, or by steam-cleaning. Drive the vehicle at low speed, so air flow will not blow the leak far from its source. Raise and support the vehicle, and determine where the leak is coming from. The following are common areas of leakage.
 a) Oil pan.
 b) Dipstick tube.

Transmission fluid brown, or has burned smell

☐ Transmission fluid level low, or fluid in need of renewal (Chapter 1).

General gear selection problems

☐ Chapter 7B deals with checking and adjusting the selector cable on automatic transmissions. The following are common problems which may be caused by a poorly-adjusted cable.
 a) Engine starting in gears other than Park or Neutral.
 b) Indicator on gear selector lever pointing to a gear other than the one actually being used.
 c) Vehicle moves when in Park or Neutral.
 d) Poor gearshift quality or erratic gearchanges.
☐ Refer to Chapter 7B for the selector cable adjustment procedure.

Transmission will not downshift (kickdown) with accelerator pedal fully depressed

☐ Low transmission fluid level (Chapter 1).
☐ Incorrect selector cable adjustment (Chapter 7B).
☐ Incorrect kickdown cable adjustment (Chapter 7B).

Engine will not start in any gear, or starts in gears other than Park or Neutral

☐ Incorrect starter inhibitor switch adjustment (Chapter 7B).
☐ Incorrect selector cable adjustment (Chapter 7B).

Transmission slips, shifts roughly, is noisy, or has no drive in forward or reverse gears

☐ There are many probable causes for the above problems, but the home mechanic should be concerned with only one possibility - fluid level. Before taking the vehicle to a dealer or transmission specialist, check the fluid level and condition of the fluid (refer to Chapter 1). Correct the fluid level as necessary, or change the fluid and filter if needed. If the problem persists, professional help will be necessary.

Driveshafts

Clicking or knocking noise on turns (at slow speed on full-lock)

☐ Lack of constant velocity joint lubricant, possibly due to damaged gaiter (Chapter 8).
☐ Worn outer constant velocity joint (Chapter 8).

Vibration when accelerating or decelerating

☐ Worn inner constant velocity joint (Chapter 8).
☐ Bent or distorted driveshaft (Chapter 8).

Braking system

Note: *Before assuming that a brake problem exists, make sure that the tyres are in good condition and correctly inflated, that the front wheel alignment is correct, and that the vehicle is not loaded with weight in an unequal manner. Apart from checking the condition of all pipe and hose connections.*

Vehicle pulls to one side under braking

☐ Worn, defective, damaged or contaminated front brake pads or rear brake shoes/pads on one side (Chapters 1 and 9).
☐ Seized or partially-seized front brake caliper or rear wheel caliper/cylinder piston (Chapters 1 and 9).
☐ A mixture of brake pad/shoe lining materials fitted between sides (Chapters 1 and 9).
☐ Front brake caliper mounting bolts loose (Chapter 9).
☐ Rear brake backplate mounting bolts loose (Chapter 9).
☐ Worn or damaged steering or suspension components (Chapters 1 and 10).

Noise (grinding or high-pitched squeal) when brakes applied

☐ Brake pad or shoe friction lining material worn down to metal backing (Chapters 1 and 9).
☐ Excessive corrosion of brake disc or drum. (May be apparent after the vehicle has been standing for some time (Chapters 1 and 9).
☐ Foreign object (stone chipping, etc) trapped between brake disc and shield (Chapters 1 and 9).

Excessive brake pedal travel

☐ Rear brakes incorrectly adjusted - early models (Chapter 9)
☐ Inoperative rear brake self-adjust mechanism - later drum brake models (Chapters 1 and 9).
☐ Faulty master cylinder (Chapter 9).
☐ Air in hydraulic system (Chapters 1 and 9).
☐ Faulty vacuum servo unit (Chapter 9).

Brake pedal feels spongy when depressed

☐ Air in hydraulic system (Chapters 1 and 9).
☐ Deteriorated flexible rubber brake hoses (Chapters 1 and 9).
☐ Master cylinder mounting nuts loose (Chapter 9).
☐ Faulty master cylinder (Chapter 9).

Excessive brake pedal effort required to stop vehicle

☐ Faulty vacuum servo unit (Chapter 9).
☐ Disconnected, damaged or insecure brake servo vacuum hose (Chapter 9).
☐ Primary or secondary hydraulic circuit failure (Chapter 9).
☐ Seized brake caliper or wheel cylinder piston(s) (Chapter 9).
☐ Brake pads or brake shoes incorrectly fitted (Chapters 1 and 9).
☐ Incorrect grade of brake pads or brake shoes fitted (Chapters 1 and 9).
☐ Brake pads or brake shoe linings contaminated (Chapters 1 and 9).

Braking system (continued)

Judder felt through brake pedal or steering wheel when braking

☐ Excessive run-out or distortion of front discs or rear discs/drums (Chapters 1 and 9).
☐ Brake pad or brake shoe linings worn (Chapters 1 and 9).
☐ Brake caliper or rear brake backplate mounting bolts loose (Chapter 9).
☐ Wear in suspension or steering components or mountings (Chapters 1 and 10).

Brakes binding

☐ Seized brake caliper or wheel cylinder piston(s) (Chapter 9).
☐ Incorrectly-adjusted handbrake mechanism (Chapter 9).
☐ Faulty master cylinder (Chapter 9).

Rear wheels locking under normal braking

☐ Rear brake shoe linings contaminated (Chapters 1 and 9).
☐ Faulty brake pressure regulator valve(s) (Chapter 9).

Suspension and steering

Note: *Before diagnosing suspension or steering faults, be sure that the trouble is not due to incorrect tyre pressures, mixtures of tyre types, or binding brakes.*

Vehicle pulls to one side

☐ Defective tyre (Chapter 1).
☐ Excessive wear in suspension or steering components (Chapters 1 and 10).
☐ Incorrect front wheel alignment (Chapter 10).
☐ Accident damage to steering or suspension components (Chapter 1).

Wheel wobble and vibration

☐ Front roadwheels out of balance (vibration felt mainly through the steering wheel) (Chapters 1 and 10).
☐ Rear roadwheels out of balance (vibration felt throughout the vehicle) (Chapters 1 and 10).
☐ Roadwheels damaged or distorted (Chapters 1 and 10).
☐ Faulty or damaged tyre (Chapter 1).
☐ Worn steering or suspension joints, bushes or components (Chapters 1 and 10).
☐ Wheel bolts loose (Chapters 1 and 10).

Excessive pitching and/or rolling around corners, or during braking

☐ Defective shock absorbers (Chapters 1 and 10).
☐ Broken or weak spring and/or suspension component (Chapters 1 and 10).
☐ Worn or damaged anti-roll bar or mountings (Chapter 10).

Wandering or general instability

☐ Incorrect front wheel alignment (Chapter 10).
☐ Worn steering or suspension joints, bushes or components (Chapters 1 and 10).
☐ Roadwheels out of balance (Chapters 1 and 10).
☐ Faulty or damaged tyre (Chapter 1).
☐ Wheel bolts loose (Chapters 1 and 10).
☐ Defective shock absorbers (Chapters 1 and 10).

Excessively-stiff steering

☐ Lack of steering gear lubricant (Chapter 10).
☐ Seized track rod end balljoint or suspension balljoint (Chapters 1 and 10).

☐ Broken or incorrectly-adjusted auxiliary drivebelt (Chapter 1).
☐ Incorrect front wheel alignment (Chapter 10).
☐ Steering rack or column bent or damaged (Chapter 10).

Excessive play in steering

☐ Worn steering track rod end balljoints (Chapters 1 and 10).
☐ Worn rack-and-pinion steering gear (Chapter 10).
☐ Worn steering or suspension joints, bushes or components (Chapters 1 and 10).

Lack of power assistance

☐ Broken or incorrectly-adjusted auxiliary drivebelt (Chapter 1).
☐ Incorrect power steering fluid level (Chapter 1).
☐ Restriction in power steering fluid hoses (Chapter 1).
☐ Faulty power steering pump (Chapter 10).
☐ Faulty rack-and-pinion steering gear (Chapter 10).

Tyre wear excessive

Tyres worn on inside or outside edges

☐ Tyres under-inflated (wear on both edges) (Chapter 1).
☐ Incorrect camber or castor angles (wear on one edge only) (Chapter 10).
☐ Worn steering or suspension joints, bushes or components (Chapters 1 and 10).
☐ Excessively-hard cornering.
☐ Accident damage.

Tyre treads exhibit feathered edges

☐ Incorrect toe setting (Chapter 10).

Tyres worn in centre of tread

☐ Tyres over-inflated (Chapter 1).

Tyres worn on inside and outside edges

☐ Tyres under-inflated (Chapter 1).

Tyres worn unevenly

☐ Tyres/wheels out of balance (Chapter 1).
☐ Excessive wheel or tyre run-out (Chapter 1).
☐ Worn shock absorbers (Chapters 1 and 10).
☐ Faulty tyre (Chapter 1).

Electrical system

Note: *For problems associated with the starting system, refer to the faults listed under "Engine" earlier in this Section.*

Battery will not hold a charge for more than a few days

☐ Battery defective internally (Chapter 5A).

☐ Battery terminal connections loose or corroded (Chapter 1).
☐ Auxiliary drivebelt worn or incorrectly adjusted (Chapter 1).
☐ Alternator not charging at correct output (Chapter 5A).
☐ Alternator or voltage regulator faulty (Chapter 5A).
☐ Short-circuit causing continual battery drain (Chapters 5A and 12).

Ignition/no-charge warning light remains illuminated with engine running

- [ ] Auxiliary drivebelt broken, worn, or incorrectly adjusted (Chapter 1).
- [ ] Alternator brushes worn, sticking, or dirty (Chapter 5A).
- [ ] Alternator brush springs weak or broken (Chapter 5A).
- [ ] Internal fault in alternator or voltage regulator (Chapter 5A).
- [ ] Broken, disconnected, or loose wiring in charging circuit (Chapter 5A).

Ignition/no-charge warning light fails to come on

- [ ] Warning light bulb blown (Chapter 12).
- [ ] Broken, disconnected, or loose wiring in warning light circuit (Chapter 12).
- [ ] Alternator faulty (Chapter 5A).

Lights inoperative

- [ ] Bulb blown (Chapter 12).
- [ ] Corrosion of bulb or bulbholder contacts (Chapter 12).
- [ ] Blown fuse (Chapter 12).
- [ ] Faulty relay (Chapter 12).
- [ ] Broken, loose, or disconnected wiring (Chapter 12).
- [ ] Faulty switch (Chapter 12).

Instrument readings inaccurate or erratic

Instrument readings increase with engine speed

- [ ] Faulty voltage regulator (Chapter 12).

Fuel or temperature gauges give no reading

- [ ] Faulty gauge sender unit (Chapters 3 or 4).
- [ ] Wiring open-circuit (Chapter 12).
- [ ] Faulty gauge (Chapter 12).

Fuel or temperature gauges give continuous maximum reading

- [ ] Faulty gauge sender unit (Chapters 3 or 4).
- [ ] Wiring short-circuit (Chapter 12).
- [ ] Faulty gauge (Chapter 12).

Horn inoperative, or unsatisfactory in operation

Horn operates all the time

- [ ] Horn push either earthed or stuck down (Chapter 12).
- [ ] Horn cable-to-horn push earthed (Chapter 12).

Horn fails to operate

- [ ] Blown fuse (Chapter 12).
- [ ] Cable or cable connections loose, broken or disconnected (Chapter 12).
- [ ] Faulty horn (Chapter 12).

Horn emits intermittent or unsatisfactory sound

- [ ] Cable connections loose (Chapter 12).
- [ ] Horn mountings loose (Chapter 12).
- [ ] Faulty horn (Chapter 12).

Windscreen/tailgate wipers inoperative, or unsatisfactory in operation

Wipers fail to operate, or operate very slowly

- [ ] Wiper blades stuck to screen, or linkage seized or binding (Chapters 1 and 12).
- [ ] Blown fuse (Chapter 12).
- [ ] Cable or cable connections loose, broken or disconnected (Chapter 12).
- [ ] Faulty relay (Chapter 12).
- [ ] Faulty wiper motor (Chapter 12).

Wiper blades sweep over too large or too small an area of the glass

- [ ] Wiper arms incorrectly positioned on spindles (Chapter 1).
- [ ] Excessive wear of wiper linkage (Chapter 12).
- [ ] Wiper motor or linkage mountings loose or insecure (Chapter 12).

Wiper blades fail to clean the glass effectively

- [ ] Wiper blade rubbers worn or perished (Chapter 1).
- [ ] Wiper arm tension springs broken, or arm pivots seized (Chapter 12).

Windscreen/tailgate washers inoperative, or unsatisfactory in operation

One or more washer jets inoperative

- [ ] Blocked washer jet (Chapter 1).
- [ ] Disconnected, kinked or restricted fluid hose (Chapter 12).
- [ ] Insufficient fluid in washer reservoir (Chapter 1).

Washer pump fails to operate

- [ ] Broken or disconnected wiring or connections (Chapter 12).
- [ ] Blown fuse (Chapter 12).
- [ ] Faulty washer switch (Chapter 12).
- [ ] Faulty washer pump (Chapter 12).

Washer pump runs for some time before fluid is emitted from jets

- [ ] Faulty one-way valve in fluid supply hose (Chapter 12).

Electric windows inoperative, or unsatisfactory in operation

Window glass will only move in one direction

- [ ] Faulty switch (Chapter 12)

Window glass slow to move

- [ ] Incorrectly-adjusted door glass guide channels (Chapter 11).
- [ ] Regulator seized or damaged, or in need of lubrication (Chapter 11).
- [ ] Door internal components or trim fouling regulator (Chapter 11).
- [ ] Faulty motor (Chapter 11).

Window glass fails to move

- [ ] Incorrectly-adjusted door glass guide channels (Chapter 11).
- [ ] Blown fuse (Chapter 12).
- [ ] Faulty relay (Chapter 12).
- [ ] Broken or disconnected wiring or connections (Chapter 12).
- [ ] Faulty motor (Chapter 11).

Central locking system inoperative, or unsatisfactory in operation

Complete system failure

- [ ] Blown fuse (Chapter 12).
- [ ] Faulty relay (Chapter 12).
- [ ] Broken or disconnected wiring or connections (Chapter 12).
- [ ] Faulty control unit (Chapter 11).

Latch locks but will not unlock, or unlocks but will not lock

- [ ] Faulty master switch (Chapter 12).
- [ ] Broken or disconnected latch operating rods or levers (Chapter 11).
- [ ] Faulty relay (Chapter 12).
- [ ] Faulty control unit (Chapter 11).

One solenoid/motor fails to operate

- [ ] Broken or disconnected wiring or connections (Chapter 12).
- [ ] Faulty solenoid/motor (Chapter 11).
- [ ] Broken, binding or disconnected latch operating rods or levers (Chapter 11).
- [ ] Fault in door latch (Chapter 11).

A

ABS (Anti-lock brake system) A system, usually electronically controlled, that senses incipient wheel lockup during braking and relieves hydraulic pressure at wheels that are about to skid.

Air bag An inflatable bag hidden in the steering wheel (driver's side) or the dash or glovebox (passenger side). In a head-on collision, the bags inflate, preventing the driver and front passenger from being thrown forward into the steering wheel or windscreen.

Air cleaner A metal or plastic housing, containing a filter element, which removes dust and dirt from the air being drawn into the engine.

Air filter element The actual filter in an air cleaner system, usually manufactured from pleated paper and requiring renewal at regular intervals.

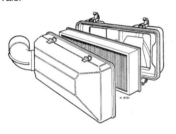

Air filter

Allen key A hexagonal wrench which fits into a recessed hexagonal hole.

Alligator clip A long-nosed spring-loaded metal clip with meshing teeth. Used to make temporary electrical connections.

Alternator A component in the electrical system which converts mechanical energy from a drivebelt into electrical energy to charge the battery and to operate the starting system, ignition system and electrical accessories.

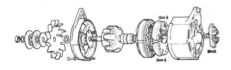

Alternator (exploded view)

Ampere (amp) A unit of measurement for the flow of electric current. One amp is the amount of current produced by one volt acting through a resistance of one ohm.

Anaerobic sealer A substance used to prevent bolts and screws from loosening. Anaerobic means that it does not require oxygen for activation. The Loctite brand is widely used.

Antifreeze A substance (usually ethylene glycol) mixed with water, and added to a vehicle's cooling system, to prevent freezing of the coolant in winter. Antifreeze also contains chemicals to inhibit corrosion and the formation of rust and other deposits that would tend to clog the radiator and coolant passages and reduce cooling efficiency.

Anti-seize compound A coating that reduces the risk of seizing on fasteners that are subjected to high temperatures, such as exhaust manifold bolts and nuts.

Anti-seize compound

Asbestos A natural fibrous mineral with great heat resistance, commonly used in the composition of brake friction materials. Asbestos is a health hazard and the dust created by brake systems should never be inhaled or ingested.

Axle A shaft on which a wheel revolves, or which revolves with a wheel. Also, a solid beam that connects the two wheels at one end of the vehicle. An axle which also transmits power to the wheels is known as a live axle.

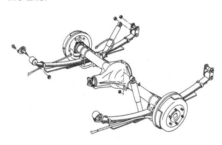

Axle assembly

Axleshaft A single rotating shaft, on either side of the differential, which delivers power from the final drive assembly to the drive wheels. Also called a driveshaft or a halfshaft.

B

Ball bearing An anti-friction bearing consisting of a hardened inner and outer race with hardened steel balls between two races.

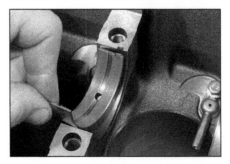

Bearing

Bearing The curved surface on a shaft or in a bore, or the part assembled into either, that permits relative motion between them with minimum wear and friction.

Big-end bearing The bearing in the end of the connecting rod that's attached to the crankshaft.

Bleed nipple A valve on a brake wheel cylinder, caliper or other hydraulic component that is opened to purge the hydraulic system of air. Also called a bleed screw.

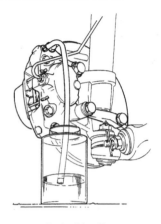

Brake bleeding

Brake bleeding Procedure for removing air from lines of a hydraulic brake system.

Brake disc The component of a disc brake that rotates with the wheels.

Brake drum The component of a drum brake that rotates with the wheels.

Brake linings The friction material which contacts the brake disc or drum to retard the vehicle's speed. The linings are bonded or riveted to the brake pads or shoes.

Brake pads The replaceable friction pads that pinch the brake disc when the brakes are applied. Brake pads consist of a friction material bonded or riveted to a rigid backing plate.

Brake shoe The crescent-shaped carrier to which the brake linings are mounted and which forces the lining against the rotating drum during braking.

Braking systems For more information on braking systems, consult the *Haynes Automotive Brake Manual*.

Breaker bar A long socket wrench handle providing greater leverage.

Bulkhead The insulated partition between the engine and the passenger compartment.

C

Caliper The non-rotating part of a disc-brake assembly that straddles the disc and carries the brake pads. The caliper also contains the hydraulic components that cause the pads to pinch the disc when the brakes are applied. A caliper is also a measuring tool that can be set to measure inside or outside dimensions of an object.

Camshaft A rotating shaft on which a series of cam lobes operate the valve mechanisms. The camshaft may be driven by gears, by sprockets and chain or by sprockets and a belt.

Canister A container in an evaporative emission control system; contains activated charcoal granules to trap vapours from the fuel system.

Canister

Carburettor A device which mixes fuel with air in the proper proportions to provide a desired power output from a spark ignition internal combustion engine.

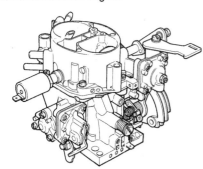

Carburettor

Castellated Resembling the parapets along the top of a castle wall. For example, a castellated balljoint stud nut.

Castellated nut

Castor In wheel alignment, the backward or forward tilt of the steering axis. Castor is positive when the steering axis is inclined rearward at the top.

Catalytic converter A silencer-like device in the exhaust system which converts certain pollutants in the exhaust gases into less harmful substances.

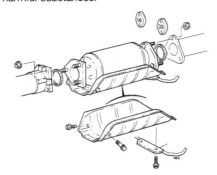

Catalytic converter

Circlip A ring-shaped clip used to prevent endwise movement of cylindrical parts and shafts. An internal circlip is installed in a groove in a housing; an external circlip fits into a groove on the outside of a cylindrical piece such as a shaft.

Clearance The amount of space between two parts. For example, between a piston and a cylinder, between a bearing and a journal, etc.

Coil spring A spiral of elastic steel found in various sizes throughout a vehicle, for example as a springing medium in the suspension and in the valve train.

Compression Reduction in volume, and increase in pressure and temperature, of a gas, caused by squeezing it into a smaller space.

Compression ratio The relationship between cylinder volume when the piston is at top dead centre and cylinder volume when the piston is at bottom dead centre.

Constant velocity (CV) joint A type of universal joint that cancels out vibrations caused by driving power being transmitted through an angle.

Core plug A disc or cup-shaped metal device inserted in a hole in a casting through which core was removed when the casting was formed. Also known as a freeze plug or expansion plug.

Crankcase The lower part of the engine block in which the crankshaft rotates.

Crankshaft The main rotating member, or shaft, running the length of the crankcase, with offset "throws" to which the connecting rods are attached.

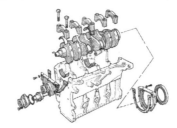

Crankshaft assembly

Crocodile clip See Alligator clip

D

Diagnostic code Code numbers obtained by accessing the diagnostic mode of an engine management computer. This code can be used to determine the area in the system where a malfunction may be located.

Disc brake A brake design incorporating a rotating disc onto which brake pads are squeezed. The resulting friction converts the energy of a moving vehicle into heat.

Double-overhead cam (DOHC) An engine that uses two overhead camshafts, usually one for the intake valves and one for the exhaust valves.

Drivebelt(s) The belt(s) used to drive accessories such as the alternator, water pump, power steering pump, air conditioning compressor, etc. off the crankshaft pulley.

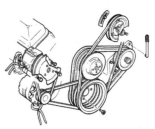

Accessory drivebelts

Driveshaft Any shaft used to transmit motion. Commonly used when referring to the axleshafts on a front wheel drive vehicle.

Driveshaft

Drum brake A type of brake using a drum-shaped metal cylinder attached to the inner surface of the wheel. When the brake pedal is pressed, curved brake shoes with friction linings press against the inside of the drum to slow or stop the vehicle.

Drum brake assembly

E

EGR valve A valve used to introduce exhaust gases into the intake air stream.

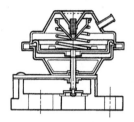

EGR valve

Electronic control unit (ECU) A computer which controls (for instance) ignition and fuel injection systems, or an anti-lock braking system. For more information refer to the *Haynes Automotive Electrical and Electronic Systems Manual.*

Electronic Fuel Injection (EFI) A computer controlled fuel system that distributes fuel through an injector located in each intake port of the engine.

Emergency brake A braking system, independent of the main hydraulic system, that can be used to slow or stop the vehicle if the primary brakes fail, or to hold the vehicle stationary even though the brake pedal isn't depressed. It usually consists of a hand lever that actuates either front or rear brakes mechanically through a series of cables and linkages. Also known as a handbrake or parking brake.

Endfloat The amount of lengthwise movement between two parts. As applied to a crankshaft, the distance that the crankshaft can move forward and back in the cylinder block.

Engine management system (EMS) A computer controlled system which manages the fuel injection and the ignition systems in an integrated fashion.

Exhaust manifold A part with several passages through which exhaust gases leave the engine combustion chambers and enter the exhaust pipe.

Exhaust manifold

F

Fan clutch A viscous (fluid) drive coupling device which permits variable engine fan speeds in relation to engine speeds.

Feeler blade A thin strip or blade of hardened steel, ground to an exact thickness, used to check or measure clearances between parts.

Feeler blade

Firing order The order in which the engine cylinders fire, or deliver their power strokes, beginning with the number one cylinder.

Flywheel A heavy spinning wheel in which energy is absorbed and stored by means of momentum. On cars, the flywheel is attached to the crankshaft to smooth out firing impulses.

Free play The amount of travel before any action takes place. The "looseness" in a linkage, or an assembly of parts, between the initial application of force and actual movement. For example, the distance the brake pedal moves before the pistons in the master cylinder are actuated.

Fuse An electrical device which protects a circuit against accidental overload. The typical fuse contains a soft piece of metal which is calibrated to melt at a predetermined current flow (expressed as amps) and break the circuit.

Fusible link A circuit protection device consisting of a conductor surrounded by heat-resistant insulation. The conductor is smaller than the wire it protects, so it acts as the weakest link in the circuit. Unlike a blown fuse, a failed fusible link must frequently be cut from the wire for replacement.

G

Gap The distance the spark must travel in jumping from the centre electrode to the side

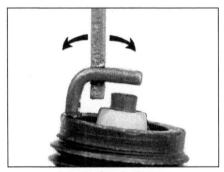

Adjusting spark plug gap

electrode in a spark plug. Also refers to the spacing between the points in a contact breaker assembly in a conventional points-type ignition, or to the distance between the reluctor or rotor and the pickup coil in an electronic ignition.

Gasket Any thin, soft material - usually cork, cardboard, asbestos or soft metal - installed between two metal surfaces to ensure a good seal. For instance, the cylinder head gasket seals the joint between the block and the cylinder head.

Gasket

Gauge An instrument panel display used to monitor engine conditions. A gauge with a movable pointer on a dial or a fixed scale is an analogue gauge. A gauge with a numerical readout is called a digital gauge.

H

Halfshaft A rotating shaft that transmits power from the final drive unit to a drive wheel, usually when referring to a live rear axle.

Harmonic balancer A device designed to reduce torsion or twisting vibration in the crankshaft. May be incorporated in the crankshaft pulley. Also known as a vibration damper.

Hone An abrasive tool for correcting small irregularities or differences in diameter in an engine cylinder, brake cylinder, etc.

Hydraulic tappet A tappet that utilises hydraulic pressure from the engine's lubrication system to maintain zero clearance (constant contact with both camshaft and valve stem). Automatically adjusts to variation in valve stem length. Hydraulic tappets also reduce valve noise.

I

Ignition timing The moment at which the spark plug fires, usually expressed in the number of crankshaft degrees before the piston reaches the top of its stroke.

Inlet manifold A tube or housing with passages through which flows the air-fuel mixture (carburettor vehicles and vehicles with throttle body injection) or air only (port fuel-injected vehicles) to the port openings in the cylinder head.

J

Jump start Starting the engine of a vehicle with a discharged or weak battery by attaching jump leads from the weak battery to a charged or helper battery.

L

Load Sensing Proportioning Valve (LSPV) A brake hydraulic system control valve that works like a proportioning valve, but also takes into consideration the amount of weight carried by the rear axle.

Locknut A nut used to lock an adjustment nut, or other threaded component, in place. For example, a locknut is employed to keep the adjusting nut on the rocker arm in position.

Lockwasher A form of washer designed to prevent an attaching nut from working loose.

M

MacPherson strut A type of front suspension system devised by Earle MacPherson at Ford of England. In its original form, a simple lateral link with the anti-roll bar creates the lower control arm. A long strut - an integral coil spring and shock absorber - is mounted between the body and the steering knuckle. Many modern so-called MacPherson strut systems use a conventional lower A-arm and don't rely on the anti-roll bar for location.

Multimeter An electrical test instrument with the capability to measure voltage, current and resistance.

N

NOx Oxides of Nitrogen. A common toxic pollutant emitted by petrol and diesel engines at higher temperatures.

O

Ohm The unit of electrical resistance. One volt applied to a resistance of one ohm will produce a current of one amp.

Ohmmeter An instrument for measuring electrical resistance.

O-ring A type of sealing ring made of a special rubber-like material; in use, the O-ring is compressed into a groove to provide the sealing action.

O-ring

Overhead cam (ohc) engine An engine with the camshaft(s) located on top of the cylinder head(s).

Overhead valve (ohv) engine An engine with the valves located in the cylinder head, but with the camshaft located in the engine block.

Oxygen sensor A device installed in the engine exhaust manifold, which senses the oxygen content in the exhaust and converts this information into an electric current. Also called a Lambda sensor.

P

Phillips screw A type of screw head having a cross instead of a slot for a corresponding type of screwdriver.

Plastigage A thin strip of plastic thread, available in different sizes, used for measuring clearances. For example, a strip of Plastigage is laid across a bearing journal. The parts are assembled and dismantled; the width of the crushed strip indicates the clearance between journal and bearing.

Plastigage

Propeller shaft The long hollow tube with universal joints at both ends that carries power from the transmission to the differential on front-engined rear wheel drive vehicles.

Proportioning valve A hydraulic control valve which limits the amount of pressure to the rear brakes during panic stops to prevent wheel lock-up.

R

Rack-and-pinion steering A steering system with a pinion gear on the end of the steering shaft that mates with a rack (think of a geared wheel opened up and laid flat). When the steering wheel is turned, the pinion turns, moving the rack to the left or right. This movement is transmitted through the track rods to the steering arms at the wheels.

Radiator A liquid-to-air heat transfer device designed to reduce the temperature of the coolant in an internal combustion engine cooling system.

Refrigerant Any substance used as a heat transfer agent in an air-conditioning system. R-12 has been the principle refrigerant for many years; recently, however, manufacturers have begun using R-134a, a non-CFC substance that is considered less harmful to

the ozone in the upper atmosphere.

Rocker arm A lever arm that rocks on a shaft or pivots on a stud. In an overhead valve engine, the rocker arm converts the upward movement of the pushrod into a downward movement to open a valve.

Rotor In a distributor, the rotating device inside the cap that connects the centre electrode and the outer terminals as it turns, distributing the high voltage from the coil secondary winding to the proper spark plug. Also, that part of an alternator which rotates inside the stator. Also, the rotating assembly of a turbocharger, including the compressor wheel, shaft and turbine wheel.

Runout The amount of wobble (in-and-out movement) of a gear or wheel as it's rotated. The amount a shaft rotates "out-of-true." The out-of-round condition of a rotating part.

S

Sealant A liquid or paste used to prevent leakage at a joint. Sometimes used in conjunction with a gasket.

Sealed beam lamp An older headlight design which integrates the reflector, lens and filaments into a hermetically-sealed one-piece unit. When a filament burns out or the lens cracks, the entire unit is simply replaced.

Serpentine drivebelt A single, long, wide accessory drivebelt that's used on some newer vehicles to drive all the accessories, instead of a series of smaller, shorter belts. Serpentine drivebelts are usually tensioned by an automatic tensioner.

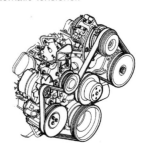

Serpentine drivebelt

Shim Thin spacer, commonly used to adjust the clearance or relative positions between two parts. For example, shims inserted into or under bucket tappets control valve clearances. Clearance is adjusted by changing the thickness of the shim.

Slide hammer A special puller that screws into or hooks onto a component such as a shaft or bearing; a heavy sliding handle on the shaft bottoms against the end of the shaft to knock the component free.

Sprocket A tooth or projection on the periphery of a wheel, shaped to engage with a chain or drivebelt. Commonly used to refer to the sprocket wheel itself.

Starter inhibitor switch On vehicles with an

automatic transmission, a switch that prevents starting if the vehicle is not in Neutral or Park.

Strut See MacPherson strut.

T

Tappet A cylindrical component which transmits motion from the cam to the valve stem, either directly or via a pushrod and rocker arm. Also called a cam follower.

Thermostat A heat-controlled valve that regulates the flow of coolant between the cylinder block and the radiator, so maintaining optimum engine operating temperature. A thermostat is also used in some air cleaners in which the temperature is regulated.

Thrust bearing The bearing in the clutch assembly that is moved in to the release levers by clutch pedal action to disengage the clutch. Also referred to as a release bearing.

Timing belt A toothed belt which drives the camshaft. Serious engine damage may result if it breaks in service.

Timing chain A chain which drives the camshaft.

Toe-in The amount the front wheels are closer together at the front than at the rear. On rear wheel drive vehicles, a slight amount of toe-in is usually specified to keep the front wheels running parallel on the road by offsetting other forces that tend to spread the wheels apart.

Toe-out The amount the front wheels are closer together at the rear than at the front. On front wheel drive vehicles, a slight amount of toe-out is usually specified.

Tools For full information on choosing and using tools, refer to the *Haynes Automotive Tools Manual*.

Tracer A stripe of a second colour applied to a wire insulator to distinguish that wire from another one with the same colour insulator.

Tune-up A process of accurate and careful adjustments and parts replacement to obtain the best possible engine performance.

Turbocharger A centrifugal device, driven by exhaust gases, that pressurises the intake air. Normally used to increase the power output from a given engine displacement, but can also be used primarily to reduce exhaust emissions (as on VW's "Umwelt" Diesel engine).

U

Universal joint or U-joint A double-pivoted connection for transmitting power from a driving to a driven shaft through an angle. A U-joint consists of two Y-shaped yokes and a cross-shaped member called the spider.

V

Valve A device through which the flow of liquid, gas, vacuum, or loose material in bulk may be started, stopped, or regulated by a movable part that opens, shuts, or partially obstructs one or more ports or passageways. A valve is also the movable part of such a device.

Valve clearance The clearance between the valve tip (the end of the valve stem) and the rocker arm or tappet. The valve clearance is measured when the valve is closed.

Vernier caliper A precision measuring instrument that measures inside and outside dimensions. Not quite as accurate as a micrometer, but more convenient.

Viscosity The thickness of a liquid or its resistance to flow.

Volt A unit for expressing electrical "pressure" in a circuit. One volt that will produce a current of one ampere through a resistance of one ohm.

W

Welding Various processes used to join metal items by heating the areas to be joined to a molten state and fusing them together. For more information refer to the *Haynes Automotive Welding Manual*.

Wiring diagram A drawing portraying the components and wires in a vehicle's electrical system, using standardised symbols. For more information refer to the *Haynes Automotive Electrical and Electronic Systems Manual*.

Note: *References throughout this index are in the form - "Chapter number" • "page number"*

A

Accelerator cable - 4A•5, 4B•2
Acknowledgements - 0•4
Aerial - 12•14
Air cleaner temperature control - 4A•3
Air deflector, rear - 11•14
Air distribution housing, heater - 3•6
Air filter - 1•15
Air vents - 3•6
Airflow sensor - 4B•2, 4B•5
Alternator - 5A•3, 5A•4
Alternator drivebelt - 1•9
Anti-roll bars - 10•8, 10•10
Antifreeze mixture - 1•17
Automatic transmission - 7B•1 *et seq*
  Fault diagnosis - REF•11, REF•15
  fluid checks - 1•12, 1•18
  kickdown cable - 7B•1
  speed selector control cable - 7B•2
  starter inhibitor switch - 7B•2
Auxiliary air valve - 4B•3, 4•6
Auxiliary drivebelt check - 1•9
Axle (rear) - 10•10

B

Balljoint, control arm - 10•7
Battery - 0•9, 0•15, 5A•2, 5A•3
Battery check - 0•15
Bearings, engine - 2•21
Bleeding
  power steering - 10•15
  brakes - 9•2, 9•3
Blower motor, heater - 3•5
Body damage - 11•2, 11•4
Body electrical system - 12•1 *et seq*
Bodywork and fittings - 11•1 *et seq*
Bonnet - 11•4
Bonnet release cable - 11•4
Braking system - 9•1 *et seq*
  bleeding the brakes - 9•2
  brake light switch - 9•16
  caliper - 1•12, 9•9
  checks - 1•12, 1•15
  disc - 9•7
  drum - 1•12, 9•8
  Fault diagnosis - REF•11, REF•15
  fluid level - 0•13
  handbrake
    adjustment - 1•15
    cables - 9•14
    lever - 9•15
    warning light switch - 9•15
  hydraulic pipes and hoses - 9•3
  master cylinder - 9•11
  pads - 9•3
  pedal - 9•14
  pressure regulating valve - 9•13
  road test - 1•13
  shoes - 1•12, 9•4
  vacuum servo unit - 9•13
  wheel cylinder - 9•10

Bulbs - 12•2, 12•7
  direction indicator - 12•8
  foglamp - 12•8, 12•9
  headlamp - 12•7
  instrument panel lamps - 12•9
  interior lamp - 12•9
  number plate lamp - 12•8, 12•9
  parking lamp - 12•7
  rear lamps - 12•8
  reversing lamp - 12•9
Bumpers - 11•5
Bushes, control arm - 10•7
Buying spare parts - REF•3

C

Cables:
  accelerator - 4A•5
  bonnet release - 11•4
  choke - 4A•6
  clutch - 6•2
  handbrake - 9•14
  kickdown, automatic transmission - 7B•1
  speed selector, automatic transmission - 7B•2
  speedometer - 12•7
Calipers, brake - 1•12, 9•9
Camshaft
  housing - 2•13
  oil seals - 2•8
  toothed belt - 2•6, 2•22
Capacities - 0•17
Carburettor - 4A•6, 4A•8, 4A•12
  GM Varajet - 4A•6, 4A•8
  Pierburg 2E3 - 4A•7, 4A•8, 4A•12
Carpets - 11•2
Central locking system - 12•12
Centre console - 11•11
Charging system - 5A•1 *et seq*
Choke cable - 4A•6
Cigarette lighter - 12•6
Clock - 12•6
Clutch - 6•1 *et seq*
  cable - 6•2
  Fault diagnosis - REF•11, REF•14
  pedal - 6•2
  release bearing - 6•4
Coil spring, rear - 10•10
Column, steering - 10•14, 10•15
Compression test - 2•5
Condenser - 5B•4
Connecting rods - 2•15
Contact breaker ignition system - 5B•1 *et seq*
Contact breaker points - 5B•2, 5B•3
Contents - 0•2, 0•3
Control arm
  bushes - 10•7
  front suspension - 10•6
  support - 10•7
Control relay - 4B•2, 4B•6
Control unit - 4B•2, 4B•5
Conversion factors - REF•2
Coolant - 0•12, 1•16
  level check - 0•12
  renewal - 1•16
  sensor, fuel injection - 4B•3, 4B•6
  temperature gauge sender - 3•5

Cooling fan, radiator - 3•4
Cooling and heating system - 3•1 *et seq*
  air distribution housing, heater - 3•6
  air vents - 3•6
  blower motor, heater - 3•5
  coolant pump - 3•3
  coolant temperature sender - 3•5
  fan, radiator - 3•4
  Fault diagnosis - REF•11, REF•13
  hoses - 3•2
  matrix, heater - 3•5
  radiator - 3•2
  sender units, temperature - 3•5
  switches - 3•4
  thermostat - 3•2
Courtesy lamp switch - 12•4
Crankshaft - 2•20
Crankshaft oil seals - 2•15
Cylinder bores - 2•21
Cylinder head - 2•9, 2•20

D

Depressurising fuel injection system - 4B•3
Dimensions - REF•1
Direction indicators - 12•8, 12•10
Discs, brake - 1•12, 9•7
Distributor - 5B•4, 5B•5, 5C•3, 5C•6
Door - 11•8
Door inner trim panel - 11•6,
Drivebelt check - 1•9
Driveshafts - 8•1 *et seq*
  Fault diagnosis - REF•11, REF•15
  gaiter - 8•3
  joint renewal - 8•3
  oil seal - 7A•3
  road test - 1•13
Drum, brake - 1•12, 9•8

E

Electric mirror - 11•13
Electric window switches - 12•5
Electric windows - 12•14
Electrical fault finding - 12•2
Electrical system (body) - 12•1 *et seq*
  check - 0•14
  Fault diagnosis - REF•11, REF•16
Electronic ignition system - 5C•1 *et seq*
Engine - 2•1 *et seq*
  bearings - 2•21
  camshaft
    housing - 2•13
    oil seals - 2•8
    toothed belt - 2•6, 2•22
  codes - 2•1
  compression test - 2•5
  connecting rods - 2•15
  crankshaft - 2•15, 2•20
  cylinder bores - 2•21
  cylinder head - 2•9, 2•20
  dismantling 2•18
  Fault diagnosis - REF•11, REF•12
  flywheel - 2•21, 2•25
  lubrication/crankcase ventilation - 2•18

mountings (engine/transmission) - 2•16
oil and filter renewal - 1•8
oil level check - 0•12
oil pressure regulator valve - 2•6
oil pump - 2•14, 2•19, 2•24
oil seals - 2•8, 2•15
piston rings - 2•21, 2•23
piston/connecting rod assemblies - 2•15
removal - 2•16, 2•17
sump - 2•13
top Dead Centre (TDC), locating - 2•6
valves - 2•22, 2•25
Environmental considerations - REF•4
Exhaust
manifold - 4A•13, 4B•8
system - 1•12, 4A•14, 4B•8
Exterior mirror - 11•13, 12•5

F

Facia panel - 11•11
Fan, radiator - 3•4
Fanbelt check - 1•9
Fault diagnosis - REF•11 et seq
Fluids - 0•17
Flushing, cooling system - 1•16
Foglamp - 12•8, 12•9, 12•10
Front hub bearing - 10•4
Front parking lamp bulb - 12•7
Front suspension strut - 10•3, 10•5
Fuel and exhaust system - 4A•1, 4B•1 et seq
accelerator cable - 4A•5
air cleaner temperature control - 4A•3
airflow sensor - 4B•2, 4B•5
automatic choke - 4A•10
auxiliary air valve - 4B•3, 4B•6
carburettor - 4A•6, 4A•7, 4A•8, 4A•12
choke cable - 4A•6
control unit- 4B•2, 4B•5
control relay - 4B•2, 4B•6
coolant temperature sensor - 4B•3, 4B•6
depressurising fuel injection system - 4B•3
exhaust manifold - 4A•13, 4B•8
exhaust system - 4A•14
Fault diagnosis - REF•11, REF•14
fuel filter - 1•13
fuel gauge sender unit - 4B•4
fuel pump - 4A•4, 4B•3
fuel injector(s) - 4B•2, 4B•5
fuel pressure regulator - 4B•3, 4B•6
idle speed/mixture - 1•10
manifolds - 4A•13, 4B•7, 4B•8
mixture (CO) - 1•10
sender unit, fuel gauge - 4B•4
tank - 4A•4
tank sender unit - 4A•4
throttle cable - 4A•5
throttle valve - 4B•3, 4B•4, 4B•5
unleaded petrol - 4A•3, 4B•2
Fuses - 12•1, 12•2, 12•3

G

Gearbox - see Manual or Automatic transmission
Gearchange lever - 7A•2
Gearchange linkage - 7A•3
Glossary of technical terms - REF•18
Glove compartment - 11•11

H

Handbrake
adjustment - 1•15
cables - 9•14
lever - 9•15
warning light switch - 9•15
Handles, door - 11•7
Hazard warning lamp switch - 12•4
Head restraints - 11•12
Headlamp - 12•7, 12•9, 12•10, 12•11
Heated rear window switch - 12•4
Heater blower switch - 12•4
Heater/ventilation components - 3•5
Hinges and locks - 1•12
Horn - 12•5, 12•6
Hose and fluid leak check - 1•8
Hoses, cooling system - 3•2
Hoses, brake - 9•3
HT coil - 5B•6, 5C•8
HT leads check - 1•9
Hub bearings - 10•4, 10•8
Hydraulic pipes/hoses - 9•3
Hydraulic system, bleeding - 9•2

I

Idle speed/mixture - 1•10, 4A•12
Ignition
system check - 1•9
HT coil - 5B•6, 5C•8
module (control unit) - 5C•8
switch - 5A•4
switch/steering lock - 10•15
system testing - 5B•2, 5C•3
timing adjustment - 5B•6
Indicator bulb - 12•8
Injector(s) - 4B•2, 4B•5
Inlet manifold - 4A•13, 4B•7
Input shaft oil seal - 6•4, 7A•4
Instrument panel - 12•6, 12•9
Interior light bulbs - 12•9
Introduction to the Vauxhall Cavalier - 0•4

J

Jacking and vehicle support - 0•6
Jump starting - 0•9

K

Kickdown cable - 7B•1

L

Light switch - 12•4
Locks
door - 11•7
steering - 10•15
tailgate - 11•8, 11•9
Lubricants and fluids - 0•17
Luggage area light switch - 12•5
Luggage boot lid /lock - 11•10

M

Main and big-end bearings - 2•21
Maintenance - see Routine maintenance
Manifolds - 4A•13, 4B•7, 4B•8

Manual transmission - 7A•1 et seq
driveshaft oil seals - 7A•3
Fault diagnosis - REF•11, REF•14
gear lever - 7A•2
gearbox oil - 1•11, 7A•1
gearchange linkage - 7A•3
input shaft (clutch) oil seal - 6•4, 7A•4
oil seals - 7A•3
reversing lamp switch - 7A•4
speedometer drive - 7A•4
Master cylinder, brake - 9•11
Matrix, heater - 3•5
Mirrors - 11•13
Mixture (CO) - 1•10
MOT test checks - REF•7
Mountings, engine/transmission - 2•16

N

Number plate lamp - 12•9

O

Oil change - 1•8
Oil filter - 1•8
Oil pressure regulator valve - 2•6
Oil pressure warning light switch - 5A•4
Oil pump - 2•14, 2•19, 2•24
Oil seals - 2•8, 2•15, 7A•3, REF •4
Oils - 0•17

P

Pads, brake - 1•12, 9•3
Parts, buying - REF•3
Pedals
brake - 9•14
clutch - 6•2
Piston rings - 2•21, 2•23
Piston/connecting rod assemblies - 2•15
Plastic components - 11•4
Plugs - 1•14, 1•17
Points gap adjustment - 5B•2
Power operated windows - 12•5, 12•14
Power steering fluid level check - 0•14
Power steering pump - 10•15
Power steering system, bleeding - 10•15
Punctures - 0•7

R

Radiator - 3•2
cooling fan - 3•4
grille - 11•5
Radio/cassette player - 12•13 to 12•14
Rear axle - 10•10
Rear foglamp switch - 12•5
Rear hub bearings 10•8
Rear light cluster - 12•10
Rear suspension stub axle - 10•10
Relays - 12•3, 12•4
Release bearing (clutch) - 6•4
Repair procedures - REF •4
Reversing lamp bulb - 12•9
Reversing lamp switch - 7A•4
Road test - 1•13
Roadwheel bolts - 1•12
Roll bars - 10•8, 10•10
Routine maintenance and servicing - 1•1 et seq

S

Safety first! - 0•5
Seat belts - 11•14
Seats - 11•10, 11•11
Sender unit
   coolant temperature - 3•5
   fuel - 4A•4, 4B•4
Sensor
   airflow - 4B•2, 4B•5
   coolant temperature - 4B•3, 4B-6
Servicing - see Routine maintenance
Servo unit (braking system) - 9•13
Shock absorber, rear - 10•9
Shoes, brake - 1•12, 9•4
Side repeater bulb - 12•8
Spare parts, buying - REF•3
Spark plugs - 1•14, 1•17
Speakers - 12•14
Special tools - REF•4
Speed selector cable - 7B•2
Speedometer cable - 12•7
Speedometer drive - 7A•4
Starter inhibitor switch - 7B•2
Starter motor - 5A•4
Starting and charging systems - 5A•1 *et seq*
Starting system test - 5A•4
Steering - 10•1 *et seq*
   angles - 10•16
   camber - 10•1, 10•16
   castor - 10•1, 10•16
   column - 10•14, 10•15
   column switches - 12•4
   damper - 10•14
   Fault diagnosis - REF•11, REF•16
   gear - 10•13
   lock/Ignition switch - 10•15
   power steering system bleeding - 10•15
   pump - 10•15
   rack bellows 10•13
   road test - 1•13
   tie-rod end - 10•12
   toe setting - 10•1, 10•16
   tracking - 10•16
   wheel - 10•14
   wheel alignment - 10•1, 10•16
Sump - 2•13
Sunroof - 11•14

Support struts (tailgate) - 11•8
Suspension and steering - 10•1 *et seq*
   anti-roll bars - 10•8, 10•10
   balljoint, control arm - 10•7
   coil spring, rear - 10•10
   control arm, front - 10•6
    bushes - 10•7
    support - 10•7
   Fault diagnosis - REF•11, REF•16
   hub bearings - 10•4 10•8
   rear axle - 10•10
   rear stub axle - 10•10
   road test - 1•13
   shock absorber, rear - 10•9
   strut, front suspension - 10•3, 10•5
Switches
   brake light - 9•16
   cooling system - 3•4
   courtesy lamp - 12•4
   exterior mirror adjustment - 12•5
   handbrake warning light - 9•15
   hazard warning lamp - 12•4
   heated rear window - 12•4
   heater blower - 12•4
   horn - 12•5
   lights - 12•4
   lock/Ignition - 10•15
   luggage area light - 12•5
   oil pressure warning light - 5A•4
   power operated window - 12•5
   rear foglamp - 12•5
   reversing lamp - 7A•4
   starter inhibitor - 7B•2
   steering column - 12•4
   throttle valve - 4B•3, 4B•5

T

Tailgate - 11•8 to 11•9
   washer - 12•11
   wiper motor - 12•11
Temperature gauge sender unit - 3•5
Thermostat - 3•2
Throttle cable - 4A•5, 4B•2
Throttle valve - 4B•3, 4B•4, 4B•5
Tie-rod end - 10•12
Timing adjustment - 5B•6
Toe setting - 10•1, 10•16

Tools and working facilities - REF•5
Top Dead Centre (TDC), locating - 2•6
Towing - 0•7
Tracking - 10•16
Trim panels - 11•6, 11•9
Tyre checks - 0•16
Tyre pressures - 0•17

U

Underbody maintenance - 11•1
Unleaded petrol - 4A•3, 4B•2
Upholstery and carpets - 11•2

V

Vacuum servo unit, braking system - 9•13
Valve lifters - 2•22
Valves - 2•25
Vehicle identification numbers - REF•3
Vent chamber, fuel tank - 4A•5
Vent grille, rear - 11•14
Vents - 3•6

W

Washer fluid level - 0•13
Washers - 12•11
Water pump - 3•3
Weekly checks - 0•10 *et seq*
Wheel, steering - 10•14
Wheel alignment - 10•1, 10•16
Wheel bolts - 1•12
Wheel changing - 0•7
Wheel cylinder - 9•10
Window glass - 11•7, 11•10, 11•13
Window regulator - 11•6
Windscreen - 11•10
   washers - 12•11
   wiper motor - 12•10
Wiper arms - 12•10
Wiper blades - 0•15, 1•12, 12•10
Wiper motor
   tailgate - 12•11
   windscreen - 12•10
Wiring diagrams - WD•1 *et seq*
Working facilities - REF•5

Preserving Our Motoring Heritage

< The Model J Duesenberg Derham Tourster. Only eight of these magnificent cars were ever built – this is the only example to be found outside the United States of America

Almost every car you've ever loved, loathed or desired is gathered under one roof at the Haynes Motor Museum. Over 300 immaculately presented cars and motorbikes represent every aspect of our motoring heritage, from elegant reminders of bygone days, such as the superb Model J Duesenberg to curiosities like the bug-eyed BMW Isetta. There are also many old friends and flames. Perhaps you remember the 1959 Ford Popular that you did your courting in? The magnificent 'Red Collection' is a spectacle of classic sports cars including AC, Alfa Romeo, Austin Healey, Ferrari, Lamborghini, Maserati, MG, Riley, Porsche and Triumph.

A Perfect Day Out

Each and every vehicle at the Haynes Motor Museum has played its part in the history and culture of Motoring. Today, they make a wonderful spectacle and a great day out for all the family. Bring the kids, bring Mum and Dad, but above all bring your camera to capture those golden memories for ever. You will also find an impressive array of motoring memorabilia, a comfortable 70 seat video cinema and one of the most extensive transport book shops in Britain. The Pit Stop Cafe serves everything from a cup of tea to wholesome, home-made meals or, if you prefer, you can enjoy the large picnic area nestled in the beautiful rural surroundings of Somerset.

> John Haynes O.B.E., Founder and Chairman of the museum at the wheel of a Haynes Light 12.

< Graham Hill's Lola Cosworth Formula 1 car next to a 1934 Riley Sports.

The Museum is situated on the A359 Yeovil to Frome road at Sparkford, just off the A303 in Somerset. It is about 40 miles south of Bristol, and 25 minutes drive from the M5 intersection at Taunton.
Open 9.30am - 5.30pm (10.00am - 4.00pm Winter) 7 days a week, *except Christmas Day, Boxing Day and New Years Day*
Special rates available for schools, coach parties and outings Charitable Trust No. 292048